In My Mother's House

THE ETHNOGRAPHY
OF POLITICAL VIOLENCE

Tobias Kelly, *Series Editor*

A complete list of books in the series
is available from the publisher.

In My Mother's House

Civil War in Sri Lanka

Sharika Thiranagama

PENN

UNIVERSITY OF PENNSYLVANIA PRESS

PHILADELPHIA

Published by
University of Pennsylvania Press
Philadelphia, Pennsylvania 19104-4112
www.upenn.edu/pennpress

Printed in the United States of America on acid-free paper
10 9 8 7 6 5 4 3 2 1

Library of Congress Cataloging-in-Publication Data
ISBN 978-0-8122-4342-0

To my grandparents
Mahilaruppiam and Rajasingam, (Amma and Appa)
my parents Rajani and Dayapala Thiranagama, (Daji and Thatha)
and Kugamoorthy

CONTENTS

NOTE ON TRANSLITERATION

Rather than use a standard system for transliteration, I have written Tamil words phonetically in English. However, the English usages I follow are those commonly used for those Tamil words (e.g. *ur* the Tamil word for home). In addition, place names and proper nouns are rendered in the text in the form they commonly appear in the Sri Lankan press.

Tamil words are explained in the text as they appear; however, readers will note that kinship terms change slightly between Tamils and Muslims, for example Tamils use *Amma* and *Appa* and Muslims use *Umma* and *Vappa* for mother and father.

Gananath Obeyesekere

It is a pleasure to write a foreword to this elegantly written, jargon free work on the ethnic conflict in Sri Lanka. For me *In My Mother's House* is the most significant contribution written to date for understanding that conflict, mostly from the perspective of Tamils and the Muslims of the north, the latter brutally evicted from their homes by the Tamil Tigers (the LTTE). I hope this work will be read not only by Sri Lankans and South Asians but also by those interested in political violence, the disrupted lives that result from it, and the resilience of those living under the shadow of terror and war, so poignantly described by Thiranagama. Thiranagama herself suffered from the war; her mother, a human rights activist and university professor, was killed by the LTTE in its "liberation struggle," which like many other liberation struggles ended up in mass violence and the targeted "rational killing" of those who refused to accept violence as an antidote to the political ills of the nation. At the time of producing her book the war was drawing to a close, but it is hard to believe that such a close will result in a closure of the issues that, from the Tamil perspective, provoked forms of resistance, including violent resistance.

Few outside Sri Lanka know that alongside the ethnic conflict there was another internal conflict in which Sinhala youths took up arms against the government, initially in 1971 and, when this failed, in yet another three-year conflict in the late 1980s. This too was a liberation struggle, and this too led to enormous violence and brutality. The JVP (National Liberation Front) practiced enormous brutalities, and equally brutal was the government reaction when paramilitary groups retaliated with scant regard to the Geneva Convention (that few I am sure had heard of) or any other decent convention. This conflict resulted in the loss of 60,000 lives according to current estimates. Statistics on violence are unreliable, but even if one reduces this figure by half, the human suffering and loss cannot be estimated through numbers. Unlike the ethnic conflict, virtually nothing of significance has been written on the short span of pain and fear erupting during the JVP youth-based insurrection. Once insurrectional violence has been unleashed, it produces its counterpart in state violence and repression, and a whole nation is thereby caught in a vortex of spiraling violence. And worse: violence can become an addiction for some participants, just like drugs and alcohol, all of which are now endemic in the nation. Liberation movements, unhappily, tend to lose the spirit of whatever idealism sparked the movements' inception. It is easy for a liberation movement to lose its soul. There is no gainsaying the fact that over the last thirty years or so, this beautiful land of ours had become a blood-besotted place. I do not know how a restoration, in the broadest sense of that term, might take place.

Thiranagama's book was completed when the long war was nearing its close and the government forces were closing in on the LTTE, and on 19 May 2009 the war was over. None among those I knew lamented the demise of the LTTE; that included my Tamil friends, although many were concerned, as was the international community, about the fate of Tamil civilians once held as hostages or human shields by the Tamil Tigers. But such concerns were overcome by the sheer relief felt by the overwhelming majority of the people. One can now board a bus without fear of a bomb; one can send children to school without being afraid of erratic suicide bomb attacks. The enshrouding fears that wars produced seem to have been dispelled. It is this sense of relief, especially among the Sinhala majority, that led to the feeling that any attempt to institute an investigation into possible violations of human rights in effect would diminish the sense of having at last overcome the LTTE terror. It is a only a very few who feel that the UN has a right and a duty to investigate violation of the rights of prisoners and civilians anywhere, whether in "just wars" or in any kind of war, as stated in the Geneva Convention, assuming of course that such an investigation is by persons of unimpeachable integrity. However, many Sri Lankan intellectuals as well as others living in this region have it seems to me a legitimate concern that is the Geneva convention is not a sacred document but ought to be revised in relation to the times in which we live. At least there should be a similar international instrument that inquires into the violation of human rights in different parts of the world, for example, the tortures and cruel punishments inflicted on women who work as low paid servants, often in effect virtual slaves, in some Middle East nations. These and even some forms of legal punishment such stoning a person to death surely must be classified as crimes against humanity, and there should be international organizations and a new set of conventions to inquire into and bring about just retribution and justice. Many would say that U.S. and NATO forces have been accused of causing civilian deaths and bombing civilian villages, but these activities somehow or other manage to elude just inquiry and condemnation.

More immediate for those of us living in Sri Lanka, whether intellectuals or ordinary folk or those in the international community, it is the specter of majoritarianism in a government that rules with an overwhelming parliamentary majority. This means among other things a fear of enveloping authoritarianism, erosion of civil rights within the nation, and impunity with which critics of the government can be muzzled. Journalists have been especially vulnerable and have been attacked or gone missing, and in one instance a TV station has been vandalized. Unlike in Thailand, here in Sri Lanka critics and intellectuals have in general been cowed into silence. Unfortunately, the criticism of the Euro-American community on these and similar issues have only resulted in an unbelievable jingoism among the majority community, the belief that the nation can go on its own, with help perhaps from India or more especially China, forgetting that altruism is hardly the motive behind international aid. No Island, unfortunately, is an island unto itself, and each is a piece of a global continent and a part of the main. One can only hope that the "we can go it alone" kind of rhetoric will give way to the reality principle of living in a globalized and interdependent world.

It seems that after the hurly-burly was over, the battle was won and then, sadly, lost. The European international community, as well as the UN, has been concerned about the delay in resettling Tamil refugees and the increasing government control of NGOs who are trying to help with that process. I personally believe that the government will attempt to resolve these contentious issues in time, and I can sympathize with any government in similar circumstances unable to stick to a hard and fast deadline. For me the more disturbing trend is the possibility of the north being recolonized, not only for Sinhala settlers but also culturally. There are currently an overwhelming Sinhala-speaking majority and a clear Sinhala-Buddhist majority in the Island, and with the latter I fear there is a conscious formulation of the idea of a Sinhala-Buddhist nation, a concept that many imagine existed in the past of Sri Lanka. It is true that many Buddhist kings of the past believed the ideal ruler was one who governed the whole island under a single umbrella. But none of our past kings could possibly have conceived of modern nationalism that consists of some form of central government control, state monopoly of resources, a sense of political and cultural unity brought mainly about by print capitalism, and in many instances a single dominant language. Thus Eugen Weber in an early study tells us that French nationalism resulted in the elimination of local languages and cultures and local forms of governance in a gradual but inevitable and brutal process of internal colonization whose end product was the creation of the modern French nation. So with Britain after the unification of England, Scotland, and Wales in 1707 that led to "forging the nation," the title of Linda Colley's book, which demonstrated the domination of Protestantism as the state religion, persecution of local Catholics, and demonization of the neighboring Catholic nation, France.[1]

But the trouble with today's world is that we are no longer living in the eighteenth or nineteenth century and there is no way that a nation-state can ride roughshod over minority religions, languages, and cultures. The attempt by the Indian BJP to create a Hindu nation based on an invented and modernized Hinduism has resulted in tragic conditions of ethnic warfare and anti-Muslim and anti-Hindu riots. I am afraid that similar attempts at imposing the dominant culture on minority religions and language groups are being currently felt here in Sri Lanka. You can squash dissent, but it is much more difficult to squash the spirit that fosters legitimate dissent. "Forging the nation" in Colley's felicitous phrase entails two things as I see it: it hammers a new sense of nationhood as in a forge; and it forges or fabricates new values, often reified as old values, that can then be imposed on the nation as a whole. A recent newspaper account (*Daily Mirror*, 6 August 2010) mentions a Buddhist monk engaged in a death fast unless, says he, the government "reconstruct Buddhist temples that were destroyed during the war in the north and resettle the Sinhalese people who were displaced during the terrorist domination of the area." I don't know the outcome of this fast but it forebodes a possible indication of "internal colonization" of the north and, worse, ignores the plight of the 80,000 Muslims ordered to leave their homes by the LTTE, and whose terrible situation in temporary homes has been described by Thiranagama. It is doubtful that the few displaced Sinhalas will go back north, but there will be many new migrants who might be waiting to recolonize that region. I can only hope that the government will listen to the voices of the minority communities and squash such attempts at internal colonization.

I have argued in my work that the movement of Sinhala Buddhist cultural colonization had its origins in the early twentieth century. In 1970 I wrote a paper entitled "Religious Symbolism and Political Change in Ceylon," a piece of ethnographic prophecy based on my witnessing a monument in the city of Colombo, erected I thought after Prime Minister Bandaranaike's triumph in 1956.[2] That regime, an early herald of Sinhala Buddhist majoritarianism, introduced a few years later "the Sinhala only act," one of the catalysts that led to fears of Sinhala domination of the North and the East and precipitated the Tamil resistance. During that period I saw a huge concrete map of Sri Lanka erected at a major intersection in Colombo. On the four sides of the map were written in English script the four great Buddhist virtues: *mettā* (lovingkindness), *karuṇā* (kindness, compassion), *upekkhā* (equanimity), and *muditā* (tenderness). In the middle of the map was a representation of the Sinhala flag, the lion holding a sword. To me, being a Buddhist of sorts, the symbolism was somewhat disconcerting, the lofty sentiments of doctrinal Buddhism being contradicted by the image of violence in the middle. But soon the obvious struck me, namely that what was being expressed here was the idea of the Sinhala-Buddhist nation, albeit in early form. That map was soon removed, but I noted that Buddha statues were being erected at similar road junctions and outside a few public buildings. Formerly in Sri Lanka Buddha statues were found in temples, and these temples were recessed from the normal village setting, somewhat cut off from the hub of communal living, expressing in symbolic terms the soteriological distance of the monk from the village and the lay folk that inhabit it. I went on to say that it seemed to me that the Buddha was being brought out of its seclusion right into the market place, a sign of things to come.

By the 1980s the Buddha in the marketplace had become an ubiquitous presence: he is found everywhere, outside public buildings, at every major road junction, at the entrance to towns, in almost every school, at the entrance to university campuses, at hospitals, and, disconcerting to me at least, even in parts of the tea country where the population is almost exclusively Tamil and Hindu. Catholics have always erected statues of Christ, the Virgin, and the saints in the Catholic areas of the west coast. The Buddhists have imitated the Catholic example in their expressions of projected nationhood, but in recent times they have even invaded the Catholic marketplace with Buddha statuary. The aesthetic ugliness of these statues, in contrast to the traditional, signifies it seems to me, the uglification of the Buddha's spiritual message and the inner uglification of the Buddhist conscience. Buddha statues have also been planted on mountain tops for all to see, some of them erected by modern private corporations, often competing with the tall and ugly telephone towers, erected by competing mobile phone companies, covering the once green and pleasant hills that range all over our land. Nowadays Buddha statues can be erected without recourse to permission; only Buddhist business-monks can build temples wherever they want, even encroaching on prime government-owned property.

Additionally there is the omnipresent Buddhist flag, invented in the late nineteenth century by Colombo businessmen inspired by the Theosophist Colonel Olcott, but, fortunately, not ugly. For Olcott the flag represented the ecumenical reach of the universal Buddhist dispensation or *sāsana*. Nowadays, the flag alongside other Buddhist symbols has become in Sri Lanka an entirely particularistic representation of the Buddhist nation. Flags and Buddha images adorn private buses and trishaws: in front for all to see are slogans such as the following: "this is the country of the Buddha." To sum up the situation in metaphorical terms: the Buddha has now become the flag of the nation. But when you put the Buddha in the market place, you are in effect transforming him from a *lokottara* or transcendental symbol into that of a *laukika* or worldly one. The latter has not supplanted the older image but it exists anomalously with the newly invented other.

Thus symbolic representations of the Buddhist-ness of the nation were happening before we won the war, but, alas, it would seem to lose the peace, when in the aftermath, Buddha images have begun to sprout in Muslim areas such as Beruvala in the Western Province and in areas in the Eastern Province where the dominant population is Muslim or Hindu. As the north has begun to open up, Buddhist temples and statuary have begun to be erected in the heartland of the Tamil country. A cultural invasion has begun, symbolically expressing the triumphalism and the possible emergent cultural conquest of the Tamil and Muslim periphery and the beginnings of the creation of a Buddhist nation. But now my prophetic sense fails me: I do not know how and when these processes will end. But as someone given to aphorisms I can say this with regard to both liberation movements and attempts to forge nations in our own troubled times: it is easy to create a monster but it is hard to kill it.

In My Mother's House

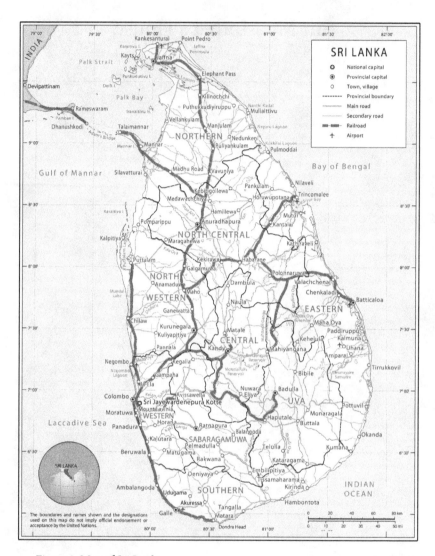

Figure 1. Map of Sri Lanka.

Introduction: In My Mother's House

On 21 September 1989, my sister and I waited for our mother to come home from work to the temporary house we were renting at the time. We were living in the northern Jaffna peninsula, by then, already a war zone. We were half minority Tamil (my mother), half majority Sinhalese (my father), but brought up speaking Tamil. The years when our Sinhalese father lived in Jaffna with us, as opposed to our once or twice yearly trip to Colombo to see him, or when my Sinhalese grandmother and uncles would travel up to Jaffna to visit or to go on pilgrimage were becoming dim memories in our almost exclusively Tamil and Muslim world. For us, our world was Tamil-speaking Jaffna.

Without being quite conscious of it, we were becoming witness to immense changes. We had already become accustomed to running into bunkers when the Sri Lankan army bombed us in 1986, were used to the idea that there were places and people we should be careful of, were cognizant that there was one really big militant group called the "Tigers," and had some dim idea of other militant groups. We had seen the Indian army arrive, heard rumors of the rapes that accompanied their arrival, seen the disordering of our world as the Indians and the Tigers fought it out. I recall in art class at school, being asked to draw pictures of beaches with coconut trees, and farmers tending their fields with cows, images that no longer described our world. At home, I drew instead pictures of being in bunkers surrounded by my family with speech bubbles of the funny things that people said while helicopters hovered. My mother mounted that picture in her office at the university. I recall having an intensely happy childhood in the midst of this war.

My mother never came back home that 21 September; her journey was ended by LTTE assassins in front of the house. Her body returned like us to "our home," my *ur*, my grandparents' house and village where she and we had been born and had lived for most of our lives. This house is still standing in

2011, though scarred like all of us by war. My childhood ended. My sister and I left Sri Lanka for London with our father who came to get us, flying on 25 December 1989. On 26 December our new lives as refugees in London began.

This is how my journey back to Sri Lanka to conduct my research began, but it did not end there. This book is not about myself and my personal journey, but instead the stories of others, and the society to which I returned a stranger over a decade later. A society which presented in its strangeness to me, new questions about what had happened and was happening. I experienced the very real sensation that I, like many others abroad, lived in memories inadequate to the task of comprehending what had happened in Sri Lanka in the 1990s. The title of this book is of course a reference to Kwame Anthony Appiah's (1992) essay "In My Father's House," which recounts his return to Ghana for his father's funeral and the fraught family and community disputes that unfolded around the requests of the dead man. Lurking behind is the Bible, which he and I too were brought up with, and one of its most quoted statements: "in my father's house there are many rooms." This book is about returning to my mother's house, but through a glass darkly, for I have put away childish things indeed. The book, while about Sri Lanka's civil war, is more largely about war itself as "a social condition" (Lubkemann 2008).

The decades long Sri Lankan civil war was waged between the Sri Lankan state and most latterly the Tamil guerrilla group, the Liberation Tigers of Tamil Eelam (LTTE, also called the "Tamil Tigers"), who emerged supreme through the elimination of all other Tamil militant groups. While there has been punctuated ethnic conflict since Independence in 1948, most would agree that large-scale violence between "armies" in the northern and eastern minority areas became a more everyday reality in the mid-1980s. It is a war that has involved the destruction of physical and human infrastructures, the permanent displacement of hundreds of thousands of people, the pitting of majority against minority ethnic groups, and the rise of insurrectionary groups who have turned from "heroes" to oppressors.

In 2009, in the midst of writing, others and I put our lives—in my case this book—on hold. In May 2009, the Sri Lankan government announced that the civil war, which had spanned almost 30 years, had ended with the final defeat of the LTTE, arguably one of the most successful, multifaceted, and wealthy guerrilla organizations in the world. The end of the war was not a quiet one. From January to May 2009, in an ever-shrinking coastal strip in the northern Vanni region the Sri Lankan government bombarded the LTTE and more than 330,000 civilians with heavy weaponry, while denying their use. The LTTE in its turn, as the Sri Lankan army advanced through the north central areas under LTTE control, took civilians with them, leading them to their death by using them as human shields. Sri Lankan Tamils ran from the advancing army, which has never offered them an alternative to the LTTE. Moving from place to place, bunker to bunker, 280,000 to 330,000 of them ended up trapped with the LTTE. The LTTE stepped up its forced recruitment of civilians, and those who escaped tell of hiding in their bunkers, trying to protect their children from roaming LTTE cadres picking up new recruits (UTHR 2009a,b). When surrounded by the Sri Lankan army, the LTTE hid and fired among civilians, refusing to let them leave.

The Sri Lankan state continued its relentless shelling of areas it had declared safe zones for civilians as well as hospitals in the war zone.[1] Escapees told the human rights group University Teachers for Human Rights-Jaffna (UTHRJ) and news agencies such as Al Jazeera and the BBC in Tamil about the heavy shelling by the state, their desperate attempts to protect themselves in the face of constant bombardment and lack of food, water, and medicine, and their disgust with their so-called protectors, the LTTE, who were willing to sacrifice them (UTHR 2009b).[2]

Meanwhile, the Sri Lankan government banned journalists and independent observers from these areas. Diasporic Tamils in Australia, Canada, and the United Kingdom mounted campaigns calling for the end of bombing by the Sri Lankan government. Increasingly, the LTTE abroad took over the management of those campaigns, and turned them into massed displays of LTTE flags and demands for the LTTE to be recognized and rescued by foreign governments. The gulf between internally displaced Sri Lankan Tamils in Sri Lanka and those in the diaspora who rallied around the LTTE was all too apparent to those of us who had done fieldwork in Sri Lanka. The support of expatriate Tamils for an increasingly delegitimized and violent LTTE meant that the protests became ineffective and the international community did not hold the Sri Lankan state to account and make it halt its use of heavy weaponry.

And so it went on. Every day in May brought more Tamil escapees from the LTTE areas carrying their elderly and children and wading through the lagoon to government-controlled territory. The events of the last days of battle and final defeat of the LTTE, especially the killing of its leader Prabhakaran, remain vague. It is unclear how the last leaders and their families died in the final days. It is rumored that they and their families were all executed by the state despite their surrender (see UTHR 2009a). The UN estimated that around 7,000 civilians may have died in these months, but this figure is in all probability conservative. After the end of the LTTE, the agony for those who survived did not end. The Sri Lankan government incarcerated 285,000 in sorely under-resourced and squalid mass camps for security clearance, not allowing them even to leave to meet family until December 2009, just before presidential elections. By mid-2010 around half had been released, but thousands still remain in camps. What happened to those taken out of camps for further questioning under suspicion of being LTTE remains a mystery. Areas where civilians once lived are now mined and scorched earth as the two armies advanced, retreated, and destroyed in their wake. The battle for hearts and minds of Tamil civilians was lost by the LTTE, and, sadly, remains the only battle the current Sri Lankan state is reluctant to initiate.

There is more to be said about these months, but I cannot say it in this book. I have no way of understanding fully what those thousands in the last war zone went through; I neither anticipated nor have privileged knowledge of the end. A book that began in the heart of the civil war somehow now tells its story from the other side of that protracted war. I have had to make the book again around a world made strange, with a new set of questions that now need to be asked.

The military war may have ended, but not the political one: the place of minorities in Sri Lanka still remains unsure. But the end of that war provides the fragile hope of new possibilities and parameters. It brings the possibility to reflect concretely on the specific social, cultural, and economic forms created in the decades of war. The accounts that will surely not survive the end of the war are those that, unlike this book, equated LTTE interests with those of the people it governed, and envisioned minority life through the pronouncements of the LTTE. The lives of Tamils and Muslims, and the complex ways people sought to live under and through the LTTE that I document here, may indeed point to why, despite many academic and Tamil nationalist claims to the contrary, when the LTTE collapsed militarily and its leader was killed it collapsed as a popular force in Sri Lanka.

War, Generation, and Home in Sri Lanka

This book is about war and the transformed physical, emotional, and social landscapes of civilians attempting to live through it. I focus on the war as mundane existence, and on the life cycles of individuals, families, and communities that are generated by and generate the social life of protracted war.

This introduction frames this enterprise through three overarching approaches. First, the book weaves together accounts of dramatic events of the war with those of life's ordinary projects. I do not focus on violence as the only primary feature of life in a war zone. Instead, following others such as Lubkemann (2008), I examine the myriad mundane (and perhaps more severe for being mundane) experiences of life in protracted wars. Second, this wartime life has been characterized by massive displacement of Tamils and Muslims. Displacement here is analyzed not in terms of facts and figures of migration flows, but as a ground of sociality, a new way of inhabiting the world. Third, I examine what kinds of new selves, generations, biographies, and ambivalences war produces—an inquiry into forms of subjectivity and individualization.

The individual narratives of war I write about in this book are self-conscious stories. People decide and select stories to tell, structured by particular political and social perspectives. I treat these narrations as commentaries, which both provide a way of understanding this war and are structured by the transformations of war to produce particular biographies. Thus the book is centrally concerned with individuals and the relationship they perceive between the self and the collective, in short, the production of selves and spaces within times of political terror.

These three larger grounding assumptions are worked through three ethnographic "how do" questions focusing on ideas of home, family, and political life. The first set of ethnographic questions tackle mass displacement through focusing on the transformations of notions of home for people who are chronically displaced in a war for homeland. I take this from the perspective of both Tamils and Muslims, the former at the heart of the struggle for homeland, the latter expelled to the margins. I explore how the loss of homes comes to endow new forms of historicity to individual and collective biographies. These concerns are braided into a second set of questions dealing with the generational divergences produced by the rapidity of transformation in the civil war, as well as the longer-term changes in familial and political ideologies. The book explores the fraught tensions between historically sedimented familial ideologies and structures and transformations in familial and generational experiences. The final ethnographic inquiries center on the effect of political terror on sociality and transforming political ideologies of militancy. I take militancy from the perspective of those who have left militant movements or of young people poised around the question whether to join, and what such movements leave in persons. The book's larger concern with sociality attempts to describe and assess the impact of violence and the stifling of internal dissent on Tamil and Muslim lives. These questions, reflecting as they do on issues of memory and the past, are nonetheless about people's imaginations of future lives and possibilities. This emphasis informs my own linking of the past to the future of Sri Lanka.

The following introduction lays out these frames and ethnographic inquiries alongside a birds-eye account of the ethnic conflict and civil war. Each chapter in the book stands for a different set of individuals/generation or ethnic group, and each presents a quite different perspective on often the same events and experiences in 1990s Sri Lanka. While all chapters deal with all three frames, some are attuned to particular inquiries more than others. Thus I discuss individual chapters in the introduction as they emerge by theme rather than by sequence.

The Social Life of War

There is an extensive discussion within anthropology around war as an object of study (see Simons 1999), and I do not intend to revisit well-worn ground (see Richards 2005b instead). Here my interest is firmly in the kinds of subjectivities, generational conflicts, and life projects produced through and in war in Sri Lanka. War here is both an object of study in itself, and at the same time a way of viewing an intensification of particular social life and process. For those I worked with, war was undoubtedly a different set of experiences from "prewar," it had its own parameters, frames, and codes, and generated different forms of sociality. Simultaneously, war did not obliterate preexisting social projects, fantasies, or social mores. Rather, it magnified and forced people, and analysts, to reconsider what those relationships and projects were meant to consist of, including their inherent contradictions as well as conflicts generated by war time. These are the moments when social life becomes revealed not as grounded by seamless shared assumptions, but as collective and individual fabrications and imaginaries, structured by larger circumstances and histories immediately out of the grasp of individuals.

This argument is not unique; it is a position in a larger debate in anthropological work on violence and war in the last twenty years. The two ends of this debate as well as the concomitant shift in focus can be illustrated by

Carolyn Nordstrom's *A Different Kind of War Story* (1997) and Stephen Lub-kemann's *Culture in Chaos* (2008), both on the same period of war in Mozambique. Nordstrom was part of a generation of anthropologists such as Daniel (1996) (though predated by Veena Das's work on India (published in Das 1997)) to place the study of war and violence firmly on the anthropological agenda. *A Different Kind of War Story* is premised on two overarching themes: that violence itself creates a shared culture, one that enables Nordstrom's short bursts of fieldwork across widely dispersed sites in Mozambique rather than indepth fieldwork in one region;[3] and that creativity and resistance emerge as ways of surviving and defeating the desertification of war understood primarily as violence. What makes war an object, a recognizable topic and process, for Nordstrom is violence and how to survive it. War, she argues, "comes into existence when violence is employed. . . . It is in the act of violence, then, that the definition of war is found" (1997: 115). In her introduction she forcefully defends such a focus on violence, arguing that discomfort with the depiction of real graphic violence and the accusations leveled against her that she aestheticizes violence reflects a discomfort with real lives and ethnographic facts, which, she argues, amounts to another form of silencing.

However, as Lubkemann argues in his refutation of this positionmost scholarship on life in war, by focusing on "how violence is organized and how warscapes inhabitants handle it," means that "our understanding of what war involves as an experience for subjects and societies thus tends to be organized almost exclusively around our understanding of what coping with violence involves" (2008: 10–11). Despite her laudable intentions, by bringing together people only as acts of violence are committed against them, Nordstrom thins the complexity of the social lives, desires, and projects of those she interviews (Englund 2005: 65–66). Social life is thicker than survival tactics, and such assertions of heroism only carry us so far in understanding.

Moreover, what is striking in protracted wars is the complexity of the violence that informs people's lives. As Tobias Kelly notes, recent accounts of armed violence in "over-determining violence" run the risk of ignoring the fraught mundanity of long-term armed conflict (2008: 353). The Palestinians Kelly works with experience the second intifada as acts of spectacular violence but also as terrible boredom, of struggling to provide for their families, worrying about how to get through checkpoints. He suggests that "if we are to understand the specific shape that armed conflicts take, with their particular peaks and troughs, we need to understand the lulls as much as the spikes in violence." Lives lived in the midst of protracted war or conflict must be understood not only in terms of spectacular violence, but also in other processes that I locate in this book: transformation of political culture, changes in kinship relations, individual conflicts between mothers and daughters about dowry and other forms of inheritance, and so on.

Lubkemann opens his book arguing for a notion of war *as a complex social condition* rather than a suspension of social life:

> In the growing number of places in which armed conflicts and displacement persist for decades. . . . For the inhabitants of such places war has not been an "event" that suspends "normal" social processes, but instead has become *the* normal—in the sense of "expected"— context for the unfolding of social life. Rather than treating war as an "event" that suspends social processes, anthropologists should study the realization and transformation of social relations and cultural practices *throughout* conflict, investigating war as a transformative social condition. (2008: 1)

Lubkemann abjures the idea of a pan-regional experience of war in Mozambique, coining the term "fragmented war." He argues that the national contest between FRELIMO and RENAMO for power in Mozambique was pursued around local struggles for power within communities and families that had little to do with the macropolitical objectives or discourses of the supralocal actors (2008: 161–86). Local actors sought to deploy and divert violence so that the civil war "became about much more than simply the violent contest for state level political power . . . it also became about the prosecution of everyday life through more violent means" (162). Through focusing on migration and marriage strategies, Lubkemann examines individual life goals and social, gender, and generational struggles as ongoing projects within wartime life that have to contend with dramatically altered social and physical environments. Thus Lubkemann argues that social projects and struggles are at the foreground of "war as social condition," and ethnography is about following "the reconfiguration of the social fields within which culturally scripted life projects are enabled" (14).

While I take inspiration from Lubkemann's notion of war as a social condition, there are divergences between my approach and his. To some extent, Lubkemann abandons the significance of the macro-political for understanding war, and, in stretching war as a social condition so broadly, ends up effacing any political specificity in wartime experiences. In this, he follows a larger trend in recent Africanist writings on war exemplified by the work of Paul Richards (1996, 2005a, b). For Richards and others working in regions that have fluctuated between periods of "war" and "peace" over many decades, to "understand war we must first deny it special status" (2005b: 3). Richards argues that war should be viewed *not* as "a thing in itself" but as a continuum, "one social project among many competing social projects." Lubkemann follows Richards in arguing that violence in wartime obfuscates the very real kinds of structural and physical violence people live with even when not at war (see Richards 2005b), and that for those studied there is little difference at times between war and peace. The insistence of the preeminent importance of preexisting social projects means that Lubkemann hovers between war as transformative and wartime life as the attempt to undertake life projects in "extremely trying circumstances."

However, in Sri Lanka, people do describe a distinct feeling of *yuttam*, war, and note enormous differences after *yuttam* from years before. Northern Jaffna Tamils and Muslims describe a total transformation of their landscapes. Stories tell of armies, such as the Indian army, the Sri Lankan army, and later the LTTE and other Tamil militants, patrolling the streets with guns. People disappeared, unidentified bodies were found. There was large-scale internal and external displacement. Aerial bombardment destroyed buildings. Sri Lanka's government institutions visibly began to break down in the war zone in contrast to other parts of the country. This is not to list only an empirical description of transformed life. By asserting that those I interviewed saw war as a thing in itself, I am paying attention to their stories and accounts, which constantly named and clustered around *yuttam*, and thus gave war a thickness, an agency, which became central to my account. I went to Sri Lanka primarily to examine ideas of home and kin, stressing these as social projects that were lived through rather than erased by violence. However, looking at these social projects returned me again and again to the ways people described war as something that had a special status in their lives, and moreover had fundamentally transformed their social and physical landscapes.

Furthermore, *yuttam* for both Tamils and Sinhalese is described differently from the continuous ethnic discrimination and anti-Tamil riots of the 1950s, '60s, and '70s, and from the mass insurrections of 1971 and 1987 in southern Sri Lanka that also resulted in thousands of arrests, disappearances, and deaths. As Lubkemann does indeed point out, violence is not a thing in itself, but always has a context and thus fashions different meanings (see above). In Sri Lanka people make qualifications and differentiations between forms of violence and its impact, from insurrections, riots, state violence, and internal violence directed by the LTTE against Tamils or by the state against Sinhalese. In fact, macro-political stories do have considerable purchase. In this book, I see war not as along a continuum with other forms of social life, but as a powerful and distinct force, period, and subjectivity, a making on a site of unmaking. Second, as later sections of the introduction will make clear, the book takes LTTE terror and its production of new forms of Tamil and Muslim life as the prism through which war is understood to have transformed social projects and biographies.

War as Making and Unmaking

In Sri Lanka, those I talked to presented the civil war as belonging to no one and yet to everyone. The war had assumed a radical exteriority, a self-propelling force seemingly out of control over everyone, which then became an existential condition, a "thing" in itself. Yet this thing, the war, which could be described through bombing, forced displacement, rape, recruitment, and so on, events that "happened" "to one," was also, as people frequently described, something that "happened inside one." One common way of describing the war by Tamils in Sri Lanka was to tell me of the fear that they felt toward other Tamils, unsure of who was LTTE and who was not. "There is no trust (*nambikkai*) among Tamils any more" was a frequent phrase. LTTE's often forcible recruitment of ordinary Tamils from families, and its widespread intelligence network and seeming pervasive presence in the Tamil community had led to a situation where networks of trust among Tamils were shrinking. The battlefields of the war were not only the frontlines where LTTE cadres and Sri Lankan soldiers died, but were also the internal lives of Tamil communities and families.

The war "happened" "to" people and at the same time made them. Every making was also an unmaking. This book documents some of these subjectivities: from new forms of individual self-making—from the LTTE promised heroic death to radical isolation and new ambivalent kinds of collective life (see also Thiranagama 2010). These new forms were built on the constantly recalled erasure of other forms of individual and collective life. Thus new forms also contained within them, the forms of their loss, whether directly experienced or inherited. I move here from Lubkemann's pursuit of life projects in trying circumstances to an insistence on the constitution of social forms and frames that give shape to the very selves that pursue life projects, whose self-evidentness has been put into question. This is an ethnographic enterprise par excellence. This book attempts to understand how people narrate themselves as wartime selves.

That identities and narrative selves produced through civil war are founded on the effects of its brutalities, losses, and destructions as well as opportunities afforded for gain, promised heroism, and sacrifice points us to the deeply fraught nature of such identities. In foregrounding such ambivalence, I take inspiration from Judith Butler's (1997) notion of "subjection" in her subtle and compelling reformulation of Foucault in *The Psychic Life of Power*. Butler discusses how, Foucauldian "subjectification" sees power that subordinates as simultaneously inaugurating. Thus, subjection "activates" or "forms" the subject through the "principle of regulation according to which a subject is formulated" (1997: 84). The subject that arises, however, is not for Butler fixed in place, it "is the occasion for a further making" (99), where she reintroduces her earlier emphasis on subject formation through constant reiteration, which, far from enabling stability and coherence, comes to constantly reinstate incoherence; "this iterability, thus becomes the non-place of subversion, the possibility of a reembodying of the subjectivating norm that can redirect its normativity" (99).

The central thrust of Butler's argument in *The Psychic Life of Power* is that if power thus forms and activates the subject, then paradoxically power is also what "we depend on for our existence" (1997: 2) . This dependency produces an ambivalent attachment to that which injures us: "subjection consists precisely in this fundamental dependency on a discourse we never chose but that, paradoxically, initiates and sustains our agency" (2). It is this ambivalent attachment that Butler goes on to explore in her theories of the psychic life of power, our attachment to subjection being the most "insidious" psychic effect of the operation of power (6-11).[4] This whole operation is made possible because subjection as such confers upon us existence, and we desire to be intelligible, we *desire existence as such* (28, 104, 129-31; 2004). Butler's account is her redirection of (Foucauldian) subjectification toward considering the place of (Freudian) desire, attachment, and libidinal investment in subjection toward, not, as she points out the more commonly theorized psychoanalytic "unconscious outside power," but the "unconscious of power" (104-5), opening up useful ways of exploring psychic and social history (see also Rose [1996] 2004).

Butler's account of the ambivalent passionate attachment to our own categorization and interpellation into the social world—because of this existential longing to be intelligible and recognized, which thus propels our subjection—speaks very strongly to how one could theorize the civil war in the lives of those I interviewed, as injurious and yet productive and constitutive. All kinds of new categories and identities had emerged precisely as a consequence of the war, deepening ethnic identification being one of them.

In this vein, the book thus argues, first, that to understand the complexities of growing up within a wartime world, one must understand the ways the war waged itself across inner battlefields that it itself simultaneously produced. Second, as a consequence, new kinds of Tamil and Muslim identities were produced that cannot just be resolved or cast away because the war ended, but now have to be negotiated anew. The war, in inaugurating new forms of subjectivity, gave life and voice to particular kinds of biographies, bodily regimes, manners of coping. This is not the same as suggesting that there was a desire for war; none of my interviewees ceased to talk of and hope for a life without war. It is rather to understand with Butler that the forces that make and unmake us are the sites of ceaselessly generative *ambivalent* attachments and investments. This account of how war grounds life even as it takes it away—producing new people, new possibilities of voice, forms of heroism—is central to the book and underlies all the individual biographies I present. Our (disavowed) dependency on such frames, because they gave our life meaning, becomes ever more pertinent now when thinking about how those produced by war can negotiate life outside it. Allied to this is a focus on a specific war formation (LTTE violence against Tamils and Muslims) and thus the specificity of the kinds of biographies, and life projects which have emerged.

Displacement and Civil War in Sri Lanka

Northern Tamils and Muslims

Sri Lanka has a basic bipartite divide of language between Sinhala and Tamil speakers. There are many other minorities who speak Sinhalese, Tamil, or English, such as the Portuguese and Dutch Burgers, the Veddas (aboriginal peoples), and so on, but they are not involved in the ethnic conflict on grounds of language or ethnicity. The majority community (around 74.5 percent) are the Sinhalese.[5] Tamil-speakers are subdivided into different ethnic groups. The largest Tamil-speaking minority, central to the ethnic conflict, are the Sri Lankan Tamils, approximately 11.9 percent (down from 12.7 percent as a result of major outmigration and deaths caused by the war). The second are the Muslims, 8.3 percent of the population. Muslims, though Tamil-speaking, are classified as an ethno-religious minority around the categories of religion and ethnicity, while Sri Lankan Tamils, Christian and Hindu, are classed as an ethnic minority around language and ethnicity. While Tamils and Muslims are scattered all across the island, they are most densely concentrated in the northern and eastern provinces, the basis of separatist claims to an independent Tamil homeland. The other most significant Tamil-speaking minority are the Malaiyaha Tamils (Hill Country Tamils), approximately 4.6 percent of the population, the descendants of South Indian plantation labor brought by the British. They too have suffered much discrimination—the first act of Sri Lanka's new parliament in 1948 was to disenfranchise them—but they are not part of the story I tell here (see instead Daniel 1996; Kanathipathipillai 2009; Bass 2001).

This book centers on bringing together Tamil and Muslim voices: the underexplored story not of the large ethnic conflict but of the transformations caused by the civil war. Because the conflict has centred on the relationship between the Sri Lankan state (as "acting for" the Sinhalese majority community) and Sri Lankan Tamils, representations of the ethnic conflict have often neglected the perspectives of Sri Lankan Muslims whose lives have also been indelibly marked by ongoing war. The Northern Muslims I worked with were all forcibly expelled from the north by the LTTE and have lived as collectively displaced people ever since. However, the north became a mono-cultural— if not mono-religious given the large proportion of Christian Tamils— Tamil region only after the expulsion of Muslims. Muslims remain, I argue, the unspoken void of the Tamil nationalist project. The breakdown of Tamil and Muslim relations in violence in the east, and in forcible eviction in the north, has been the major fissure of the 1990s war. Any possible peaceful future in northern and eastern Sri Lanka has to contend with Tamil-Muslim relations (McGilvray 2008).

I have *not* written about Tamil and Sinhalese relations and not contextualized what I have written in relation to the highly complex and equally geographically and politically divided southern polity. This is not a sectarian choice, but it is a choice. First, there is much research on the south and some on the east, but little elsewhere given the difficulties of fieldwork with minority communities in the war zone. Second, while the conflict between the state and the Sri Lankan Tamil community is well known and well documented, the experiences of Tamils vis-à-vis the LTTE, the inside of the community so to speak, have been little written about. Tamil academics faced the possibility of real persecution by the LTTE unless they toed the LTTE line, while non-Tamil academics like Margaret Trawick (2007) and Peter Schalk (1992, 1997), who have written about the LTTE, have relied on the LTTE to gain access and their work accordingly bears the consequences. I had an easier route than many researchers. I am Tamil, and my mother's political history in opposing both the state and the LTTE made it easier for people to trust me and talk about the LTTE without thinking I was a stooge of the Sri Lankan state.

Third, tellingly and very sadly, the war has had a polarizing effect on Tamil and Sinhala relations. Quite simply, after the onset of the war, many of those I interviewed had little contact with ordinary Sinhalese until they came to Colombo. The Sinhalese they described were army and navy personnel, where the coercive apparatus of the Sri Lankan state stood in for Sinhalese civilians. I set out to document an increasingly insular world created as a result of long-term discrimination and intensification of militarization. I tell the story as Tamils see it, not withdrawing my critical eye, but not enforcing a transformed ethnic conviviality between Sinhalese and Tamil.

Furthermore, that this book is about *northern* Tamils and Muslims is to highlight another contested assumption of pan-regional Tamil and Muslim identity. The pan-regional Tamil identity enshrined at the heart of contemporary Sri Lankan Tamil nationalism is historically problematic and regionally contested—most evidently in the schism in the LTTE on regional (north versus east) lines in 2004. Sivathamby (1984) identifies three distinct Sri Lankan Tamil regions: the "North," " East," and "Vanni" districts of the North Central province.[6] This regionalization is also important for Sri Lankan Muslims, who can also be subdivided regionally into "Eastern," "Northern," and "Southwest" blocs, though Muslim dispersal across the island, especially in highland Kandy, makes the southwest bloc more permeable. Northern and eastern Tamils and Muslims differ in the ways they reckon caste, mosque membership, folk dialects, and family structure (Pfaffenberger 1982; McGilvray 1982, 1998).[7] Despite national ethnic identities, at a local level northern Tamils and northern Muslims are more alike in social and familial structures, as Tamils and Muslims are in the east. Not least, one of the most immediate differences between north and east is the highly diverse nature of the east coast, with Sinhalese, Tamils, and Muslims each comprising roughly a third of the population (McGilvray 2008), while the north is primarily Tamil and (formerly) Muslim.[8]

Northern Jaffna has been always viewed as the primary ideological and physical battlefield of Tamil nationalism. While the war shifted progressively toward the East over the 1990s, Jaffna nevertheless persists as an image of "Eelam" (the putative Tamil homeland) central to the imagination of a Tamil identity. Jaffna Tamils dominated nationalist movements throughout the twentieth century, and Tamils from other regions have often complained with justification about discrimination by Jaffna Tamils. East coast Tamils consistently express a distrust of Jaffna Tamils, concerned that the latter would largely control any separatist state (Whittaker 1990; Pfaffenberger 1994; McGilvray 1998, 2008). Among Muslims, it is the numerically stronger eastern Muslims who dominate representations of Muslim identity, not the small Muslim minority from the north.

While Jaffna is highly overwritten in political and public discourse as personifying "Tamilness," in fact there has been little actual fieldwork carried out among Jaffna Tamils or Muslims.[9] Jaffna past, present, imagined, and future, has emerged as hegemonic through an *assumed* knowability created by constant citation and elision as the site of war, violence, and nationalism if not the site of fieldwork research.[10] Sources on the daily lives and wartime events of minorities have been written not by anthropologists but by human rights activists and NGOs who have taken on the task of documenting and research, often of the highest caliber.[11] My research with northern Tamils and Muslims, given the chronic displacement that characterized northern life, was carried out in the southern Colombo and north central Puttalam districts.

Movement and Migration

My research was with those on the move. This is far from unknown in Jaffna. Jaffna has not stood still for over two hundred years, if ever. For Jaffna Tamils, becoming displaced (*idam peyrntha*) with little control over one's movement was played out against a longer history of migration as a means of economic and social mobility. The Jaffna peninsula is notable for consistently high rates of out-migration throughout the colonial and postcolonial period. Economically marginal to the emerging Sri Lankan plantation economy, and overpopulated (Arasaratnam 1994),[12] the area remained largely rural and underdeveloped, while its highly educated young men and (later) women became salaried labor within the colonial administration in the rest of the island and in the wider British empire of South and South-East Asia (Bastin 1997)[13] and to a lesser extent Africa. The economy was heavily dependent on remittances, with over 600,000 rupees remitted from outside the island in 1903 (Bastin 1997). By the twentieth century "a spirit of migration mostly by middleclass Tamils, became built into Tamil cultural aspirations" (McDowell 1996: 69). Within the island, Colombo, the capital city, was the favored site of internal migration flows from Jaffna for those seeking salaried work, the flow between Jaffna and Colombo being one of the most consistent migratory flows into Colombo throughout the twentieth century (Don Arachchige 1994: 30). Thus what I describe is not a largely sedentary group of people, Jaffna Tamils to whom movement was unknown, but a people for whom the possibility for *chosen* migration was always valued. In contrast, until their eviction in 1990, Northern Muslims were far more sedentary and less migratory.

Since the 1980s, outmigration from the Jaffna peninsula has been increasingly due to worsening conflict.[14] Almost two-thirds of Jaffna's population live elsewhere, and many living within the peninsula are themselves internally displaced. As a whole, one in two Sri Lankan Tamils has been displaced and nearly one in four lives outside the country (Sriskandarajah 2004).[15] Displacement has varied in intensity, often occurring in waves after forced movements, military operations, and riots. In February 2009 there was a floating population of around 495,000 displaced people, mainly Tamils and Muslims; this figure dramatically rose after the last battles in May 2009 (IDMC 2009).[16] The majority of internally displaced Tamils are in camps in the north and east in both LTTE- and government-controlled areas; a considerable number who are not formally registered as Internally Displaced Persons (IDPs) live in a variety of rented, temporary, and sometimes permanent housing in the capital Colombo. The majority of displaced Muslims are from the north, though as a result of communal tension in the east, the number of Muslim IDPs in the east is rising. Northern Muslims were all displaced when they were ethnically cleansed from the north by the LTTE in 1990, and the majority ended up in refugee camps in the Puttalam district in the north-central district. For both Tamils and Muslims forced, aimless, and continual displacement were experienced as profound cultural shocks, within which people tried to pursue—by whatever means possible—culturally valued strategies of going abroad or elsewhere for work.

Overseas migration by Tamils matches internal displacement. In 2002, Sri Lankan Tamils were among the top ten asylum seeking groups in the world.[17]

Significantly, this large, visible, well-organized diaspora meant that the Sri Lankan civil war became globalized. Phases of emigration corresponded to the ebbs and flows of the severity of the war in Sri Lanka (Sriskandarajah 2002; Daniel and Thangarajah 1995). Since 2000, it has become ever more difficult to migrate abroad, as I was told by those Tamils I interviewed in Colombo waiting in limbo to find means to migrate. I call them "the shadow diaspora." The majority of academic work on Jaffna Tamils has been on overseas diaspora communities, and by dint of arguing for a continuum between diaspora communities and their former homes, seeks to extrapolate experiences of diasporic Tamils as fully representing Tamils in Sri Lanka (see Cheran 2001, 2007). I begin with the opposite and more productive assumption of no such easy, naturalized cultural continuum between Tamils in Sri Lanka and Tamils in diasporas abroad. In this book I focus on the internally displaced, though I have carried out fieldwork in Canada and Britain, to highlight rather than subsume the very different experiences of those still living in Sri Lanka (see also Thiranagama 2010). The differences between diasporic Tamils and those in the war zone became most evident in the differences between protesting diaspora Tamils under LTTE flags as the battle raged between the LTTE and the state in 2010, and Tamils in Sri Lanka who denounced the LTTE as they fled from them (Rajasingam 2009; UTHR 2009a,b).

Writings on migration and displacement, as Ranabir Samaddar points out, often play the numbers game, stressing facts and figures but failing to take these as creating new sociabilities as well as matrices of state and extrastate power (1999: 199–212). When one begins research on mass and individual movement in Sri Lanka, one cannot avoid the moral, experiential, and emotional dilemmas of displacement that have created new orientations toward the world. Throughout this book, displacement is taken not simply as something that happens to people, but through its ubiquity, as a way of inhabiting the world. Displacement has become a reality that families and individuals undergo, and, at the same time provided the dominant metaphor and story of change that those I interviewed used to describe the civil war and the entanglement of personal fortunes with collective futures. An individual struggle to find a stable place to live, for a Tamil or Muslim, is a personal story and also a collective story; the violent making and unmaking of place and home in Sri Lanka is about the right to belong as members of a minority. I position this displacement within the larger biography of the spirit of migration and movement, to emphasize the extent to which displacement was experienced as "forced movement" in a universe where migration provided social mobility. The opposite of internal displacement for those I worked with was not always resettlement but in fact greater mobility.

Ur-*Home*

In approaching displacement, I foreground one of the most celebrated aspects of personhood in northern Sri Lanka: the notion of *ur* (home/natal village). *Ur*, home, is an *everyday* and often used Tamil word. On meeting someone else, Tamil or Muslim, one of the first few questions asked is almost inevitably "what is your *ur*." It refers to one's natal village, most often one's mother's village though not exclusively so. It is the soil on which one is meant to have been nurtured, eaten food from, taken in the air and properties (Daniel 1984). *Ur* stands in contrast to *kiramam* (village) and *tecam* (nation), which Daniel (1984) argues are "bounded, standard, universally accepted and constant spatial units. For the South Indian Tamil villagers that Daniel studied, *kiramam* referred to a fixed universal and context-free space, while *ur*, that which expressed oneself, was person-centric, contextual and fluid.[18] Knowing the *ur* of someone can reveal to you the person's *kunam*, character, and thus *ur* can provide a repertoire of guesses about character and possible interaction (Daniel 1984: 102). These *ur* were named places in Jaffna where "there are also a few proverbial sayings about the characteristics of the inhabitants of particular villages" (Banks 1971: 71). As persons who came from the same *ur* shared characteristics through their nourishment in the same soil this provided a more collective identification of people from that *ur*.

This book foregrounds particular notions of home, *ur*, rather than a generic home per se found in more philosophical discussions (e.g., Rouner 1996). In doing so, I write against a dominant thread of work whereby too often the common scholarly and popular assumption is that in separatist wars ideas of home and homeland are congruent emotive and political concepts. Home is assumed to be a smaller version of homeland, the latter a scaled up imaginary. In fact, homeland and home did not exist on the same layers of imagination for those I worked with; they had parallel lives, invoking different moments and senses of the self. In one encounter in Toronto, a group of elderly women and I were chided by one of their grandsons for talking about Jaffna. He rebuked us and told us we should be saying Tamil Eelam instead. As he walked away, his grandmother apologized for him and his Canadian ways, and we all went back to talking about Jaffna, for, as one of the women said, "that's our *ur*."

Homeland, Tamil Eelam, is a firmly mono-ethnic concept enforced by ethnic cleansing, occupying a different emotional terrain from ideas of home. It is for Tamils and named by Tamils as such, an imaginary geography par excellence. Here, I show that the potent emotional force surrounding *ur*/home, like the Tamil language itself, was mobilized by both Tamils and Muslims—especially in relation to each other. *Ur* has the possibility to be used across ethnicity and caste, though the question whether the same *ur* in social terms exists across caste and ethnicity for the same geographical entity is more vexed, beckoning to the idealized hierarchical structured interactions within Tamil life, which were increasingly unsustainable through war and displacement.

This book explores what work ideas of *ur* do in the context of large-scale displacement. Taking discourses of *ur* away from Daniel's more general discussion of substance, personhood, and the drive toward equilibrium in Tamil life, I focus instead on the specific historical and political trajectories of the people I work with, which shape their ideas of *ur*, and the way the language of *ur* came to condense within it a multiplicity of narratives about who we were, who we are, and most significantly who we are becoming. All those I talked to assumed that because one is a person, one has an *ur*, and because one has an *ur*, one must either love it or feel obligated to love it. *Ur* here became about an everyday language of love, affection, sentiment, and memory, which, produced as it was around an assumed cultural good that was by its very nature highly mutable, was highly potent but also a generator of contradiction. Rather than seeing the effects of mass displacement as placing the notion of home in crisis, instead the book points to the ways in which people sought to fix and make larger meanings out of this fluid person-centric discourse of assumed love and affinity. The potency and yet problem of *ur* as a means of belonging was the loss and fluidity built into its very practical life as transferring and transmuting, marriage after marriage, move after move.

This difficult translatability and potency was particularly acute in the case of Northern Muslims. Chapter 4 focuses on notions of *ur* and how Northern Muslims related to their former homes after expulsion, as well as their discourses about the un-homeliness and homeliness of the camps and settlements they were living in. I examine how the seeming incommensurability of transmitting *ur* and the absolute necessity of doing so became the focus of intense emotional work within families. How could ethnically cleansed Muslims pass on a sense of home to their children growing up in a different *ur* in refugee camps and settlements, given that this *ur* was both what they had lost and what was left to them now that they were barred from the narrative of the Tamil-only homeland? Chapter 4 and others are guided by an emphasis on the futural bent of stories about lost homes. In a situation of mass displacement, what people talked about in their allusions to past homes, was the search for a future home where could one be at home.

This emphasis on what home could be in the future responds to another problem in anthropological and philosophical literature on "home." Discussions of being at home in the world as an existential condition play to a normative schema that privileges nostalgia for sedentism by those on the move (see Malkki 1995 and Jansen and Lofving 2009 for a good discussion) rather than a consideration of homeliness as an always potentially disappointing ideal type (Hage 1997) or as an ever present material concern about self-perpetuation. Instead here, I privilege very particular notions of home, an understanding of the emotional potency and thus fraught availability, of this notion for larger discussions about belonging, as well as the possible failure of *ur* to be the felicitous space that Bachelard argues images of houses and domestic belonging often are (1994 [1969]: 7–10).

Questions of what could be future homes are treated in greatest detail in Chapter 6, which focuses in on Tamil life in Colombo, the de facto capital of Sri Lanka. I examine the (long) history of Colombo's heterogeneity and the securitized mapping of the city around the anticipation of violence. to come up with a phenomenology of Tamil Colombo and the possibilities of homeliness in a Colombo that is home to multiple minorities. I try to confront what the ethnicized notion of homeland as the derivative for political rights could mean, confronted with a city like Colombo where minorities might have homes but not homelands, and where the home in the future might not coincide with a home of the past. These questions are deeply consequential because of the ways individual and collective displacement and futures have come to be intertwined in Sri Lanka.

Ethnic Conflict and Civil War

Sri Lanka's ethnic conflict has been extensively covered (e.g., Tambiah 1986, 1996; Sivanandan 1984; Spencer 1990a; Krishna 1999; Manogaran and Pfaffenberger 1994). What has emerged most coherently from this vast literature is that the ethnic conflict is not a primordial conflict expressing an ancient enmity between Tamils and Sinhalese. While nationalist commentators, academic and popular, in Sri Lanka continue to elaborate this myth (e.g., Bandarage 2008), others have comprehensively demolished this as a factual story (see Tambiah 1986; Spencer 1990a; Nissan and Stirrat 1990). Tambiah puts it most elegantly when he points out that "Sinhalese and Tamil labels are porous sieves through which diverse groups and categories of Indian peoples, intermixed with non-Indians. . . . have passed" (1986: 6). The story of ancient enmity, and the positing of stable "ethnic" identities to these formerly rather fluid labels, is itself the product of a more recent history of colonial historiography, the racialization of Sri Lanka's diverse population, and postcolonial ethnic conflict and discrimination (Spencer 1990a; Jeganathan and Ismail 1995).

Sri Lanka, formerly Ceylon, was the longest colonized country in South Asia for three colonial powers, the Portuguese (1505–1658), Dutch (1658–1796), and finally British (1796–1948). When the British defeated the Kandyan Kingdom in 1815, they were the first power to unite the island under a common administration and it was the first time the island had ever existed as a unified political and spatial territory. The British encountered and made sense of Sri Lanka's immensely socially and religiously heterogeneous population through popular Victorian ideas of race, linking this to religious and language differences (Rogers 1990; Nissan and Stirrat 1990; Gunawardena 1990). While it is clear that the British did not "invent" ethnicity in Sri Lanka—there is clear evidence that groups have categorized others in various forms over the centuries—identities assumed more solid and "ethnic" form as they became linked to concrete political structures (Wickramasinghe 2006: 44). The categories Tamil and Sinhalese came to assume great significance and substance in the political and administrative structures of the island (Wickramasinghe 2006; Nissan and Stirrat 1990). These were elaborated and entrenched by scholarly work on philology, ancient history, and archaeology, all of which premised clearcut categories of difference (Gunawardena 1990; Rogers 1990; etc.). Ethnicity became a highly meaningful political category in colonial rule, continuing though transformed after independence.

Sri Lanka's postcolonial history was dominated by a populist policies that brought into being a comprehensive universal welfare state providing free education, health care, and other benefits for its (multi-ethnic) population, which at the same time was undergirded by a strong Sinhala nationalist rhetoric that privileged the ideal beneficiaries to be the majority community (Spencer 1990a,b). Given an enormous gulf between a postcolonial English-educated political elite and its voting population, Spencer (1990a: 20) argues, the political elite turned to the language of emerging Sinhala nationalism, purified Buddhism, "racial authenticity," and the feeling of having been the "sons of the soil" but exploited by colonial rule. This meant the opportunistic use of the perception by the majority community that those minority groups, Tamils, Muslims, and Christians, perceived as having undue influence under the British, must be "kept in their place" (Tambiah 1986: 66–86). Thus education in Tamil and Sinhalese was politically couched as a "Sinhala-only" policy in 1956. This and other discriminatory policies against minorities, such as the university standardization system[19] and the 1972 constitution, which removed the constitutional guarantees of protection for minorities (section 29) contained in the previous constitution and made Buddhism the official state religion (section 6, chapter II), led to increasing tensions around ethnic relations (Krishna 1999; Tambiah 1986; etc.).

The symbolic and economic effects of state restrictions in the 1960s and 1970s were immediate: "the Tamils . . . well established in commerce, public service and the professions. . . . [were] edged out of their niches as the State was largely Sinhalicized and the economy partly socialised" (Moore 1990: 349). The most visible and polarizing effect of ethnic discrimination and Sinhala nationalist rhetoric was the presence of regular anti-Tamil riots, in 1956, 1958, 1977, 1981, and 1983. All the Tamils I interviewed had a family member involved in one riot or another. This brought not only loss of life, but displacement, anxiety, and the constant anticipation of further violence. When the 1983 anti-Tamil riots occurred, often named by many as the beginnings of the protracted war, it seemed only to confirm that Tamils were not safe in southern Sri Lanka

Increased ethnic discrimination and the growing welfare state were also accompanied by growing challenges to state authority and growing violence. From the 1970s onward, the Sri Lankan state faced challenges from radical Sinhalese youth (as well as later from Tamil militants), with an insurrection in 1971 by the Janatha Vimukthi Perumuna (JVP), an armed revolt of university students and rural peasants, and its renewed and transformed reappearance in 1986. The 1970s to 1990s marked an increasingly authoritarian face of the state. The SLFP (Sri Lanka Freedom Party) government of the 1970s had used the pretext of a new constitution to extend the life of its parliament, had brutally suppressed an insurrection and had ruled under emergency legislation for most of its tenure. The 1977 UNP (United National Party) government took political repression to new heights. Between 1977 and 1994, under UNP rule, saw two more anti-Tamil riots, passage of a repressive Prevention of Terrorism Act, an executive presidency formed and the parliamentary term extended under a rigged election and referendum, and military intervention in the north and east. The 1987–1989 conflict between a resurgent JVP and the state left the south in a state of terror and chaos with around 60,000 reported missing in two short years. Party reorganization and economic liberalization increased state patronage in the distribution of economic and political resources (Moore 1990). The state's incursions into the north and east by the late 1980s were on a full war footing, involving aerial bombardment, a counterinsurgency campaign, and curfews, boycotts, and restrictions on the supply of food and goods to these areas.

The Tamil "National Liberation Struggle"

Two major factors are significant in the rise of Tamil nationalism and Tamil militancy. The first is the growth of pan-regional Tamil identification across the north and east.[20] From the 1950s onward, a frontier of poor Sinhala peasants was settled in the dry zone and further east into already populated Tamil and Muslim areas. This succeeded in cutting the proportion of Tamil and Muslim votes in their traditional constituencies, and dividing the east between different ethnic constituencies (McGilvray 2008), with rising identification with a larger pan-regional discriminated against Tamil community. Anti-Tamil riots reinforced the feeling that one was a target across class, caste, and region, purely on the basis of being Tamil (Tambiah 1986).

Second was the failure of Tamil parliamentary parties to provide material and political resources for young Tamils. Political parties and MPs controlled access to all kinds of resources, leading to the state being subsumed by politicians and their alliances. As Nissan and Stirrat put it, "access to the resources of the state became a matter of access to politicians" (1990: 36). While Muslim politicians made alliances within the major Sinhala parliamentary parties, patronage networks that brought state resources to rural areas were inaccessible to Tamil parliamentary parties and thus to northern and eastern areas.[21] Tamil parties were pushed further toward declaring for full independence, hamstrung and frustrated by the inability of successive Sri Lankan governments to resolve discrimination (McGilvray 2008).

The impotence of the Tamil parliamentary parties, such as the Federal Party and its successor, the Tamil United Liberation Front (TULF), prompted the creation of many small Tamil militant groups with a plethora of acronyms in the 1970s. As Krishna points out, "Tamil militant groups regarded moderation and compromise with the political establishment as oppositions that had been tried repeatedly and had conclusively failed" (Krishna 1999: 77). Militants called for the creation of a separate Tamil homeland comprising the Tamil majority areas of the north and east. This was also an important social transformation, as young people of all castes turned away from the older elites in the Tamil parliamentary parties. After the 1983 riots, recruitment to the militant groups swelled into the thousands, and the Indian central government began to play a (double) role. It offered itself as the mediator between the Sri Lankan government and the militants, and, it secretly began training and arming Tamil militants through the Research and Analysis Wing (RAW) (Krishna 1999). These moments of transformation have often been referred to superficially but left unexamined ethnographically. As Tambiah remarked in 1990:

It is likely that there are internal tensions taking place on three fronts: the relationships between generations, between sexes, and between castes. These changes among the Tamils may be as dramatic and fateful as the more dramatized and accented ethnic warfare between the Sinhalese and Tamils. (Tambiah 1990: 28)

The secretive, highly disciplined, and militarily effective LTTE emerged as the self declared "sole representative of the Tamil people" in 1986, when it proscribed or absorbed other militant groups (e.g., TELO, the Tamil Eelam Liberation Organization, and EPRLF, the Eelam People's Revolutionary Liberation Front) and families associated with them in a year of intense fratricidal conflict. They labeled militants from the other groups and their families, not freedom fighters, but "traitors to the Tamil nation." This climactic and bloody struggle has been sparsely documented even though it is central to the rise of the LTTE. The subsequent alliance of these other militant groups with Indian rule in the north (1987–1990) and attendant misrule also soured the reputation of these groups among the civilian population.

After 1986, the LTTE and the state intensified their campaigns against each other, leading to heavy bombardment and a pacification campaign against the Jaffna peninsula in 1986 (Fuglerud 1999: 36). India intervened more directly in light of pleas by Sri Lankan Tamils. The Indian Peace Keeping Force (IPKF) entered in 1987 to broker and maintain a settlement, but relations between the IPKF and the LTTE broke down into a bloody war. The atrocities committed by both are well documented in the book *Broken Palmyrah* produced by the human rights group UTHR (Hoole et al. 1990).

In 1990, after a bizarre alliance by the Sri Lankan state and the LTTE, President Premadasa channeled arms and aid to the LTTE and the IPKF were forced to withdraw. By the time the Indian army left in 1990, the death toll amounted to some 10,000 civilian deaths and displacement of 750,000 people as internal refugees, with a further 100,000 seeking asylum in the West (UTHR 1994). Soon after peace talks between the Sri Lankan government and the LTTE collapsed into Eelam War II. The consequences of this period of authoritarianism, violence and opportunistic politics were seen in subsequent years when, in 1993, President Premadasa was murdered by an LTTE suicide bomber, paradoxically bringing a caretaker government, fresh elections, and the restoration of normality in southern Sri Lanka. In 1991, Indian Prime Minister Rajiv Gandhi was blown up by a female LTTE suicide bomber bending to give obeisance at his feet. These were the years that people began speaking of war.

The Rise and Fall of the LTTE

The period described in this book is from the late 1980s onward, the rise (and now fall) of the LTTE. In 1990 the LTTE assumed virtual control of northern Jaffna and north central Vanni, as well as parts of the east. In Jaffna they established a taxation system, a judiciary, a police force, and other systems and institutions such as orphanages (Fuglerud 1999: 53, 2009). The Tigers were focused in both real and symbolic senses on their leader, Vellupillai Prabhakaran. The military wings included a conventional land and artillery army, a navy (the Sea Tigers), intelligence wings, and special suicide squads (the Black Tigers). Its primary features were: a pyramidal structure, use of suicide bombings and cyanide capsules, an extensive intelligence network, and a prioritization of eliminating traitors within the Tamil community; thus, its reliance on fear and intimidation to control Tamil politics in Sri Lanka and the diaspora. This was accompanied by increasing fetishization of themselves, use of flags, uniforms, its own law code, a constant stream of propaganda, relentless pursuit of a "party-line," and ritualization of the Tamil calendrical year through public events and celebrations devoted to its martyrs. Fear of its intelligence network, divided into military and internal intelligence, was widespread. "Intelligence" was involved in surveillance, incarceration, and elimination of both LTTE cadres and the general population. Cadres infiltrated and mobilized others to inform on their neighbors, kin, and fellow cadres.

Cadres were both voluntarily and forcibly recruited. Forced recruitment rose in the 1990s, particularly focused on recruiting children. The extensive LTTE recruitment and use of child soldiers, the infamous "baby brigades" as it names them, have been internationally and locally criticized. The 2002 ceasefire did not halt such recruitment; families in eastern Sri Lanka were told that each family should contribute one child to the LTTE. This large-scale conscription, whether voluntary or forced, means that most families had a connection to or a family member in the LTTE. Uniformed cadres were separated from the civilian population, renamed, and their loyalties reoriented toward the movement. However, the LTTE also possessed a more civilian face; the Tigers were also one's brother, sister, son, cousin, as well as the uniformed young men and women patrolling the area or demanding taxes from you in your house. Given its intimate ties within Tamil families, the LTTE occupied an intimate space within the family and the community rather than an external one such as the Sri Lankan state was imagined to inhabit.

The LTTE also militarized and inserted themselves into civilian space in other ways. Not only were there undercover cadres, but they also maintained a loose network of long-term and short-term loyalties and informers, who offered information for gain or as a result of coercion. Civilians caught in the struggle for survival existed in a state of constant complicity. This intimacy of LTTE presence among the civilian population led to a situation where networks of trust were increasingly shrinking while fear of other Tamils expanded. Other Tamils could always have been informers ready to denounce, or LTTE cadres in civilian garb.

This book examines the identification of Tamils and the LTTE by focusing on how the LTTE forced new ways of thinking about Tamilness and ethnic identity and affiliation around itself from the 1990s onward. The 1983 riots made it possible to feel Tamil across caste and class lines, by virtue of being targets of mob violence and state discrimination, but this solidarity was reframed by LTTE policing of its own population. The LTTE reconfigured being Tamil around the ethnic cultural intimacy produced by shared knowledge of itself (LTTE) and the possibility of its rule over you—wherever you are—simply because you were Tamil. Whether you were in Toronto or in Sri Lanka, the LTTE was with you. Every Tamil had to have a position on the LTTE as either "pro" or "anti," which no Muslim or Sinhalese necessarily had to (Mannikalingam, personal communication).

Tamils talked to each other knowing that there was a possibility that any other Tamil could be an LTTE cadre or informer. Being Tamil meant that everyone shared the same secret: "the LTTE." Being Tamil, everyone assumed, put you in possession of the same secret alongside them. It was assumed that you would know that conversations were multilayered, allusive, double-voiced. Even if Tamils could not trust other Tamils, they nonetheless believed that only other Tamils could understand the predicament that all found themselves in, because only other Tamils were subject to LTTE surveillance and power. When I interviewed people, I was told that they could talk to me because I could "understand." What this understanding meant was that I too "knew" about the LTTE and would be careful, and that I was risking myself, as a Tamil, as much as they were in talking to me. Only other Tamils were presumed to know the rules of the game and could read between the lines. Thus, "outsiders," Sinhalese and foreign journalists, who reported that Tamils seemed to publicly support the LTTE were regarded with disdain: they "weren't in the know," "they didn't know the rules of the game," and they saw clarity in ambiguity (Thiranagama 2010).[22] "Knowing" the LTTE defined the inside of the community; Tamils who could always be targeted by the LTTE as potential traitors were more like each other than the Sinhalese and Muslims who could speak out against the LTTE and not be considered traitors by the LTTE.

Aside from its coercive nature, the Tigers have intervened in temple quarrels, in relationships between parents and children, in the decision on who and how to marry, on who is considered dangerous to know, on whether you leave your home or not. This alone calls for a sober examination of the LTTE in *ordinary* Tamil life. However, increasingly scholarship has been fascinated with the *self-pronouncements* of the LTTE, the structure of its former quasi-state, its ritualization of its actions, and particularly its female suicide cadres (e.g., Schalk 1992; Trawick 2007; Stokke 2006; Natali 2005; and see Fuglerud 2009 for an excellent critique). The LTTE's claim to represent Tamils, and its roots in "deep" Tamil culture (e.g., Roberts 1996; Trawick 2007) are uncontested in these accounts.

This is most evident in the work of Margaret Trawick (2007), whose *Enemy Lines* is the only book-length ethnographic account of war and the LTTE. Trawick's fieldwork was in LTTE-controlled area of eastern Sri Lanka and was primarily with Tiger cadres. Trawick's uncritical stance and political naïveté regarding the LTTE has rendered the book controversial in Sri Lanka. Despite empathetically rendering the voices and stories of Tiger cadres, throughout the text she refuses to note, let alone probe the many instances where the LTTE's coercive strategies were all too plain to see. This is baffling, as after

the 2004 split in the LTTE into northern and eastern wings, the latter following self-appointed "eastern commander" Karuna, many young cadres left the
eastern LTTE in droves and parents openly protested for the release of their
children in precisely the area she discusses (UTHR 2004). Instead, Trawick
filters the stories she receives through the literary and cultural tropes found in
ancient and medieval Tamil literature central to her work with South Indian
Tamils (Trawick 1992). In representing the LTTE as an *innate* expression of
Tamil culture, she fails to acknowledge (and thus underestimates) not only
the LTTE's coercive nature but how in the 1990s it set up an office devoted to
researching Tamil culture to *self-consciously* evoke and borrow from cultural
themes to evolve an LTTE calendrical year, ritualized burials, and valorizing
death and sacrifice for the nation through joining the LTTE (Schalk 1997).
Not least, as Sankaran Krishna points out, "imputing unchanging characteristics and continuity to "the Tamil" across centuries marked by dramatic
transformations [are]. . . . violently reductive and essentializing" (1999: 65)
fails to understand a modern guerrilla group like the LTTE or even politics
itself "as an open-ended, agentive process."

This book examines the LTTE's insertion of itself at the heart of Tamil
society and to some extent northern Muslim life without collapsing Tamils into the LTTE or Muslims into Tamils. I take two events, the Eviction
and the Exodus, as the climactic and symbolic events of the new war in Sri
Lanka. In the north, in October 1990 the LTTE forcibly expelled all 70,000–
80,000 Muslims from the northern areas under its control—this is called the
Eviction. This was predated by and further accompanied by LTTE pogroms
against Muslims in eastern Sri Lanka, which inflamed tensions between the
communities, heightened when the Sri Lankan state attempted to use this by
recruiting from the Muslim communities and using those "home guards" in
its operations against Tamils. Tensions remain high, and Tamils and Muslims
increasingly segregate themselves. The Eviction of northern Muslims was
matched five years later to the day in 1995, when, after the failure of peace
talks in 1995, the Sri Lankan army began marching on Jaffna city, determined
to take it. The LTTE in response announced in October 1995, as the army
advanced, that everyone must leave, and cleared its reluctant population of
around 450,000—known as the Exodus.

In Chapter 1, I take the memories of those who were adolescents in 1990s
Jaffna. I examine their accounts of what it was like to grow up, imagine, and
pursue life projects with the LTTE as a highly normalized alternative "government." The chapter documents the overwhelming control over individual

movement, as well as the Exodus and stories of immense forced collective movement. It begins a focus on generational relationships, gaps, and conflicts that dominates the book as a whole. I explore a particular generational biography of war, asking at the same time how that biography grounds life for these young people. In Chapter 3, I extensively explore Muslim ethnic formation throughout the nineteenth and twentieth centuries and the Eviction as producing a new demographic: "Northern Muslims." In Chapter 4, though examining the kinds of new collective selves and experiences that came into being through this forced movement, I examine the changing configurations of ethnicity through the experiences of war. In Chapter 5, I examine the stories of Tamils who joined *all* the militant movements (not just the Tigers) in the 1980s, to inquire further into the changes in generational, caste, and gender relations that these entailed (Tambiah 1990). I particularly focus on the most common narrative of the Tamil militancy, that those who joined fled from oppressive families and from a deeply gender conservative society, to understand the relationship between militant kinship and household kinship.

Given the current focus of some scholars on female LTTE cadres as a sign of resistance to gender oppression in Tamil society, I discuss why it is that even as the LTTE advocated radical forms of relatedness within the movement as forms of exceptional life, it increasingly policed and regulated a vision of the conservative normative Tamil family for those who were not cadres. This sustained focus on LTTE practices is part of the book's emphasis on understanding ethnographically what life was like under the LTTE for Tamils and Muslims, and what kinds of political, generational, and familial transformations were produced through the LTTE war of the 1990s.

The fall of the LTTE itself, though seemingly sudden in 2009, was presaged by dramatic changes occurring at the time of my fieldwork. I came into Sri Lanka some years after, in 2002, at the time of ceasefire, at a key moment to observe and listen to stories of the long-term social life of war. My sustained period of fieldwork in Sri Lanka was in 2002–2003 (followed by stints in Toronto in late 2003 and London in 2004), and was supplemented with four short trips back to Sri Lanka in 2004. This was combined with new fieldwork in London and Toronto with ex-militants in 2005 and 2006. In 2002, I was lucky to arrive at a ceasefire period, when in fact many security regulations had been relaxed, and there seemed a faint hope for a cessation in violence. People were reflecting on stories and their lives at a moment of respite. However, as I continued my fieldwork, assassinations by the LTTE

and Sinhala nationalist currents began to be apparent again. Toward the end
of my stay, the third set of peace talks, instituted by the UNP government
in 2002, went the way of others and were suspended in April 2003. In April
2004, the LTTE split into two factions along northern and eastern lines, ex-
posing bitter resentments in eastern Sri Lanka. Karuna, who was in charge
of the eastern wing of the LTTE, formed his own short-lived eastern branch,
LTTE (K), accusing Prabhakaran's northern LTTE of discriminating against
the east, the ever-growing toll of LTTE dead from the east and Vanni areas,
and the dominance of Jaffna people in the LTTE hierarchy. The LTTE (Prabhakaran) and LTTE (K) fought a short-lived war in the east, "won" by LTTE
(P). We watched on TV the amazing sight of parents protesting their children's recruitment in the LTTE, and even on one occasion the (orchestrated)
burning of pictures of Prabhakaran in the east. LTTE (K) transformed into
an armed Tamil political party propped up by the Sri Lanka state called the
TMVP (Thamil Makkal Viduthalai Puligal) engaging, like the party EPDP
the other major Tamil ally of the government, in all kinds of state-sanctioned
paramilitary activity. I had left Sri Lanka by the time a massive tsunami hit
Sri Lankan coastal areas in December 2004. A major part of the damage was
in the war-affected east, particularly in Muslim areas. While both the LTTE
and the state attended to civilians immediately, wrangling over aid and aid
distribution were just one of the many things that pointed to the unresolved
nature of political sovereignty in Sri Lanka.

After new presidential elections, the SLFP-led government of Mahinda
Rajapaksa pursued an increasingly military strategy to end the war, and it
was in this context that war resumed in 2006. Despite a series of high profile
and daring attacks on Colombo, including the unveiling of its air force, the
LTTE was much weakened. It had attempted to re-recruit cadres who had
left the movement in the 2002 ceasefire period, but many resisted rerecruit-
ment (UTHR 2009b). They had to push harder to force Tamils back into war.
In 2008 and 2009, the Sri Lankan state's military campaigns became highly
successful as a result of its alliance with eastern commander Karuna and the
state's ruthlessness toward Tamils and "domestic" dissent in the south.

It won that war, and defeated the LTTE. But the political struggle for a
more equitable and demilitarized Sri Lanka is only just beginning. Reflecting
on the transformations of Tamil and Muslim political, familial, and collective
cultures is integral to understanding what can happen in the future. If until
now, we have dwelt on the large productions of nation and ethnicity, now we

turn to the other key aspects of fraught self-making that inform this book: familial life and ideologies, and, the individual.

Individuals and Families at a Time of Terror

My grandfather watches the popular South Indian soap *Kudumbam* along with thousands of others. Most South Indian Tamil soaps popular in Sri Lanka and India are about families, their intrigues, poisoned relationships, failed dowries and debt, and most of all, as my grandfather never fails to comment on, effete men and evil dominating women. As the soaps very often show, it is the elders in the family, male and female, who are ideologically central, either saintly venerables or spiderlike calculators with young men and women in their thrall.

Academic work on South India has heavily concentrated on kinship; the debate on "Dravidian kinship," relationship terminology, and categorical relations dominates much of this production (e.g., Dumont 1953; Trautmann 1981; Good 1991, 1996; Busby 1997.).[23] In this book, I tend toward the reading of kinship that South Indian soaps are acute in rendering: emotionally fraught hierarchical relations of power, gender, and transmission. For all those I interviewed, family was most at risk from the privations of displacement, child recruitment, death and terror, yet it was also family which seemed to provide that which could survive such privations in its unceasing desire to perpetuate, continue, survive. I also, like those I interviewed, emphasize generational divergences, not only because these are latent within gerontocratic kinship systems but also because the life cycle of protracted war can also be traced by the production of distinct generations.

Kudumbam, uravu (kindred), linked to *sontakarar* (kin, those you share an affinity with, belong to) coming from *sontam* (affinity, possession, compatibility) as Kapadia argues in South India, is represented as axiomatic to society as " the greatest good in life" (Kapadia 1995: 40). One is empowered by having kin and one suffers economically and socially without kin. To live without family close by, as many related to me, was to be lonely which could bring you close to madness.[24] Yet, as Kapadia also relates, this social good is by its very nature hierarchical and unequal; the obligations of kin weigh more heavily on women (and juniors), who are taught from a young age to subordinate their interests to the family and to exalt their suffering and self-sacrifice.

Kapadia writes that in South Indian Aruloor, where she worked, while "in-equality has been well hidden in the public discourses of Tamil kinship that have represented marriage and affinity as life's greatest goods. [I]t has not been hidden from women, however, which is why, though their frustration is seldom spoken, they continue to warn that "kinship burns" (1995: 42).

This book takes up this doubled life of kinship and family as it emerges in the stories I tell, while the greatest good, source of affinity, care, trust, it is also the site of difficult emotional labor, disappointment, inequality (Peletz 2001). Thus the book foregrounds the constant necessity of what Arlie Hochschild calls emotion work: "the time consuming and arduous emotional labor in-volved in forging, deepening and repairing relations" that kin relations neces-sitate (quoted in Peletz 2001: 427). As Peletz points out this "emotion work" is itself necessitated by expectations and frustrations within intimate kinship, arguing that "all emotional attachments are conducive to the realization of ambivalence; intense attachments are *thoroughly* suffused with mixed emo-tions" (2001: 432).[25] Thus different chapters pick out how individuals negoti-ate relationships to kin dead and alive, relationships that require enormous obligation that simultaneously afford the possibility of much desired recogni-tion (Bourdieu 2000: 507–13).

Moreover, familial and kin bonds are innately differentiated, and dif-ferent relations—sibling and parent-child being central to this book—have different though interrelated emotional and material circuits and may come to seriously threaten each other (Kapadia 1995).[26] Sibling relations real and imagined in Tamil and Muslim kinship concern both the obligation to pro-vide dowry for female siblings, and the seeming horizontal equality between juniors in opposition to their seniors, epitomized in the adoption of sister and brother as forms of address in Tamil militant movements. These, in Chapters 2 and 5, are talked of as relationships of opposition, protection, solidarity, and sometimes, in the case of militant movements, betrayal. Chapter 1 and 3 trace the complexities of parent and child relations, in the midst of the profound social change that makes parents and children face each other from different worlds. This is true of the young Tamils who grow up only knowing Jaffna in wartime, in contrast to their parents, and the young Muslims who grow up in refugee camps and whose relationship to their northern homes their parents were expelled from, is that of memory. This more generic issue within fami-lies, what Bourdieu calls the contradictions of inheritance (1999: 507–13), is heightened in its ever more difficult passage at times of war, rupture, and displacement.

Questions of inheritance, material, social, and psychic, were at the heart of family relationships and anxieties. One was a set of inquiries about the possibility of dowry, one of the preeminent forms of material and social reproduction in northern Tamil and Muslim life. Inability to give some form of dowry puts a crucial part of social recognition within kin, as well as the community, at stake. Dowry in Sri Lanka varies significantly from dowry in Tamil Nadu, South India in its emphasis on the transmission of land as mother-to-daughter dowry.[27] The absence of a significant population of Brahmins and thus the repressive Dharmashastric system practiced in Tamil Nadu means that many brahminical customs, including the ban on widow remarriage, sati, and seclusion, are completely absent in Sri Lanka (McGilvray 1982; Thiruchandran 1997). In Tamil Nadu, immovable property, such as land, is not part of dowry, and land is considered a male right (Kapadia 1995).[28] Conversely, under the Jaffna customary code Thesawalamai, the woman's dowry land is considered her property with her husband considered the manager of the land.[29] Both Tamils and Muslims prioritized land for female dowry; sons were expected to marry land and their sisters inherited land.[30] Muslims observe these practices though they do not express any affinity to Thesawalamai.

However, as war and displacement has worsened and overseas migration by Tamils increases, Tamils have been turning to liquid (thus transnational) cash, as a preferred donation straight to the groom and his family over Jaffna dowry land, whereas among displaced and expelled Muslims dowry was ever more imagined as land. Among Muslims land epitomized familial continuity and safety, where it was precisely their right to belong on and transmit northern land that the LTTE had erased. Living on state land and camps, the possession of one's own land seemed imperative to ensure stability. In the book, dowry relations and property relations were thus polysemic ways of talking about all kinds of relationships of transmission, belonging, and inheritance (Spencer 1990c). Whilst dowry relations were a commitment to an idealized normative family, they were also practical and material ways of talking about, negotiating and sometimes blocking the reproduction of the family in the future.

Chapter 2 looks at the fraught relations of power, love, and ambivalence within families as well as the ongoing tensions concerning reproducing the family in the midst of war and immense violence. It focuses on the life history of one woman, Malathi, and her relationship to her mother and daughters in the aftermath of personal tragedy and displacement. Thus Chapter 2 also initiates a question about what has been called *transgenerational haunting*, about what it is that we can inherit or pass on—conscious and unconscious histories, disappointments, secrets and loss. These were not questions I teased out of interviews; these were question that people asked themselves directly, given that war seemed to heighten latent fears about the difficulties of self-perpetuation.

This emphasis on the anxieties surrounding future perpetuation, as well as the very real differences between generations produced through and in the war, is central to every chapter in the book. The rapidity of social change in the Jaffna peninsula was folded into inter-generational structures (Daniel 1996: 171). I argue that the transformation of the political and physical land-scapes through war meant that generations simply did not share the same experiences any more, with generations after 1980 having no knowledge of peacetime Jaffna or a life outside war. This led to the differences of memory between generations migrating or evicted and their children and grandchil-dren growing up in other places. The book takes generation as an axiomatic topic providing a line of inquiry in every chapter.

This leads me to the second component of this emphasis on the new forms of collectivity produced through the war: a concomitant inquiry about individuality and my focus on individual stories and the ways political terror shaped what an individual was understood to be. It is after all individual lives and their reflexive understandings of their lives, relationships and the war that comprise my attempt to understand what a (generationally differenti-ated) war time biography might look like. This is not to make the individual the same as the subject by any naïve literalism (Butler 1997: 14). Instead, I argue that LTTE's political repression produced a particular structural iden-tity for the individual among Sri Lankan Tamils; a particular form of alien-ated individualism as well as an intense and heightened sense of sociality.

The Individual

South Asian scholarship, as Mines (1994) points out, dominated by the shadow of Louis Dumont, has viewed Indian society as possessing a weak notion of the individual subordinate to the collectivity, and posited a sharp break between Indian and Western ideas of the individual. As Mines argues, this does not mean that there are no individuals or a strong sense of indi-viduality in South Asia, merely that this is of different kind from the Western notion of the individual (1994: 6). In South Asia, he argues, there is no dearth of evidence in South Asia to show the importance of the individual. Mattison Mines's *Public Faces, Private Voices* is specifically about the significance of "big men" in civic life in Chennai, Tamil Nadu. For Mines, the critical difference between "Western" individualism and the kind he describes in South India is that in India people do not believe that all are born equal; all are born differently placed in hierarchies of gender, caste, *ur*, class, and so on. Individuality has to be earned through a lifetime of achievement. Thus to be a big person or a prominent individual is to actively cultivate individuality through a public life, and some are more able to do so than others. Mines's interviewees continually reflect on the pressure of achieving individuality and the imperfect marriage of the interior, "private self" and the mediation that needs to be effected in relation to the collective pressures of enacting this self within and through a community.

Mines reminds us that relationships between individuals and collectives are rarely seamless but constantly negotiated, and that, moreover, individuals are at the nexus of many different, sometimes conflicting forms of collective life. We might even destabilize the picture of absolute difference between the "West" and the rest. The Euro-American West has been characterized as cultures of individuality, seen as necessarily identical with the growing interiorization of the self in the eighteenth, nineteenth, and twentieth centuries (see Dumont 1994; Giddens 1992; Taylor 1989).But equally, Georg Simmel (1972) talks of this growing individuality in European life as a social form which, while manifest through new kinds of interior selves, is also repeatedly produced through social encounters and interactions. In short, individuality has to be continually worked on. Taking for granted the assumption of absolute individualism as a pre-given structure in Euro-American life, against which the different dividualism of the "rest of the world" is oppposed (Strathern 1990; see Thomas 1991 for the larger debate and Strathern 1992 for an incisive commentary) itself exists in uneasy tension with the anxieties surrounding "mobs," "crowd mentalities," "mass movements," and some of the other major themes in western social theory. These anxieties point to expressions of individuality, even posited in its western absolute form, not only as a particular historical form (see Taylor 1989) but also ebbing and flowing (rather than constant accumulation) within particular social and political structures.

I ask here the more general question: under what conditions do particular notions of the individuals come to have meaning as an idea that seem to be imperative at some times and at other times not? Can particular moments of social transition, extended or rapid, propel some meanings with more urgency than others? What I proffer is both an acknowledgment of the empirical phenomena of multiple persons, historical and social agents, who register and negotiate larger struggles and discourses, who are not wholly reducible to their various social properties or membership of groups (Holland and Lave 2001), and a particular understanding of what it meant to be an individual within this specific political juncture in Sri Lanka.

Wartime Individuality

LTTE placed landmines in civilian areas because they saw people like they saw the land in their maps of combat actions and battles. But while when something awful happens the natural thing would be to tell one's neighbors, because of the way things are, you won't tell your neighbors if you discover there is a landmine near you. Instead, without telling anyone you would move and go and live somewhere else and wait for something to happen instead.

I can understand why people choose to only focus on some things, on survival, on day to day, because if they look at the whole picture then you see the hopelessness of it all. But then you have to go further, then you have to make things so that this world seems real . . . you come to know what you do to survive and what is a danger. Everyone then hopes and tries to survive as individuals. . . .

We felt powerless caught between the Sri Lankan army and the LTTE. (K. Sritharan, human rights activist, UTHR(J))

When I arrived in Sri Lanka to conduct research as a young Tamil woman, I found myself under considerable constraints as a woman in a city where public spaces for women are restricted. To visit people I crossed Colombo on hour-long bus journeys for appointed times. By six all my interviewees would tell me to go home before it got dark. I could not hang out in tea-shops practicing my participant observation skills because the men in the shop were made uncomfortable by a young woman sitting down alone in the tea-shop. The limits to my own mobility also shaped the kinds of interviews I was able to carry out. However, the primary constraint was the political situation and fear of the LTTE, which meant that open and formal ethnographic participation, household surveys, and questionnaires were out of the question, as information gathering enterprises that potentially put those who talked to me at risk—one does not have to do much to be called a traitor by the LTTE. I could not work openly within Jaffna or even Colombo without compromising the safety of those I interviewed.

Thus, my work with Tamils was primarily through individual stories, in contrast to the large group and individual interviews I was able to conduct with northern Muslims. In the camps Muslims spoke openly about their experiences under the LTTE, among Tamils these were secret stories. My methodology was thus integrally produced by how sociality in Tamil and Muslim communities was differently organized by LTTE terror. The book's split soul, between Tamils and Muslims, between individual narratives and a bustling sense of the collective, reflects this paradox: one community (Muslims) had the right to speak, the other (Tamils) the right to belong, neither had both.

I had to use exactly the trust networks and story-telling practices that people themselves have generated to deal with internal terror. The political conditions that shaped the possibilities of my inquiry became the problem I was seeking to explain, an inquiry into political culture and authoritarianism, the relationship between secrecy, speech, and public worlds, and ultimately the ways in which people thought about collective life and the possibilities of being, speaking, and living together.

First, the war has reinvented the possibility of being an individual in unexpected ways. Bearing in mind, Mines's suggestion that it is commonly believed among South Asians that all individuals are not born equal and that individuality has to be achieved, I suggest, the immense upheavals of war and displacement have altered traditional routes of achievement of individuality. The inability of fixed caste hierarchies to be maintained in residence, given displacement and the opening of overseas migration through political asylum to a wider category of people, meant that mobility and to think of one as an actor with individuality was thrown wide open. Not least, the LTTE with its promise of power through recruitment promised another route to achievement, given that the traditional route, education, was no longer available to the same degree. Among northern Muslims, the Eviction accentuated pre-existing marginality and inequalities within the communities, but did also allow some to start again.

Second, and equally significant, internal repression by the LTTE has also rendered new ways of viewing collective life, and "the individual" as a site of "tactical contraction" (Donzelot 1979). As the LTTE stamped down on public protests and independent organizations, expressions of discontent, dissent, and sharing of secrets moved into the home and interior spaces and small networks of trust, which in turn became expanded in significance and potency. Distrust of other Tamils, fearing that others could be undercover LTTE or report one to the LTTE, meant that people were constantly on guard in conversations with others and public encounters. Conversations required a participating self and another self inside who constantly evaluated the other person and his/her intentions, and decided what could be shared and not. K. Sritharan of the UTHR (J) told me, "everybody is reading between the lines, thinking that you are fooling them and they are fooling you." I found sarcasm in private and double and secret intonations in public were pervasive features of public life, as has been reported widely elsewhere in repressive regimes (e.g., Wedeen 1999; Watson 1994). War has rendered the multilayered nature of trust, truth, and evaluation in social life more obviously as a treacherous reality to be navigated, putting individual negotiations and navigation squarely on the table.

If targeted violence used by both actors in the war has been to police and impose public acquiescence, this has imbued expressions of oneself as an individual as potential expressions of dissent, investing such expressions with significance and power. The Sri Lankan government treated all Tamils as possible "Tigers" and individual Sinhalese as potential traitors and dissenters to be targeted. The LTTE on its part regarded all Sinhalese as uniformly the enemy, killing them at random, while with Tamils it focused on individuals and their actions. Selective targeting of individuals functioned as warnings about what happens to those who do not toe the line. This served to render the "other" as random "groups" and monolithic collectivity and to invest "the self" (Tamil or Sinhalese) with individual responsibility and thus potency. Thus individuals and political actors were aware of the simultaneous vulnerability and power of individual dissent.

Thus, the LTTE's targeted terror at individuals and families—albeit for such a large range of activities that anybody could become potentially targeted—put individuals at the center of dissension. The shutdown of independent collective political and social organization and the reification of the LTTE as the supreme collectivity—where greater heroism, patriotism and devotion was professed to abound, and where individuals were seemingly swallowed into the service of the collective—only further emphasized dissent as a matter of individual alienation and selfish refusal to join. For the LTTE, refusing to pay taxes, be recruited, saying public criticisms among other activities were all marks of selfish individuals who chose themselves over the greater good of the Tamil nation and its necessary collective sacrifices. Thus,

I encountered in interviews an even greater consciousness of the complexity of relations between the self and the collective, and frequent expressions of frustration, alienation, and the sensation of a dissonance between private and public speech. The equivalence made between acting as an "individual" with one's own moral compass and being a dissenter meant that the individual life histories I recorded were also attempts to think through and narrate biographies that automatically qualified the relationship between one's beliefs and actions in relation to others.

Moreover, if we understand public expressions to be ones that are allusive and double-layered, then we have to consider the nature of political life and public support for an unelected organization like the LTTE as somewhat more complex than has been represented by recent commentators who see participation in LTTE rituals and its quasi-state as tantamount to popular support (e.g., Trawick 2007). Seeing unequivocal popular support deduced from the absence of open resistance (the latter's absence unsurprising given the normalisation of heavy repression) is redundant at best and or at worst is political naïveté compliant with LTTE imaginations of its own power and base. As Wedeen argues, trying to equate participation in a system with belief in the system has stymied attempts to understand many authoritarian regimes (1999, 2004). She argues that the Syrian Asad regime did not require its subjects to believe in Asad's proclamations. All it had to do was ensure public compliance with them. Syrians do not have to believe in the State's proclamations; they merely have to act "as if" they do (1999: 6). Wedeen argues that internal terror suppresses dissidence, not by suppressing people's actual experiences of disillusionment or discomfort, but by producing a politics where people internalize the potential consequences of talking about these experiences openly (1999).

Thus regimes—through circulation of fear and punitive policing of transgressions—are able to maintain a system where, without having to believe in what they do, people enforce conformity on themselves, what Havel (1986) calls "the principle of social auto-totality" (1986: 52). The simultaneous presence of individual dissent with public compliance, rather than constituting meaningful resistance to the regime, draws people into a cynical and morally complicitous (through disavowed bad faith) pact with the regime (Wedeen 1999). So I do present individual narratives not as straightforward signs of resistance, but *forms of individualisation as generated by particular political regulation, which are both complicit with but also exceed this regulation.* As I argue in Chapter 1, the younger generations who grew up with the LTTE as a repressive quasi-state rather than a liberation group saw the LTTE not as a vehicle for meaningful utopianism but only as a pragmatic necessity. This means that they may not rush to resuscitate it now, unlike diasporic youth for whom it is utopian still.

Instead of focusing on the atomization and silences produced by authoritarianism (see Yurchak's 2006 critique) in this book I have tried to do the opposite. I have tried to represent the dense texture of speech that came to life in particular spaces, and the immensity of people's belief in and longing for social life in the face of repression. In a country where, as Spencer (2000b) points out, politics is a form of life, the desire to discuss politics and the knowledge that the vicissitudes of war govern sometimes even minute details of one's routine, mean that politics is not banished from conversation. I found stories, gossip, and jokes proliferating within small trusted circles and inside houses as people attempted to make sense and second guess their public worlds and possibilities in an ongoing war. Thus, like Wedeen (1999), I also argue that political regulation, far from producing an inherently atomized and deadened social landscape, instead invests everyday life, sociality, and commonplace information and events with enormous significance and secrecy among trusted friends and family (1999: 45). Intense and hushed sociality in shrinking circles of trust becomes ever more discussed, a potent dream of an imagined future and nostalgic past.

To do this, I believe that in Sri Lanka we need new and imaginative ways of looking and writing about what is going on. Developing this kind of imagination took me on journeys I would have never anticipated otherwise. I took the kinds of spaces that were opened up for research and the methodologies I had to put into practice as reflections on the complex politics of narrating oneself to others. I wanted to write something that brought out how I, and those I interviewed, experienced the moment of telling, and to go beyond their understandings to create relationships between them in this text. The topics I have dealt with were those crafted by people to reach out to others, told to be shared, not just within conversations but with audiences outside the immediate conversation. The task I set myself was to find how to express these in such a way that their tellers would understand how I did it. I tell these stories so they can stay long after one leaves a house, that they would leave a trace in you, as they did for me.

CHAPTER ONE

Growing Up at War:
Self-Formation, Individuality, and the LTTE

> Over the years I will probably learn to have an understanding with myself
> about what I went through. When you are living in that time, living in
> this closed place, that is what life is about. So you never know anything
> different. I certainly didn't. I don't know if anyone else did. That was
> normal because that is what you are growing up with
>
> —Vasantha

I begin here in the middle of a conversation with Vasantha, a Jaffna Tamil in
her mid-twenties living in London. Our interviews, running over months,
were themselves in the middle of a long, loving, and complex friendship. I
have known Vasantha since we were five-year-old neighbors, classmates, and
best friends in Jaffna, our mutual home. My sister and I left Jaffna in November 1989, and I didn't see Vasantha for twelve years. As we started to
reconnect and talk of our homes, she consented to be interviewed. On these
occasions, she dwelled exclusively on her adolescence in Jaffna. This book
thus starts with the most intimate of relationships, though from here it proceeds into ever more uncharted territory. It begins with the story of someone
whose life was intertwined with my own, and with the story and temporal
perspective of a generation I call my own.

Jaffna in the 1990s was unique. In 1990, the LTTE embarked on an ex-
periment to turn themselves from an insurrectionary group among many
(see Chapter 5) into a quasi-state entity in the north. Between 1990 and
1995 movement out of Jaffna was highly regulated, while within people were

frequently displaced and under constant military bombardment from the state. They lived crammed next to each other. This did not make them any more intimate; stories tell instead of fear of other Tamils. Vasantha, as she says above, did not know if anyone else knew whether their lives could be considered "not normal," a sentiment many expressed as a retrospective judgment, when I talked to them later on in their lives.

Vasantha was born in 1979 in the northern peninsula of Jaffna to a middle-class, upper caste—though a mixed caste marriage—family. Her mother was an outspoken and hardworking professional, her father a gentle semi-retired man who devoted himself to Vasantha and her sister Sakuntala. Vasantha's parents were central in her narrative, navigating her move from childhood to adolescence at a time of enormous change. Her adolescence in Jaffna, until her departure in 1998 after the death of her parents, was precisely during the years when Jaffna was to undergo enormous transformation as militarization and war intensified.

Vasantha's stories were highly reflexive and individualized, and, at the same time, marked by a collective experience and particular subjectivity that emerged from "that closed place" which she was "growing up with." These are the subjects of this chapter, the emergence of a generation of young people who were distinct from their parents by virtue of growing up in a full-fledged war which, as I argue in the Introduction, didn't just happen to people but was making them too. Young people I interviewed linked their biographical stories continually to others—their families and peers. Individuality appeared not as the right to possess one's own story, but as the isolation resulting from the inability to understand what others thought, even as all were enjoined to behave publicly the same way. Not least, young people were also the central focus of LTTE control and attempts actively to create new subjects of an ideal Tamil Eelam (Tamil Homeland), subjects who had to willingly sacrifice their lives to die on the battlefield. Young Tamils spoke of their experiences, and were imagined by others, as the personification of the war itself.

This chapter twins Vasantha's story with Anthony's, whom I met still living in Colombo in 2003 and whose life in Colombo, and failed attempts to leave Sri Lanka, I return to in Chapter 6. Anthony was from a Catholic fishing caste family. His family, like others from the villages surrounding Palaly airport and the Sri Lankan army camp, were forcibly evacuated from their homes when the Sri Lankan army created a high security zone around the airport and military camp, the only area they were in possession of in the early 1990s. In 1990, Anthony and his family moved to a refugee camp in

Jaffna town. From there, they moved to live with his aunt, but also registered with a refugee camp as they had no income for food or basic supplies. While Anthony's family left for India as migrants in 1995, Anthony remained before leaving Jaffna for Colombo in 2000 to try to migrate abroad.

These two stories are of different intimacies with me and thus different possibilities. Vasantha's conversations with me, her friend, were an emotional account of adolescence seen through changing interior realizations, an intense picture of an alienated observer in an exterior world. Anthony and I were curbed by all cultural restrictions of intimacy between unmarried young men and young women; he instead told me his life as an example, presenting aspects of his life that he felt typified his peers and their lives. For Anthony, full personhood was marriage, supporting one's family, and as long as he lacked the resources for both, he represented his life as a partial person, only as that which lacked. His account turned interiorization inside out. I choose to bring together these two stories because of their differences in social locations, caste, and desired futures, as well as their marked similarities, to illuminate the predicaments individuals in this generation faced.

I treat their stories as both commentaries and realizations of a particular psychic and social history. Koselleck remarks in his analysis of the three hundred dreams collected by Charlotte Beradt from 1930s Third Reich Germany, that these dreams were not just "simply of terror; they are above all dreams in terror ... forms of the realization of that terror itself" (2004: 211–12). Koselleck's essay reflects on and espouses historical explanation that neither prioritizes structural external causes without understanding the uniqueness, singularity, and contrariness of experience, nor reduces historical action and event to the inner motivation of individual actors and their despotic fathers and anxious mothers. Here I attempt to work out such a psychic and social history, weaving together both synchronic and diachronic explanations. This first part of the book (Chapters 1 and 2) takes individual stories as constituted through both self-reflexively recognized experiences and the new kinds of practices of self-making that protracted and unpredictable political repression and war brought into being.

Two experiences featured prominently in all the interviews I conducted: (1) the intense focus on recruitment by the LTTE and the staged nature of childhood and adolescence within the LTTE, and (2) the experiences of total control over movement—from the restricted pass laws keeping young people trapped in the Jaffna peninsula to the forced mass movement of the 1995

Exodus. I suggest that these two came to create particular kinds of under-standings of childhood, and distinct forms of individuality and collectivity.

Rather than use the term "youth" as self-evident, I follow Durham (2000) in thinking through youth as a culturally specific and laden category that is constantly made and regulated through claiming it for oneself or nam-ing others as youth. My characterization of youth (throughout the book) implicitly rests on Philip Abrams's (1970) useful characterizations of "age spans." Abrams suggests that an "age span" (e.g., infancy, youth, middle age) is a culturally demarcated institution distinct from the individuals passing through it (1970: 183). Abrams argues that within age spans one can then mark "age groups" that strive to articulate, present, and crystallize common predicaments in relation to other age spans (182). Yet, most often, he argues, as individuals pass out of the age span they "abandon the attitudes and affili-ations" of the age group (183). Thus, this chapter is framed around the speci-ficity of "youthfulness" and what makes the young people I talk of, following Mannheim (1952), a sociologically significant generation.

While Mannheim argues that common social location (*lagerung*), a com-mon place in social and historical processes, is the basic denominator (1952: 288–292) which can make "mere contemporaneity" "sociologically signifi-cant" (298), not every generation "creates new collective impulses and forma-tive principles original to itself and adequate to its particular situation. Where this does happen, we shall speak of a *realization of potentialities inherent* in the location, and . . . the frequency of such realizations is closely connected with the tempo of social change" (309).

Contemporaneity is transformed into sociological or political signifi-cance when destabilization or politicization occurs to such an extent that those experiencing them feel that they share a common set of historical or social problems—"*participation in the common destiny* of this historical and social unit" (Mannheim 1952: 303). The young people I talk of here shared a set of sociologically significant experiences that were fundamentally dif-ferent from their parents, not only because they had different perspectives by virtue of different location, but also because they, as young people, were the *target* of such experiences. However, here I talk of "youth" to distinguish them from generation in its fullest sense; where a "generation" represents "a more fundamental freezing of consciousness" who will carry forward its experiences and their impetus beyond their age group (Abrams 1970: 183) as in Chapter 5, where we encounter ex-militants from the 1970s who continued in middle age to speak of singular generational commonalities through different age spans.

The importance of youthful experience in self-formation can be understood in sociological (as well as Freudian) terms. As Mannheim points out, experience is "stratified;" we do not just accumulate experiences, they are articulated in relation to structures, and they are dialectically articulated within our life cycles in an uneven manner (1952: 288). Whether one encounters experiences when one is young or older is significant in what is called on in terms of memories, relations to others, and other structures in determining how experiences are rearticulated within self formation (Bourdieu 1992: 52–66, 80–98). Thus, youth as an "age span" has a particular charged valence within this dialectical articulation, the shuttling back and forth between experience, relations, structures, and selves that Mannheim describes for the self and, Abrams argues, has particular and different cultural articulations.

Here I also trace how this generation imagined themselves as distinct from their parents, in their distinct temporal and personal subjectivity in the world of war, which they experienced not as anomaly but as inheritance. The chapter reflects thus on a war in which young people constituted themselves around living a life that they thought was normal but which turned out post facto not to be, and to feel that they had lost what they had never possessed, Jaffna in peacetime.

The War, the World

Jaffna changed dramatically in the 1980s and 1990s. Landscapes were crisscrossed by different military powers, under aerial bombardment, with open battles conducted inside villages and towns. New forms of navigation came into being as people moved back and forth from places of refuge to their homes. Temples, churches, and schools were bruised and broken by shrapnel and shell damage. Coastline areas were cordoned off as high security zones for either the Sri Lankan army or the LTTE. Nearly two-thirds of Jaffna's population found ways throughout the 1990s to leave the peninsula, though many were stuck between 1990 and 1995 (McDowell 1996). Neighbors changed. New caste configurations pushed at strictly controlled residential caste restrictions. A younger generation knew an entirely different landscape from their parents, though they lived in the same place.

Combat between Tamil militants and the Sri Lankan state intensified in the late 1980s. The state enforced food shortages, curfews, roundups and, in 1986, a brutal aerial bombardment called Operation Liberation (Hoole et al. 1990; Fuglerud 1999). India intervened by negotiating the Indo-Lanka Accord and sending in the Indian Peace Keeping Forces (IPKF) in 1987 to implement political reform and devolution for northern and eastern areas. Anthony recalled his parents discussing Tamil militancy and the 1983 riots, but for him war entered his life with the arrival of the IPKF. Between 1987 and 1990, the LTTE and the IPKF were engaged in all-out war. The Tigers waged war from amid the civilian population, drawing fire onto them, and the IPKF responded with a full counter-insurrectionary drive, resulting in hundreds of deaths, arrests, and rapes by Indian forces (see Hoole et al. 1990). The IPKF had governed with the assistance of other Tamil militant groups, such as EPRLF (Eelam People's Revolutionary Liberation Front) and TELO (Tamil Eelam Liberation Front), PLOTE (People's Liberation Organization for Tamil Eelam). In the last days of combat with the LTTE, the Indian intelligence wing RAW forced Tamil militants allied with them forcibly to conscript young men into a Tamil National Army to fight the Tigers. Anthony's friend was one of those. This forcible recruitment along with the partnership with the IPKF was one of the reasons popular support declined for those non-LTTE Tamil militant groups (see Chapter 5). In 1990, the IPKF withdrew after the LTTE were given surreptitious aid and support by the Sri Lankan government. When the LTTE took power, it killed and detained most of the TNA and Anthony's friend died. As Anthony recalled:

The IPKF (Indian Peace Keeping Force) left, that was when I was coming to an age of understanding 16, 17. I didn't maybe understand everything, but enough to understand what was going on in the country . . . then we started looking the troubles in the face. . . . The LTTE took people who had no party anymore; they captured and then murdered them. . . . Whether someone was in a party, or not, if they spoke freely or not, they took them and murdered them. Because we had not been able to see the troubles before, we did not really understand. . . . In 1990 to 1995 we experienced fully what it was like to live under the LTTE.

When peace talks between the LTTE and the Sri Lankan government broke down in 1990, the LTTE consolidated its power by taking full control of northern Jaffna (and north-central Vanni) and partial control of the east between 1990 and 1995.[1] Anthony and his family then became displaced to Jaffna town after the Sri Lankan army was confined to part of the coastline areas where they lived. The Sri Lankan government continued to pay salaries of government workers such as doctors and teachers but the LTTE co-opted preexisting structures of governance into its own systems as well as building a parallel police force and judiciary. One young Jaffna Tamil man, Krishnan, remembered "they showed their power in every aspect . . . they had their own courts, judges, and judgments." The Tigers had comprehensive taxation schemes on goods already subject to government tax, and regular forced "donations" for its National Defense Fund. LTTE cadres patrolled the streets in their distinctive uniforms, "uniformed" and marked even when in "civil dress"—female civil dress was no earrings, hair short or in plaits crossed and pinned up, and long shirts belted over trousers. Cadres regularly mediated disputes. The Tigers also placed their own "people" and supporters in fishing and farming and other collectives. Regular LTTE recruitment drives were enforced in schools. Thus, the LTTE sought to actively reform sociation, including work, school, and community, around its own structures. This quasi-state integrally depended on the Sri Lankan state's presence as a ghoulish other—manifested in Jaffna Tamil life as a bomber, soldier, and banner of basic goods. The state as aggressor ideologically softened the privations of life under the LTTE by giving the LTTE seeming necessity, and in its absence, making the enforcmentof law and order in Tamil by Tamils, the LTTE, seem desirable in the midst of chaos.

Vasantha recalled the war games that all the children played, and the ones she played with our other childhood friend M, who later joined the Tigers and died,

> At the back of the house we used to play games. We used to have these training sessions. We would have camp and camp attacks. This was when I was ten, eleven. I used to play with the boys. When you left, I was alone, I didn't have any other friends and you remember the other girls don't you! I was too scruffy for them. I had to go with the boys and M was my ally.

The LTTE had also begun a Tamilizing program, insisting that certain words of foreign origin (English, Sinhalese, etc.) had to be replaced. For example, the English word "ice cream," was literally written as such in Tamil script, was changed to "kuli kully" (meaning cold sticky substance).[2] While this rule was later softened, the LTTE in Jaffna banned foreign movies and music, even South Indian Tamil movies and music, producing and circulating Tiger films and music instead. Thus, the LTTE military regime was also aural and visual. Interviewees told me that one went to school and tuition classes, played cricket, football, and other school games, and listened to LTTE music and watched LTTE films.

Bombs, shells, and the arms on the street were an everyday reality for young people. While militarization was repressive, it was also "normal." Vasantha recalled a critical moment when the Sri Lankan government used a new kind of "supersonic bomber." She remembered this, not because it was a bomber, but because this bomber was silent unlike the others and took them by surprise, as their adaptive reactions were attuned already to detecting the approach of bombers through their sound.

> I remember the first time Supersonic bomber bombed. We were just sitting there and then dedum, we didn't hear it, and we were like "what's happened?" Then we were just sitting there shocked. Nobody moved, nobody ducked we were just sitting there. Then somebody screamed. And then one prefect saying "they haven't bombed us yet, go and hide" . . . it was very close to us, a few yards away.
>
> Normal day would come and go and then you would have all these moments. For a long time I thought that was normal, just how a human being is going to live. That's how my life is going to be.

Life, Vasantha related, intertwined daily tasks and routines and the predictably constant unpredictability of bombing, shelling, and death.

> The schools were going on as usual. If there was bombing in your area then you wouldn't go to school. They will say they are going to have fights. On other days we would go.

The normal life of daily tasks and routines, however, was not an idealized other; daily tasks and routines themselves were characterized by improvization around LTTE recruitment possibilities, government military attacks, and lack of most foodstuffs and imports. Normal in some senses, then, signified civilian adaption to exigencies, the art and techniques of everyday life—which was morally considered abnormal by those living it—and at the same time it could signify the predictability of the unpredictable and arbitrary violence and death that also characterized life in Jaffna at the time.

Krishnan was a soft-spoken middle-class Jaffna Tamil, now in his early thirties and living in Colombo. He recounted to me the various techniques of managing civilian life that ordinary people evolved to cope with the goods embargo imposed by the government, from the soap made of local Palmyrah tree products, to the adjustment of car engines to run primarily on kerosene oil. Krishnan was expert at making homemade coconut oil lamps to save kerosene. Anthony recalled these privations bitterly:

> Our lamps were jam jars with a little kerosene and wick; that is how we studied. Yet those who were high up in the LTTE had their generators, they lived in the light. There are children who went to study by the light from the ICRC (International Committee of the Red Cross) safe areas.

These stories from young people were also filled with pride while recounting methods of survival, how they and their parents turned themselves into everyday bricoleurs.

For Krishnan, these managements and new skills, as well as the ceaseless attempt to maintain school-going and other activities was "the life of normal life, civilian life." At the same time, he told me, "on the other side there was also bombing, shelling."

> We were used to that. We were not scared. I was personally not scared to die. I was just doing daily living, going to school and class as normal.

Years later, when Krishnan had moved to Colombo, in 2007 the LTTE bombed Colombo with their self-assembled lightweight Czech aircraft.

> When the airplanes came to Colombo, Sinhalese people were so frightened. I was so used to that. I was brought up like that. Every night if you didn't hear the sounds of shells and bombs at night, then *that* is the different thing.

In Jaffna, Krishnan said,

> I thought I may die, but I didn't care much. It was not a big priority. We were just trying not to take any risks.

Death was numbingly normal, it receded into the always possible whilst other stories emerged brighter in their possibility.

Stories of bombing were part of other stories too, of being together in adversity, and even titillation. Vasantha recalled the beginning of regular bombings through the neighborhood building of bunkers:

> I remember as a child, I remember building the bunker in-between those two houses. It was like an overnight event. S—— Aunty had lots of girls staying with her and I loved hanging around there. It was in our house that we were building the bunker. We had the big lanterns, really powerful, and people were making tea and everything. . . . We went to bed so late. . . .
>
> My father always used to let me sleep in the morning. He used to say "kids only grow if they sleep properly." Once in the morning they started bombing and everyone was in the bunker. Half an hour later . . . everyone realised that I was not there and I'm still in bed. . . .
>
> My mother was screaming. My father was waking me up and by the time he got me up there was a helicopter. It was literally in front of our home. My father is rushing me into the bunker and I could see the man's face in there. He didn't shoot because it was just me and my father and everyone in the bunker was screaming because they thought they were going to bomb us.
>
> I remember being so scared and also at the same time like "cool I saw the army." [laughs] It was so stupid. Then I remember my mother giving me a hug and then a slap. "How could you not get up, how stupid." I was like "none of you saw the army," and my father was "yeah, yeah that was cool." My mother was looking at both of us like she could kill us. That was a moment I remember well.

Krishnan, too, talked of how his family would rush into the bunker:

> My brother and I, we would not like to go to the bunker, we like to go out and see the bombers. We would look at them and watch for the small thing that would come out when a bomb would be dropped, and we would be like excited "oh they put a bomb now." And we would look out for the different helicopters and bombers. We collected all the shells and caps. We had a collection. That was a common thing for youngsters at the time.

In the refugee camp, Anthony's characterization was darker. When I asked him about the greatest changes he noticed as a young person, he told me that life had become harder, it had become *kodumai* (tyranny, harshness, cruelty). The real thing that had changed him, he returned to again and again, was that he and others had looked war in its face. I could not even imagine, he told me, what it was like to see people with missing, legs, arms, eyes. . . . "There was death everywhere," he said, "you suddenly see people die, people with their insides exposed," indicating with his hands on his own body the turning inside out. For Anthony as a child, living in and out of refugee camps and rations (rather than within family houses as with Vasantha and Krishnan), death presented itself as an ever present disordering of the living.

All the young people I interviewed talked of tight LTTE control. Even for those who favored the LTTE, all words outside small circles of trust had to be guarded. I met Rajesh in Colombo, when he was seventeen and had with much effort gained admission to university. He was the eldest of four children and had also taken on the responsibility of helping his parents with his siblings. He was cynical about the life they lived in Jaffna, as he told me:

> Now can I say to somebody high up in the LTTE, what you have done is wrong, this is all wrong? Can I say that? No. Tomorrow I will not be there. So I cannot talk about my opinions or my beliefs freely. I have not got free speech or freedom to write. I can't criticize them in a paper.

He continued ever more emphatically on the costs of survival,

> You can't talk about it in public. We must talk about it, but nobody will talk. Nobody will talk about the Tigers. Not any kind of Tigers. Even if you're against them, you'll talk in support, because we're frightened.

He did, Rajesh said, talk about these sorts of matters within the house, "in our house we talk about it," but "outside, nobody talks about it." For them as young people, still within familial homes, it was the family that afforded protection and stability (though as we see in Chapter 5, for older people the family was not automatically the holder of secrets).

Anthony's stories only confirmed Rajesh and others. Anthony himself had come close to joining the LTTE, but

It was watching the way they acted toward us, that I began to be re-
pelled by them and what their ideas were. They were not fighting for us
but for themselves. Even so, their acts toward ordinary people . . . they
snatched our freedom to speak and to write from us.

If I joined these people what is the point? Even inside them there
is no freedom of thought or speech. There are so many prohibitions
and rules and oppressive rules.

He felt, too, that the only safe place to talk freely was within the home:
"they are my *sondakaran* (kin), we can talk freely among ourselves." When I
asked him about friends, he told me that some could talk among themselves,
but one could never argue with a friend who was pro-LTTE, "you have to be
careful because if they are in or involved in the movement they will tell local
command." "Home" he instructed me, is "trustworthy because it is your relations, in public you never know who is a member of their intelligence . . . you
never know who will report you." There was a sense in which this risk management, these skills of survival came to children as a matter of course. They
did not have to be learned afresh; they were part of the injunctions of society
at large. Children were vulnerable to the new world, but they understood it,
because it was their world.

Vasantha grew up with sharp eyes toward adult hypocrisies and the
openness war afforded in breaking down some barriers. War, she told me,
had changed some experiences. It had brought many closer together as they
shared common fears and risks. This was more than evident in her account
above of building bunkers in her neighborhood and being together with others. Yet, intimacy was still structured by social differentiations, from the ethnic one of Tamil and Muslim to that of caste, which governed the residential
segregation that war and profound displacement constantly threatened. One
of the moments Vasantha remembered most vividly was of another bombing
that had caused a bunker to collapse close to where she had lived. A family
had been trapped inside, and as events transpired it became clear that the
family was from a dalit/"lower caste." The municipal workers had to be called
to dig them out. Vasantha recalled how her neighborhood stood outside their
houses discussing what had happened and waiting for the municipal workers
to arrive, instead of rushing to help personally as they would have done in the
case of any other family, especially as there were children trapped in the bunker. Her mother had become so angry that finally she had forced two young
men to come with her and start digging the family out.

This moment haunted Vasantha particularly when she saw this turned against her. In her mid-teens, she had pursued a relationship with a boy of another caste. Those of her neighborhood came constantly to inform her father of the relationship, and to tell him that they did not want "such people" to be hanging around in their crossroads. Her father, much to Vasantha's relief, refused to countenance such conversations. In a peninsula that was transforming rapidly, caste could not be contained under manageable residential distance any longer. It became openly visible as displacement and war threatened to constitute overwhelmingly collective experiences. Fear of this enforced "mingling" constantly reinstated and hid caste and caste segregation, even while narratives of common suffering under war were reproduced.

Anthony was not from an upper caste. When I talked to him of how people asked me which village I was from, he told me immediately that they were "trying to find out what kind of person I was." When I looked at him inquiringly, he qualified this impatiently, "what caste you are, if they ask you what street you live on then they want to know what caste you are." Unlike South India (where caste names are often retained within proper names) and southern Sri Lanka, caste is not discernible through one's name in northern Jaffna given a trend toward more uniform naming practices in the last 50 years. It is a guessing game played primarily through guessing the place one is from. In Jaffna, caste is heavily residential, with wards composed of particular castes. Different wards of the same caste, as Banks (1960) points out, also maintain intense competition with each other. If one knows Jaffna and its social geography then one can know what caste someone is by asking what street they live on. Displacement has disrupted this ordered caste universe within Jaffna. The mass migration of upper caste "big" vellalas (farming upper caste) and some of the artisanal castes out of the peninsula has meant that Jaffna's "small" vellalas, artisanal and oppressed castes, have become more visible as they are swept up in mass internal displacement and reduced access to migration. The good aspect of the war, Anthony told me, is the fact that refugee camps are unable to maintain caste differentiation and many castes reside mixed together. This, he pointed out, led to the unwilling breakdown of many barriers between castes, disrupting the ordered maps of caste geographies.

Young people talked more often of these contradictions, I noted, than their parents did. Not unaware of the dangers and risks their parents constantly worried about on their behalf, nonetheless Vasantha and Anthony both intimated they and maybe even other young people had keener eyes for their new world and its own possibilities of disarray and disorder even as the adults in their world attempted to police it.

Both Vasantha and Anthony described in one way or another a complete disconnect with an older generation's world. Both Vasantha and her mother could see the immense difference between the everyday life that she knew and that her mother knew. Her mother had studied at a university outside the peninsula, and Vasantha remembers how her mother told her about her college friends and how they went to see films and walked around. For Vasantha, her mother's life seemed like a fairytale, an instructive fable. It gave her another source of life, but it also accentuated the differences between them.

> My mother was really worried and she was trying to tell me that there was this other life that she grew up with this pressure. Even though they had racism, they had problems with riots and things but she was saying there was no worrying about what you can read or write or what exactly what you can talk about. . . . You know, my mother would tell stories and it was like magical days, but that was normality but I just didn't know that was normality. I think for my mother it was such a sad thing because she felt like she couldn't let her children enjoy all these things in life.

Her life was, for her and her mother, empty of "something" that she had never known, to be imagined in its absence.

It was here that children's lives and the experiences they lacked seemed to characterize for many adults, and later children when they became adults, the war itself as a social field. Moreover, children's relationship to their parents and adults was complicated by the complete inability of adults to protect them. In situations of bombing, curfew, and raid, adults were equally vulnerable as children and the desire for safety and protection had to be counterbalanced with the knowledge that very few could provide it. Vasantha describes this and her parents, with tenderness,

> Even though there were struggles and things we were going through . . . they [her parents] were there. It doesn't make sense, my father is not superman, he is not going to stop the bombs falling on us, but they were there to take care of us.

In contrast to Vasantha's close and loving relationship with her mother, Anthony felt abandoned by the older generation, not only because of their physical inability to protect him, but also a moral inability to show him something other than the world he had. He reflected,

> When I was young, people went to join the movements in armed struggle. Truly if I had been older at that time I would have also joined the movement. When the movements started they started with the purpose of elevating people and fighting for their freedom and to liberate them.

Anthony and other young people inherited a vocabulary of liberation mouthed by the LTTE, yet without any ability, he argued, to achieve that liberation. After 1990, he told me, he felt a resounding silence settled over Jaffna. Those who had thought differently or talked openly, had been killed, or had left. His generation, he told me, was truly "one alone." When he was in his twenties, Anthony had begun to read more widely. It was then that he looked back and regretted the "emptiness" of his childhood:

> The problem was at that time there was not the situation to make a foundation for myself. to meet people who were knowledgeable. When I was going to school I never had the opportunity to meet these people. Later I was inspired by Marxism and Leninism but we need a foundation for that. The old people who could have helped are not there.

Instead, he grew up in a world where adults exhibited fear and conformity,

> Jaffna's people always adjust, in order to carry on with their lives and their work they will give themselves to be oppressed by anyone, and not talk against them. This is the kind of people we are. There is not a situation to talk against anyone, they will just say ok and yes. The only situation that is there for Jaffna people is to go behind whoever arrives in Jaffna. There are only a few people who still think about right and wrong.
>
> This is the awful situation that Tamil people face now. We didn't get liberation.[3] Our houses, bodies, rights, everything has been erased. The little freedom we had has been taken away from us and we now live as refugees in far flung places, separated from each other.

Thus Anthony came back to what others also agreed on; he told me of the older generation, "their ideas and experiences are different, our experiences and ideas are different." What was for Vasantha (and Krishnan too), close bonds with their family and the feeling of mutual besiegement, was for Anthony a more profound betrayal by an elder generation toward his future. This cleavage of "experiences and ideas" is most concretely illuminated by the new role the LTTE offered to young people through recruitment that bypassed their families.

Soldiers of the Future

Our situation was that only the LTTE was there to fight. The Sri Lankan air force was bombing us. People were dying and the houses were being smashed. The Navaly Kovil (temple) was hit. In this situation when you see the bodies of those who have been killed brought past you, when you see them, then you feel like I must join the LTTE and fight against the Sinhala army and the Sinhala government. I thought about it, I came close to the decision to join. (Anthony)

In Sri Lanka, youthfulness is marked by the emergence of a new demographic in the 1970s of unmarried, educated, aspirational youth between sixteen and twenty-four, a newly extended transitional period between "childhood" and the "adulthood" produced by significant marriage delay and the expansion of universal schooling (Kearney and Miller 1985). This generation's frustrations and unfettered status have been extensively analyzed as filling the ranks of the dramatic Sinhala (and Tamil) youth insurgencies of the 1970s (e.g., Spencer 1990c; Peiris 2008; Kearney and Miller 1985).[4] In the 1990s, the LTTE shifted this popular characterization of unfettered youth viable for political action downward to an even younger category of Tamil youth, male and female, who were enjoined to die for the nation rather than experiencing political awakening per se. This line was demarcated through recruitment into the LTTE.

Voluntary recruitment had fallen in the late 1980s, and so the LTTE stepped up a campaign that was targeted at a younger age range. By 1991, harsh pass laws imposed controls on those aged ten to twenty-five (which varied somewhat between areas but was generally 10–23 for girls and 10–25 for boys) (Amnesty International 1996, 8).[5] Some were informed that this applied to those up to thirty-five, though officially it was twenty-five. One could only leave the peninsula if one left another child. Vasantha's parents were told that her parents and sister could leave Jaffna if they left Vasantha behind for the LTTE or found an equivalent child as a guarantor. One option offered to leave was if one took an undercover LTTE cadre with them through the army checkpoints, which could result in indefinite detention and torture for the civilian family. Those who were able to circumvent these pass laws were either connected to the LTTE or able to bribe LTTE cadres, and already with connections and families abroad. Even those who managed to get an LTTE pass still had to navigate the Sri Lankan army checkpoints on the other side of the border, where young Tamils suspected to be LTTE members were at risk of arrest and horrific torture. All the young people I interviewed talked of "feeling stuck" because of the pass laws. These delineated an age span and cohort, as youth, through their possibility of being recruited. Ironically this has reinforced life cycle ideals; some families in eastern Sri Lanka under pressure in 2002 to give one child to the LTTE, arranged early marriages to push their child into marriage, and thus adulthood and hopefully beyond recruitment (Boyden 2007).

Most significantly, as Jo Boyden points out (for eastern Batticaloa), the LTTE's emphasis on recruitment rendered childhood a "highly politicized and contested social space" (2007: 26). To be a young Tamil meant that one could be recruited into the LTTE and could die for the nation. To be young was to be in the power of adults who could not protect one from the LTTE or the vicissitudes of war. To be a young person born in the late 1980s onward was also never to have known Jaffna in peacetime. Young Jaffna Tamils perceived themselves as inhabiting terrain of common presents and potential future distinct from their parents, marked specifically by the prospect of recruitment.

Traditionally, one of the preeminent life stages in Jaffna Tamil life is "schooling." Young people's role in families was to study hard even if many could not always achieve these strictures. Education as a social good is deeply embedded in the Jaffna peninsula. For two hundred years, people of the peninsula told its children that the primary means of advancement was through education and government service. A dense network of schools dates from nineteenth-century (especially American) missionary activities (Wickremeratne 1973; Russell 1982).[6] Arasaratnam (1994) argues that in the nineteenth century every village in the Jaffna peninsula regardless of size had a Christian mission school.[7] The Hindu revivalist movement also concentrated many of its efforts on education, setting up non-mission schools such as Jaffna Hindu College, which also taught in English and followed British mission standards. Education led to employment for Jaffna Tamils. Well-educated English speaking Jaffna Tamils, freed from overpopulated land and a declining market economy, travelled all around the island and in British colonial territories as civil servants, overseers, and clerks, becoming "a nation of pen pushers" at a time when "there was a great demand for pen-pushers all over the British Empire" (Arasaratnam [1982]1986: 40).[8]

In the twentieth century, the prioritization of education continued despite state discrimination. In the context of rising school attendance in the postcolonial era across Sri Lanka, in 1971 Jaffna had the highest percentage of children ages six to fourteen attending school, 79.5 percent (Kearney and Miller 1985: 90). The "desire for education" is a classic story Jaffna Tamils tell about themselves. All social classes and castes sought education until the advent of mass militancy as the means for upward mobility and improvement.

This desire for education and the importance of education continue as the primary way in which Anthony and many others imagined a future. Even when conditions militated against the fulfilment of their desires, they struggled to study. When I asked Anthony why he had carried on going to tuition classes and studying for his exams after displacement, he reacted passionately. Education was important, he said, "if you didn't do your O levels or A levels, there was nothing you could do." He said, "maybe if you had some technical jobs you could work. But then if you didn't have these things you would be stuck doing menial jobs; there was a standard you had to live up to still."

Anthony's story was filled with bitterness and regret for an education he felt he could not pursue, and a future that had disappeared alongside it:

I did my O levels at the age when I should have been doing my A levels.

I was studying hard for my O levels but then one of my friends was captured by the EPRLF [for the TNA], I was very sad and depressed over that and my studies were affected. Because we had to move as refugees and I had to leave school my studies were all muddled up. . . . This way everything was delayed, all the time.

The mind grows old when you don't do things on time, you became more unable to study or do the exams and so things were slipping back and back.

Like this there were so many young men. They were working in Jaffna studying by first kerosene and then when there wasn't any kerosene anymore by a little bit of oil in a bottle with cotton, some-times coconut oil. That is how they were studying.

Because of my sadness and the moving I didn't get [good] O level results. Then with all the disturbances and the war even though I tried to study for the A levels, I didn't get the results. Now what can I do? At least I have some technical training in wiring. There are so many who have nothing. Now what kind of job can I hope to get? My future is over.

In launching recruitment drives in schools, the LTTE thus targeted one of the most socially significant spaces in Jaffna society: young people struggling to fulfill the expectations of their families and society at a time of privation, with little possibility of education leading to jobs or further success. These were spaces filled with desire, aspiration, guilt, and fear of failure, as well as of camaraderie and alliance against adults. The LTTE presented a different route to status and power, which all had access to. Frustrated education was placed in opposition to glorious "heroism."

Children were saturated with images that valorized militarization. The Jaffna Kittu memorial park for children was built with seesaws in the shapes of machine guns (cf. UTHR 1994. In this period, as UTHR documents, one of the most common pictorial representations of the LTTE posted all over Jaffna was of an LTTE cadre holding children and walking toward a hilltop with a gun planted upside down (UTHR 1994. Krishnan recalled that his school was asked to keep the last period free for whenever the LTTE came to recruit. The LTTE would show videos of death, rape, and destruction. The videos mixed current bombings with older ones, with narratives about the necessity to oppose the Sinhalese and the need for young people to fight. Krishnan described these videos as hypnotic, and the feelings aroused of shame, guilt, anger, and desire. As he said, "You get the impression that all Sinhalese people are bad, that they are really bad people, they want Tamil people to be slaves and kill us." This was not a far stretch for those watching. They had little if no experience with Sinhalese who were not part of an army bombing them: they were in the middle of an intense military campaign and the Sri Lankan government and the south as a whole were unfamiliar to them.

Vasantha recalled her own instinctive revolt, not as one about whether Sinhalese people really could be evil, but even more fundamentally about the lack of a future outside death and dying promised to her by the LTTE. In one recruitment event at her school, female LTTE cadres had come to give their "usual talk" of the honor of dying for their nation (see Sornarajah 2004). Vasantha had in the midst of the talk looked amused and had smiled. Immediately one cadre had turned on her and demanded to know why she was smiling and not taking this seriously. Stung, Vasantha had stood up and said "I was just wondering if we are all meant to be dying for Tamil Eelam, who will be around to enjoy it?" Other girls had concealed their smiles, and the cadre had rejoindered, "it is people like you who let down our nation." Later, Vasantha had been summoned to the headmistress's office and upbraided. From that moment on, the LTTE-supporting girls in the school contrived to find ways to bully her.

Others I interviewed talked of being cornered by LTTE cadres and scolded and sworn at for being traitors, for not being patriotic, for letting down others who had died in the war. As young men, Krishnan and his friends did not "hang around" too much in the streets. On one occasion, confronted by the LTTE, he and two others endured for hours lectures on their cowardice in not joining the LTTE, being berated and sworn at for being "traitors." The pressure to join was such that many did indeed stand up and pledge themselves at these collective sessions.

Vasantha told me that stories did circulate though among young people about what could happen if one joined the LTTE and how having once joined one could not leave. Rajesh told me,

Because of my family situation, I didn't even think of joining. They were always coming to our school, though, and giving us trouble. They held meetings asking us to join. There were those who joined and those who didn't. Those who joined could not come back. Now take me: if I had said yes, then within five hours I couldn't go home again. Once you've joined, you've joined. If you try to come back again, there will be punishments.

Many young people did end up in precisely this predicament: having joined the LTTE, they were unable to leave and return home at the risk of harsh punishment for desertion. The 2004 Human Rights Watch Report on Child Soldiers noted that "once recruited, most children are allowed no contact with their families. The LTTE subjects them to rigorous and sometimes brutal training. They learn to handle weapons, including landmines and bombs, and are taught military tactics. Children who make mistakes are frequently beaten. The LTTE harshly punishes soldiers who attempt to escape"

(HRW 2004). The HRW report details numerous testimonies of escapes and consequences. By 2003 when I was there, desertion w: ing such a problem that the LTTE shaved the heads of new female ɪₑᵤᵢ uɪₜs to make them visible on desertion. The LTTE promised many that ten years service would suffice, so many attempted just to serve out their term, though this promise was not always kept. One former senior LTTE cadre, Ranjan, told me that after ten years in the LTTE and rising in the ranks, he was imprisoned by the LTTE for two years on his departure, as he "knew too much."

However, I found that young people talked not of open opposition but of considerable moral ambivalence toward the LTTE. New structures of power instituted by the LTTE promised a different route toward power, status, and heroism, albeit a dangerous one that particularly appealed to the teenagers it was designed for (see Trawick 2007 and a more nuanced account in Boyden 2007). It promulgated images of itself as highly disciplined, self-sacrificing, and heroic. Rather than brushing aside death, it valorized death as the ultimate sacrifice (Thiranagama 2010). While the Tamil word for suicide was *thatkolai*, the LTTE renamed it as *thatkodai*, the gift of oneself (Schalk 1997). Most of all, the LTTE represented an ordered authoritarian vision of society; it promised order and stability at a time when debilitating change was a permanent pervasive feature of growing up.

Through recruitment, the LTTE inserted itself between children and their families. The guns on the street entered the family house as a constant threat from within. Within homes, parents lived in the fear that their children would be forcibly conscripted or voluntarily run away from home to join the LTTE. Rajesh, who had no interest in joining himself, told me of his and his parents' continual fear that his teenage brother would join. Parents, even while supporting the LTTE, feared recruitment, as Rajesh told me:

> Now outside they'll talk: one person will tell another person's child, you go and fight for the movement, but will they let their own children go? Of course not. That's how they are. When it comes to themselves, they won't think that way.

I heard stories such as of one prominent LTTE supporter who when his own son was recruited went to the camp begging him on his knees to return home. The person who related this story commented that he "deserved it" for encouraging other people's children to join.

Those I interviewed all told me stories of young people who would threaten their parents that they would join the LTTE if they did not get their way (see also Boyden 2007 for similar accounts in eastern Batticaloa). Krishnan told me,

> If you have fought with your father and mother, then they threatened their family that they would go to the LTTE if they didn't get what they wanted. We were teenagers and we did not think about consequences. It was childish acts. There are many who joined the LTTE because of a small conflict at home. But it's a one-way thing, once you go to them then you can't come out.

Family disputes did indeed push many young people toward the LTTE (Boyden 2007), but these stories were also apocryphal. Stories of children being able to demand things from their parents through the LTTE became stories about generational relationships for the young people who passed these stories on. Awareness of the LTTE's power over adults lay like a ghost within the family. Youth became imbued with a diffuse agency in potentia, which was at the same time the curse of being young, and which became paramount to their public lives within LTTE control.

Vasantha traced her own alienation from the LTTE to her family background. Her parents, particularly her mother, were very critical of the LTTE's repressive side and so she had access to a world at home where opinions circulated more freely. Vasantha also has an instinctively rebellious streak. Never "a good girl," she refused to conform, evident in her story of defying the LTTE cadre in school. But, as Vasantha herself pointed out, her own sense of growing dissonance came alongside a tacit acceptance that this was their world.

> The rest of the school boys and girls this was all they grew up with, so the Tigers was part of the government for them, even for me. I did not know anything different until you come and see the other side. But I can still see that some of the things they were doing wasn't right. It's almost like living in a place where everything is controlled. . . .
>
> I knew, when you are thirteen, fourteen, you are learning. I could see things changing. And I'm thinking Ok, is this how the rest of my life is going to be? Showing ID, going to sentry point. And you just think that's how it's going to be. It's not something you can change so you accept it.

Within this prosaic and alienated acceptance of reality, trying to discern dissent is less a matter of open rebellion and more a subtle understanding of dissent but also accommodation with, what was for young people, common sense. Krishnan told me,

> I personally never realized this when I was in Jaffna. We were young and kept in the dark. We just went around. Personally I only realized what I had undergone when I went to Colombo. We had undergone displacement. But we were teenagers. My father didn't have a job. We just thought it was coming to a new place. You get on your bike and go around. . . . We never thought about it.

Young people saw the LTTE not as an emancipatory oppositional force like their elders (see Chapter 5) but as a deeply normative force, a "government" in their lives providing normalized routes of power and recognition. No wonder that young people described their lives also characterized as such by others, as examples of the ambivalent agency of war. They were "powerful" and they were "hunted."

Threaded through these accounts were stories of closeness, friendship, neighborliness, but also fear of others and the opacity of other's people's motives and thoughts. As Vasantha said in the comment with which I opened this chapter, she didn't realise that her life was "not normal" but didn't "know if anyone else did." Anthony told me of guarding oneself against others, biting one's tongue continually. Life with others was, for these young people at least, life lived together with warmth but also awareness of separation and withdrawal. This stood in great contrast to their accounts of the upheavals of mass displacement.

The Mob and the Migrant: Displacement and Departure

The most common experience of war related by all Tamils is movement. While Jaffna itself was historically the site of migration for employment from the nineteenth century onward (Arasaratnam 1994; Bastin 1997; McDowell 1996), the war saw unprecedented internal displacement and an external refugee diaspora. Jaffna itself saw two of the largest forced movements in Sri Lankan history, the 1990 Eviction of Muslims from the north (70,000–80,000) and the 1995 Exodus of Tamils from Jaffna city (450,000–500,000), both instigated by the LTTE.

The young people I talked to put forward accounts of forced movement and internal displacement as their events of political awakening, in contrast to the stories of riots and militancy put forward by older Tamils (see Chapter 5). This was part of a differentiated generational grammar. Young Tamils stressed watching, waiting, accepting; the feelings of having things happen to them and the refusal of responsibility for a world that they felt they had inherited but not created. Displacement in Vasantha's story was not individual, it was her experience of "being Tamil." It was also when she discussed displacement that she moved most easily between the collective and the "I." Her stories of collective displacement are of immense suffering, but unlike her other memories, they are also of brief alliances and survival measures taken together—experience fashioned en-masse.

Eviction and Exodus:
"We watched them go," "It happened to us"

On 28–30 October 1990, the LTTE forcibly expelled all 70,000–80,000 Muslims from the northern areas under its control (see Chapters 3 and 4). Tamils I talked to talked as if Muslim expulsion was out of their hands. What was for Muslims a singular site of community and personal tragedy was woven by Tamils into more generic (Tamil-centered) stories of "powerlessness" and apathy, especially by young people. Vasantha recounted,

> Then it was the Muslims leaving that I remember . . . I had a friend in fifth grade called Mumtaj. She was the only Muslim girl in my class and we were really good friends, because we both rode the blue van to school. I remember talking to her a lot. And she would tell me about Ramadan and other things. Then I remember the day her parents came and picked her up from school. That night she had to go. She didn't come back to school and I was quite upset about it because I didn't know why. Her parents were so nice and I remember thinking why?
>
> I remember we were all standing outside and the neighbors were crying, whether you were Hindu or Christian. I remember all these Muslims crying. I was about ten or eleven. . . . They were walking down the road with their two bags that was all they were allowed to

take. Sometimes they went past in vans looking out of the window. Not all people were sad, but we all stood out and watched them go, when the vans were going carrying them away.... I remember my mother and father talking about it and being so angry about it, and I didn't really understand at that time, now I do.

Vasantha's mother's attempt to talk about the Eviction to her students met with the reply "we are Tamils we are fighting for a *Tamil* Eelam" from the LTTE supporters.

Instead, for many Tamils, the Eviction was recalled most strongly in their own forced displacement, "the Exodus," on the same day (30 October) five years later. Rajesh was just one of many young Tamils who linked the Eviction to the Exodus: "This happened to us because we let the Muslims go," he told me. The UTHR (1995) special report on the Exodus described how

Forced in the night and under heavy rain, on 30th October ... one clear refrain was readily heard and assented to: "This is happening to us today because we did it to the Muslims exactly five years ago." Some recalled that they were given four hours to vacate, while the Muslims were given two. (UTHR 1995)

The failure of the 1994 peace talks between a newly elected government and the LTTE had led to renewed war. In 1995, the Sri Lankan army was dispatched to capture LTTE-controlled Jaffna city. The army indiscriminately bombed the north, including places of shelter, with refugees fleeing from rural areas toward Jaffna Town for safety (UTHR 1995). On 29 October the LTTE had come to collect money "owed" them for the National Defence Fund, "from government servants they took 5,000 rupees, from the people they took money and jewels. For the big war they said," Rajesh told me. Those with family members abroad had to donate extra.

As the army approached Jaffna Town, the LTTE announced on 30 October that the entire population of Jaffna Town must leave. It told the international audience that the people had chosen to leave of their own volition, unable to face living under the Sinhalese. All Jaffna Town's long-term residents and refugees had to leave. There were two routes, through the narrow Chemmani-Kandy road to the areas of Chavakachcheri and down through the narrow bottleneck of the peninsula, or in boats straight across Kilali lagoon to the

LTTE's new headquarters in the north central Vanni district. The latter was particularly treacherous, Rajesh told me.

> They would tie together 5 or 6 boats and only one boat would have a working engine and that would pull the other boats. If there was any trouble the first boat would cut the rope, the rest were left in the middle of the lagoon. That was the kind of frightening situation we were in. That's how they told us to go to the Vanni.

Families who took the lagoon route faced continuous bombardment by the Sri Lankan army as they tried to make their escape. Krishnan told me "some of my good friends have died at that time crossing the lagoon at night. The army was shelling, people fell into the lagoon and there is no one to rescue you. My friend and his family drowned."

Around 450,000 people left Jaffna city on foot, on the Chemmani-Kandy road through the bottleneck of the peninsula (UTHR 1995). The LTTE rounded up individuals, broke down schools to force out groups hiding in them, went through camps. Some junior doctors and nurses in Jaffna Hospital attempted to stay with their patients. However, the ICRC withdrew protection from the hospital, and so patients and doctors too were forced to leave the peninsula (UTHR 1995). The ICRC transported some of the most severely ill by ship, but many were left stranded.

People stubbornly resisted. It took the LTTE two weeks to clear a recalcitrant, unwilling population out of Jaffna Town. Increasingly desperate, they brought buses to transport the last resistors in mid-November. Finally the last two places hiding both Hindu and Christian refugees, the Methodist church and the Christian Chundukuli Girls School, capitulated after the Methodist pastor was assaulted by the LTTE (UTHR 1995). Those inside the school pleaded with the Tigers to let them stay, but to no avail. The last refugees, including my grandmother, were bussed away in tears from Jaffna town.

By the time the Sri Lankan army arrived on 16 November, Jaffna Town was empty for the first time in 600 years. The Exodus is an unforgettable event for Jaffna Tamils; every family has an Exodus story. There are so many to tell. They talk with the same intensity of walking, of violence, hunger, fear, and anger. Rajesh's parents could not get food for him and his brother, not even milk for his twin infant sisters. One middle-aged couple, Murugan and Thangamma (see Chapter 6), told of sleeping under trees, and related how

people drank water collected in umbrellas. Schools with limited
were housing hundreds of people. In this chapter, I concentrate on
story of the Exodus, but hers is only one among thousands.

Vasantha's Exodus

Vasantha was studying for exams when the army dropped leaflets announcing their arrival: "We were meant to be taking our GCSEs (sic) and I was
very under prepared . . . I was hoping they would delay it. That was naïve
and stupid of me I know." Vasantha's father had just returned home after a
serious heart attack. It was then that the LTTE announced that all had to
leave. As her father was too weak to travel, Vasantha's parents sent Vasantha,
her sister, and the girl who worked in their house with a family friend to join
others walking. The only road wound over one small bridge across the narrow bottleneck of the peninsula. It was monsoon time and the roads were
muddy and the sea high.

> I started to cry. . . . I'm going to Chavakachcheri and they [parents]
> say that they are going to come later, but I don't know what's going to
> happen. . . . Then I see the LTTE blocking half the bridge. . . . Half is
> occupied by the LTTE and half by the people. So the people are going
> on bikes, little motorbikes, and bullock carts and walking with bags
> on their heads and all the things they could take and they don't know
> where they are going, to a school or whatever it is, they are moving
> there. And then we see the LTTE's cars and vans and all the things
> they confiscated from the people and they are filled, filled with stuff.

Accounts of the Exodus (see UTHR 1995) tell of the increasing ruthlessness
of the LTTE in their determination to keep people moving to protect their
own movement, and the shock as Tamils realized the LTTE was not fighting
for them. Vasantha recalled,

> They [LTTE] were using us as human shields. They didn't fight for
> us. They were moving faster than we were because they had vehi-
> cles . . . trucks and trucks filled with kerosene oil.[9] . . . They are not
> just leaving they are taking all the things they had.

She recalled the bustle of conversation in the mob being pushed forward,

> They were ruthless and that time people were very angry. People were
> saying "are they not fighting? Why are they withdrawing?' Because
> that's what it looked like. People were starting to talk about it. I remem-
> ber asking this uncle who was taking us "Why are they withdrawing?
> If they are going to fight for us then why are they withdrawing?" and
> then this other man who was passing by, and he turned and looked at
> me. I'll never forget his face because it's sort of agreeing with me but
> he never thought about it straight away but I had said it out loud. So
> he's thinking now "why?"

Vasantha remembered this moment vividly. In another's eyes, she traces
the recognition that she had said out loud what he was thinking. At the moment of complete erasure as families, individuals, a new strange sense of collectivity briefly flared. For Vasantha, who had been feeling alienated from
others and at odds with what she saw as prevailing opinion, it is here that she
finds a moment of acceptance.

As a mob, Tamils started to throw off the conformity of previous years,
shouting and protesting and showing open anger:

> In one of those long bread queues in Chavakachcheri one man blew
> up: "We are being treated as slaves. If this is their behavior now, how
> would it be when we get Eelam?" Unlike in other times ... others
> joined in ... the [LTTE] police arrived and ordered the first speaker
> to get into their vehicle. The man was vocal in his refusal. Finally he
> was dragged inside. (UTHR 1995)

Vasantha's parents failed in their attempt to stay in Jaffna. The LTTE insisted
on clearing them with all the others who had begged to stay in their homes,

> People didn't want to go. People said "we live or we die, let us die
> in our own home," especially old people. And also they didn't know
> where to go to ... my mother begged them "if I take my husband he
> will die, he is really ill, he can't move." But there was no arguing with
> them, they had guns and they were ruthless, they are started beating
> up some man who was arguing so it came to a point where there was
> nothing they could do, they might as well leave.

Vasantha's parents left, her mother pushing her scooter with her father mounted on it,

> my mother said that people were stepping on people . . . a woman had actually dropped her baby, my mother couldn't see her but she could hear her screaming . . . nobody could stop and help her out because you couldn't move. . . . Nobody could rescue anyone. It was raining so badly that day and nobody had boats. . . . My father's state was bad, he was really tired. . . . This is one of the reasons he [later] ended up having another heart attack.

Walking inch by inch, her parents and others took hours and days to travel small distances crammed in together. Vasantha's family were luckier than most, ending up at one end of the peninsula which was where her father was originally from, rather than in the north central area of the Vanni where the LTTE had moved its new headquarters to and where refugees moved into makeshift camps. Vasantha, like others, began preparing for her now postponed exams,

> They were saying the army is going to capture Jaffna and then you will have an exam. So I was still studying while being displaced because I know that any moment they will announce it, and I will have to have my GCEs . . . we took them in December 1995.

Hundreds of Jaffna children took their exams in 1995, just as in 2009 a month after the war ended hundreds of Tamil teenagers in the refugee camps sat for their GCE exams. Six months after the 1995 Exodus rumors started to spread that the Sri Lankan army was allowing people to return to Jaffna Town. From all directions Tamils fled back home to forbidden army territory. The LTTE was unable to prevent over 200,000 going back.

> The Tigers had told us that they were still fighting for it [Jaffna] and that the army wouldn't let you in. So nobody tried to go back. Then these few families were the first to go. They literally packed up their bags and escaped. And what they had found is that the army is letting people come and one of them came back to get his family and the news spread. And then we keep hearing this, my mother was saying "let's go, I'm not staying here."

If you go, everybody's idea was, if you go in there, then you can get out wherever you want to go. If you go into the area controlled by the government then you can move, there is no pass system. As soon as they started running planes or running trains. You see a lot of families were separated but they were stuck because the LTTE would not let them out.

Vasantha's dream of "you can get out wherever you want to go" was testimony to how chosen movement was the dream of those who had only grown up with acute control of movement.

When Vasantha and her family went home, their house and all the other houses in the neighborhood had been raided by the LTTE, opportunistic looters, and the Sri Lankan army.

We saw their materials and things; they had sat in our home eating. When we got home all our clothes were piled up like a mountain. They had been through our stuff they had taken stuff. Even tables they had turned the other way around. . . . It was everyone's house. . . . It took us weeks to clean. . . . There were four houses around us, and then we all came in, all our stuff was in this private lane, so we were all picking up our stuff as we were coming in. That was horrible. Tables and sofas you can't pick up, but you're looking, "that's ours," "that is yours." . . . When we left we all got lost, so none of us knew what had happened to the others.

The Jaffna Tamils who returned were cautious, especially those like Vasantha who simply had little if no experience with the Sri Lankan state:

When we came back it was the start of something new. You see, for years and years we had never been part of the government. . . . We heard these scary stories that the army is going to rape you or kill you.

Indeed, life was difficult upon return, with young people under constant suspicion by the Sri Lankan army. There were indeed high profile atrocities, such as the Krishanthy Kumaraswamy case where a schoolgirl was raped and killed by army soldiers and the members of her family who went searching for her were also killed. When I went to Jaffna in 2003 the stark divisions between Jaffna people and the soldiers stationed there were still clear. The LTTE also returned in 1996, mingling with civilians and posting bombs as warnings to Tamils not to collaborate with the Sri Lankan army. Two successive mayors of Jaffna were killed by LTTE bombs (UTHR 1998, 2003).

Writing about the Exodus is even more painful after the last battles of 2009, when the LTTE again forced civilians to march with them as human shields and the Sri Lankan army used heavy weaponry on those civilians in their bid to destroy the LTTE. In both, civilians proved to be the LTTE's last resort. It was only in such moments that Tamils could see that their individual survival was linked to collective survival, and that both were inimical to the survival of the LTTE. The 200,000 who returned to Jaffna in 1995 were luckier than the thousands who desperately fled LTTE territory in small family groups in April and May 2009, even as the LTTE shot at them while they escaped. It was not the LTTE nor the Sri Lankan government who ensured the safety of Tamils in 2009 (or 1995), but unarmed individuals and families, without adequate water or food, who nonetheless ran, waded, and hid in small groups and attempted to protect themselves and their children (UTHR 2009a, b). Paradoxically, it is in these moments of erasure that some forms of collectivity have flared, even if evanescent, and new forms of experience have emerged through rupture.

K. Sritharan from UTHR, who gathered accounts of the Exodus, told me that in 1996 Tamils in Jaffna and Colombo openly talked with anger of the Exodus. But soon these stories stopped being told, as the LTTE bombs in Jaffna showed their presence again. Official accounts by Tamils carefully weeded out the LTTE order and the origins of the Exodus, leaving it as an event of immense suffering that had to be shorn of any of its details to be related. K. Sritharan's own conclusion was that the trauma of the Exodus became even greater because of its abruptly stunted public life. This stood in contrast to the public memorialization of the Eviction by Northern Muslims that I describe in Chapters 3 and 4. Sritharan told me,

> There was no public debates, no discussions no space for arguments. Also the newspapers were hiding a lot of things which were absolutely obvious. So there was an obvious lack of truth within public. If people had gone through a period of discussion and debate then it would not be as traumatic an event as it still is. . . . Time goes on, they suppress the memories, or at least their anger.

His argument about public acknowledgement was one expressed by many Tamils (discussed intensively in Chapter 5). When I went to Sri Lanka,

I found a community of people who were frightened to talk in public spaces and as public people, for fear of being called a traitor and thus potentially arrested, taxed, or murdered by the LTTE, or of being taken for LTTE by the Sri Lankan army. What I did not find was silence. There were stories everywhere. People told me their experiences, subversive jokes, political thoughts, feelings of love, of betrayal, of anger and sorrow. They just never told me in public, only in private safely constructed spaces and after tests of my trustworthiness. Dealing with the political climate in Sri Lanka was to understand that silence was not absence of speech, but pregnant, it beckoned to a many-layered notion of social space and safety. What people most desired was to make their individual stories jointed to others, to make them public stories (Watson 1994). Indeed Vasantha herself did not talk of whether she had a story to tell or not, or the problems of expressing it, but rather of "whom to talk to"—which frames allowed her private story to become a public story of collective experience.

Vasantha's father died of a heart attack in 1997. Six months later, in 1998, Vasantha's mother was attending a meeting between the army and local Jaffna council officials, including the mayor, when an LTTE bomb designed to destroy collaboration killed them all. After Vasantha's parents died, she and Sakuntala were sent to her mother's sister in Britain.

> We got to Colombo by ship. I remember that day well because it was just me and my sister leaving, we are standing there waiting for the Red Cross people and they called our names and I was feeling responsible for the first time in my life. My sister was only eleven. I remember our godfather saying "be good girls, be very good girls." I think he was so sad . . . my uncle got a trishaw and the private lane that we were going on, all the people stood out and waved and everyone was crying. We were so close to the neighborhood and everyone crying. We were crying and we felt this great departure of our life. . . . It's like a movie because we were leaving. You are not sure what the destination is going to be, you don't know who is going to come and pick you up. Everything was uncertain, trusting someone you don't know and you are leaving.
>
> I remember getting on the ship, my first ship journey. . . . Once the ship started going, I went on the deck and stood there really getting scared. It didn't sink in until about an hour after I got on the ship that I realised, that I don't know what the fuck I am doing. I don't really have anyone in Colombo. I can't speak the language, I don't have that much

money, and if these people don't come to get me [her mother's in London] what the hell am I going to do? Really, really terrified remember hugging her [my sister] and telling her "it's going to be right I will look after you," because she started crying halfway through the journey. I was really feeling the responsibility and thinking I just want a sister I can fight, because that was the story previously; an annoying little sister. But then I had to take care of her. It was a scary feeling.

Vasantha presents the two common motifs of departure that occur in most of the stories I heard. She leaves in the Exodus, surrounded by others; they walk as a mob toward a collective unknown destination. This image of mass displacement and memory of forced migration contrasts with her departure to go to Colombo and abroad. Here she and her sister leave by themselves waving goodbye to others, leaving the neighborhood, their departure traces the slow hemorrhaging of population from Jaffna. She arrived thus in London.

"I Miss It . . . [That Life]"

On arrival in London, Vasantha and Sakuntala initially stayed with her mother's family, but Vasantha ran away after bad treatment at their hands. She found herself a job and put herself through university, doing a BA and an MA. Forbidden to have contact with Sakuntala by her family, nonetheless Vasantha succeeded in making a home in which Sakuntala joined her. Now a successful and dynamic professional, Vasantha has made a new life and friends in a new country. Yet, as she told me,

> Who would I talk to? The people who live here, unless you go through it with someone. . . . I talk to you but you have a particular interest in the subject; there is no way that Aunty would understand. Even though I can explain to Sam and Mona, they would never understand the extent of this thing, for them it's like the Lord of the Rings III. It's not something they can grasp. It's not their fault. I don't have Sri Lankan friends who used to live there.

In the position of the complete author of her own experiences to her friends, where she was the only voice and the dictator of all terms and meanings of her experience, Vasantha nonetheless found herself feeling disempowered. She explained to me that she ended up sounding as if she was telling "story of tragedy after tragedy," and yet it had not been like that for her.

Her problems with "Aunty," the middle-aged Sri Lankan woman she lodged with after leaving her maternal family, were different. The Sri Lankan community in London was composed of a number of different phases of migration from different periods in the civil war with concomitantly quite different understandings of the conflict and the Sri Lanka they had left behind (see Daniel and Thangarajah 1995; McDowell 1996). Often different sets of migrants found each other's experiences difficult to understand in such a rapidly changing situation. Not least, Vasantha rebelled against the diasporic reconstruction of conservative forms of community through food, cultural events, temple visits, arranging marriages, and so on. She found that most diasporic Tamils were pro-LTTE and unwilling to listen to her stories of LTTE-controlled Jaffna.

Vasantha's difficulties are also not uncommon. There was something about the intensity and specificity of her experiences that made it difficult for her to share them with those who had not experienced them. This is a much wider phenomenon, especially for those who become refugees cut off from their former worlds. This was one of the reasons that when I started interviewing Vasantha, she concentrated almost exclusively on her experiences growing up in Sri Lanka, mostly abjuring stories of London. Krishnan also told me that he had enjoyed talking about his experiences: "it's different with someone who knows," he told me; otherwise his life would sound like "fiction." Anthony and Rajesh, surrounded by Tamils with similar stories in Colombo, desired no such sense of recognition from me for their stories. Anthony wanted his story to be a public document from one who was not frightened to speak. Rajesh at seventeen was young and angry and wanted to express his sense of injustice to an outsider; just on the brink of starting a new life in university in 2003, he feared that war would return (as it did in 2004 and 2005) and interrupt his future (which I hope it did not). We return to Anthony again in Chapter 6; for now I end with Vasantha.

Vasantha experienced profoundly mixed emotions toward her past life. She had only lived in wartime Jaffna, so her past life in Jaffna is about living in and at war. In our first interview Vasantha told me, "I don't have feelings of home any more . . . it has nothing to do with what I have become." Jaffna was too far away, she said. However, another time she told me of the impossibility of forgetting her experiences in Jaffna; "I can't forget it, how can I? It's a part of me, it has shaped me, and I can't forget any of my experiences. How can I?" Vasantha's new life is laced with reminders of her previous existence and profound guilt about escaping that life and those she left behind. As she told me, "it's like another life. I miss it sometimes. It's weird, as shitty as it was, I miss it." On another occasion when Vasantha and I talked intensely about Jaffna, sharing memories and stories, she talked about her parents and her loneliness in moving to London, a move that coincided adulthood with orphanhood.

In this chapter, I attempt to understand the relationship between, first, the reflexive consciousness of the individual, and second, the social and political conditions as well as narratives (of power) out of which selves can become visible. Here, through Vasantha's and Anthony's stories among others, I have sought to illustrate how war, in Sri Lanka as elsewhere, produced particular forms of self-formation and creation, new forms of individualism, as well as new forms of collectivity and recognition. A new generation was brought together by shared ruptures and thus a new sense of temporality and everyday life, creating new frames of becoming, and thus new biographies. This chapter pays attention to what such generationally and caste differentiated wartime biographies might be.

These young people's stories are accounts of their own individual negotiation with particular experiences (which given the closed society they lived in were forcibly similar), which were constituted by frames that lay outside their own individual choices. They are, as I suggested in the Introduction, the way people talked of the war as both "happening to them," as an external force over when they had little power, and as "making them," experiences which were formative in making them who they are, waged within communities and families. The war thus was experienced as external, and as internal.

However, there was ambivalent agency in that war, and it would be a mistake to understand it as only stories of immense loss and trauma. It was a war in which young people found their own agency valorized, even as this agency was that of the potential to die for the nation. The kinds of losses young people talked of were losses that took from their parents' stories of a life that young people themselves had never experienced and longings for what "should be." That is why in this chapter I emphasize the common sense of the world that those I interviewed grew up in, to show that our imaginings of the world, our feelings of loss, are always larger than just what we experience, though they are fundamentally constituted around them.

Perhaps it is not then surprising that Vasantha felt so ambivalent about

Jaffna; it was what she had fled from, and yet it was everything that she sought to retell when I asked her about her life.

> There are times when I feel I owe a lot to my country, how I was brought up, how it made me strong and able to cope, but then I think maybe I have a lot to thank my parents for, but not my country . . . we have no choice; we cannot forget. I wish I could forget a lot of things that has happened. Even though there are plenty of good memories of my childhood, little things.

Vasantha repeats what I encountered with others, that the desire "to forget" was more often mentioned than "to remember." Yet, if granted, that forgetting was in fact of her own "becoming". This is the ambivalence of being shaped by war: the kind of person one becomes to deal with that war are at the same time one's trauma, and marks of that war. War grounds life even as it takes it away, what may injure us also sustains us (Butler 1995).

This ambivalent attachment, if we are to imagine a new future now for Tamils *sans* LTTE, is fundamental to how and why new practices and thus political and generational cultures have come into being and at the same time the ways in which these were constantly tested, remade, interrogated from within by those who were products of that very same process. Perhaps, this younger generation were precisely the ones who saw little alternative and heroism in an LTTE they only knew as quasi-state, enough so that when it collapsed in 2009 they will not be the ones that reinstate it.

CHAPTER TWO

The House of Secrets:
Mothers, Daughters, and Inheritance

We had lost the most, Amma [Mother] and I, but we couldn't come back.
How could we come back to this house? We were forced to stay in Jaffna.
But we kept the land in Colombo. They asked us to sell, there were offers
from Colombo. Amma refused to sell. She had revenge in her heart still.

Malathi's tone was measured. Malathi is in her mid-thirties, living in Colombo with her mother, her husband, and her two daughters, Ovia and Rosa.
Malathi and I often meet, but our more formal interview takes place over
two houses in two kitchens. In the first kitchen (and our most extensive interviews) we discuss the building of the second house, which was at the time
waiting empty for the family to move in. This second time, we were sitting in
the kitchen of the house she had just moved into. It was in one of Colombo's
busy, thriving old neighborhoods, on a sandy road that leads off a main street
to this cluster of houses jostling for space. The house is newly built, but it is
built on another house that Malathi once lived in. That house was burned
down and her father and eldest brother murdered by Sinhalese rioters in the
1983 anti-Tamil riots in Colombo, when more than two thousand Tamils
were killed.

   After 1983, Malathi, her remaining brother Keeran, and mother Analuxmi
were displaced to Jaffna, the northern Tamil majority area in Sri Lanka. In
the 1990s, Malathi and her mother became displaced back to Colombo from
Jaffna. This was after Keeran, a member of the Tamil militant movement
EPRLF, died in combat and the LTTE began to arrest members of other Tamil

militant groups, dissidents, and their families. These events mapped Malathi's journey from Tamil nationalist politics to profound disillusionment with its consequences. In Colombo the family lived in a variety of rented houses until, twenty years after the riots, Analuxmi, Malathi's mother, insisted on rebuilding their original house in Colombo to pass it on to her granddaughters, Malathi's children. So the house in which we sit is in the same house and neighborhood in which Malathi's father and eldest brother had been murdered in 1983. The twenty-two years between Malathi's departure and her "return" to this house is a life history that provides a micro-spatialized account of Sri Lanka's war.

What is obvious for most Sri Lankans living through the war is that personal and larger collective political futures, personal and collective displacement, are inextricably linked. The struggle of an individual, whether Tamil or Muslim, to find a place to live is both a personal story and a collective story. The violent making and unmaking of place and "home" in Sri Lanka is also about the right to belong as members of a minority. Malathi's story is about both past displacement and dislocation and the possibilities of finding a future in which people can flourish individually and together. Thus, this chapter tells a personal life story that could have only emerged through a larger collective story of being Tamil in Sri Lanka.

Lacing this together is a story of secrets, familial conflict, and generational reconciliation—battlefields staged within the house as well as the country. I explore how families deal with loss and how they "store" memories and secrets. What happens when one returns to the same place that was once "home" and attempts to make "home-in-the-future?" What will Malathi's daughters inherit? The last section of this chapter deals with the question of "return" and what this question asks of the future, both feared and fantasized about.

Childhood

When I listen to the tapes of our interview again, Malathi's voice wavers in and out of focus, interrupted by the sounds of grinding and rattling. Malathi makes lunch; I help whenever she doesn't notice, otherwise she shoos me away from the cooking. Instead as she cooks, she puts food into my mouth. The kitchen, like most Sri Lankan kitchens, is crowded with the myriad pots and pans in which things are placed, a plethora of spices and miscellaneous leaves cut up directly on the tile work surface. Kitchens are about intimacy;

they enjoin upon those within unusual and intimate positions of sitting, stooping, squatting. I now realize that Malathi talks about how one makes food to give to others for celebrating death anniversaries, the importance of nurturing relationships, the time her mother refused to give her food, all while cutting up and cooking food for lunch. I only recall now that her voice and hands talked to and against each other.

The children come in and out of the kitchen. We cut up the ends of vegetables so that they can use them as block prints for painting; they bring their paintings for regular examination. The older, Ovia, is a serious and responsible eight-year-old. Rosa, five years old, with her sunny smile is charmingly mischievous. Malathi breaks off whenever the children enter, but there is no door for the kitchen and sound echoes through the house. Do they hear her? How do they come to understand the silences that are transmitted to them? Analuxmi, Malathi's mother, is not there. I realize that had she been there, much of the conversation Malathi and I have would not have been possible.

> I was close to Appa [Father]. He didn't help out at home at all. . . . It was Amma [Mother] who cooked and cleaned and looked after us, but I was closer with Appa. 'Til he was dead, I was his pet. Amma was more attached to my brothers. . . . I used to go out with Appa all the time, not with the boys. . . . Amma was open and closed at the same time. I was more attached to Appa.

Malathi's father moved his young family from Jaffna to Colombo after he began to work there. The house in Colombo was bought with the proceeds of the sale of her mother's dowry house in Jaffna, so in effect the house in Colombo became her mother's dowry house. Malathi was a toddler at the time, so her childhood memories are of Colombo, interspersed with family holidays in Jaffna. Consequently, she speaks Sinhalese and Tamil with equal fluency.

While Colombo is the capital city of Sri Lanka and part of the southern Sinhalese heartland, in fact it is also a city where large numbers of Tamil-speaking minorities live. These include both recent Sri Lankan Tamil migrants from the north and east like Malathi and her family, Tamils from Colombo itself not claiming origin anywhere else, Malaiyaha/Hill-country Tamils, (Tamil-speaking) Sri Lankan Muslims, and so forth. Moreover, the city was a classic migration site for Jaffna Tamils throughout the twentieth century (see, e.g., Don Arachchige 1994; Jayawardena 2002).[1] Many of the Jaffna Tamils who came to Colombo were government servants, clerks, and professionals like Malathi's father. Some did settle in Colombo, but many came for the week on the train from Jaffna and returned home on the weekend.

Given its internal diversity, riots in Colombo (1956, 1958, 1977, and 1983) took an immense toll.[2] Malathi's story is such a case. In 1983, Malathi's mother Analuxmi was abroad. Malathi and her two brothers were at home with their father when rioting began. The riots were prompted by the LTTE killing thirteen Sri Lankan soldiers in northern Jaffna, and the return of the bodies to Colombo. Violence occurred in many phases. The army and the police watched without intervening. High-profile government members were implicated in the violence, and there is considerable evidence that some action against Tamils was pre-planned, as in the second phase rioters came armed with voting lists and addresses of Tamils (Tambiah 1986, 1996). Some rioters were transported in buses. Waves of violence moved upward from Colombo toward the Malaiyaha Tamil plantation areas and towns and Trincomalee with its large mixed Sinhalese and Tamil population. Tambiah reports that, despite the official death toll of 470, probably around 2,000 to 3,000 were murdered (1996: 94). In Colombo, more than half the city's Tamil population, around 100,000, were displaced. Malathi recounted:

> The thugs on buses, with their voters lists, they knew how to find the houses, particular houses, particular numbers. Even I didn't know the other Tamil people in the neighborhood. They had spotted them; they came with their voters lists. If the government had not assisted there is no way that they could have done such mass destruction in three days. . . . It was obvious to us that it was a well-planned and government-aided massacre.

It was Malathi who found the charred bodies of her father and elder brother in the hallway of their house. She and Keeran, her other brother, hid with one neighbor and watched their house being looted by others. They then lived in the makeshift refugee camps set up in temples and schools in Colombo, where refugees were first housed and then sent in successive boats to the north and east. Malathi and Keeran arrived at the Pillaiyar (Ganesh) Kovil (temple) in Bambalapitiya. This was a time when families were pulled apart and separated from each other, unsure of what had happened to other family members. In the camps the refugees made new alliances, friendships, and kinships, telling stories of their experiences of the riots to each other and helping each other in camp life. The riots made possible a feeling of Tamilness under attack across caste and class. Different kinds of kinship, both personal and political, were being constructed.

Malathi and Keeran became even closer, united by their experiences. They were drawn toward another family in the camps, whose two eldest boys had studied with Malathi's brothers prior to the riots. The family had escaped intact, but they had lost everything and had watched their house being burned to the ground. The eldest son, Neethi, and Keeran became active in the organization of the camps, registering people, allocating food, and sending people on the ships. Malathi, who was without her mother, spent her time with this family. Finally both families were boarded on one of the refugee ships. Malathi and Keeran went to her father's village in Jaffna, where their mother could rejoin them. The arrival of ships of Tamil refugees to the north and east brought about what we can now see as a momentous change. Refugees arrived irrevocably transformed by their experience of violence, and the circulation of their stories would in turn alter the destinies of thousands of Sri Lankan Tamils.

The 1983 riots were the cataclysmic event of the ethnic conflict. The riots comprehensively transformed Tamil public support for newly emergent Tamil militancy (see also Tambiah 1986; Daniel 1996). After 1983, Tamils lost faith in the Sri Lankan state, given clear evidence of state collusion, cover-ups, and support for "keeping the minorities in their place." The riots were the impetus for the geographic polarization of Sri Lanka, with Tamils fleeing to the north and east and large numbers going abroad and forming a major Tamil refugee diaspora (McDowell 1996). Large-scale displacement, which has characterized the conflict ever since, began in earnest in 1983. Significantly, the 1983 riots were cited as grounds for the insistence of the LTTE that Tamil people must have their own state, that they could never live at peace with the Sinhalese in a Sinhalese-majority country. For Malathi and her family, like many, 25 July, called "Black July," is both a public and private event. Malathi remarked once on the importance of telling her children what happened in the riots, because otherwise "They don't know much about it, so the sad thing is that if it is only [LTTE leader] Prabhakaran that tells them 'this is what happened,' that will go into their heads, no?" Her point is not that the facts of death, arson, and violence would be altered, but that the teller lays claims to interpreting the frames by which future action and interpretation of the position of Tamils in Sri Lanka could be understood.

The 1983 riots were always mentioned in my interviews with those who became militants in the 1980s. Stories of witnessing violence and anti-Tamil riots were the constitutive events of biographies of militancy and Tamil nationalism. Recruitment to the militant groups swelled—groups that could be counted in tens became thousands. It was 1983 and 1984 that were the peak years of recruitment to militant organizations (see Chapter 5). While many young Tamil men and women had experienced riots firsthand, equally many young people joined because of the stories of other Tamils, especially refugees who returned to tell of the horrific violence directed at all Tamils, evidently with some state collusion. The 1983 riot condensed numerous experiences, collective stories about the discrimination of Tamils, previous anti-Tamil riots in 1956, 1958, 1977, and 1981.[3] Tamils no longer felt safe in Sri Lanka, and this allowed a collective identity to coalesce and stabilize that hitherto had been divided by region, class, and caste.

The role of state-led riots and violence in creating political subjectivity is well known. Begoña Aretxaga (1997) describes in *Shattering Silence* the way in which experiences of violence shaped the entry of young people into the IRA and gave their biographies moral force: "witnessing violence ... [had] the force of self-evidence, the power of knowledge that cannot be contested and needs no further elaboration; a kind of knowledge that defies linguistic containment to infuse instead a form of political transcendence" (1997: 89). For those who were teenagers and learning about ethnic difference in Northern Ireland, their feelings were then linked to their parents and grandparents' experiences of riots and thus embedded within a collective memory, providing a history that seemed to repeat again and again. For the women Aretxaga interviewed, it was not just the experience of violence itself that was preeminent in their biography, it was the role of witnessing such violence that came to constitute them "as republican political subjects." Vijitharan, whom I interviewed, remembered that for his school class, the 1983 riots initiated discussions about militancy and prompted his decision to join the LTTE when he was 15. The 1983 riots gained their force by their possible non-singularity as the latest in a cycle of post-colonial anti-Tamil riots, a cycle that seemed to point only to reoccurrence. Ranjan, who became a senior figure in the LTTE, lived as a child in the border area of Anuradhapura. His family lost everything in the 1977 anti-Tamil riots, ending up in Vavuniya. He told me (of his decision to join the LTTE)

> I was emboldened to go and join because of the government. Because of their racism. Because of the ethnic discrimination. If I had lived

in Anuradhapura, I didn't understand Tamil; sometimes I may have said that I didn't know any Tamils. I only knew Sinhalese. If I had stayed there, who knows, I may have even joined the army! Become a commander. Because my basic language was Sinhalese. I would have become a Sinhalese. The reason I am here speaking Tamil to you and thinking of myself as a Tamil is because of the country's ethnic problems. I would not have had the opportunity to go to the LTTE otherwise.

Thirteen-year-old Malathi and twenty-year-old Keeran were among the thousands that joined militant groups. Yet this is not the end of Malathi's story, nor is it the end of biographies of political awakening for Tamils. As I discuss through Malathi's life, the effects of 1983 are rather more complex when viewed twenty years afterward. Not least, the civil war that resulted from these years has in turn created very different kinds of biographies of militancy and political subjectivity from those that could be read from the 1983 riots.

I Belonged in Jaffna

[In Colombo] one day there was a big trouble in our house because Anna [elder brother referring to Keeran] was running around with the movement [EPRLF] and Appa had found out. . . . They had such hopes for him; he was so clever and studied hard. . . . Appa hit him and then cried, and then we all went to sleep. But Anna did not give up on it.

Keeran had already been a member of the Marxist EPRLF, one of the many Tamil militant movements, while in Colombo. Malathi, as a schoolgirl in Jaffna, joined the EPRLF women's wing: "I was a little involved [in politics]. I was not like Anna, a hardcore member of EPRLF, but I knew them and I identified with their theory more than any other [group]." The militant movements were youth movements, openly rebelling against a gerontocratic kinship system and exalting inter- and intra-group sibling relations. The dominant image presented was one of a horizontal family, of brothers and sisters fighting for the same cause (see Chapter 5). Malathi and Keeran reconsecrated their sibling relationships through their new closeness after "1983."

Following the riots, Malathi fully identified with the militant cause:

> After we went to Jaffna, I became more concerned and I supported
> him [brother] fully. What happened in Colombo pushed us to think
> then that we can't live with the Sinhalese and we have to have auton-
> omy. We were so young then, but I had a feeling of revenge.

For Malathi, Jaffna, the site of her growing political awareness, becomes
"home."

> I gained a sense of identity in Jaffna ... I loved being in Jaffna, that
> was the main time for me. In Colombo I was only there as a small
> child, only up to thirteen years ... When you are thirteen, fourteen,
> then you start looking at the world. Until then you need your family.
> That I had. But when that time came, I had lost everything.
>   I think that it was then in Jaffna that I filled this need. Then it was
> only Amma, Anna (elder brother), and I. At that time Anna was in-
> volved and people were coming in and out. From thirteen to twenty-
> two, until I came back to Colombo ... In that time you have a need,
> you know, as an individual. It is a confusing moment. You are not a
> girl or a woman, not a big person, but not a child, you are in between.
> At that time what I needed, or what gave it to me ... it was Jaffna so-
> ciety that fulfilled me. I feel more like I belonged there.

In Malathi's story, Jaffna presents itself as a choice, a desire, or, as she
says, "an identity." It centers on a community and a society. In Jaffna, she and
her family lived in her father's natal village, and it continued to provide her
with a sense of connection and belonging traced through her father, who appeared socially present even though physically absent. Often at odds with her
mother, who had rejoined her brother and herself in Jaffna, Malathi's attachment to Jaffna was also about having ties of school, friends, and neighbors
that provided refuge from her troubled family. After the 1983 riots, Malathi
emerged with a new sense of what it meant to be Tamil, and she tells me that
she filled loss and liminality with a feeling of society, collectivity, and growing political awareness. Jaffna is for Malathi that which brought her "into the
world." When I asked, "Why belong in Jaffna and not Colombo?" she replied
immediately that Colombo never felt like her city.

In saying this, Malathi is part of larger Tamil conversations about

Colombo as a city *of* minorities but not *for* minorities, as I explore in Chapter 6. Colombo, her childhood home, was a difficult place to be Tamil. It was in Colombo that the major anti-Tamil riots began. Up until the cease-fire in 2002, Tamils from the north and east were subject to special regulations. They Tamils had to register their address with local police stations and carry a police certificate at all times; they were liable to arrest if they were found at a different address. Sinhalese were encouraged to report on "strange Tamils" in their area. The Tamils I interviewed in Colombo told me of the years in which women were afraid to wear the *pottu* (the vermilion mark on the forehead) or speak Tamil on the streets. Lodges, temporary housing where Tamils rented by the room, were regularly raided by the police at night. Colombo was for many Jaffna Tamils a transient city, a marginal waiting place. Most of the Tamils I interviewed in Colombo in 2003 had come in order to find a way to leave the country and go abroad. Some had been "waiting" for more than ten years. Everyday exclusions reinforced a feeling of not being able to be at home in Colombo if one was a minority Tamil (see Chapter 6).

However, by 1991, Malathi had returned to Colombo, and to date she cannot return to Jaffna. The question of being-at-home and the quest for a place to belong is evidently important for her and her continuing dislocation. Moreover, homemaking, rather than just being invested in one place or another, depends on the interplay between places. Homeliness also depends on the possibility of finding a home-for-the-future. It is this home-for-the-future, as the rest of this chapter discusses, that Malathi and other Tamils are striving for.

Leaving Jaffna

Malathi's story of leaving Jaffna strikes at the heart of the political awakening, community, and sense of being Tamil she acquired in Jaffna. In 1985, cracks had begun to show among the militant movements, and rumors of internal killings abounded. In 1986, internecine fighting took a new intergroup turn when the LTTE banned all militant groups not allied with it, first TELO and eventually EPRLF, TEA, and so on (Hoole et al. 1990; Swamy 1994; and see Chapter 5). The LTTE exhibited the bodies of TELO members in the street, and some were publicly burned with tires around their necks (Swamy 1992; Hoole et al. 1990). Hundreds from the other movements were arrested or killed, and members and their families increasingly persecuted. For Malathi, this marked another key event in her life, when "things changed":

When they (LTTE) first banned TELO, it was inside them all the time, but when everyone saw it publicly was in 1986. . . . Anna [elder brother] was also very upset, and I was able to see his pain. That was the first thing, the shock. Internally these things were happening in PLOTE and TELO, but for one organization to ban another organization and murder its leader,[4] and to catch their people and burn them with tires around their necks. . . . They did it, as if they were others, as if they were an enemy group.

For Malathi, who had come from Colombo in search of some sort of community, Tamil nationalism, far from an inclusive refuge, was, in its splintering becoming increasingly the brand of one group, the LTTE. In the midst of the internecine warfare, Malathi heard that Neethi, the eldest son of the family she and her brother had become close to in the camps, had been killed by the LTTE despite the fact that he was not a member of the militant group TELO. Neethi's younger brother, to whom Malathi had been very close, had protested and publicly condemned the killing. He too was shot by the LTTE a couple of years later. The parents survived. and the youngest daughter left for Switzerland. Malathi's tone as she recalls this family is of mingled sorrow and guilt. After arriving in Jaffna the two families had become separated.

Anna never took me there because by that time he was involved with EPRLF, so he was busy. I used to ask Amma if she would take me there. He [the younger brother] had come a few times it seems, and when he had come I was not there. He had come and introduced himself as "Neethi's little brother, is Malathi there?" Amma said she would take me, but because she didn't really understand the importance she had never actually taken me. "We'll see," she would say. We never went. Then he died, he was shot. After that I felt really bad, that we had never gone to the house. When Neethi died I felt really bad, and then within 1 or 2 years they had shot his brother too.

For Malathi, the still-new kinships were being destroyed, from that of the militant movements to the alliances and kinships created through the time together in the refugee camp and the shared experiences of the 1983 riots. The uniqueness of the latter and the guilt that Malathi still feels about her separation from that family still lingers now.

I used to tell Amma. Amma was not there for the riots, she was abroad, so sometimes, I used to think she didn't understand what had happened to us, the importance . . . , I tried to explain to her, "he was in the camps with us."

The relationship between mother and daughter became more strained after another blow was struck to the family. Malathi's brother Keeran died in a military operation at sea. She and her mother were the only two left in a family of five. We will return later to how Malathi and her mother came to deal with these new tragedies and the recriminations and unspoken charge implicit in the statement above: "Amma was not there for the riots."

In the years following 1986 and LTTE warfare against the Indian Peace Keeping Forces in the 1987–90 war, leading to the withdrawal of the Indians in 1990, the LTTE organization consolidated its power. Assuming full control over Jaffna in 1991, it continued to eliminate anyone considered a political dissident and or associated with other militant movements and their families. Malathi left Jaffna for Colombo fearing for her life, as people even peripherally involved with alternative political movements were in danger. Many of those she knew were killed or arrested, most by the LTTE, some by the Sri Lankan army, some in wartime bombing. EPRLF carried on, but after the LTTE ban of other movements the women's wing was deactivated. Malathi had intended to go back to Jaffna, but it became clear after 1992 that the LTTE had taken Jaffna as its own, and her exile from the place "she belongs" began.

While most accounts (e.g., Tambiah 1996; Spencer 1990a; Krishna 1999) agree that the 1983 riots and the Sri Lankan state's role and response had immediate and consequential effects in moving Sri Lankan Tamils decisively toward militancy and thus war, this does not mean, mythicized though the riots have become, that there was a uniform response to the riots, nor does it mean that the 1983 riots are not memorialized in completely different ways now. As Jansen (2002) argues in relation to Bosnia, explanations that reiterate narratives that posit straightforward causality between present conflict and recollections of past events and traumas run the risk of such events becoming "canonized." Such resignification has to pay critical attention to how collective memories can sometimes progressively shape themselves around nationalist narratives, sometimes even adopting these frames of explanation, uncritically erasing any contradictory personal memories (see Amin 1995's insightful examination of the canonization of the events of Chauri Chaura as resistance to colonial rule in India). The memorialization of particular events over time, short and long term, as well as the theorization of their effects, are not self-evident. Memorialization is also about the constant political re-symbolization of the riots by the LTTE and Tamil nationalists to make them emotionally effective, as well as the indifference shown to such memorialization by the Sri Lankan state, which continue to make the 1983 riots not a Sri Lankan but a uniquely Tamil tragedy.

Since major events continue to reshape lives, and we continue to ascribe and assume causal relationships between particular cataclysmic events and subsequent attitudes and behaviors, this attention to the difference between the short-term and the long-term phrasing of recollections is essential. Here 1983 is placed within Malathi's life-in-progress and her move toward the Tamil nationalist movement—itself built on memories of 1983—and her subsequent alienation from it. Malathi's experiences emphasize the complexities of the event, and the importance of marking the different ways in which particular events are *rephrased* in individual lives to acknowledge the changeable nature of the life process (Das 2000), and being cautious not to equate political effects of events as subsequent self-evident emotional and subjective consequences of those events. Here, Koselleck's notion of "the temporal structures of experience" and his suggestion that experience continually "leaps over time" (2004: 260) is particularly illuminating. As Koselleck suggests,

> Events . . . have occurred once and for all, but the experiences based upon them can change over time. Experiences overlap and mutually impregnate each other. In addition, new hopes or disappointments, or new expectations, enter them with retrospective effect. Thus, experiences alter themselves as well, despite, once having occurred, remaining the same. This is the temporal structure of experience. (262)

This attention to the "temporal structure of experience" is essential in understanding how Malathi's experiences and evaluations of the 1983 riots shift continually in relation to her relationship with her mother and daughters and through her relationship with Tamil nationalism. The short-term effect of her experience of the 1983 riots was her move toward Tamil nationalism and militancy. Now, more than two decades after 1983, she still bears the scars of the event. Her family and her sense of belonging have been restructured, but she no longer lays claims to Tamil militancy in the same way, having found herself excluded by the LTTE from Jaffna. Thus the conventional story

told of how Tamils came to identify with a collective discriminat
through the 1983 riots, at once explains and fails to explain the place ᴏ.
riots in Malathi's (or others') lives as time passes and the riots are continually
reinterpreted though new limits and possibilities.

The ways such moments of violence are written into experiences of place,
family, and self mean that understandings of "home" and homeliness are
also constantly shifting. One can easily complicate the picture I have drawn
hitherto of "being-at-home" as one of "community," where Jaffna represents
"community" and Colombo "alienation." However, as Hage argues, it is forgotten in many theorizations of homely structures that "home has to be a
space open for opportunities . . . so that one can perceive opportunities of 'a
better life': . . . to develop certain capacities . . . personal growth . . . the availability of opportunities for "advancement'" (1997: 103). This sense of possibility is what I attribute to making home-in-the-future. How, then, is "home"
made meaningful in a war fought for "homeland," in which, as one person
told me, "we have no home or land any more?" Ongoing war, recruitment
of their children by the LTTE, and lack of resources and facilities mean that
many do leave Jaffna, their "home" where they are the center of the imagined
Tamil nation. Almost half of those from Jaffna now live outside the peninsula.
Jaffna, as "home" and specifically "home" for Tamils, offers a story about former sociality and emotional and spiritual sustenance, but Jaffna is also a place
that people continue to attempt to leave because it cannot offer them a future,
and this has been the case for nearly a century. Those who remain in Jaffna
are most often those who are unable to mobilize the resources to make it out
of Sri Lanka. Colombo was a transient place where people felt they did not
belong, but it also offered relief from the war and, most important, it had an
international airport to take one out of Sri Lanka to dreams of "foreign" destinations that might offer Tamils some sort of future. Homeliness, of the past
and the future, was discussed through the interplay of these places: Jaffna,
Colombo, and "abroad" (as we return to in Chapter 6).

 As Katy Gardner points out in her discussion of *desh* (home) and *bidesh*
(abroad) for Sylheti migrants from Bangladesh, "localities" are more than physical places; these places are used to "discuss both the past and contemporary
change and the future" (1993: 1) and are associated with different power and
socioeconomic relationships. "Home" for Tamils as a place where one could
belong was then not always synonymous with a Tamil homeland where the
future was bleak and uncertain. The paradoxical effect of the fight for a Tamil
homeland has been the constant stream of Tamils attempting to leave that

"homeland." Thus, conversations about "home" and belonging are also conversations about "senses of possibility," about the expectations and possibilities of flourishing in the future. As Hage highlights, these are conversations about ideal types and approximations, because homely structures, far from existing in reality, are also aspirations and "ideal goal guiding practices" (1997: 104).

"Home" and homeliness are also produced through our interactions with others, kin and intimates, those others with whom we share houses and neighborhoods. It is this to which I move in looking at mothers and daughters living through the aftermath of violence and massive loss, particularly the question of how one inherits and transmits secrets, substances, memories, and dowry, a condensed expression of all of the above.

Mothers and Daughters: The Living and the Dead

Amma was not there for the riots. She was abroad, so sometimes I used to think she didn't understand what had happened to us.

The relationships of Analuxmi and Malathi to Jaffna and Colombo were quite different. Analuxmi had sold her dowry property in Jaffna and bought the house in Colombo. In northern Sri Lanka, dowry, the passage of land from mother to daughter, is a significant way of imagining belonging. Land and jewelry are the favored components of mother-to-daughter property. Dowries imagine future continuity, and Analuxmi's was moved to Colombo. In Jaffna, Malathi recalls,

> We ended up in Appa's *ur* (home), they were not kind to her. . . . We were surrounded by his people. Everyone in *ur* is related to us. Amma was the outsider. It would have been easier for me than for her. Everyone liked me because I was his daughter; people would take me and give me food . . . I was one of them. *She was an outsider.*

Malathi's relationship with her mother also became tense in Jaffna around her brother's involvement in EPRLF.

Amma used to have arguments with Anna about being in the movements. "What does it mean you are in a movement and you are still going around with them? Why don't you go abroad? I have some money saved too." Amma would tell him, "You have a little sister, you are responsible for her."

Analuxmi was powerless to stop her son being involved in the movements even through using the ultimate appeal of the authority left to her: the responsibility to provide dowry and the responsibility toward family in perpetuation and transmission. In these discussions, Malathi supported her brother against her mother:

> I used to tell Anna, "You go and do what you want." Amma was so angry with me because she was trying to stop Anna and using me as the reason. If you have a sister in our normal Jaffna society it is the brother's responsibility, if there is no father, for giving dowry and for looking after her. She used to tell him, "I only have your father's pension. If you go and die in the movements, what are we to do? Aren't there enough deaths in the family?"
>
> Because I was in full support for him, Amma was so angry with me. And then he died of course. And then Amma was even angrier with me. If I hadn't given Anna such support maybe he would have gone abroad, maybe he would have lived.

Malathi's sense of sorrow, memory of guilt forced on her by her mother, lingered in her tone.

> She can be very arrogant and rude, but now I can see her reasons behind it and the way she was with me. Because I supported Anna, Amma may be blaming me inside. Now she is okay with me, him [Malathi's husband], and the children. But those days she was really angry and took it out on me. Sometimes she would not cook for me. I used to be very angry with her.

By withholding food, Analuxmi withheld nurture from Malathi, who tells me this as we sit in her kitchen and as she cooks for her own daughters. She puts food in my mouth as I help. She talks of her mother and herself, and how the same ghosts and the same places say different things to them.

Malathi's changing relationship with her mother mediated her understandings of herself and facilitated the constant revaluation of her experiences. Each noticeable phase she introduced in her story of how "she was coming to be" was also an introduction of another phase of her relationship with her mother, who withholds nurturing but represents the unbreakable bond of family too. Her life process was marked by a continuing dialogue with her mother, one that was often of misrecognition and recriminations on both sides. This relationship was characterized by feelings of binding obliga- tion and also profound misrecognition and unhappiness. While their rela- tionship is specific to their personalities and situation, it also highlights more generally the heightened pressures and tensions which can be said to be an integral feature of kinship relations, an ambivalence which is, as Peletz (2001) argues, a central, if often unacknowledged theme in kinship studies.[5]

Meyer Fortes (1970) suggests that all societies distinguish relations be- tween non-kin and kin along the "axiom of amity," moralized feelings that kin are meant to *feel* toward each other and which create "inescapable moral du- ties and obligations" (1970: 242).[6] However, Fortes points out that "we must not misunderstand the ideal that kinfolk should love one another" (237). Fortes suggests instead that "what the rule posits is that 'kinfolk' have irresist- ible claims on one another's support and consideration in contradistinc- tion to 'non-kinsmen,' simply by reason of the fact they are kin" (238). In fact, his seminal writings on the axiom of amity draw out a number of latent conflicts involved in many kinship ties such as siblingship, where in fact "the dogma of amity is supposed most stringently to prevail." These latent conflicts have everything to do with the varying structures of inequality, differentiation, and conflict present in kinship relations and ties.

This latent conflict also arises because kinship ties themselves are not in- ternally consistent. In Trawick's (1992) *Notes on Love in a Tamil Family* she suggests that, in the South Indian Tamil families she studies, bonds between generations, between siblings, and between spouses often came into conflict: "at certain times in his or her life, these different kinds of bonds are likely to pull an individual in different directions . . . the longings for freedom and longings for continuity cross-cut each other" (157–58). This is clear in my account of Malathi and Analuxmi's relationship around the question of Mal- athi and her brother Keeran's involvement in the militant movements. In Analuxmi's attempt to prevent her son's involvement in the militant move- ments through his responsibility to provide dowry for his sister, and in Mal- athi's support for her brother against her mother and her prioritization of sibling solidarities independent of the duties of perpetuation, two different models of kinship bonds become inimical. This conflict has left an indelible trace on the relationship of mother and daughter.

Kinship creates a set of highly moralized ideas about expectations and obligations and longings, ones which may be hard to live up to, or which are inherently emotionally, socially, and materially hierarchical and unequally fulfilling. The active presence of jealousies, struggles of status, and conflict in a moralized domain that is ideationally distinguished from other domains makes life with kin doubled, necessary, and yet constricting. Kinship, in this account, constitutes a distinct "structure of recognition," which retains a distinct moral force and generates self-referential social relations and longings (Bourdieu 1999).[7]

This is nothing new; this idea of the emotional ambivalence and tumult of the family has long been central to Freudian psychoanalysis (e.g., Freud 1918 [1914]). Emotional ambivalence within kin relations should not be seen as a failure, an example of "bad" kinship to be contrasted with "good kinship," but should be viewed through the understanding that in our relationships with other people, especially kin, there is an element in which, as Trawick puts it, kinship "creates longings that can *never* be fulfilled" (1992: 152). For Malathi and Analuxmi, these longings and obligations through the death of all the men in the family are rendered unfulfillable and impossible from the outset. They cannot find refuge or give one another what the other wants, the return of a family, neither can they be son or father to each other.

Throughout this book I pair a parallel examination of kin and intimate relations with a study of political biographies and processes. Part of the intention is to emphasize not only how these two fields calibrate, interpenetrate, emplace each other, but also to show, by keeping them separate, how conflicting demands between political action and public life, and familial intensity, obligation, and love can also generate demands which pit these two fields against each other, even as they are transformed together by this conflict. War and political conflict have, in the case of Malathi and Analuxmi, reshaped and reemphasized a latent conflict that is integral to kinship relations themselves, between siblings and parents, freedom and obligation, nurture and claustrophobia, inequality and love, and recognition and misrecognition.

Inheritance

Edmund Leach (1961) once argued in his book on Sri Lanka, *Pul Eliya*, that kin was just a way of talking about property by other means; here I use dowry and inheritance in the broadest sense to think about how, as Spencer (1990b) argues, property is also a way of talking about status and personhood, here kin, by other means.[8] I use inheritance to think of how families and individuals perpetuate themselves, how parents and children imagine, transmit, and inherit (or not) not just material wealth, but social positions, desires, and recognition.[9] Analuxmi and Malathi's relationship breaks and is reconciled around what can be inherited and what cannot. For Analuxmi especially, belonging and continuity were also phrased through the idealized inheritance of land passed down through mother and daughter as dowry.

Malathi's already difficult relationship with her mother turned into full estrangement when Malathi married Ketheswaran in Colombo after she left Jaffna in 1992. As far as Analuxmi and her siblings were concerned, Ketheswaran's caste status was ambiguous. For them, he was clearly not from the top of the Vellala caste, but from a lower rank within it. Malathi, for whom caste was not a concern, told me how her uncles and cousins had threatened to break Ketheswaran's legs. For Analuxmi, Malathi symbolized the recipient of all property in the family, the only child for whom responsibility can be borne, the only child for whom a marriage can be arranged, the only child whose children will perpetuate the family, and the child for whom dowry must be provided. It was a heavy set of inheritances to bear and the relationship between mother and daughter broke after Malathi defied Analuxmi. For Malathi, her mother and her mother's family's involvement in the matter of marriage was even more difficult given Analuxmi's anger with her and her intermittent refusal to nurture her.

> Because I was the only daughter in the family, the only child then, they thought that he was marrying me because I would get a good dowry and then he would use that for his family. There was also this thing that my mother thought that I was the only living child and she had responsibility for me. She also thought, how can she decide for herself for her own liking, she is only a little girl. We are here to select. Those were her thoughts.

After marriage, Malathi and her husband moved away from Colombo to eastern Sri Lanka. There she found a job and became pregnant, but missed her family: this family, though uneasy, was still a part of her life that she needed. Being cut off from her mother's family also meant that the remembered relationship between herself and her father and brothers became blocked. Malathi's recollection of this time is not happy: "Amma cut me off completely and refused to give me dowry. I was very isolated and depressed for a long time then."

By severing dowry transmission through Malathi, Analuxmi had signaled her attempt to end the relationship. Property, land, and inheritance are polysemic "goods" in Sri Lanka; they speak of the possibility of making relationships of continuity and transmission as well as of status, both material and immaterial relations of sustenance (Spencer 1990b: 101).[10] The key distinction between Sri Lankan Tamil Jaffna and Batticaloa and South Indian Tamil Nadu is that in Tamil Nadu, land and immovable property is held as a male right and women's dowries never consist of land (Kapadia 1995; Tambiah 1973). The reverse holds true in Tamil Sri Lanka, where dowry is also immovable property. Here, for Analuxmi and Malathi, mother-daughter relationships are themselves constituted around the passage of dowry and nurture, and thus the withholding or the regeneration of one or the other is braided with, expressive of, and worked through with the other.

Malathi returned to Colombo with one daughter while pregnant with her second daughter. They lived with Analuxmi, but soon moved out. Analuxmi and Malathi argued, separated, then reconciled and met, fell out again and so on. However the key difference is that Analuxmi increasingly took an active role in caring for her grandchildren and began to build a relationship with them. The desire for transmission finally became the basis of Analuxmi and Malathi's reconciliation, around Malathi's daughters, Ovia and Rosa, to whom Analuxmi decided to give dowry. I turn now to the renewal of relationships around the next generationo, including the question of the psychic, and social inheritance Ovia and Rosa themselves might receive.

To Inherit Ghosts

Malathi began to reevaluate her relationship with Analuxmi after she became a mother:

> Then I didn't understand. Now I am a mother I can see, think about her feelings. Now we talk about things that we never talked about before. Now she tells me that those days, our relatives were jealous that she had two sons. In her family there are five girls and one boy, so that when she got two sons straight away there was jealousy. And then she ended up with only the girl.

We also didn't do counseling or anything, we didn't know about things like that. Maybe someone should have talked to Amma about these things.

For Analuxmi, her granddaughters presented the possibility of inheritance, and she sought to reintegrate Malathi's daughters into the family, giving them the dowry she refused Malathi and taking them with her to commemorate the dead family they did not know. Thus, Analuxmi tied the children into her own family through the commemoration of the 1983 riots, substantializing the relationships between the children, herself, and those absent.

Commemoration of the dead very often occurs in Sri Lanka through food, and the distribution of food in the names of the dead.

On the annual date we do something at the temple. Amma does it for Appa [Father]. When a young unmarried male or female dies, you can only give in their name once . . . so that these young men and women will be born somewhere else. If we carry on giving, it will be like they have not been released from this life. Their "soul" (*atma*) will struggle. . . . So Amma gives not for my brothers but for Appa. These two [daughters] go to those. So Amma does one for July twenty-fifth and she makes ten or twenty food parcels for beggars on the road. . . .

When she goes to the temple she takes the children and they know. The little one knows "Black July." "That's when something happened to your father, isn't it Amma?" she'll ask me. I started to tell them little things now and then. Then they used to look sad.

I don't tell them much. . . . They don't know much about it, so the sad thing is that if it is only Prabhakaran [the LTTE leader] that tells them "this is what happened," that will go into their heads, no? . . . They are small still. But I will tell them later what had happened, they should know their roots. We must not forget these things. Thirteen, fourteen, they might understand better.

It is Malathi's two daughters who make this telling of the story possible. The children present to Malathi and Analuxmi the possibilities of renewal, a perpetuated and whole family, pulling them toward the future, away from the past. Ovia and Rosa make it possible for Malathi and Analuxmi to begin new relationships.

The two girls also reorder relationships to the dead. Malathi sees the possibility of telling stories to Ovia and Rosa about her dead father and brothers as a way of remaking the relationship, bridging the gap between material and nonmaterial webs of relationships. There have never been any funerals in Malathi's family. The bodies of her father and brother were not officially cremated, and her other brother's body was never recovered, commonplace in Sri Lanka, where war means bodies are rarely recovered. Rituals that most people carry out to commemorate the dead also create the dead for Malathi and Analuxmi. However, as Malathi points out, while there is no permitted commemoration of her unmarried brothers' deaths, their names unspoken, that does not suspend the relationship between them and herself; unmarried men and women continue to be remembered by the living despite the inability to ritualize their deaths. The inability to acknowledge them in ritual does, however, point out how, in contrast to the acknowledgment of her father, relationships to those young and unmarried and thus without children to remember them are always unclear. Thus remembering her brothers by tying them to their nieces Ovia and Rosa is very significant. However, the reverse is also true; ways of remembering the dead still remake relationships for the living.

> I had some differences of opinion with Amma and I did not go there for a while. Then I went once when she had called the *aiyer* [Brahmin priest] for the twenty-fifth of July. She was doing it in Appa's name, she keeps my brothers' photos there but the *aiyer* will not say their names. Three kilos of rice and seven kinds of vegetables are given, and when she gives, Amma says the name and gives; "I am giving this for the *atma* of . . . "
>
> I went after a long time and then I saw the photos and then I started crying. As soon as these two little ones came home, they told their father, "Amma saw a photo and she cried." From then I was able to talk to them about this more. . . . I didn't know that they had observed it for so long. In one sense I was happy because I knew they share my feelings, it has affected them that I cried.

Memories of riots, defiance, and neglect irretrievably pull Malathi and Analuxmi together toward a family that only they are left to remember. Though they do not speak the names of the dead in order to release their souls, the dead have not released the living yet. Malathi's children's observance of her grief gives her the hope that they will understand her later on.

Analuxmi and Malathi are reconciled again, tied together by relationships to the dead, and to the living: each other and Malathi's children. Malathi and Analuxmi, who saw themselves as a family only through others, are forced to construct a relationship as those others who could have defined them as a family die and new ones are born. As relationships with her father, or brothers, collapse or disappear in the tangible present, the mother and daughter reassemble themselves and entomb the lost relationships within their remaking. These constantly negotiated relationships bearing the knowledge of loss coalesce around the possibility of new life for Analuxmi and Malathi: the two little girls, Ovia and Rosa, watching, observing, puzzling through their family.

These two little girls run in and out of the kitchen whenever I talk to Malathi. I often wondered exactly what they thought of all the secrets that they do not "know" about people and the house they live in, but which nonetheless structure their lives. For Ovia and Rosa, memory is being passed as allusions, secrets, and absences. Between generations, memory is being handed down without direct speech through the contours of relationships and interactions. Their watching ears, their knowing without being told, and the patchy histories they must be putting together force us to think about the multiple ways families transmit knowledge and memories. The key moments in which the past histories of their mother and grandmother reveal themselves to the children are transmitted not through direct speech but through unexplained photographs and observed tears.

If Malathi and Analuxmi carry within themselves the memories and ghosts of others around which their relationship is constantly made and unmade, then what of Ovia and Rosa, who never knew their uncles or grandparents? The girls grow up with the consequences of their grandfather and uncles' murders and deaths imprinted on everyday interaction in the house. Of course this can only be speculation, but trying to think about memory and inheritance through Rosa and Ovia's perspective, the two little girls who without direct experience will inherit their mother's and grandmother's ghosts, provides some imaginative ground to think of the wordless transmission of one generation's "pain" to another. This intergenerational transmission, the ways the goals of one generation are partly shaped around the previous generation and its ghosts and secrets, our political histories tell us, is perhaps one of the most complex and yet consequential aspects of the social world.

In suggesting this, I do not at all mean that such transmission is always conscious or that it is inherited consciously. Indeed, for psychoanalysts Abraham and Torok, as Jacqueline Rose describes, "transgenerational hauntings" are "forms of remembrance—most often of hidden and shameful family se-crets—which hover in the space between social and psychic history, forcing and making it impossible for the one who carries them to make the link" (Rose 1996: 5). One generation finds itself performing through the unspo-ken secrets of another, without being consciously aware of it. A sense of loss as experienced, not through direct experience of events, but through living with the desires, secrets, and silences of a previous generation's experience of those events, is obviously evident within writing on the Holocaust in par-ticular (e.g., Apel 2002). Transmission from one generation to another is not just about direct speech; transmission can take place equally through unex-plained tears, photographs, gaps, silences, and secrets. Children can come to know something without ever consciously "knowing." While Abraham discusses this from a clinical perspective, his notion of the "phantom" still provides a compelling trope by which we can think through this. Abraham argues that if a child has parents "with secrets . . . whose speech is not exactly complementary to their unstated repressions" (Abraham 1994: 140n1), the child will receive a "gap" in its own unconscious, one it is unable to articulate fully or be cognizant of because it is a result of "repression" not on its part but on another's. Abraham suggests that "the buried speech of the parent will be [a] dead [gap] without a burial place in the child." The phantom that haunts us may sometimes not be our own dead "but the gaps left within us by the secrets of others" (1994: 171). The subtle observance of the tensions and se-crets contained within the relationship of adults without knowing the specific content of these is one of the most commonplace and yet consequential ex-periences of childhood, texts of sociality which, voiced or unvoiced, become imprinted in us, ghosts we carry around.

These questions of multiple forms of inheritance for families and nations, psychic, social, and material brings me to the question of "return" and how Malathi and her family took the almost unheard of step of coming back to the house that Malathi fled when she was thirteen and where the second part of our interviews were conducted.

Return

Amma said she was going to save her money and started to build a new house. I knew nothing of this, for a long time no one told me. But I had nothing to do with it at all, she was the one who built it up.

Malathi had heard from others that Analuxmi had begun rebuilding the house in Colombo. She describes Analuxmi's actions ambiguously. On the one hand, she expressed admiration for Analuxmi's gesture of defiance, that it was her house, her dowry, and she would not give it up because of the neighborhood. She talked of Analuxmi's pain at not being there in 1983 and returning to find everything lost. However, Malathi is nonetheless conscious that Analuxmi was absent for the riots. It is part of the tangled knot of misapprehensions and recriminations between mother and daughter. Malathi tells me she herself would not have chosen to return to the neighborhood and the house. "She said from the time she went back, people were talking, passing comments, staring at her. Now she says there is nothing, she says that some neighbors are even good to her now. It must be the guilt, I think."

Malathi's house is a repository of secrets and memories that do not offer themselves readily to narrative. It is a new house built on the old, not the same house, but near enough to offer a strange doppelganger effect of the past and present enclosing the secret. In the past in the old house, Analuxmi was a mother and Malathi a child. In this house, Malathi becomes a mother and the house is once again a family house. However, I remember well that this new (old) house was rather beautiful: brightly painted with a large balcony running around and a profusion of flowers encircling the front courtyard. Malathi told me that the children loved the new house.

I say this because the house is not a dour gray cage of memory. This is not a story of despair. When I began writing, I worried that Malathi's tone, which is measured and meditative, could be interpreted only as a voice of tragedy and horror. But Malathi is not a character in a novel, so she is not trapped within the motif of the text. She is not trapped in solipsism in contemplation of herself. Equally, her memories of the house, her memories of her past, her present, and her future, do not confront her with continual pain every second in the way that we might imagine. The best example is the one I mention at the beginning of the chapter, that Malathi tells me of preparing food for the dead in the celebration of death anniversaries *while cooking*. The association is unmistakable. But it would be ridiculous to say that every time Malathi cooks, every time she cuts up things and makes food, she thinks about the dead. At times, associations present themselves unmistakably; at another time, in another mood, they are not associated. When she cooks, she also cooks for the living, for her children, and for the future. Thus, living in the house and in the neighborhood and with the memories of the riots is a little like cooking, at times undeniable in their associations, at other times, commonplace. Haunting, as Rose (1996) characterizes it, is not only about absence, it is about uncanny persistence, a presence that hovers in an extraordinary, but also commonplace and everyday way.

Very few families reinhabit the houses that were burned in 1983. Nonetheless, while Malathi's case is unusual, her return still presents us with Sri Lanka's own haunting, a haunting that hovers and makes the everyday life of "coexistence" possible even as it undermines it continually.

While in Sri Lanka perpetrators are hard to find, bodies are often lost, and deaths are reported in name, when Malathi first started visiting the neighborhood again she was confronted again with the neighbors she knew had taken their possessions and caused the deaths of her father and brother.

> I went with Amma, to the house down the road. There were lots of people in the first house, lots of boys around my age then, as soon as they saw me they became very anxious and went into the house. I was wondering why they were doing this. I thought that it was because I was an unwelcome person to the neighborhood . . . I realized it was because they had so many of our house possessions in their house. It was only one wall that separated us and there were four boys, they had taken from our house and put in their house. Now when they see me they are feeling guilty, that is why they are running inside.

Becoming permanent residents in the neighborhood and assuming ownership of land was, she recalls, the issue that had provoked hostility twenty years before. It was this that first sparked resentment between her family and the Sinhalese families in the neighborhood, particularly her neighbor from the house in front, who led the mobs in the neighborhood in 1983.

> The neighbor from that house [in front] came to talk to me. I told him, "So you thought in 1983 that the troubles would be solved by threatening us and sending us all back to Jaffna. Have the troubles been solved?" He told me, "I never did anything to your father. If I had been there I would have looked after your father. He was such a nice man, I knew him." He is a cunning man, just trying to tell me tales . . . he is just an old UNP [referring to the United National Party, in government in 1983] thug, now he is a little like a snake with its fangs drawn because he is old. But I knew we would have trouble from him one day.

When Appa used to go by on his bike, he would look at us with hostility, and he would tell tales. He was not at all happy with us. We were the first Tamil people to buy land there and build a house. There were other Tamil families after a while, but we were the first, so he always had a problem with us.

Malathi told me of her first encounter with this neighbor:

He said, "It seems like you are a familiar face, like I have seen you before." I told him, "Why are you even thinking about it, I am the daughter of——." Then he asked me, "Who was that?" He had understood, his face changed when I said it.

I said, "You killed him didn't you? I'm his daughter." He said, "I was not there; I wouldn't have done something like that, I was somewhere else. If I had been there it would not have happened." I said "You would have gone somewhere else to cut somebody else up."

The riots draw neighbors into histories that cannot be disentangled from each other. "When they see me then they start to be anxious. Amma was not there then, but I was there. But also I know, Amma is old now, but I am young, and if I go and live there." Malathi makes many trips back to the house as it is being rebuilt, and as she points out, the Sinhalese neighbors are anxious about her presence for two reasons. First, she reminds them of a past they wish to forget, and second, as a young woman, she represents a future of residence, ownership, and possibly continuity that they also wish to avoid. The neighborhood is willing to accommodate an elderly woman living out the rest of her life. Malathi and her family, however, are young, like the family they were when they first resided there. They have children, to whom the bought house and land will pass. They present the past to the neighborhood, and they present the future through the possibility of their continued residence there. Their presence reminds the neighborhood of a guilt it cannot contain.

Riots happen in localities, concrete places; they tear apart intimate face-to-face daily relations. Memories of neighbors acting on neighbors, from direct physical violence and looting to standing silently by, reside in such sites. "Returning" not only stirs these memories, it forces neighbors into an unwilling confrontation with the past and the necessity of repair for the future. Malathi's experiences illustrate this "after," when the dust has settled and people cope and create new lives and new histories. In addition, if not in Malathi's case then in other stories I recorded, for many this is made easier by memories of those Sinhalese neighbors who braved the mobs to protect and give shelter to strangers and friends. These are the other memories of riots. Malathi's experiences were less positive.

> He [the neighbor] had said in Amma's hearing to someone else, "The children are lovely and innocent but their mother is a real trouble maker." Because I had scolded him . . . They want to forget. Even we Tamil people have that too. . . . We want to hide it and forget about it all. . . . In 1988–1989 there was a huge massacre here [in the south] with the JVP (Janatha Vimukthi Peramuna), sixty thousand people, but nobody is talking about that. Everybody wants to forget the past. Our people [Tamils] keep memories alive for a little, but who talks about the TELO massacres now? We still remember a little more, though. So much we don't forget . . . It may be easier if we forgot a little bit.

In Sri Lanka in the south, as Malathi points out, 60,000 went missing between 1987 and 1989 as a result of fighting between the Sri Lankan state under the UNP (United National Party) and the southern insurrectionary group, the JVP. Both the UNP government and the JVP were in parliament at the time we spoke. What Malathi alludes to is the operation of memory within the larger political context of the present, and also the future. The neighborhood's reluctance to recognize her and act as they remember their own roles in her life and asking *her*, instead, *to forget*, is for her the preeminent sign of the unhealed wounds of 1983. Their deliberate forgetting, while a tacit and unspoken acknowledgment that the riots will never happen again, does not seem like reconciliation for Malathi. For her, their desire that *she forget* and not "make trouble" is their attempt to avoid a future that acknowledges this past. These are the difficult memories of violence that local(e)s contain and that only large-scale political change, still unavailable in Sri Lanka, can make into stories of the past.

Recent research in anthropology, focusing on suffering and violence and on the individual traumas of living through (and engaging in) violence, often talk of the relation of individuals to the past, to their former experiences, and to their attempts to work through, to mourn, to reinhabit the world (e.g., Das et al. 2000). In situations of ongoing violence, as in Sri Lanka, the necessity of "working through" and "surviving" is well understood, but the desire not to have to survive in this manner is of equal importance. The necessity of the constant work of repair is far from valorized, it is read as the result of ongoing acts of violence. Veena Das suggests that anthropologists pay careful attention to how those we work with "resume" ordinary life along with the creation of a public sphere that acknowledges the suffering of victims and allows trust in community, state, and social world also to be "resumed." She suggests that "remaking self-creation on the register of the everyday is a careful putting together of life—a concrete engagement with the tasks of remaking that is mindful of both terms of the compound expression—everyday and life" (2006: 218). Here, the "resumption" of everyday life becomes possible not only because of concerns within the micro-life of communities but also that of the state, as Das (2006) alludes to.

Everyday life and its remaking, as it is experienced, is not always a refuge. The constant remaking of life—a task ceaselessly embarked upon in Sri Lanka—is as much a sign of violence as it is an act of "healing." In situations of ongoing war and violence for those like Malathi, what is desired, in order to make these histories memories of the past and not expectations of the future, is some transformation of the political structures. In my attempt to understand "re-inhabitation" I wish to understand the desire not just for the subject to reinhabit the world, but for the world to change for the subject.

Sri Lanka struggles under the weight of "expectation for the future," a desire for social transformation that still remains unrealized. This desire shows most brutally in the two insurrections in the south and the ethnic conflict and war in the north and east. They form concrete measurements, if tragic and most often repressive, of popular desires and mobilizations for political change. This desire, as it emerged in my life history interviews with displaced Tamils and Muslims from the north, strongly conditions the ways people regard the past. All persons I interviewed had been displaced, had undergone traumatic experiences over the last twenty years, talked of "home" and the loss of their homes, but recounted all this through their constant attempts to imagine or even fear what the future would look like. Where could one belong in the future? How could one imagine "home" until the violence stopped, until a future where one does not have to flee again could be ensured? I found reiterated again and again in individual stories the perception that actually only large-scale political change could effectively actualize and frame the unceasing attempts of individuals to try to move into a desired future.

The failure of three peace processes in Sri Lanka and the constant anticipation of future violence meant that at least in 2003, despite Malathi and her family's return to their former house, the possibility that violence may once again tear open their lives was always on the horizon. Perceptions of political stasis were constantly woven into individual stories of personal fortunes and possibilities. Those I talked to directed emotional energy into imagining totally transformed political landscapes, which could, only by virtue of their transformation, ensure that they would not have to endure new displacement, death, and crisis. People told me that the past was the past, it had happened and unable to do anything else they were dealing with it and carrying on. What they wanted to know was that it would not happen again. Even though the war ended in 2009, ongoing harassment and detention of Tamils, alongside the lack of any political reform and demilitarization of the north and east by the state in 2011, means that violence from the LTTE may have ended but the fear of the Sri Lankan army, police, and state is far from over. Until Tamils are more than second-class citizens, individual "repair" can always be undone. Now that the war seems to be over, with the end of the LTTE's military presence, if not their ghost in remission, what then for those like Malathi? Can Sri Lanka offer a home-in-the-future for minorities to inhabit? The intimate lives of Tamils always beckon to the intimacy of the effects of the riots and the war, forcing new reimaginings of feeling-at-home through place and people.

If questions of ethnicity, generation, and inheritance play a large part in the life of individual Tamil families, the next two chapters move onto to discuss these questions in the life of northern Muslims with whom northern Tamils were once neighbors and friends. The lessons I draw from Malathi's life story in discussing how home and relationships within families can be marked and constituted by a series of violent experiences and multiple displacements become even more urgent in what follows. As with Malathi, northern Muslim stories of home do not just reflect on the past, but envision and dream of a flourishing future and the possibility of return. There too, to be at home for a Northern Muslim entwines with it the necessity of imagining the transformation of collective political structures to accommodate belonging for all minorities.

CHAPTER THREE

From Muslims to Northern Muslims:
Ethnicity, Eviction, and Displacement

In 2003, I went to the northwestern province of Puttalam, home to thousands of Muslim refugees ethnically cleansed from the north by the LTTE. All 70,000–80,000 Muslims had been forcibly cleared from the five districts of the north that the LTTE (at the time) controlled in October 1990 within 24–48 hours, in an act now known as the "Eviction."[1] The majority of northern Muslims, around 65,000 and growing, live in refugee camps and settlements in the Puttalam and Kalpitiya districts curving under the disputed northern territories that they still call home.

On my first trip, I was taken to one of the major camps holding Jaffna Muslims. With male unemployment rife, the camp in the morning was filled with men but very few women. The women, as one man explained to me, had already left early in the morning on the trucks to go and do daily work plucking in the fields. They would be back in the late afternoon, when their waged labor would end and their household labor would begin. A plastic chair was found for me outside one thatched hut, and soon a curious group of men were sitting around to talk to me. My guide, Farook, a young Jaffna Muslim around my age, introduced me to whomever we met with the following formula: "name, Sharika, *conta ur*/(natal home) Nallur, Jaffna, she also has *known*[2] the LTTE so you can talk freely and trust her." With that short introduction I found, to my amazement, people were willing to talk. The men began to retell me their experiences of the Eviction and their lives in Puttalam, taking it in turns to relate individual experiences but also gesturing to each other about commonalities, weaving collective stories. Many of the men had formerly been tailors (a predominantly Muslim trade in Jaffna), and they evoked the dusty Jaffna town market with its open front shops where men would sit among their clacking sewing machines, the symbiosis of the street and inside. They had all left their machines and shops behind and, as they explained to me, there was little tailoring work in Puttalam.

In the late afternoon, a long debate was precipitated when I asked them what they would like to title their stories and whether they had any preferences for the names I would give them. In my previous fieldwork without exception Tamils had asked for anonymity. To my surprise, half the men wanted anonymity and the other half wanted their names and details to be used so that "the world could know what had happened to them." This discussion was finally resolved by Thachitha coming home from work. When she began to tell me her name, one man stopped her, saying that I was recording and explaining the debate. Thachitha laughed, took my microphone in her hand, and told me her name, her former residence in Jaffna, and present residence in Puttalam. She then said, "They [LTTE] have taken everything away anyway." I watched the men's faces change. Farook leaned forward, turned his hands together, then parted them, palms open to the sky, and told me "life comes and life goes, use our names if you want." They all nodded; the die was cast, I could choose, but they wanted their names to be recorded. I thought long and hard about the decision I did make in the end to give them false names. Unlike them, I could not summon the courage to take responsibility for anything happening to anyone as a result of my work—however slim this possibility was.

Such an open discussion about the LTTE or political events, or even that conclusion would have never been possible among Tamils. Living and working with Tamils meant that the LTTE and their actions were always spoken about with hushed voices after trust had been established. In the Muslim refugee camps I could interview people on doorsteps, on thresholds to houses, on roads walking in the camps and settlements. Even children would talk to me about their experiences. I, and others, could speak my heart and mind about politics as a matter of course. This was ethnography of open spaces, the only time in my fieldwork when the world was not being brought indoors.

This experience illustrates the crucial political conditions of possibility that different groups of people face in Sri Lanka (and also the way people can consistently exceed or transform the limits placed on them). Tamils feared the LTTE and each other; they had the right to belong to the Tamil nation but not the freedom to speak. Muslims evicted by the LTTE from their homes, by being outside the "Tamil nation" were thus not subject to individual internal terror by the LTTE. They did not have the right to belong, but they did have the freedom to speak. These sorts of differences are part of the new transformations in sociality and ethnicity in the last twenty years. This chapter and the next are about such transformations: how Muslims from the north are becoming "Northern Muslims" and the stories of the Eviction they tell to outsiders, themselves, and their children, how a cataclysmic event founded a collective story and future.

Sri Lankan Muslims are 8 percent of the population, the second largest ethnic minority in Sri Lanka, and the second largest resident ethnic group in the northern and eastern Tamil-speaking disputed territories. This has meant that, despite academic and political neglect of Muslim perspectives on the civil war, the everyday lives of northern and eastern Muslims are inextricably caught up in the ongoing conflict from a perspective of being neither Sinhalese nor Tamil.

Part of my research is motivated by an ethical, academic, and political obligation to document and reflect on an event, the Eviction, which has had enormous consequences for those involved, but with those consequences and concerns left out of the (two) peace talks subsequent to expulsion and little represented in academic work. These stories have been rendered invisible, not because of the traumatized silence of those involved—any visit to the refugee camps shows the desire of Northern Muslims to speak about and narrativize their lives—but because of a rigidity of representation of the conflict and of who are considered its victims and subjects.[3] The stories of Northern Muslims force us to rethink the ways the Sri Lankan conflict has been historicized and theorized around the two poles of the "Sinhalese" and "Sri Lankan Tamil" and the underlying causes of the war (see McGilvray and Raheem 2007 's excellent discussion of this). I argue that Muslim minorities are not at the margins but the key problem for Tamil nationalism, crucial to understanding the polarization of Sri Lanka and deepening ethnic identification. Muslims are the absent but pregnant emptiness in the heart of Tamil nationalism. The north, easily assumed to be a mono-ethnic Tamil space, was only created as such after the assertion of its mono-ethnic status through the expulsion of Muslims, even though the LTTE tried to make the outcome "Tamil Eelam" the immanent cause.

Second, examining the Muslim communities of the north and east forces us to move beyond the conceptual structure of the nation as Tamil or Sinhala, or even Sri Lankan, which underpins this current separatist war. Ethnic authenticity is accorded to those who have a place that they can call their own, itself rooted in a late colonial ordering and vision of Ceylon as an already racialized geography. Muslims, while considered an ethnicity, have no *one* place that is considered Muslim, even though there are many places where Muslims are concentrated. The wide ranging regional dispersal of Muslims across Sri Lanka means that any proposal for an area which is solely Muslim, a Muslim self-governing region (MSR) that was proposed by some eastern Muslim politicians, has found little favor among island-wide Muslims, as it would involve the forced movement of one or another Muslim community (McGilvray and Raheem 2007). There can be no "Muslim Homeland." In a war fought over ethnic territory and homelands, where do Muslims belong? It is only through examining the evolution and location of Muslim ethnic formation that one can denaturalize the parameters of one kind of nationalist story about ethnicity projected onto territory, which dominates the conceptual matrix of the current war.

The often ignored relationship between Tamils and Muslims is at the heart of this chapter, especially since the violent breakdown of village level neighborly relations between Tamils and Muslims, as well as the more recent attacks on Muslims by Tamil militant groups. The Eviction has meant that these relationships can only be grasped through tropes of catastrophe and conflict, resulting in, as I found, the idealization of Tamil-Muslim relations by Northern Muslims and the embarrassed guilty silence of northern Tamils. What is the nature of Tamil and Muslim relationships as they appear now, the differences, the secrets, the loyalties, and the betrayals? In the aftermath of the Eviction, Northern Muslims are left to constantly probe this wound.

In the first section I retell the well-known history of the entrenchment of ethnicity into political and social structures alongside the spatialization of ethnicity, through the eyes of Muslims, the constant exceptions, figures who oscillate in and out of different stories about ethnicity in Sri Lanka. I then trace ethnic relations in the context of growing state discrimination, as well as the uneasy and now fateful effects of Tamil militancy in the north and east on Muslim communities, moving to a detailed consideration of identities created as a result of new events. It is patently clear that the war itself has set into play new kinds of classifications and identifications, both the result of polarization and the reaccentuation of regional conflicts as they have been integrated into the current politics of Tamil militancy. The second half of this chapter addresses the Eviction, and through Eviction stories I begin tracking the emergence of a new category of people called Northern Muslim, and loss as a form of historicity.

"The Nation and Its Muslims"

In the British colonial period there were officially five different Muslim groups, differentiated on the basis of "racial origin": Ceylon/Sri Lankan Moors, Indian/Coast Moors, Malays, Borahs, and Memons.[4] While there has been some breakdown and intermarriage among these groups, Muslim ethnic consciousness has primarily coalesced around the group referred to as Ceylonese/Sri Lankan Muslims, who are seen as both "indigenous" to Sri Lanka and of a different ethnicity from Sinhalese and Tamils.

There are two major specificities within the Sri Lankan Muslim ethnic identification. The first is the appellation of Muslim as a category encompassing both religion and ethnicity. Muslims are a Tamil-speaking minority, the other major ones being Sri Lankan Tamils and Malaiyaha Tamils. However, Tamil-speaking Christians, like me, are considered ethnically Tamil while Muslims are not. As Nuhuman explains, in Sri Lanka the major differentiation through which Muslims emerge is neither through language, dividing Sinhalese and Tamils, nor through religion, between Hindus and Muslims, but through "two different categories of language and religion" (1999: 5).[5] It is Tamil nationalists who have insisted that there is no difference between Tamils and Muslims, and that Muslims should be content to be represented and thus subsumed by Tamils in the north and east, even as they are treated as pragmatically different, and often inferior, in local contexts. This pattern has a long and singular history: attempts to gain political recognition by Tamils and Muslims from the British colonial regime were constantly through reference to each other, tacitly or at times more obviously, drawing lines of separation. As traced in sections below, Tamil and Muslim late colonial and postcolonial ethnic identities are inextricably linked.

The second important peculiarity is the wide regional dispersal of Muslims across the island. This regional differentiation and demography give Sri Lankan Muslim identity formation and history some of its distinctiveness, both within Sri Lanka (Kearney 1987) and in relation to Muslim groups across the southern subcontinent (McGilvray 1998).[6] There are both urban and rural agrarian populations, often separated from each other; central and western Muslim are scattered rather than concentrated (1998: 446). These dispersed populations vary greatly in occupation, kinship structures, wealth, and regional position vis-à-vis other ethnic groups—Tamils are the majority population for eastern and northern Muslims and Sinhalese the majority for southwestern and central Muslims. This dispersal and heterogeneity is significant because of the spatialization of ethnicity in colonial and postcolonial Sri Lanka. It has meant that from the start Muslim identity formation has contended with the effects of a pan-island ethnic identity and a deep regional schism and contestation over that identity. In a war rhetorically fought about earmarked ethnic territory, Muslims are in "too many places," and thus in none specifically.

The relationship between Tamils and Muslims nationally and the linking of place and people alongside ethnicization of identities are the legacy of new forms of being governed and understanding oneself in the late colonial British regime. Here we explore three significant factors in understanding the location and formation of Muslim ethnic consciousness and the conjoining of race and religion in the late colonial period: (1) religious revivalism in the context of island wide religious revivalism and a larger subcontinental wave of Islamic reform movements and nationalism; (2) the way race guided how spatially Ceylon was made legible for rule; and (3) how race was made the basis for representation.

Religion

Religious difference was the key marker by which Muslims were identified long before ethnicity as a concept became key to all social groups in Ceylon, now Sri Lanka. When the Portuguese arrived in 1505, they encountered a medieval Sri Lanka that was "remarkably cosmopolitan, a veritable polypsest" (Russell 1982: 2), ethnically and religiously heterogeneous with many different immigrant populations, shifting populations, warring kingdoms, and so on. The Portuguese "recognized" Muslim groups as "Mauros"/Moors with whom they had a long history of competition across world trade routes. Thus the identification of Muslims as a separate category is of rather long standing though significantly not ethnicized, as it became in the nineteenth century. McGilvray identifies the roots of this "Moor community" in both the pre-Islamic seaborne trade between South, South East Asia and the Middle East both Arabic and Persian, and Arab Muslim mercantile trade in the southern subcontinent subsequent to the dawn of Islam in the seventh century (1998: 436).[7] Muslim communities were scattered throughout the island. As early as the fifteenth century and very definitely by the seventeenth century there were large populations of Muslim farmers established on the east coast (McGilvray 1998). There is clear early archaeological evidence for seventh- and eighth-century "Muslim" settlements in the north (Hasbullah 1996).[8] There was large-scale Muslim migration to the central inland of the island after the Kandyan kingdom offered protection from Portuguese persecution (Dewaraja 1994), as both the Portuguese (1505–1658), and the Dutch (1658–1796) who followed them persecuted Muslim communities to break their trading practices and alliances across the Indian Ocean. It was in fact under the British (1796–1948) that many of these restrictions were lifted, and Muslim communities began to become more prosperous, though this prosperity was largely restricted to the southwestern elites.

However, as Samaraweera (1979) points out, this religious identity was multifaceted. While Moors from India, so called "Coast Moors," were assimilated into Ceylonese Muslims through marriage and residence, nonetheless, throughout the nineteenth century a distinction was always maintained between "native born" "Ceylonese Moors" and "Indian Coast Moors," both in the census and in how representatives of Ceylonese Muslims spoke of their community.

The late nineteenth-century Muslim revivalism was primarily, like Buddhist and Hindu revivalist movements, inspired by and preoccupied by ideas of "upliftment" and education. Hindu and Buddhist religious revivalist movements initiated nascent anticolonialist opposition first through opposition to Christian proselytization. They fought for state protection and establishment of religious boards and temples and set up Buddhist and Hindu English language schools to break missionary control of education. Muslim religious revivalism, coming later, concentrated on the same objects without the same feelings of besiegement, not least because of low rates of Muslim (unlike Buddhist and Hindu) conversion to Christianity (Samaraweera 1979).

Muslim elites, due to reluctance to be educated in Christian mission schools and thus with less access to English medium education and mass literacy, had not participated as heavily as Tamil and Sinhalese elites in the politico-administrative and educational structures of colonial Ceylon (McGilvray 1998: 448). However, an emerging small mercantile and middle-class Muslim elite based in Colombo and Kandy began to be heavily involved in religious revivalism and educational societies (Nuhuman 2003). In the late nineteenth century, Muslim revivalism was in full swing under Siddi Lebbe, a lawyer and the figurehead of Moor revivalism (Nuhuman 2003; Zackariya and Shanmugaratnam 1997).[9] Papers such as the *Ceylon Mohammedan* on 3 January 1901 stressed that "in order to take the proper place among our fellow country men we should educate our children" (Samaraweera 1979: 372) and were pressing for educational reform, English language education, Islamic reform, and increased political authority. However, the religious and educational revivalist movements clearly favored southern Muslim elites, with not a single school established for East Coast Muslims (Samaraweera 1979; McGilvray 1998). The large numbers of Muslims living outside the southwest were largely excluded from these developments.

This religious revivalism in Ceylon did not occur in a vacuum: throughout the nineteenth and early twentieth centuries, South Asian Muslims were engaged in revivalist and reformist movements. In Ceylon, the presence of Arabi Pasha, exiled to the island in 1883 after an unsuccessful revolt against the British in Egypt, undoubtedly provided a catalyst for nascent Muslim elites (Samaraweera 1979; Ismail 1995). While Ceylonese Muslims seemed unaffected by the actual revolt in Egypt, on his arrival in Ceylon Arabi Pasha was greeted by large crowds and feted by newspapers and local Muslim populations. His modernist ideas about upliftment also undoubtedly influenced activists such as Siddi Lebbe (Samaraweera 1979: 299). In 1900, Ceylonese Muslims also participated, along with Indian Muslims, in the celebrations of the Golden Jubilee of the Sultan of Turkey's accession to power. However, identification with Islam and Muslim identities outside the Island, which came to the fore in the late nineteenth and early twentieth centuries, were also part of political struggles for representation in the British colonial regime in Ceylon.

Race, Space, and Representation

While medieval and renaissance Ceylon was highly socially and religiously heterogeneous, ethnic/racial categories were not the basis of inclusion or exclusion. A wide variety of social groups were asymmetrically clustered around monarchies in "dissimilar ways" (see Nissan and Stirrat 1990: 26). Nissan and Stirrat suggest that a polity in which different groups are differentiated through a series of "objective" classifications and factors in relation to each other as well as to the center came only in the British colonial era, when social groups became differentiated into differently *entitled* racial groups. This was also made possible by the centralization of Ceylon under the British. The Portuguese and Dutch colonial regimes could not occupy the central Kandyan kingdom, and essentially only adapted and modified already existing hierarchies and ranks from the former kingdoms of the Maritime Provinces (Samaraweera 1973). The British gave a radically new form to Ceylon. After the conquest of the Kandyan kingdom in 1815, the whole island was placed under a common administration, and its highly heterogeneous population was differentiated in a system of communal representation.

Many have written extensively about this nineteenth-century fixing of race and representation (see Spencer 1990; Jeganathan and Ismail 1995); here I take the figure of the Muslim to examine the contradictions in how race and space were made legible in colonial governance. Under the British, one genealogy can be summed as race = representation, another as space = race. In the figures of Sinhalese and Sri Lankan Tamils, these two equations were brought together. However, while Muslims were recognized as legitimate race with thus limited rights to representation, they had no specific place, thus were absent in the second mythical story, in which certain kinds of people are considered to emanate organically from certain kinds of places, and to have a legitimate "voice" is to have "a place of your own." It is the tension between these two representations that Muslims expose.

Racial Geographies

The 1815 unification of the island as a unitary political and spatial territory was solidified under the 1833 Colebrooke-Cameron reforms, which introduced executive and legislative governing councils and a new spatial order for the island. The island was structured into 5, then 9 provinces with mini-regional capitals, all answering to Colombo, placed at the center as the new imperial city (Perera 1998: 45–47).[10] Different areas were administered as racio-linguistic regions, in either Sinhalese (southern and central provinces) or Tamil (northern and eastern provinces) according to the preponderance of speakers. One example is Anuradhapura, which was shifted from the Northern Province to a newly created North Central Province by Governor William Gregory in the 1870s, attributing the perceived neglect of the town partly to "the fact that this portion of the Northern Province was Kandyan in its population whereas to the north it was Tamil, and generally ruled by a

Government Agent who was more conversant with Tamils than with Sinhalese" (Gregory quoted in De Silva 1973c: 257). Anuradhapura had become understood as Sinhalese after the British excavated ruins of an ancient and extensive irrigation-based kingdom there. This move implicitly demonstrated that certain areas were seen as linked to certain people and different ethnic provinces posed different (incompatible) welfare issues. This despite the fact that the new town of Anuradhapura that had emerged through British rule and British archaeological excavation of its ancient ruins was a highly mixed frontier town with large Muslim and Tamil as well as Sinhalese populations (Jeganathan 1995) and only "cleansed" of its minority Tamil population in anti-Tamil riots in 1977 and 1983. Now Anuradhapura is commonly referred to in Sri Lanka and in scholarly and journalistic writing as a "border town." The border referred to is that between Sinhalese and Tamil lands, revealing how deeply such identifications have become naturalized and lived.

Each region was governed by a combination of British and Roman Dutch law, with customary law applied to all instances where the former were silent Particular regions were considered the territory of particular groups with common understanding of inheritance, property, caste, and kinship; for example, the Jaffna Tamils governed by the Thesawalamai. One of the major exceptions to this regionally dimpled application of law were Muslims. Sri Lankan Muslims were instead subject to an island-wide "Mohammedan" code, though practically speaking, this code was adapted to the regional practices of different Muslim communities.[11]

As Wickramasinghe (2007) remarks, the Colebrooke-Cameron reforms, intended to break down social and cultural division and introduce a more homogenized European nation-state space, in fact introduced constant differentiation at a local level,[12] reinforcing assumptions about Tamilness and Sinhalaness while at the same time creating new configurations that gave rise to new supra-local ethnic identifications. The eastern province historically was not connected to the precolonial Jaffna kingdoms in the north. Some parts of the eastern area were under the jurisdiction of the pre-British large Kandyan kingdom and a swath of small chieftains, the Vanniyar, held some parts of the north central and eastern belt, offering fealty to the Kandyans. Now however, the north and east were (and are now) commonly imagined as a naturalized Tamil (speaking) homeland. Another prominent example is the collapse in the first half of the twentieth century of a historically highly significant distinction between Low-Country and Kandyan Sinhalese into an island-wide identification as Sinhalese. Thus this "racialized geography" of rule (Stepputat 2008) with its simultaneous differentiation and pan-island homogenization of ethnicity is the precursor of today's postcolonial ethnic conflict, in its demarcation of Tamil and Sinhalese as bounded, politically significant ethnic collectivities with their own naturalized homelands. The boundaries of the LTTE-claimed Tamil homeland, as many commentators (e.g., Spencer 1990) have pointed out, exactly follow the 1889 northern and eastern provincial boundaries.

Muslims were, however, from the beginning excluded from the kind of ethnic reckoning that linked people and place, which is of course one of the most compelling imaginaries of national communities (Malkki 1995, [1992] 1999). The regional affiliation of Muslims or Moors was considered incidental to their ethnic classification, even though at the village level in the north and east, as we explore later, Muslims shared kinship and inheritance practices with neighboring Tamils. Muslims thus could claim regional homes, but were not accounted as living in places that were "their own." Sri Lankan Muslims are an important example of an ethnic collectivity that emerges without a place of its own, and, as we shall see, one that can also be defined through narratives of displacement in the case of the Northern Muslims. Perhaps even, paradoxically, Northern Muslims have gained their place through losing it. Loss has made substantial what was formerly hidden and unrecognized; it has in some peculiar way allowed Muslims to claim the homes they always lived in.

Race and Representation

Muslim ethnic identity instead took root not through regional identity but through the new centralized structures emerging after the 1833 reforms. The reforms instituted two councils to keep the governor in check: an Executive Council responsible for running the core machinery of the state, and a Legislative Council of a limited number of nominated unofficial members drawn from the governed population at large to represent distinct "races." The significance of the legislative council was that, while it was envisaged to have a rather limited function,[13] as K. M. De Silva points out, "from the start the unofficial members of the Legislative Council tended to look upon the Legislative Council as the local Parliament" (1973a: 229). The Legislative Council was always constituted around communal representation though this was later overlaid with some territorial representation too.[14] In 1931, when communal representation was totally abolished in favor of territorial representation and universal suffrage, it was in a context where, for more than a hundred years, representation had been on the basis of representing one's own race's interests, alongside others representing their races. The state provided a stage where struggles over representation could only be legitimate insofar as they were racialized. As Wickramasinghe remarks, "colonial knowledge did not imagine identities or construct them; rather, it opened up a new realm for political identities to blossom" (2007: 44). Enumerating these new social identities in censuses and legislation and fixing them in space, solidified and fixed these identities and made them possible to be categorized, systematized and identified with (Cohn 1987; Wickramasinghe 2007).

The beginnings of a debate on separate Muslim racial and political representation date from the late 1860s. In 1883 the three unofficial representatives nominated were a Tamil, a "low country Singhale," and a Burgher. The Tamil representative Ramanathan was presumed also to represent the Tamil-speaking Moor minority. In 1889 after considerable agitation two new members were added: a Muslim and a Kandyan Sinhalese. It was precisely this development that prompted the famous Ramanathan-Azeez exchange, seminal in elite Muslim identity formation. In 1885, to forestall the rumored selection of a "Moor" member, Ramanathan made a speech to the Legislative Council (published in 1888 as a paper to the Royal Asiatic Society, Ceylon Branch entitled "The Ethnology of the Moors of Ceylon"), arguing that the "Moors" were not a race (read thus not eligible for a seat on the Legislative Council) as they were Tamils, who looked like other Tamils and were Tamil-speaking. Ramanathan argued that "taking 1) the language they speak at home in connection with 2) their history, 3) their customs and 4) physical features, the proof cumulatively leads to no other conclusion than that the Moors of Ceylon are ethnologically Tamils" (quoted in Ismail 1995: 67). I. L. M Azeez, a prominent Moor leader and lawyer, immediately rejoindered with the comment that

[Ramanathan's] object in calling Moors Tamils in race was to dissuade the government from appointing a Moorish member in the Council, it having leaked out then that the government were contemplating to appoint such a one, and to make them understand that there was no such necessity for taking such a step, as the Moors did not form a distinct race. (Azeez in 1889, quoted in Samaraweera 1979: 374)

In 1907, Azeez instead published a reply to Ramanathan that attempted the first systematic formulation of a clear racialized history of the Sri Lankan Muslim community. Azeez argued that the "Moors" were indeed a distinct race from Tamils, with Arab, not South Indian, origins. They were, he argued, the descendents of Hashemites from Arabia who had acquired Tamil through the marriage of Arab men to Tamil women and for the purposes of trade. Eager to claim distinctness from Tamil political hegemony, Azeez also found himself trying not to emphasize the "foreignness" of Muslims against a Sinhala nationalist movement that had denounced Muslims and particularly Indian Muslim migrants, as outsiders and foreigners (Ismail 1995).[15] As Ismail concludes, Muslim identity formation in this period was beset already by the contradictions forced on it and embraced by it by "Moorish" relations to "Tamil" and "Sinhalese" elites and the construction of racial identity as political representation by the British. In rejecting Ramanathan's claim, Muslim elites were forced to repudiate any similarities between themselves and Sri Lankan Tamils. The simplification of the complex heritage of Sri Lanka's Muslim community thus erased Persian influences, downplayed the importance of language and the similarities between Muslim and Tamil village-level practices outside the Southern based urban Muslim elite, and promoted instead "a hypostatised Arab 'racial' pedigree . . . to separate Moorish from Tamil and Sinhala 'races' " (McGilvray 1998: 450).

This Arabicized pedigree and image has left a profound and contradictory legacy. Still potent and powerful as a representation of Muslim difference and pedigree, acting to make the community cohere, nonetheless this image also exposes profound internal differentiation. The image of Muslims as a trading community with Arab origins, while congruent with a southern Muslim elite's perception of itself, sat very uneasily with a larger island-wide Muslim community. The vast majority of Muslims living in northern and eastern regions were not in fact traders, but engaged in fishing and farming, and did have historically strong links with South India.[16] The southern Muslim urban elite attempt to transform themselves from a *regional elite* to a *national elite*, speaking on behalf of all Muslims throughout the nineteenth and twentieth centuries (Samaraweera 1979), precipitated constant struggles over representation. A widened franchise in the 1930s and Independence in 1948 made divisions between Colombo elite leadership and provincial Muslims even more pronounced; "differences between the leadership in Colombo and the Muslims in the regions (living outside the centre), became sharper due to conflicts between the older and younger generations on the issues of power and control over community affairs" (Zackariya and Shanmugaratnam 1997: 9). In discussions surrounding the 1931 Donoughmore constitution[17] instituting territorial representation, eastern Muslims supported territorial rather than communal representation in an attempt to wrest control away from southern Muslim elites (Asad 1993).[18] Thus, Muslims mobilized themselves both around the same kinds of communal logic Tamil and Sinhala national elites pursued in trying to constitute themselves around seemingly homogeneous ethnic identities, and, also along a similar internal/vertical struggle for communal representation.

Muslims and Tamils

In the twentieth century, many of the debates outlined above have become transformed and reaccentuated. The question of Tamil-Muslim relations, nationally and regionally, has moved beyond nineteenth- and early twentieth-century obsessions with whether Muslim was a primarily religious or an ethnic category. Now Muslims are more concerned with establishing their rights as a minority of whatever ilk, in the face of Tamil nationalist hegemony and state indifference. In the northern and eastern war zone areas, the question of who Tamils and Muslims are *to each other*, politically and socially, has become one of the most pressing questions the current ethnic conflict and war have forced. The accentuation of conflict in the north and east has also accentuated and remodeled the conflict within the Muslim community around representation. Southwestern Muslims and their elites have lost ground to the pressure, particularly from eastern Muslims, to seize control of Muslim political participation. These new debates are key to understanding contemporary Muslim lives and here I trace the transformation of Muslim, Tamil relations, the regional struggles within Muslim political parties, and the significance of regional differentiation for the emergence of Northern Muslims. In this and the next chapter, I also attempt to show how, while conventional genealogies of the ethnic conflict begin with the colonial era and stop in mid-twentieth century, positing continuing anti-Tamil riots and civil war as natural consequence, in fact the civil war has itself instituted new kinds of identities and fissures that transform the parameters of the ethnicization of the previous century. This chapter argues that "Northern Muslims" are a new kind of demographic and collectivity created through the war from Muslims from the north.

Being the Second Minority

The Muslim community's vulnerable position as a minority sandwiched between Sinhala and Tamil nationalisms shaped Muslim participation in Sri Lankan politics throughout the twentieth century. Moreover, the question of who were the majority, Tamils or Sinhalese, in different Muslim communities exposed crucial regional differences within the Muslim community, a community that was never "one." As McGilvray and Raheem emphasize, "the cultural, economic and geographical diversity of Sri Lanka's Muslims has always meant it would be a heterogeneous community with divergent interests and plural political adaptations at the local level" (2007: 2). Given this, one can observe two major trends in Muslim political participation in the twentieth century: the policy of accommodation politics in the South and Muslim coalition politics more generally (Ismail 1995; McGilvray 1998); and, as the democratic franchise opened to include the voices of rural Muslims from the nonmetropolitan areas of the island and the ethnic conflict intensified from the 1980s onward, the progressive shifting of the political heart of Muslim politics toward the Eastern Province.

In 1915, Sri Lanka had its first anti-minority riot. A Sinhalese pogrom against Muslims in the south saw Muslim elites seeking protection from the British state, with Tamil and Sinhala nationalist politicians clearly excusing the Sinhalese rioters (Roberts 1994; Ameer Ali 1981). Fear of such riots cast a long shadow. The first elections for Independent Ceylon, in 1948, clearly favored Sinhala majoritarian parties; seeing this and the defeat of many Muslim candidates, the Muslim elite then shifted allegiance to a policy of accommodation with the Sinhala-dominated state (Ismail 1995). Muslim politicians developed considerable ingenuity at coalition politics, switching between the UNP and SLFP national Sinhalese governments to win concessions and protection for Muslim minorities. This reflected the high levels of everyday racism against Muslims in Sinhalese majority areas. The 1983 riots in Colombo undoubtedly raised the possibility that attention would turn from Tamils to Muslims. This "subtext of fear" governed part of the accommodative politics in the South (Ismail 1995). This accommodative politics saw nominal participation of Muslim politicians in State political structures, but not much in actual rewards for ordinary Muslim communities. As McGilvray points out, rewards from Sinhala majority parties secured the election of a few rich southwest coast Muslim politicians to cabinet positions but not much else:

> as an educated Muslim middle-class began to emerge in the 1970s and 1980s its demands for practical socioeconomic concessions (university admissions and job quotas, for example) were placated with a broad array of Islamic religious and cultural self-esteem programmes, some of them funded by rival Sunni and Shia regimes in the Middle East, which cost the government nothing. . . . [this]might have continued indefinitely, if not for the fact that after 1983 the government could no longer guarantee the lives and property of Moors in the East coast Tamil guerrilla combat zone. (McGilvray 1998: 456)

While southern Muslim politicians in the southwest and central provinces attempted to negotiate their place in Sinhala majoritarian areas, northern and eastern Muslims faced very different pressures. From the first, their concern was how to manage a highly intimate neighborly life with Tamils, their ethnic majority.

East coast Muslims form around a third of the total population of Sri Lankan Muslims, and the east coast as a whole represents the most considerable concentration of Muslim population. Within the Eastern Province Muslims form a territorial bloc with some parts Muslim majority areas: Amparai district is about 40 to 42 percent Muslim. This means the possibility of concentrated and powerful voting constituencies and influence in municipal structures. Moreover, when state-sponsored dry-zone colonization from the 1950s onward settled a frontier of poor low-country Sinhalese peasants in eastern areas. This altered the population balance of the Eastern Province and cut into Tamil and Muslim constituencies. Muslims emerged holding the delicate balance of power. Tamils form 42 percent of the east, Sinhalese 26 percent, and Muslims 32 percent. In the current conflict, any possible devolution of the northeastern region thus has to take account of the Muslim minority in the Eastern Province. Not least, any referendum on the merger of the north and east as a single Tamil region rests on Muslim consent. Tamil-Muslim relations, particularly in the east, have thus assumed loaded significance.

Village level relationships between Tamils and Muslims are culturally intelligible while segregated. Tamils and Muslims not only share a language in the north and east, they also—unlike Muslims and Sinhalese, and Tamils and Sinhalese—share kinship and neighborly structures. It is not just that both speak Tamil as their mother tongue. McGilvray (1998, 2008) has extensively documented how east coast Tamils and Muslims have a common kinship structure organized into matrilineal clans, similar understandings of sexuality and substance ideologies, and so on. East coast Muslims and Tamils both operate under the *kuti* system, where *kuti*'s are exogamous matri-clans and men acquire the *kuti* of their wives on marriage. Muslim Mosque and Hindu temple membership are passed on through these matri-clans (McGilvray 1998: 467). While residential separation, reduction of intermarriages, and a bifurcated school system have led to less direct interaction between eastern Tamil and Muslim communities (McGilvray 2008), Tamils and Muslims continue to be who they are in relation to each other.

This fact is also apparent if one considers the contrast between northern and eastern Muslims. Northern Muslims and Tamils do not operate under a matri-clan system but under a more bilateral caste and mosque structure with similar sorts of dowry patterns. Regional differences between north and east thus transcend ethnic differences. Northern Muslims and Tamils, and, eastern Muslims and Tamils, share more with each other *intra-regionally* than *inter-regionally*.

Moreover, the size and scale of the eastern Muslim community gives it a different confidence in its dealings with Tamil neighbors. In the east, the general pattern of residence is alternating Tamil and Muslim villages. One commonplace saying compares Tamil Muslim relations to "puttu," a staple favored by both Tamils and Muslims, long steamed rolls of rice flour cakes glued together with alternating stripes of grated coconut. Tamils and Muslims are said to live together like rice and coconut, integral but separate. In comparison, there were very few Muslim-only villages in northern areas, with Mannar district with the greatest concentration of northern Muslims the only exception. Northern Muslims and Tamils shared villages which were internally segregated. As we shall see, the multi-ethnic nature of these village homes came to assume great significance for Northern Muslims after the Eviction. Thus the shifting of the moral heart of Muslim politics to the regions and the eastern coast is both fueled by and magnifies the oscillation between intimacy and betrayal in the complex nature of relationships at the village level, between Tamil and Muslim politicians, and most recently between Muslims and Tamil militant groups.

Politics in the East Coast

Muslim politicians and youth also participated in the rise of Tamil nationalism in the north and east, though this became ever more uneasy as Tamil nationalist politicians explicitly moved toward exclusivist ethnic ideologies. In the 1950s high profile eastern Muslim MPs such as M. M. Mustapha, M. S. Kariapper, and M. C. Ahmad became members of the Tamil-dominated Federal party and stressed their relationship to the broad linguistic nationalism of Tamil-speaking areas and a larger eastern Muslim consciousness. On one occasion M. M. Mustapha, addressing (Senator) Razick Fareed the dominant southern Muslim politician, argued that "we [Muslims] in the Eastern Province don't speak "Arabic-Tamil" but "the purest form of Tamil" (Ismail 1995: 86). This move also opened up the divisions between southern and eastern concerns, part of the push by eastern politicians for a greater stake in national politics.

Muslim inclusion in Tamil parties was short-lived. Tamil nationalist parties could not sufficiently address the concerns of Muslims and sought to subsume Muslims under a broader umbrella of Tamil-speaking people that tacitly sought to suppress Muslim identity and present them as (in effect) lesser Tamils. When Mustapha and other Muslim politicians moved to switch between the two national parties UNP and SLFP, they were immediately accused of being *thoppi pirutu*, or turncoats (literally, switching hats), by Tamil politicians, despite the fact that some prominent Tamil MPs were also members of the UNP. This set in place a script, trotted out whenever convenient by Tamil politicians, of Muslim "collaboration" with the "Sinhalese."

In the 1980s, Muslim politicians began to turn to the formation of Muslim-only political parties, this communalization of identity coming much later than that of the Tamils and Sinhalese. As McGilvray and Raheem (2007) point out, the formation of an exclusively Muslim political party in turn reflected the inability of the UNP and SLFP parties to move away from a core Sinhala Buddhist constituency and ideology. Significantly, the two Muslim political parties formed came from the east coast and reflected very specific issues with regard to east coast political realities and the rise of Tamil nationalism and militancy. The initial impetus for the formation of these parties came out of protest against the UNP government's alliance with Israel and its proposal of merging the Muslim constituencies in Amparai within the Sinhalese-dominated Uva province, effectively disenfranchizing a significant proportion of eastern Muslims. The more significant of these two parties was the Sri Lanka Muslim Congress (SLMC), formed in 1981, consolidating in its registration as a parliamentary party and its successful contestation of the Provincial Council elections in 1989 (which the LTTE had demanded Tamils and Muslims should boycott). Its charismatic leader Ashraff himself had

briefly been part of the Tamil parliamentary party, the TULF (Tamil United
Liberation Front) before forming the SLMC (Jeyaraj 2000). The other major
group was the East Sri Lanka Muslim Front (ESLMF), later the Muslim United
Liberation Front (MULF), which attempted to negotiate more explicitly with
the LTTE. Both parties, especially the SLMC, represented the increasingly
politically articulate voice of eastern Muslims, a voice which grew through a
violent "dialogue" with Tamil nationalist politics.

Tamil militant movements emerged in the northern provinces before
quickly taking root in eastern areas, as a more generalized disenchantment
with the Tamil parliamentary parties spread through the north and east.
While the small Muslim minority in the north did not pose a significant threat
or problem for Tamil militant politics, all Tamil militant movements realized
that in the eastern provinces the Muslim minority in one way or another
represented a key constituency. The first phase of militancy saw the attempt
to incorporate Muslims into the militant struggle as combatants through a
larger ideological notion of Tamil-speaking peoples that would hold both
north and east as their traditional homelands. As Taraki[19] commented:

> the most progressive thinking during the early years of Tamil mili-
> tancy that was possible within the Tamil Nationalist thinking was to
> ensure the proportional representation of the minorities in recruit-
> ment. The Muslims were subsumed from time to time under vari-
> ous politically-convenient concepts such as "Tamil speaking people,"
> "Eela-Muslims," and "Islami Tamils." ([1990] 1991: 28)

Indeed, the intensification of the government military campaigns against
the northeast meant that alliances between the two communities formed,
with some young Muslims also joining the major militant movements.[20]
However, from the mid-1980s, militant movements began to impose increasing taxes on Muslim businesses and advance more exclusivist ethnic ideologies. Muslims began to fear for their own safety and also their right to reside
in the east as minority communities with well articulated rights of their own,
not subsumed under a majoritarian Sri Lankan Tamil identity. In April 1985
the first riots between the Tamil and Muslim communities broke out in the
east, with violence spreading outward from Kalmunai to other areas.

One attempt to deal with the bad blood between Tamils and Muslims
was an agreement brokered in 1986 in Madras, South India. It was facilitated

by Dr. Baddiuddin Mahmud, the highest ranking Sri Lankan Muslim politician (minister of education for the Sri Lankan government, 1970–1977) and signed by Kittu, LTTE political commander of Jaffna, and M. I. M. Mohideen of the MULF (Muslim Liberation Front). The agreement stated that the LTTE recognized Muslims as a distinct ethnic minority group, and that the northern and eastern provinces were also to be seen as their homeland with significant protection of their right to political representation and land and resource allocation. This agreement has often been forgotten in recent history. What is significant about it is that it was forced and brokered on the basis of eastern concerns, where Muslims do form a large minority, and where the terms of their rights were to be defined *territorially*.[21] This is revealing for current *northern* Muslim concerns, because this agreement, though broken in the most brutal fashion possible, was on the basis of a Muslim community being numerically and territorially strong, which northern Muslims have never been.

In fact, in the 1980s Muslims tended more toward the LTTE than other movements and Muslim-LTTE relationships, while shaky, were nonetheless strong. Muslims saw further diminution of their rights in the years of Indian army occupation and the provincial government system it instituted (1987–1990). As the EPRLF led eastern province government persecuted some Muslim communities, some saw the LTTE as potentially more lenient. Furthermore, the Muslim community found that the Indian army did not recognize them in brokering devolution programs. The Indians saw them as similar to the Indian Muslim community, and rank and file soldiers in some instances persecuted Muslims (Jeyaraj 2002). In this period there were many Muslim cadres in the LTTE. Not least, Taraki points out, the LTTE survived the Indian offensive in the east chiefly because eastern Muslims maintained supply lines through Muslim areas to feed guerrillas in the jungle ([1990] 1991: 71). The Indians identified some Muslim villages as Tiger strongholds.

Nonetheless, in 1990, when the LTTE gained control of the north and east after the Indian army's withdrawal, it seemed to have decided to take a different attitude to the Muslim community. This was particularly fueled by the successful contestation of the 1989 elections by the SLMC, who not only defied the boycott but also garnered a significant electoral victory, marking its arrival on the eastern political scene. Taraki argues that this was because the Muslim community in the east always posed a deep unsettling crisis at the heart of the nationalist project for a unified, pure Tamil northeast homeland:

The East can always be a region that will cause fissures in the LTTE's project of total domination. The reasons for this are many and varied. Some can be tentatively summarized as follows: The question of Tamil Nationalism which seeks, however subtly, to assimilate the Muslims. The question of Muslim ethnicity its scope and limits. Village level Tamil and Muslim relations. (Taraki [1990] 1991: 27)

As war began with the Sri Lankan government in June 1990, the LTTE embarked on a series of massacres of Muslims in Eravur and Kattankudy. In 1990 it decided to evict Muslims from the north. Numerous LTTE massacres were accompanied by the machinations of the state Special Task Force in arming home guards, naming them "Muslim home guards" in order to destabilize the east. The cycle of killings and counter-killings in the east makes grim reading. Tamil and Muslim relationships broken down at a village level leaving great scars within the east, stoked continually by the LTTE.

The LTTE continued to harass Muslim communities in the east, attempting to break Muslim economic power, right to cultivate and fish, land occupation, and political strength Furthermore, in the 2002 peace talks the LTTE successfully ensured that Muslim parties were only allowed limited participation, clearly excluding them as stake holders (see McGilvray and Raheem 2007 for an extended discussion of this). Eastern Muslim communities were trapped between Sri Lankan army and LTTE fighting and bombardment resulting in mass displacement (such as in Mutur in 2006[22]) with neither side caring to guarantee the safety of Muslims. Moreover, after the suspicious death of Ashraff in a helicopter accident in 2000, Sri Lankan Muslim parties have been in disarray, constantly splintering among different factions and coalition partners.[23]

Northern Muslims

In discussing Muslim ethnicity in Sri Lanka it is telling that I have not hitherto been able to discuss Northern Muslims hitherto; this shows their marginalization within the larger Muslim political community. In the story of Tamil Muslim relations in the war zone, eastern stories and concerns have consistently dominated. Indeed, articles that discuss Muslim identity in Sri Lanka mention the eviction of Northern Muslims as an adjunct to discussions about eastern Muslims (McGilvray 1998), and mention only two regional blocs as of significance: Southern Muslim elites and Eastern Muslims (Ismail 1995).

Muslims from the north possess neither the numerical strength of the east coast Muslims nor the historical dominance of urban southern elites. The only northern district to have numerical strength is Mannar province, 26 percent Muslim. The question of a "place of their own" is also thus more heightened amongst northern Muslims. However, while Muslims only formed 5 percent of the total population of the north, they were significant minorities nonetheless; the Mannar district is given its distinctive character within the Northern Province by its large Roman Catholic population, Muslim community, and sacred Catholic and Muslim sites (*Talaimannar*). Jaffna Town's Moor Street complex was famously part of the town with its distinct architecture and history. With the exception of a few Muslim-only villages in Mannar district, Muslim communities lived in mixed ethnic villages; thus Muslims and Tamils were not only well integrated but direct neighbors. Thus their ideas of minority relations do not stress the imperatives of numerical strength (as do east coast Muslims) or harmony through coexisting Tamil and Muslim villages, but more general rights for minorities irrespective of numbers. Consequently, northern Muslim issues very often have been elided under discussion of east coast Muslim concerns, a point Northern Muslims resent considerably. The following sections seek to rectify this gap through detailing Northern Muslim stories of their former life in the northern districts and their lives in the refugee settlements as the displaced, clearing space for those who have been aptly called by Hasbullah (1996) "Sri Lanka's forgotten people."

Ahathi! (Refugee)

One day five years ago, the blow fell on our people in the north. . . . Without any warning and without any kind of charge or accusation against our people, the LTTE announced that every single Muslim man, woman, and child must leave their homes and go out of the province. They were ordered to leave their possessions behind. All their money and jewellery and household goods had to be left behind. If anyone disobeyed the order, the penalty was to be death.[24]

Nachiya was standing at the door of her house in Jaffna with her young children when the LTTE cadre came. Amina was a five-year-old playing and eating mangos with her brother in her house in Kilinochchi when she remembers seeing her parents crying, "but what they were crying for we didn't know.

The next-door Tamil people were coming, crying and then leaving, why are they crying, where we are going . . . we didn't know." Separated by two generations and two districts, Nachiya and Amina share in their individual and collective story of Eviction, a moment of becoming. They became in October 1990 *ahathi* (refugee) and Northern Muslims as they described themselves, and in the parlance of international law, IDPs (Internally Displaced Persons).[25] I refer to them as IDPs and as *ahathi* refugee depending on the context.

In 1990 the five districts of the Northern Province contained 75 distinct Muslim settlements with more than 75,000 Muslims, around 100 mosques, and 48 government schools with a majority of Muslim children. In October, the LTTE announced by loudspeaker in the five districts of the north—Kilinochchi, Mullaithivu, Mannar, Vavuniya, and Jaffna—that all Muslims living within the Northern Province must leave within 24 to 48 hours. The timing of the eviction announcement varied from 15 October in the Chavakachcheri section of the Jaffna Peninsula to 30 October in Jaffna Town. Here I give a brief picture of events in Mannar and Jaffna.

In Mannar Island, the LTTE had already begun to harass the Muslim population, and announced on 24 October that all Muslims must report to the LTTE office and leave on 28 October. Despite protests by a delegation of local Tamils and Catholic clergy and a purported extension of stay to November, on 26 October the LTTE sealed off the large village of Erukkalampiddy and all dealings between Tamils and Muslims were forbidden. Muslims from four villages were assembled on a beach and left without food, water, shelter, or sanitation facilities and forced to make their journey out of the North. On the Mannar mainland, the LTTE announced on 25 October that Muslims must surrender their vehicles, fuel, and electrical items, register with the LTTE office on the 26th, and leave. The limit set in Mannar was five travel bags per family, one gold sovereign, and 2000 rupees. They were then checked at Madhu and Pandivitrichchan, where cash and any jewelry above official limits were removed and receipts given. At the final checkpoint in Vavuniya, further items were removed despite guarantees about possessions. Most of the 38,000 Mannar Muslims evicted from the mainland and island went to the Kalpitiya district, 60 miles south of their homes.

There were close to 15,000 expelled Jaffna Muslims. In Jaffna Town, Muslims were summoned to Osmanii College grounds on 30 October for a 7:30 a.m. meeting and told to leave by noon. They were only allowed to take some limited possessions and 500 rupees. Jaffna Muslims' route through the town was carefully mapped out and took them through LTTE checkpoint after checkpoint where they were searched and stripped of their possessions ranging from land deeds, jewelry, electrical goods, and bicycles to thermoses. Thirty-five rich businessmen in Jaffna were held for ransom, as were other rich individuals in other districts (UTHR 1991). Jaffna Muslims had the longest route: they came through the land route to government-controlled Vavuniya, where most were transported to Puttalam district. Sixty-five thousand of the evicted Muslims ended up in Puttalam district, in the Puttalam and Kalpitiya divisions The north had been ethnically cleansed. By November 1990 a new population of displaced people called "Northern Muslims" emerged.

A survey by the northern Muslim NGO RAAF (Research and Action Forum for Social Development) in 1991 to record facts and possessions taken for future legal cases attempted to calculate the financial loss of the population. The losses are staggering. The final calculation puts the collective loss at around U.S. $110 million (Mohideen 2004) of residential properties, commercial and industrial establishments, religious institutions, agricultural lands, gold and jewelry, livestock, and so on. One of the most common things people tell you in Puttalam is that they all arrived with nothing. The Eviction had a tremendous leveling effect, as more or less the whole population was impoverished.

The Eviction order had come all the way from the top leadership, and many local LTTE cadres were caught by surprise. I heard stories of cadres who boarded themselves up in their houses so they would not have to do the eviction. I heard one man's story of the young LTTE cadre he had known all his life crying as he told the family to go. In some places cadres were moved from their local area to other locations so they would not have to evict their neighbors. One man from Mannar told me "we did not recognize the faces of those who came to evict us." The LTTE obviously did fear that its cadres could potentially disobey the Eviction order. In Jaffna, eastern cadres (Karikalan group) were brought to execute the Eviction.

The reaction from the local Tamil community was also one of shock and surprise. There was no indication that it was the result of communal tensions between the two communities. There is no evidence of Tamil civilian collusion. Since then Tamils have remained silent, refusing to outwardly condemn the Eviction, though privately most northern Tamils I interviewed spoke of it with discomfort. It was thus a decision to forcibly remove a whole community without any attempt to legitimize it through any popular feeling. The Eviction was a comprehensive LTTE-only military operation and no reason was ever offered.

One popular supposition is that the LTTE, faced with the numerically and politically stronger eastern Muslim minority, decided as a warning to evict the

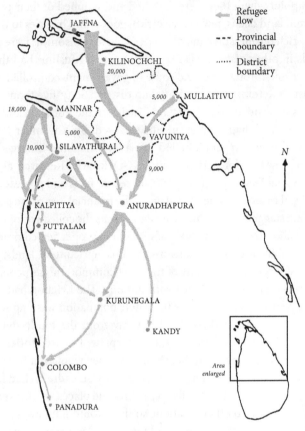

Figure 2. Routes taken by Muslim refugees, 26–30 October 1990. Courtesy of
Dr. Shahul Hasbullah.

much smaller and more politically vulnerable Muslim minority in the north.
In Jaffna, some Muslim men were told that the Eviction was happening because of problems in the east and they were being evacuated for their own
protection, which angered and confused them, Rajeeb (Jaffna) told me:

> Karikalan came from Batticaloa (the East). I don't know what was going
> on there, but it wasn't the same in Jaffna. He wasn't over us. When we
> heard the news, and when we started walking, we came through the sea-
> shore. Tamil people came out crying and hanging onto us and saying we
> shouldn't go. They said "this is your home, don't go" but we had to leave.

Many Tamils were told by the LTTE that the Muslim community could not be felt to reliably belong to a Tamil polity, and could, if not now, maybe in the future be a "fifth column."

By this act of ethnic cleansing, in November the north became fully ethnically Tamil, the first plank in the LTTE's renewed war for Tamil Eelam, the promised Tamil homeland. The Eviction stood as a guarantee that Eelam was for Tamils only. That the Eviction occurred without popular support and with checks against its own cadres' disobedience suggests very clearly that Tamil Eelam as a practical possibility was processual rather than primordial. This was an act that sought to create its own reason post facto.

Anton Balasingam, the now deceased LTTE political ideologue, at the onset of the 2002 peace process admitted in a public statement that the eviction had been "a blunder" on the part of the LTTE and that the Muslims were indeed "our brothers." However, despite this seeming apology, in 2002 less than 10 percent of evicted Muslims were actually able to return, as the LTTE simultaneously refused to guarantee that the Muslims would not be evicted again or recognize Muslim political rights as a minority. When I was there in 2003, many Muslims had at the beginning of the 2002 peace process attempted to find work in the north and travel between the refugee camps and the north, but abandoned this after imposition of a tax of up to 10 percent on profits by the LTTE and harassment by LTTE cadres. However, now in 2011 now that the LTTE has been destroyed (in 2009), thousands are contemplating or have already returned.

Retelling the Eviction

Those times . . . we can't tell about that kind of life. Now when I think about it I have to laugh. When I think of it I feel frightened. That's why we have to guard our lives carefully. It should never happen again. It won't happen again and it should never happen again. They say it won't happen again.

Nazleen trails off. She resumes,

These thoughts will always come again and again. Some things you can forget, some things you can never forget. We think about Tamil people still and their difficulties back home. We were used to them; we all lived together. Only after the Eviction did we think about that.

The Eviction for northern Muslims is truly, in Veena Das's categorization, a "critical event" after which "new modes of action came into being which redefined traditional categories such as codes of purity and honor, the meaning of martyrdom, and the construction of heroic life" (1995: 6). First and foremost, the Eviction created a whole new demographic community. Northern Muslims were "born" in the aftermath of an unthinkably traumatic event that broke one set of communities in the north and created another. Previous to the Eviction, there were no Northern Muslims; there were only Jaffna Muslims, Mannar Muslims, and so on. The term "Northern Muslim" came into currency only after the Eviction and denoted a community traumatically born through it; it gave them an origin in a place, a region after they had lost it. "Northern Muslims" are a community created around (1) common origins in the northern districts of Sri Lanka, (2) a shared collective experience of "the Eviction," and (3) a common experience of internal displacement within refugee camps or as the UNDP called them "welfare centers."

The strength of this collective identification and the density of stories of the Eviction in Puttalam cannot be underestimated. Diverse individuals, families, and villages found that their lives became pulled together in such a way that, even though their pasts were dissimilar and multiple, their futures would be intertwined. Hitherto in this chapter we have traced a more conventional account of ethnic identification from colonial racialization to postcolonial discrimination. However, in the last twenty years ethnic identification continues to transform as ever new stakes and histories that draw together new collectivities come into being. The Eviction is one such major event. It redrew the ethnic map of the north, making it Tamil in a way it had never been before, it tore apart Tamils and Muslims giving them now a history of fissure rather than sometimes uneasy fusion and coexistence, and it created a new community of people with a common genesis. Muslims from the north had become Northern Muslims.

Nazleen was only one of many who spoke of the Eviction as something that should never happen again. She articulated this together with the uncertainty that indeed perhaps it could happen again, that the Eviction could never be forgotten, altering the basic frames of certainty and life itself. The Eviction is the reason, refugees point out, that they became refugees and all their savings, property, homes, and livelihoods were taken away from them. They told me that if Northern Muslims did not tell these stories, then no one else would. While there was undoubted reticence on the part of parents to express fully their feelings to their children and me, I found that there was

not a house where the larger story of the Eviction as personal and social loss
was not narrated. Children too young to have been part of the Eviction would
tell me that their family arrived in Puttalam as a result of being evicted by the
LTTE. Eviction stories form part of a collective story of becoming.

All Eviction stories concentrate on three major themes: the experience of
being expelled from their natal villages and recounting the moment of rupture; the journey; and the experience of arriving with absolutely nothing. I
recorded and listened to countless Eviction stories, here I retell two, both
of which exemplify Jaffna Muslim stories, on which I concentrated in my
research.

Nachiya's Story

I was visiting Amina and her family when I met Nachiya. Amina's mother and
aunt were retelling their journeys from Kilinochchi district when Nachiya
came into the house on her way home from work—coolie labor plucking and
weeding in onion fields. When she heard what I was doing, without prompt-
ing she immediately began to speak into the blazingly hot afternoon. The
other women fell silent to listen to her. Her voice moved sharply between
anger and bitterness, only pausing in the hours that followed to spit her betel
into the pot provided with various expressions of disgust. She brought her
hand up, shaking a single taut finger to make her point, or cradled her forehead with her palm, gestures the other women responded to and I too was
caught up in. The next time I went, she called me to her house, where I sat in
the one-room cadjan leaf-thatched house where all her children and she and
her husband live, separated internally into rooms by strung-up saris. Giving
me tea, she told me that I must also come to lunch at her house and not just
other people's houses. Maybe I could even stay one night with them, she told
me. Her husband and she broke into an argument when I was there and her
little son rolled his eyes drolly at me. I like Nachiya and how she knots her sari
tightly as she speaks and her defiant attitude to the world.

"Is this the house your father's mother built?"

On the 29th of October my relative from Mannar came. He said "How
are things Akka [elder sister]? How are things going? Then he told

us "They will tell you to leave suddenly from Jaffna, when it is I don't
know, you get ready." We thought "as if they are going to tell us something like that in Jaffna!"

Then I'm standing at the shop at about seven o clock washing the
pots when they came around announcing from house to house; "a big
person has asked you to come." They said they wanted us to come to a
meeting. . . . They told us that the man coming would not talk for long.
He would not say much, he would tell us just two sentences. . . . So he
came on his motorcycle and stopped it. "Everyone must leave in two
hours." There was no talk. That's all he told us. He was a big guy in the
Tigers [Karikalan]. Karikalan told us "you must leave in two hours."
Did the motorcycle stop! He didn't get off, he didn't sit on a chair, and
he didn't even stop the motorcycle. The motorcycle was still on start,
he stood up "you have to leave in two hours." That's all he said.

After that then what could we do? We came crying and lamenting.
Then we saw they were coming from house to house asking for things.
I asked them; "is this the house that your father's mother built?" You
have to ask! I am asking them straight, *"is this the house your father's
mother built? Is this the house the leader of the Tigers built? Have you
come all this way to take from us, us who built this house, this threshold,
who brought these things? Now if you want to go and catch a country,
you do that. Take the country. Who would come and ask from people
these things?"* They told me "so you can talk a lot, but there is someone
bigger than us who has come," I said "I don't care, whether there are
six of you or a hundred, it's still a loss to me! If you are doing this then
just wipe us out as a family, you shouldn't do this." They became angry
and demanded that I give them the key. I wouldn't give it to them.
I locked the door. They asked me "what do you have, what kinds of
things?" I told them "you don't need to know such things, we may
have this or that but that is not for you to know" . . . as he watched I
threw the key, holding my children in my hand . . .

So then I went to join him [her husband]. He had been told that
he couldn't go this way, he couldn't go that way and he couldn't go
home. . . . I was coming up to Osmanii College. I said, "come let's go
and get our things, get our certificates." But they wouldn't let us there
either. They wouldn't let us even cross the roads, because they wanted
to take things. After that we couldn't do anything, so we went.

As we were walking, everyone was being stopped. You know those boxes, those crates you get from abroad. At every junction there were six of these boxes. . . . There were three such junctions [lists the junctions]. . . . Jewelry, money, possessions, cycles. Everything was taken. They didn't allow us anything. I had a suitcase of clothing for them [the children]. They asked for it. I put it down. We had money, we had 25,000 there. So we were thinking how to get it. So we were watching them take all the jewelry off people and watching them being put in the boxes. So somehow I took a little of that money and I put it in the hands of my youngest daughter. I kept it with her and then kept quiet. They asked us to take everything off. Two rings I had, by god's grace I was living fine in Jaffna, then my earrings, then the children's earrings, and she (her daughter) was wearing a ring. . . . They took all our jewelry what were we going to do? My man had brought 4 or 5000 rupees from the goat meat business, he had to hand it over straight into their hands.

From Karaithivu there were lorries charging money to take us by the sea route. It was a small lane; it was five rupees for children and ten or fifteen for adults. We took it, five rupees for each child and ten each for me and my man. It was the route where many children fell off and died along there. Then we came to Pooneryn. My man asked me; "Shall we stay here?" Can we stay in Pooneryn? It's their [LTTE] land isn't it! Can one live there? I said, "you stay then I'll take the children." So he came and we went on. . . .

From Pooneryn then we came in lorries. It was so much money. Mother! It was so difficult; it took us four days to get to Vavuniya. God! What difficulties! God only knows the journey. We were so hungry. Then we arrived in Vavuniya, we bought four parcels of food, each parcel was 50 rupees, so we paid 200 rupees. We took four parcels of pumpkin and rice. How those children suffered, without food and water. There was no water, only rainwater. . . . Thinking of the difficulties I could not even raise my head. . . . Then we went to the [Sri Lankan] army camp in Vavuniya. They gave us each a packet of biscuits and tea and asked us what happened. Then they sent us in their lorries to Vavuniya town. There we stayed in a school, then they asked us where we wanted to go and we told them Puttalam.

. . . we came to Puttalam town . . . when the Grama Sevaka[local government] saw us . . . they looked me over, my sari, the way my children looked . . . I went to the well and I washed and washed. . . . Then the people gave us something, biscuits, bananas, powdered milk. . . . Others were looking me over. What am I to do? I am in a worse situation than them, could they not see what situation my children and I were in? There is always competition.

I asked someone whether I could go for coolie work, and then went to work and took a house for rent. We couldn't stay in the school. Then after two months we got another house, we lived there for four years. I needed a house. Whatever work I did, even if I didn't eat, I needed some peace of mind, somewhere for me to sleep, for the children to rest, to live in freedom. If people gave me things, others would say, why are they giving you things, you who have taken a house for rent? There is always competition. Then we came and built this hut/ *kottil*. How many difficulties!

Nachiya's story drew together themes of many different stories. While I have greatly shortened her account, in fact telling the story of the journey, the places passed through, the privations of every step was critical to Eviction stories. The painstaking detail of the journey condenses all the emotion of the Eviction, perhaps because of the bleakness and sparseness of the Eviction order. Stories like Nachiya's often begin without genealogy. Muslims could not find a reason for their Eviction. The lack of communal tension prior to the eviction and their long histories of coexisting with Tamils meant that there were no signs, no signals that they could find in the past to explain the present. Nachiya had rebuffed her cousin because the idea that they would be asked to leave Jaffna was so unbelievable. The Eviction order itself was summary. Karikalan did not even, Jaffna refugees recount, pause to explain in any detail what was happening to them. After the order was summarily announced, Muslims found cadres within hours ready to supervise their eviction.

While the Eviction emerges in stories as profound rupture, it is rupture of a particular kind. Let us return to Nachiya's questioning of the LTTE cadre:

Is this the house your father's mother built? Is this the house the leader of the Tigers built? Have you come all this way to take from us, us who built this house, this threshold, who brought these things? Now if you want to go and catch a country, you do that. Take the country. Who would come and ask from people these things?

Nachiya's questions capture the way in which the idea of the "local village"/
ur was embedded in many Eviction stories as both the stage for LTTE action
and the ideology and refuge that defied them. In her story "the country" and
"the house," "the LTTE" and "ordinary people" become counterposed. It was
the village that was the stage for the Eviction. It was in the common spaces of
the village that Muslims were summoned and it was in well-integrated Tamil
and Muslim villages that Muslim departure was visibly paraded. Muslims
were ripped out of the social fabric of the local in a few hours. The looting of
houses, checkpoints, and personal body searches emphasize the invasion of
the intimate. This is one way in which the Eviction as a foundational event is
seen as complete rupture, break, and crisis.

Eviction stories also named the LTTE as the primary perpetrators. Tamil
neighbors are commonly represented as passive watchers, sometimes weep-
ing but standing silently by, also a potent comment on the failure of the local.
The clarity and precision of this accusation against the LTTE and the differentiation between Tamils and the LTTE is present in every single Eviction
story I heard. As a result, the local can also be a potent symbol of defiance as
in Nachiya's statement. Representations of "the local" construct a harmonious
locale before the moment of the Eviction. These images are possible because
the Eviction both happened in the space of the locale and simultaneously
did not happen at the level of the local; it was enacted by LTTE cadres, not
neighbors. Thus the home and the neighborhood were represented as places
of dense sociality united by neighborhood ties, and the moment of rupture
was a moment of invasion. The relationship of belonging to a land that is now
only for Tamils, ethnically marked and not linguistically marked and shared,
came from the outside, defined by a macro-force, the LTTE. Thus stories related how everyday relations were put into question by military and nationalist decisions but also became an idiom that defies the potency of such claims.
Nachiya asks the cadre, "Did the leader of the Tigers build this house?" This
stress on the rupture of the local from the outside by the LTTE, the imagination of a rupture itself provided the hope for refugees that one day, at the stage
of neighborhood and home, relations could be social again.

This idiom of home, villages, and neighbors defined by everyday living
as opposed to the LTTE, provided in Puttalam a powerful story of loss and
future renewal and has become a potent way of structuring belonging in the
present and in the construction of a story of future return as I discuss in
Chapter 4. An emphasis on the rupture of the Eviction as a rupture of the

everyday life of now idealized villages is critical to understanding Northern Muslim identity as it unfolds into the future. However, this was always
couched and understood as material and concrete losses, as Tareek's story
illustrates. Tareek, formerly a tailor in Jaffna, was one of the most irrepress-
ible and vehement of the men I encountered in my first public gathering in
the refugee camps.

Tareek's Story

Little sister, do you want to know how we arrived here? My wife came
with her blouse torn and her sari streaming behind her.

When we were living in Jaffna, the Indian army burned our house
there. When the Indian army came, there were 150 cadjan houses.
We left for work in the morning and then they burned the houses
all down. Then we became displaced. We saw our homes burn. We
saw our houses razed to the ground. We asked "why"—apparently the
Indian army had seen some houses at the front with some posters of
Prabhakaran so they'd burned the whole line of houses. . . . We were
living in Osmanii College. The women slept inside, the men outside.
The Indian army took away four Tamils and Muslims for four days.
There was also heavy firing, so we couldn't leave the college.

[Then] we were in Jaffna when they asked us to come to a meeting—they said men only—so all the men went to the meeting. Two
people came from the LTTE, from the Karikalan group; they said that
there had been trouble in Kathankuddy in Batticaloa for Muslims [the
East][26] so they, the LTTE, in order to protect the Muslims of Jaffna,
had decided to ask them to leave for their own safety. This was the
excuse they gave. They said "you have to go or we will shoot you, take
whatever you can carry."

People believed you could take what you could carry, but at every
junction the LTTE took things from us. That time, my eldest son was
not even one, they took even the milk packets that we had for my son.
As they did, they told us "if you ever talk about this, we will shoot
you." In the end, we had only the clothes we were wearing. I had two
unmarried younger sisters. They need things to get married—clothes,
jewelry—things we'd saved over the years—we put all these things
in a trunk so we could take them—I told them to go on ahead and

returned home to get their things. There were LTTE people standing in the door of the house, they said "if you have left the house you
can't come in again." They took my shirt and pushed me out. I went to
talk to somebody important [in the LTTE]—they said "you go; we'll
send the trunk later." The trunk never arrived. In the end, my younger
sisters had not even the jewelry they were wearing. They even took
earrings from their ears. For us Muslims, it's a big thing when these
young men are touching our women's ears and necks to take the jewelry off. When the women cadres searched our young women, they
took them behind a screen. God knows what happened. Inside, they
took all the money. . . . We came here with bare pockets. That's like
everybody behind us. Even those who had things from abroad, or had
been abroad and brought things back had to leave them all.

Tareek's recounting of pre-Eviction displacement and Indian army action
is familiar. The 1980s had seen the massive rise of violence and war in the
northern districts. Cycles of displacement and violence were becoming familiar experiences. Many Muslims I met around my age discussed our mutual
memories of curfew and bombing in the north. A few told me of how after arriving in Puttalam they continued to write poems and stories in school about
their wartime experiences, completely incomprehensible to children growing
up on the other side of the war zone border in Puttalam. Long biographical interviews of Northern Muslims revealed many commonalities between
noncombatant Muslims and Tamils in their pre-1990 war experience. There
were of course crucial differences; while a few Muslims did join the militant
movements, it was not at all to the same extent as Tamils. But I heard repeatedly that Muslims from the north had been not unlike Tamils in being
broadly supportive of the militant movements in the 1980s. As one man told
me, "we supported them like everybody else, we also gave food and some
of our young people joined them and the other movements." Some women
recounted surreptitious cooking for young militant men. These stories of discrimination and war against Tamil-speaking people from the north had also
been part of Muslim biographies.

The Eviction severed Muslim experiences from a general history of the
north. It threw them outside these stories, and ethnicity has differentiated
between the kinds of wartime stories that Tamils and Muslims can tell. Muslims were now left with only one story to tell, their making through forced
expulsion. This is why in this book I insist on the Eviction as a story about the

making of the north, to restore the history of Muslims back into an account of the transformation of the north through the war.[27] The Eviction is a story of the north and how both Tamils and Muslims were made.

Tareek's story, however, does not just allude to the wartime prehistory of the Eviction and the stripping of these commonalities and histories from Tamils and Muslims. It also captures a very particular story of socioeconomic impoverishment: the stripping of dowry goods. These were expropriated from all Muslims, but for Jaffna Muslims this is a story of how women were stripped of jewelry and goods as they went through the checkpoints. All Jaffna Eviction stories stress the stripping of land deeds and jewelry from women at the checkpoints. Many possessions were taken, people had to leave the entire contents of their houses, the tools of their trades, open shops, but again and again stories come back to the loss of land deeds and jewelry.

Northern Muslims, like northern Tamils, gave both movable and immovable property as dowry: land, jewelry, and cash (as donation). Gold jewelry is also in Jaffna "woman's property," not only necessary in dowry but also, after marriage, capital to be sold or pawned, and to be melted down for children's puberty rituals and in dowry. Stripping Muslim women and their children bare at the checkpoints meant the cadres were stripping their bodies of connection and regrowth in the land where they were living. The relationship to land in Jaffna has always been mediated through the relationship to dowry and thus in relation to women (see detailed discussion in Chapter 5).

One woman told me how her sister had been forced to remove all her jewelry, but when it came to her necklace and ring given to her in marriage she had started crying and saying she would not leave. Their cousin had told her repeatedly he would buy her some more jewelry, but she refused to go until they gave her ring and necklace back. Finally, one of the LTTE cadres agreed, and she had to plunge her hands into a crate filled with rings to find hers. When she described it, the woman was laughing incredulously; she asked me to imagine these crates filled with different types of gold jewelry and the wealth contained at one checkpoint. Her sister went on with her journey with her jewelry. Not all were so lucky. I heard how LTTE cadres had taken gold chains and childhood bangles from their children's necks, hands, and feet, and people's attempts to hide jewels in thermoses and sewn into their children's clothes. As Nazleen told me fiercely, "they didn't get them all, there are some who got them through, they didn't get everything."

As Tareek says, refugees arrived in Puttalam "with bare hands." The

Eviction had an immense leveling effect; economic impoverishment was almost total. The consequences of this and how refugees remade their lives are fully explored in the next chapter. However, economic impoverishment in relation to dowry goods also carried a more symbolic and psychological charge. Belonging to a place is also about the possibility of regrowth and renewal. In Jaffna, settlement and belonging are also about being able to circulate and acquire land through dowry. Some of the Jaffna Muslim men I interviewed went back to casual work in Jaffna, but reinvestment in Jaffna as home can only come at the moment their whole family goes back and they are able to marry their daughters within Jaffna. This is also why many Muslims, even though they were not able to press their claims to land in Jaffna in the Tiger courts, continued to refuse to sell their dowry property there. It was the last link, even if symbolic, with home. It was the ability to make continuity in the future within Jaffna that the stripping of land and dowry property endangered. As Tareek says of his sisters, "They need things to get married—clothes, jewelry—things we'd saved over the years."

These objects and land carefully collected over the years were about imagining quotidian futures, now overwhelmed by an event that could not have been predicted. In the Eviction, all these savings, symbolic and material, the bridge between residence and family in the past and making residence and family in the future, were wiped out in one day. While Chapter 4 moves to consider how this and the long-term consequences of the Eviction are lived through in Puttalam, here I point to the way these concerns are introduced and staged through the effects and accounts of the Eviction and a future the Eviction has brought into being.

Becoming Northern Muslim

When we lose certain people, when we are dispossessed from a place or a community . . . maybe when we undergo what we do, something about who we are is revealed, something that delineates the ties we have to others, that shows us that these ties constitutes what we are, ties or bonds that compose us. It is not as if an "I" exists independently over here and then simply loses a "you" over there, especially if the attachment to "you" is part of what composes who "I" am. If I lose you, under these conditions, then I not only mourn the loss, but I become inscrutable to myself. Who "am" I without you? (Butler 2004: 22)

Eviction stories stress a complete rupture between the past and the present, and most importantly, a rupture between their former homes and their putative futures. This rupture was of both person and place. Nazleen's hesitation in an earlier quotation, "They say it won't happen again," is a small pause in speech that represents an abyss of meaning. Once the Eviction happened, it could never be forgotten and its suspicion seeps through newly made everyday relations (Das 2000). Northern Muslims emerge in a world where it is possible for Northern Muslims to exist. They, and the manner of the world in which they do not belong, were born together.[28] Being Northern Muslim means an entirely different disposition to the world, to home, to place, to person. In Puttalam, displacement and the Eviction posit the Eviction as a massive crisis through which all meanings are now defined. The next chapter explores exactly how a new everyday reality is lived in the refugee camps, and the nature of this new disposition to the world conditioned as it is by the experience of being internally rather than externally displaced amongst those, Puttalam Tamils, Muslims, and Sinhalese, whom one looks like but feels completely different from. Here, Judith Butler's insights into the impossibility of a self-sufficient subjectivity and her question "Who 'am' I without you?" are especially pertinent in thinking through the Eviction as an event of the north. Who are Tamils without Muslims and Muslims without Tamils? This is a question that, as I have attempted to demonstrate throughout this chapter, has been continuous with a history of ethnicization of social and political life in Sri Lanka. Muslims are far from marginal from the story of the ethnic conflict in Sri Lanka; they are the hidden other side of Tamil nationalism, the intimate but refused other. This shadowing of each other, while often ignored, is at the heart of everyday life in the north and east.

What does it mean that relations between Tamils and Muslims have broken down? Eastern Sri Lanka presents a different history and paradigm, as McGilvray's (2008) account shows. In the case of northern Muslims, relationships and coexistence with former Tamil neighbors are emphasized. Unlike those in eastern Sri Lanka, most northern Muslims lived in mixed Tamil-Muslim villages, even as they clustered together. Nazleen had not as yet visited her former home in Jaffna, but she had heard stories from others who had returned:

Everyone says, you can't see Jaffna, it's too much sorrow. And also in Jaffna, so many Tamil people have left for Canada, France, UK, family after family have left.

She had recently seen a video another family had made of the Moor Street complex where most of Jaffna's Muslims had lived clustered together,

> Moor Street . . . you can't even see that we lived there. Where we lived in Muslim College road, we were encircled by Tamil people and we lived in the middle. There was always light. Now that road, to look at it on the video, it is like looking at ghosts.

This image of being encircled, separate but together, is constantly stressed by Muslims, as we shall explore in the next chapter. Life in Puttalam's refugee camps was filled with reference to idealized other neighbors who loomed in a romanticized past of who we used to be. Yet this was also a world that everyone knew had vanished, even if this easy coexistence without discrimination against Muslims had not existed in the way that now was being narrativized. Tamils too were leaving Jaffna. When Muslims visited former homes again after the 2002 ceasefire time, many of these homes were being squatted in by displaced persons like themselves. Moreover, meeting the Tamils one knew again was sometimes emotional and touching but at the same time it constantly opened up the wound of the Eviction because it also made it clear that Muslims did not belong in the north any more. The Eviction had altered history, and now Tamils and Muslims had to confront each other across this abyss.

I finish here with the story of a letter sent by an old Tamil man to a Jaffna Muslim family in Puttalam in 2002. I had met the daughter Shafiqa, exactly my age, now married with a child. When I asked Shafiqa whether she remembered her home, she responded immediately with, "How can I forget? My first day at school, my friends, our house, the teachers who taught me and when we all celebrated [the Tamil Hindu festival] Thaipongal. How can you forget these things?" Shafiqa asked me if I really wanted to ask her about these things. She was not an educated and learned person, she told me; she could only tell me so much. Once, she said, she had been very good in her studies. Since she came here, she had not been able to study and all these things had gone. She had written a poem here in Puttalam when she first came, about her experiences. She tried to remember, struggling with her memory; she repeated a few phrases to me, but it wouldn't come. She kept on shaking her head in frustration and we looked at each other while she was at the point of tears. I asked her if she had written anything else, or, if she kept on writing, and she shook her head in exasperation at me: "How can I? I am up looking after the child all morning and cooking and cleaning, I don't even have time to think." She pointed out that my question arose because I was not married myself.

Shafiqa's happy memories of Jaffna and her childhood center around an old Tamil man who had helped raise her and her brother as children. For twelve years after the Eviction nothing passed between neighbors. In 2002, after the ceasefire, a letter came carried by many hands to Shafiqa's family from the old Tamil man. The letter told of his own displacement in the 1995 Exodus and his recent return to Jaffna. He too was now an IDP living in a cadjan hut; the Muslim family should, he wrote, come home to where they belonged so they could be neighbors again. Her parents had made a trip north to visit him, but Shafiqa, married with a child in Puttalam, tells me that though she wants to return, she cannot return now. When I ask her what she wants, she picks up her child and says that she wants for the child to have a good future. I ask what she wants for herself, and she turns her face away from me and her daughter, and says nothing. The Eviction has altered everything.

In the next chapter, I turn to this dilemma that Shafiqa and others face. In this journey to remake one's life after the Eviction, new senses of self, memory, kin, and homeliness along with anxieties, fears, and hopes are emerging. The real question, as I explore now, is not who Northern Muslims were, but who are they becoming?

CHAPTER FOUR

—————

Becoming of This Place?
Northern Muslim Futures After Eviction

Meditate that this came about
I commend these words to you
Carve them in your hearts
At home, in the street,
Going to bed, rising;
Repeat them to your children,
    Or may your house fall apart
    May illness impede you,
    May your children turn their faces from you
—Primo Levi, *Survival in Auschwitz* (1996: 11)

Farook and I were in a Jaffna Muslim majority refugee camp in the Puttalam district one evening in 2003. We had arrived there late, dusk was approaching fast, and the camp rang with the busy sounds of the women beginning their household labor for the evening. The camp leader explained this to us, asking me to come another time. Looking at me, while Farook explained my purpose in the camps, the leader had the same question for me that all the refugees had begun with "what was my *sonta ur*?" By *sonta ur* he meant my "real/ancestral" home, where I was "really from" rather than where I lived at any given time. *Sontam* itself is a term that denotes and mutually implicates ownership and kinship. I knew and recognized the terms of the question, not only because I had been answering it continually through my time in Puttalam, but because I knew how to ask that question too. When I told him that it was Nallur, Jaffna, he looked at me again intently in recognition of our shared home. The road I grew up in, as it gets into the heart of Jaffna Town, ribbons into the famous Moor Street complex, where the large majority of Jaffna's 15,000 or so Muslims had lived.[1] He turned me to face outward from the camp with him. Beyond the half glimpsed abandoned salt fields, was a distant black palmyra tree splitting the sky open. The palmyra is the famed symbol of the Jaffna peninsula, a familiar sight to anyone who has grown up there and the symbol most often used to represent it. Pointing at the tree he told me, "they call this S—— B camp, we call it the one palmyra tree camp. Every morning we wake up and look at it and we remember our homes and we remember what we have lost."

This was not just a poignant story of loss; it was also about the kinds of objects in which loss could be read. It was a story of internal displacement and the physical and psychic landscapes of proximities. For internally displaced people such as Northern Muslims, there was, and the palmyra tree was the symbol of this, no absolute separation from the object of their memory. They lived in the peripheries of landscapes they once knew and still knew. Puttalam and Kalpitiya in the northwestern province were not so dissimilar in physical appearance from the northern districts with which they are contiguous. The palmyra tree was a distinct reminder of how close home was, and yet how different Puttalam was, even though it shared much of the same landscape. The uncanny unfamiliarity of the seemingly familiar physical landscape thus also mapped an alienated social and interior landscape. Puttalam district itself was highly mixed, with large numbers of Muslims. Articulating difference from others, Tamil, Sinhalese, and especially Puttalam Muslims had to be on the basis of practices that were not exotically other, but had to be put to work in such a way that differences not apparent to outsiders could seem to those inside as crucial and cataclysmic. These had to sufficiently express the alienation of the like us, but not us.

Proximate displacement, as is common in civil wars, creates very different ways of inhabiting loss from that of external displacement. Research I had carried out with externally displaced Tamils in Toronto, Canada, immediately stood in stark contrast (Thiranagama n.d). For those who have left the country, "home" can remain in a static time left at the point of departure, with tantalizing scents, memories, sounds of another landscape markedly different from the one they inhabit. This is highlighted in Bahloul's (1996) *The Architecture of Memory* centered on her maternal family, the Senoussi' and their memories of their former home Dar Refayil, shared between Jews and

Muslims, in colonial Algeria. The monograph itself is focused on the quotidian practices that become memorialized when taking the house as a frame, but it also points out how the geographical and temporal estrangement of the Senoussi' from Algeria means that remembered quotidian practices, while constantly evoked in family gatherings, have become symbolic in the move to France. Remembrance and the object of remembrance have been irreversibly separated, and "the past urban landscape has disappeared entirely from the sensory experience . . . memory has taken over the space left empty in sensory experience. [I]t is a distant and intangible relation to the past" (Bahloul 1996: 132). In contrast, Northern Muslims' geographical proximity meant that their past landscape had not disappeared from sensory experience but remained just on the horizon. Furthermore, whenever they could, in ceasefires, they visited their homes and saw them decay over time. They lived close enough to their homes to note the work of time in them, but too far in time and space to be politically welcomed back into those homes. Both place and people were engaged in simultaneous processes of transforming and becoming, both not entirely of their own volition.

Here I trace the ways internal displacement (made through this contiguity and haunted proximity) created new social, moral, and physical landscapes. In doing so I focus on how particular kinds of spaces were imagined and reimagined within others, alongside how people traced the temporal process of becoming something else. I am inspired by Bakhtin's (1992) exposition of the connectedness of space-time, because, for dislocated people, time and space are critical measurements of belonging, as indices of loss. Loss itself provides historicity (Carsten 2007). People continually discuss what five years, ten years, and thirteen years away from home mean. Five years may not have meant the same thing in Jaffna as in Puttalam. Here space thickens time and gives it flesh (Bakhtin 1992). We accrete relations in places. Relationships accrued, denied, and allowed in Puttalam district for those who arrived as "people out of place" were seen as of a completely different kind from past relationships in the north. I take displacement itself as an orientation, a way of inhabiting the world, a chronotope (1992).

This chapter is about the human problems of "begetting and belonging" (Spencer 1990b: 253), as they are reconfigured in the aftermath of violent and foundational events such as the Eviction. I examine the material ways in which Muslims from the north are becoming Northern Muslims and the ongoing dilemmas produced by the struggle to make new persons and places. The chapter points to the centrality of ideas of *ur*, ordinary understandings of a particular notion of home/natal village, in restructuring new residence and ideas about proper sociality in displacement. Former *ur* structure material residence in Puttalam, provide the basis of differentiation between *ahathi/* refugee Muslims and local Puttalam people including Puttalam Muslims, and provide for internal differentiation among refugees on the basis of different *ur*s in the North. Stories about *ur* also map ideas about sociality, proper mixing and intimacy, and thus the way these emerge as concerns about women's bodies in the refugee camp. I track the transformation of lives, through the war, as people habituate themselves as permanently displaced.

Moreover, this becoming is itself structured generationally and temporally. If, as is the case for Northern Muslims, different homes/*ur* are felt to produce different persons, then what happens when children and parents come from different homes? The chapter examines through the constantly open landscapes of return, the possibilities of forgetting home/*ur*, as it is mapped onto internal structures within the family and different generations. I discuss how the question of return comes to divide generations, and how these generations are marked by different attempts to negotiate perceived disjunctures between modes of transmitting personhood.

As with all the chapters in this book, we begin anew, with a new stance on the world, a new habitation. Yet houses, kin, violence, and generation thread these stories together again and again. The memorialization of the Eviction and the creation of future generations that did not forget were the stories and injunctions first repeated within the home. It was precisely about and in one's children and one's houses where, in the absence of official sponsorship, memory could become subject formation. In this chapter, more than any other, I take on the subjects—internal displacement, breakdown of relations between Tamils and Muslims, and concrete material dilemmas of refashioning lives, marriages, and children—that an ethnography of the Sri Lankan civil war can avoid only at its own peril. Accounts of a longer running ethnic conflict figure only Tamils and Sinhalese, Tamil militants and the state, but this war has produced the profound, often ordered displacement of Tamils and Muslims as its primary subjective experience. This chapter is about that displacement and its consequences.

Living with Your Own People

In November 1990, after the forced Eviction of the 70,000–80,000 northern Muslims from the north by the LTTE, IDPs (Internally Displaced Persons)

poured into Puttalam district. Some Northern Muslims went south to Colombo, some to other areas in the northwest, but the large majority arrived
in the northwestern district of Puttalam and settled in hurriedly constructed
refugee camps in the Puttalam and Kalpitiya divisions. In 2006, the Sri
Lankan government recorded that 63,145 persons still lived in 141 welfare
centers, while others had taken the opportunity to move into settlements.[2]
Northern Muslims were officially designated IDPs by the government and
UNHCR, but they frequently referred to themselves as *ahathi* (refugee). To
that end I use IDP and refugee interchangeably depending on the context, not
in reference to legal categorization.

In 1990, the refugees were welcomed with open arms to Puttalam district. The mayor provided transport from Vavuniya to Puttalam; local people
sheltered and fed the refugees. Puttalam district itself had a large and visible
Muslim presence. IDP arrival changed Puttalam's demography considerably:
the percentage of Sri Lankan Muslims rose by 8.8 percent from the 1981 to
the last census carried out in 2001 (the next is in 2011).[3] In 2001, the Puttalam
district was 73.8 percent Sinhalese, 6.9 percent Sri Lankan Tamils, 0.3 percent Indian Tamils, 0.3 percent others, and 18.7 percent Sri Lankan Muslims
(Consortium of Humanitarian refugees 2003). Whereas Sinhalese are obviously the large majority of the district, settlement patterns provided a different ambiance to the area. The majority of the Sinhalese lived in outlying rural
areas; the Puttalam urban area was 67.4 percent Sri Lankan Muslims and only
18.7 percent Sinhalese and 12.3 percent Sri Lankan Tamils. In the Puttalam
and Kalpitiya divisions where the IDPs settled, Sri Lankan Muslims were 58.7
and 57.9 percent of the population respectively.[4] These figures mean that in
the areas where the IDPs live, the spoken language on the street was Tamil
and the physical presence was overwhelmingly Muslim.

By the time I first visited the camps in 2003, relationships between locals
and refugees had soured significantly. An influx of around 62,000–65,000
refugees had dramatically changed the political and social economy of a historically underprivileged and economically stagnant area, albeit one that experienced a brief period of agricultural intensification after the IDP arrival
(Shanmugaratnam 2000). Locals began to resent the IDPs and their seeming
"well-off status," receiving rations in a desperately poor region.[5] These are
the classic fault-lines of refugee camps set up in impoverished areas.[6] There
were clashes between the host community and the refugee settlements,[7] some
violent. IDPs also complained of continual discrimination in the administrative and bureaucratic structures of Puttalam. Despite the influx of a new

Tamil-speaking population, the bureaucracy had remained rigidly Sinhala-speaking and Puttalam locals of all ethnicities were Sinhala-competent. unlike Northern Muslims, who tended to be only conversant in Tamil and bitterly resented the language discrimination they faced. They found themselves unable to read their own identity cards, issued to them written in Sinhalese instead of Tamil and Sinhalese, which Tamil and Muslim minorities are entitled to in Sri Lanka. Furthermore, most refugees were registered as locals not in Puttalam district but in their former homes, so money allocated by the central government for them went to their former homes and not to Puttalam (Brun 2003: 377).[8] In some areas of Puttalam district, only more recently have IDP men been allowed to drive three wheelers and engage in trades such as bakeries, and government service remained largely off limits to IDPs (CPA 2003a; see also CPA 2003b).

Distinctions between the "locals"/host community and IDPs, however, went both ways. IDPs themselves argued for social and moral distinctions between "locals" and *ahathis* even across ethnic lines, with Puttalam and *ahathi* Muslims also divided into local/refugee. For refugees, however, not all Muslims were of the same kind. Being with "your own people" meant primarily being with other Northern Muslims, preferably those from the same district as yourself. Intermarrying between Puttalam Muslims and Northern Muslims has become common over the last 20 years, but it is not openly advocated. Northern Muslims also attempted to differentiate themselves clearly from Puttalam Muslims, whom they saw as part of the local "host" community. IDPs represented themselves as more "sophisticated" and "refined"; they talked of being more "educated" than local Muslims. In 2008, as my friend Nazima took me through a settlement with many new Jaffna Muslim houses, she talked about the style of the new houses as "Jaffna style" with large verandas, pillars, and open doors, very different, she suggested disparagingly, from Puttalam Muslims, who built "dark and small houses" with indirect entrances like the other Puttalam locals. Northern Muslims drew clear status distinctions between themselves and locals. At the same time, Puttalam Muslims complained about the lack of piety among northern Muslims and the seeming laxness of their control over women. When IDPs arrived, the young girls who were accustomed in their northern homes to walk to evening tuition classes and ride bicycles found their movements restricted after local Muslim complaints and their families' embarrassment at being called bad Muslims. These sorts of tensions, attitudes, and differences meant that Muslimness as an ethnic category, if not as religious practice was, for most I interviewed, hyphenated by place and a local/refugee distinction even as intermarriage threatened it. Refugees foregrounded separation on the basis of different regional origins, which they argued made different kinds of persons. Northern Muslims saw themselves as different kinds of people, and the language of these differentiations was that of *ur*, the former home. In Northern Muslim active attempts to "recover a shattered social geography" (Bahloul 1996: 28), their former homes were not just located in a now uninhabited geography, they were lifeworlds that the refugees brought with them and they tried to mobilize in Puttalam.

"An *Ur* Known"

The symbolic qualities evoked by notions of home has been extensively philosophically explored (e.g., Bachelard 1994; Rouner 1996) and often forms the trope around which social scientists prefigure discussions of migration and displacement (cf. Jansen and Löfving 2009 for a discussion). Home in my work is the Tamil (language) notion of *ur*, a specific embedded notion with very real significance for social life among those I studied. I approach *ur* here through joining as Illana Feldman succinctly puts it in her study of Palestinian refugees in Lebanon, "the articulated and the enacted, that gives attention both to what people say about home and what they do with it" (Feldman 2006: 12).

As I discussed in the Introduction, *ur*—translatable most properly as home or natal village—is one of the most ordinary (thus evocative) words in colloquial Tamil. For the refugees, *ur* is an often-used Tamil word. It evokes an everyday emotive language of expectation, love, and sentiment. For those I worked with, because one is a person, one has an *ur*, and because one has an *ur*, one must either love it or feel obliged to love it. The only comprehensive exposition of *ur* comes from Valentine Daniel's (1984) ethnography of (South Indian) Tamil personhood, *Fluid Signs: Being a Person the Tamil Way* (from which the title to this section is taken). Daniel explores the link between a person and her natal village (*ur*), concretely expressed in the shared substance of soil and body that comes from physical presence in the place of origin. As Daniel argues,

> One of the most important relationships to a Tamil is that which exists between a person and the soil of his ur. . . . "Ur" is defined to approximate to a named territory that is 1) inhabited by human beings who are believed to share in the substance of the soil of that territory, and

2) a territory to which a Tamil cognitively orients himself at any given
time. (1984: 62)

Ur, Daniel argues, represents cognitively shifting and contextual spatial orientations that have to do with the person, not with an abstract collective (1984:
68) in contrast to kiramam (village) and tecam (nation), which are "bounded,
standard, universally accepted and constant spatial units" (69).

People tell you that persons are formed by the particular ur in which they
reside and have been nourished. This is, as Daniel points out, through relationship to both the imagined properties of such soil and those others who
are assumed to share this with you, those more like you than are people from
other ur. Wherever I went in the camps and settlements, my introduction
always began with the statement of my ur, Nallur, Jaffna, and if omitted it
would be the first thing IDPs asked when we began speaking in Tamil. While
most of the time the distinction between Tamils and Muslims held, sometimes Northern Muslims from Mannar or Mullaithivu would direct me to
Jaffna Muslims, because coming from the same ur we were considered more
similar. The common nourishment of people from the same ur means that
referring to somebody's ur is also an easy shortcut to discussing the nature
of the person. Ur not only make person-centric places, they also make place-
centric persons. These ur are known places located in dense social geographies, which territorially refer to villages, but conceptually to a neighborhood
and residence, and are said to have different soils and different kunams (character traits), and thus to produce different persons. Animated within a known
social geography where very small distances index not metric measurements,
but forms of sociality which different ur create, these discourses locate place
and person simultaneously, as constituting each other through residence.

This ordinary language of ur was significant in many ways. First, conversations about ur and the descriptions of the emotions aroused by ur partook
in a language and register shared by Tamils and Muslims. Ur was about the
ordinary form of living, eating, marrying. It was a materially emotive way
of reckoning belonging that was in sharp contrast to the mono-ethnic concept of Tamil Eelam, homeland. Often scholars working on separatist wars
assume too quickly that homeland and home are congruent concepts, that
homes scaled up can become homeland. Yet, as I discovered in my own
fieldwork, home ur and homeland Tamil Eelam occupied very different conceptual registers. While both through displacement and civil war, could be
said to be imaginary landscapes—one marked by loss, the other by constant

projection—*ur* was shared by Tamils and Muslims. Even while Tamil Eelam proposed a Tamil-only origin and future for the north, Tamil stories of *ur* tended to focus on specific villages rather than describing Tamil Eelam as *ur*.

One can also read the Northern Muslim insistence on the importance of *ur* in relation to the exclusiveness of Tamil Eelam. As I argued in the previous chapter, stories of Eviction insisted that it was the LTTE, not local Tamils, who had evicted Muslims, to keep "the local," the former "neighborhood" an untainted repository of possible hope and return. However, despite these narratives of neighborliness, in the aftermath of the Eviction relations had changed cataclysmically. Questions about one's relationship to former neighbors and the LTTE were disquietingly always present, always possible. However, while relations with Tamils and the LTTE were now uncertain and uncomfortable and had to be asserted against a bewildering new reality, place could still be owned through residence and material practice. It could not in effect be erased. Thus place carried the potential to empower *all* social relations, including *new* ones. Refugees reached out again and again to this narrative of home, a home located in the past and in space, where Tamils and Muslims had all lived together.

This seemed especially significant to refugees because at the time I was there in 2003 it was not clear whether refugees would ever return to those places in the north. Tamil refugees in camps in Vavuniya, I was told, also clustered in camps and settlements centered on their former homes. But while displacement was foundational for Tamils too, their right of return to the north had never been symbolically severed in the way it had been for northern Muslims. Northern Muslims had been both materially and symbolically dispossessed. Thus, their enactions of *ur* in Puttalam anticipated the possibility of "not returning" and clung onto the notion of a home that was not homeland. Attachment to *ur* thus provided a belonging that superseded present political possibilities, ties that continued to exist despite the severing of their right to return and the ethnicization of the North. It was *ur* that northern Muslims had lost, and it was *ur* that they clung to as an inalienable belonging that could not be taken away from them.

Living Side by Side

Refugees lived in four different types of spaces: "welfare centers," which I refer to, following northern Muslims who sidestep the niceties of the UNHCR, as "refugee camps"; new housing settlements (involving voluntary relocation of families by purchasing housing land); relocated areas (camps on state land); and rented houses and houses of friends and relatives (Shanmugaratnam 2000: 9). Camps, settlements, and relocated areas were clearly demarcated from Puttalam local residences, and were mostly filled with people originally from the same northern locality. Even when some settlements were a little more mixed than others, people were immediately able to navigate me around residences, effortlessly naming where people were originally from. Thus I found it surprisingly easy to locate Jaffna Muslims. Nazleen, one Jaffna Muslim woman, told me:

> When we first came we couldn't make our lives properly. Everyone lived side by side in camps with their sorrows . . . we thought of moving only with our people. Wherever you go, people live together; Jaffna people, Mannar people. We can help each other. Mannar people live with Mannar people. Jaffna people with Jaffna people, side by side.

Differentiation between local and refugee on basis of regional origin thus also worked to allow internal differentiation *between* Northern Muslims from different districts and villages. Districts such as Jaffna, Mannar, and Mullaithivu became scaled-up *ur*, given flesh and body by the way one resided and classified residence, how conversations about home could flourish in the midst of your "own people."

Moreover, while the majority of Jaffna Muslims had lived within Jaffna Town itself and thus came from the same area, Mannar and Mullathivu Muslims were distributed among a number of different villages, and their settlements reflected these smaller locales. Thus, Shanmugaratnam (2000) relates how Alankuda village, prior to the Eviction, had been a Puttalam Muslim village with one mosque, and was seen by locals as one village. After IDPs moved into Alankuda and established settlements, the village changed radically. It became seen by the refugees who lived there as composed of twelve mosques and twelve clustered settlements. Each settlement and mosque was centered around a village of origin in Mannar or Mullaithivu. Thus all refugees were seen as similar to each other in sharing common origins in the north, and the discourse of home/*ur* also provided a place- and person-specific set of emotions and relations, which articulated difference *within* the refugee community.

This internal differentiation was significant because Northern Muslims themselves were not homogeneous communities, but were marked with all kinds of preexisting social rivalries. In the camps, Jaffna Muslims would frequently point to the wealthier and more numerous Mannar community, and the preponderance of Mannar Muslims among local NGO and rising politicians, as signs that they were neglected by even their own Northern Muslim people. Mannar Muslims would joke about Jaffna Muslims and their assumption of their own refinement coming from Jaffna.

Thus, the Eviction and the importance of *ur* were not just stories; they were reproduced in spaces in which the idealization of neighborhood was being written into the seams of life in Puttalam. Children in the settlements who had never even seen Jaffna would grow up in "Jaffna" in Puttalam. This reordering is far from uncommon among long-term refugee dwellings. Renee Hirschon (1989) observed in her study of Asia Minor refugees in camps and settlements in Greece after expulsion that regional identification with former villages "provided a means of orientation and adjustment, a way of creating a familiar geography out of an unchartered expanse . . . [and its] persistence into successive generations is impressive" (1989: 23). Discourses of home evoked by those suffering collective displacement, emerging as they do within processes of *collective resettlement*, constantly resituate these within those material processes and attempts to find ordered sociality in rapidly disordered worlds.

Living in Puttalam

If I tell you my difficulties who's going to listen?
      We've lived here for 13 years with nothing to prove it. We have no deeds; we don't own the land we live on. There are five parties in this area, but none of them care about us [Jaffna people]. They told us we can't take work away from the host community. We mainly do coolie work. People can mainly only do coolie work. Wherever there is a camp here, there are men with unmarried children. We live in *olai* [cadjan/thatched] houses. Since we have come, things have got more and more difficult. When you look at us, they won't say we are Jaffna people. Our children don't study. How can they study here? They walk maybe a mile to school. The bus sometimes won't stop for refugee children. The children hang around with nothing to do. There we were studying from 6 until 9.

As Rajeeb, a middle-aged Jaffna Muslim, talked, the other ten men sitting around us nodded in assent. I was in another Jaffna refugee camp, on a main road bordered only by other camps and abandoned salt fields. While some refugees had moved out to settlements, thus assuming ownership of land, those in the refugee camp felt completely transient. Rajeeb, like others, saw his difficulties—the feeling of transience through not owning land and living in temporary shelters, the problem of unmarried daughters, and the inability to educate and motivate children—not only as economic deprivation, but as deprivation of the resources for personhood: "when you look at us, they won't say we are Jaffna people." Male unemployment, I soon came to realize, was endemic. Of the adult IDP population surveyed by the Sri Lankan government in Puttalam, 61 percent reported that they were unemployed.[9] This was a very young population too; 41 percent of IDPs were under eighteen in 2006. The little work available in Puttalam was for women. Tractorization has rendered men's work in agriculture defunct, leaving "women's work" of plucking and weeding. The ready availability of displaced women as cheap labor served to intensify agricultural production in Puttalam, and push down wages for local workers, creating much resentment (Shanmugaratnam 2000). Women planted, watered crops, and collected and cleaned the harvest. Crops were mainly onions, sweet potatoes, and chilies. In the refugee camps, every morning the truck arrived to take the groups of women to the field. The women were paid low wages by local farmers[10] for heavy and intensive "coolie"/daily labor, and were nonetheless expected to return home and perform the majority of household labor, though some child care did shift toward men. Shanmugaratnam found that male IDPs did not complain about the low wages paid to women because this was in keeping with their ideas about the lower value of women's work. This meant that, like the oppressed caste women Skjonsberg (1982) worked with, the combination of waged and household labor reflected women's centrality in household production but also their disempowerment in the denigration of female coolie work and the additional burden of household labor. The other major source of income for women was waged labor in the Gulf as housemaids. I had frequent conversations with women about this in the refugee camps and settlements, but this was always devalued as "dangerous" and potentially "immoral" work.

Undoubtedly before the Eviction there had been Muslims in the north living in transient housing, without means to educate their children, and women working as coolies. It was clear from some of my conversations with some women that they had resumed coolie work they had also previously done. One woman, whose husband had long abandoned her, and her three daughters cooked for a local eatery, and they told me of a life before Eviction that was not dissimilar to their current life. What was significant after the Eviction was the leveling effect of mass appropriation and the ways individual difficulties became collective difficulties. It was not just a few men out of work; it was almost all the men in the camps and settlements. Moreover, even working-class families had made sure that what savings they had were invested in jewelry and other dowry goods for daughters, and these precious savings were also wiped out when the LTTE confiscated Muslim goods in the Eviction. The effects and experiences of the Eviction were overwhelmingly collective, and searches for jobs, upliftment, marriage, and security were already staged as collective narratives.

However, even as stories of collective deprivation united Northern Muslims, differentiations of gender and class and their translation into issues of residence, possibility, and narrativizations of *ur* continued to exist in tension within this collective "becoming." There was growing internal differentiation between those still living in camps and those who had moved to settlements, those who had to pawn their ration cards and those who had found independent incomes.

Conflicts about the resources to achieve the familial and gendered obligations that were valued also translated into conflict between international and national NGOs, as the influx of IDPs was accompanied by the rise of local and national NGO groups concentrated in the area (when I was there, there were around 36 and growing). People attempted constantly to link themselves to INGO and NGO projects, as, given the high unemployment rates, these were in large part the sole resources available. NGOs vied with each other to get funding projects. People constantly suspected others and other Northern Muslim districts as having an advantage in getting this help. Much of the cultural and social energy of communities was thus directed through NGO activities.

This channeling of community building through NGO projects contoured representations of the community in public space and in relation to non-Muslims such as myself. Most projects trying to get national or international funding emphasized Muslimness as an ethnic category, need, and displacement as preeminent categories, rather than holding up piety or Islamic practice, given this was the time of the second Iraq war, the war in Afghanistan, and the American "war on terror." Furthermore, relationships between Northern and Puttalam Muslims was also rather complex, given local resentment of the large influx of northern Muslims with their different mosque committees and community links. Each northern area brought with it its own mosque committee, even if the mosque the committee was attached to had been left behind or no longer existed. I got used to seeing a board hanging up over a temporary building or corner announcing a northern mosque committee. The mosques in Puttalam were divided between those that accepted IDPs and those IDPs set up themselves. These sorts of religious negotiations also became caught up in the local/refugee struggles, and the push by NGOs to deemphasize Islam in order to attract general funding.[11]

As a woman and a Tamil, many of the men kept me on the periphery of these debates; it was assumed that if I wanted to know about northern Muslims *as a community*, then mosque debates were not to be placed center stage. Instead conversations, particularly from women, highlighted struggles over social mobility, inequality, and hierarchy along with narratives of the Eviction and collective existence. These conversations pinpointed (along with male unemployment) education and mobility as two of the most major transformations in status in Puttalam.

Education—secondary, technical, vocational, and university—due to overpopulation, land scarcity, and so on had been a prime symbolic and material component of social mobility for those in the north, particularly Jaffna (Arasaratnam 1986, 1994). This was also evident in Puttalam, where, as Shanmugaratnam observes, "the IDPs placed a high value on education as reflected in their generally higher levels of literacy, especially among women [compared to local women]" (2000: 40). At first, Puttalam schools could not cope with the influx of children. For the first generation from the refugee camps, education was minimal. Mumida, from Mannar, recalled,

> I studied, after a fashion. Those days we could only study for three hours after school in the schools. But we couldn't take part in any of the activities that we would have for our age, sports meets and activities. Local people studied in the morning, we studied in the afternoon. Some people here are very nice, but some were difficult. . . . Because we came here and studied only three hours a day, I didn't even finish the syllabus. That's how I studied for O levels and A levels. That's how I sat the exam here. My learning suffered here at the crucial age. My sadness is that I have wasted those days. If I had been at home, I would have competed and studied. At home all my family went to university, here not one has gone. Here the difficulties are many.

Others told me of the hostility they faced from other children. Amina said, "they would take things from us and we couldn't say anything because we were refugee children." This situation has been regularized, though as a whole Tamil-medium education is chronically understaffed.[12] Open hostility by the local community was replaced with increased competition for educational resources, due to the positive valuation of education among local Puttalam people, especially local Muslims, after IDP arrival (Shanmugaratnam 2000). Education too became key to emerging class differences between camp refugees and those who moved to refugee settlements, the latter children being educated to higher levels while children in the camps often had to contribute to family incomes.

For young women, the normative expectation of schooling had in the north enabled some measure of free movement. Mumida and others told me of their arrival in Puttalam and the increasing restrictions placed on their movements as local Muslims complained about young IDP girls walking together unescorted for tuition classes. Regardless whether this was true, many of the young women I talked to perceived and represented life after the Eviction in the refugee camps and settlements as one of increasing control over their movement by their families. I now turn to the stories of these young women, and to what their stories critically implicated—the question of dowry. The ongoing feelings of transience that many felt in the camps, the inability to own land, to protect their daughters from what was seen as uncontrolled mixing, and particular discourses of *ur* were linked by the imagination of permanence as the transmissibility of land. Temporary houses were seen as lodging between lost dowry houses of the past and dowry houses of the future. These discussions were critically concerned with the need to contain and order appropriate sociality and intimacy for women. They also highlight how while displacement has made more women economically powerful in the household, it also reinforced preexisting gender hierarchies.

How Many Troubles in a Camp

While the majority of refugees were settled in camps upon arrival, in 1995 the Sri Lankan state and NGOs offered assistance for settlements, and by mid-2000, thousands of refugees were living in variegated settlements (Shanmugaratnam 2000: 4).[13] One of the primary reasons cited by refugees when they moved to settlements was fear of inappropriate sexual intimacy and lack of privacy.

I noticed that the most immediate difference between refugee camps and settlements was the appearance of fences. There was no difference between settlements and camps in actual mixing and moving in and out of houses. Furthermore, houses in settlements were no less temporary. In 2006, the Sri Lankan government recorded that 62.9 percent still lived in thatched houses;[14] it was only when I returned in 2008 that I saw more permanent brick structures. However, camps were unmarked open tracts of land, with the boundaries marked around the camp and not between houses. Settlements had neatly fenced houses and clearly separated spaces, and bore the marks of active human labor on the environment, transforming open tracts of land into neighborhoods. Fences marked practices of ordering and separation; they enforced the proper relations of intimacy and avoidance that the camps were thought to lack. Thus when Nazleen, who had bought land in Puttalam, told me about a proposal to go back to Jaffna to live in a refugee camp she told me:

> They say that we can go and live in a camp there again and try and build up our houses there. Can we go live there in a refugee camp again? Look at her [pointing at a young woman] she was brought as a young child, now she is a young unmarried woman. Can her father and mother take her there and live among other refugees and young men? How many troubles! If we go and live in a camp now, should the husband stay and look after his daughters and protect them or go and look for work? How many troubles in a camp! We don't want to live in a camp again, we said instead give us assistance and we will build our house ourselves again.

Many young women I interviewed had come to refugee camps at precisely the point when they were considered to become women. Their memories of the north were also thus tinged with the nostalgia for a childhood that was free of control. Most, however, stressed the extent to which they felt new control over their movement as a result of living in refugee camps. The only desirable work (as opposed to the denigrating work in the fields) was the highly sought after NGO work, or the possibility of education, which was hard to access for the first generation of adolescents in the refugee camps, given the critical age at which they had suffered dislocation. Many young women felt themselves moved farther and farther indoors, even as they lived a life which was constantly more exposed to the elements, both human and natural.

In the refugee camp housing Muslims from Mullaithivu that I visited in 2003, there were fifty families for each toilet. In the Jaffna camp that Tareek lived in, bathing was initially public with little division for men and women. Children and adolescents without regular schooling hung around, giving rise to parental fears about illegitimate sex. Muslims told me that the marriage age in the camps was dropping as parents married off their daughters at a younger age to protect their reputation.

Shafiqa, then in her early twenties, recalled her childhood in Jaffna with affection and sadness, reflecting on the feeling of freedom she associated with her former *ur*.

> When we were there we lived in freedom. We lived on the street running around with all the other children; we even used to go to the [Hindu temple] kovil sometimes with them. Our parents didn't worry about these things and most of the time they didn't even know the things we did. Now we are all closed inside doors, those days we lived a life of freedom. . . . The culture is different here and we have had to fit in.

She had an insecure existence, married without dowry to a man from another northern district, and with a fifteen-month-old daughter.

Shafiqa and others represented movement into the camp as the feeling of constant surveillance, outside by Puttalam Muslims and inside by one's own neighbors, engaged in the acute competition over resources and marriage prospects. For Shafiqa (and many other young women) Puttalam Muslims were more conservative than northern Muslims, and the alteration in their circumstances had to do with the "culture of the land." She herself longed to ride a bicycle, as was common for Muslim girls in Jaffna. In rural and more conservative Puttalam, Muslim girls and women did not ride bicycles when I was there; only in the last two years, I am told it has begun. Then, bicycle riding was something that "Tamil girls" living in "Puttalam Town do."

These perceptions were exemplified in one conversation I had with three others, two young women, Amina and Mumida, and one older woman, Nazleen, who tellingly only had sons.

> *Amina:* From the beginning for these people how to raise girls is a
> big thing, should they live in freedom or not. We don't have that
> now, not for women.
> *Mumida:* Before they trusted us, what time we are coming home.
> Now even we are frightened.

Amina: Since we came from our motherland, girls are being kept
   close. In their (parents') minds there is fear. That if their
   children go around there will be flirtations or harassment.
Mumida: It is happening too. One thing is that this is a Sinhala area;
   we can't talk to anyone. At home we were surrounded by our
   kin, so that if anything happened we were all right.
Amina: We are scared of Puttalam autos; we will get into a refugee
   auto without fear.
Nazleen: Now we are becoming more like kin people, our people are
   marrying them with them. . . . There is no harmony here. *Living
   with your people is good, we help each other and we can keep
   young children and unmarried women safely.*

Nazleen finished this particular conversation, against the grain of the complaints by the others, by reiterating the necessity of keeping women safe, that
is to say, chaste.

Refugee camps were made larger *ur*, surrounded by a seemingly hostile
host community outside. Within, the community itself constantly policed
women to maintain the integrity of these *ur* as ordering schemas for sociality.
Thus, *ur* provides both the model of order that is valorized in the camps and
the story of "freedom" young women use to talk about their mobility. *Ur* thus
could continue to be imagined always to be associated with "felicitous images" (Bachelard [1960] 1994), even if these ran counter to each other. It was,
however, also no surprise that stories of active community building always
raised the question of dowry and marriage. In the temporality of familial reproduction, constituted around a community made through historical loss,
women and marriage were prime vehicles by which historical and familial
loss and regrowth could be linked together and at the same time threaten the
possibility of return home.

Marrying with Dowry

Nachiya told me "I still live in difficulty." Amina immediately jumped in
with an explanation—"she has four daughters, two of them are married now
but two are still unmarried." As an afterthought Amina added, "she has four
sons too." Throughout my stay there I came to recognize this moment, when
people told me how many daughters they had, or how many sisters they had,

accompanied by the same worry—how were they going to get married? When I asked Nachiya whether one had to give dowry, her reply was incredulous, "of course, without dowry they can't get married."

While officially under the Sri Lankan Mohammedan code, Muslims do not give dowry, unofficially Northern Muslims give dowry. Some are ambiguous about its origins, arguing that Mannar Muslims brought it to the camp, but there is enough oral evidence to show that dowry giving like Tamils was common among Muslims, with the attempt to marry within families an attempt to avoid more onerous dowry giving. Moreover, dowry practice among the refugee Muslims, many told me, had increased after displacement.

Providing dowry, as we discussed in Chapter 2, has always been a potent symbol of status and personhood, given that marriage is the preeminent social relation of kinship for Jaffna Tamils and Muslims, as for southern subcontinental communities more generally (Kantawala 1930; Tambiah 1973; Kapadia 1995). Both movable and immovable property are dowry: land, jewelry, and cash (as donation), though land was the prized symbolic core (Tambiah 1973). Dispossession was imagined as the stripping of dowry and the reproductive potential between place and kin. As I described in Chapter 3, Jaffna Muslims dwell again and again on the stripping of land deeds and jewelry by the LTTE at their checkpoints. Chapter 3 details how for many, what stripping Muslim women and their children bare on the checkpoints meant was that LTTE cadres were stripping their bodies of connection and regrowth in the land they were living, stripping them of the ability to transmit dowry located within the north.[15] In addition to trying to acquire dowry land in Puttalam, many Muslims also told me that even in absence and without being able to claim or transmit it, they symbolically refused to sell dowry property in Jaffna.

Northern Muslim stories of a good life, and of belonging more generally, idealized possessing and passing on a dowry house in marriage, mother to daughter. Giving dowry was also to establish oneself as a person and to fulfill one's obligations to one's family. Without this, men and women were but half-persons.

Since the onset of the civil war and the mass migration of Tamils abroad, eminently liquid and transportable cash donations have come to supplement land dowries for Tamils. Jaffna land is no longer a treasured component of elite dowry practices. It was among displaced Muslims that land and jewelry, rather than the more impersonal cash, retained their symbolic value as dowry. Critical to understanding how houses are ideally imagined for Northern Muslims is to see every house as a potentially discarded or appropriated dowry house. Those that cannot be owned, that are temporary because they cannot be transmitted, even if they are the spaces by which quotidian life is structured, are always in the shadow of a potentially owned house in the past or future.[16]

People explained to me why dowry was demanded through referring to their present living conditions. One cannot embark on a new life as a married person on nothing. You need somewhere to live, you need money, and one doesn't have the support or employment one could depend on before. Providing dowry was central to economic strategies. Rashima, who lived in a two-room kottil partitioned by hung up saris, shared it with her two married daughters, their husbands, their children, and another unmarried daughter. She herself had worked in Saudi Arabia twice, for two years each time, to get money for her first and second daughters' dowry. When I met her we were discussing the situation in Iraq and wondering whether she would be able to go back for a third time to earn for her third daughter's dowry. She like many others spoke longingly of giving land, of relieving her overcrowded existence.

Thus in the refugee camps conversations about giving dowry and marrying one's children traveled between the interlinked symbolic potency of dowry as regrowth and reproduction and its material life as the primary means of capital accumulation in kinship. This is encapsulated in a word: when one owned land, it was called *sontam*, a Tamil word that means both to be "of one's own" and to "be kin." To become kin with land was also to pass it on.

However, becoming *sontam* and giving dowry in Puttalam, while necessary, implicated one in making kin relations in and with Puttalam. I have argued hitherto that Northern Muslims rebuilt their lives structured around invocations and reconcretizations of former homes. These homes thus never disappeared into the past, but continued to generate homes in the future. This was what made northern Muslims Northern Muslims, not just Puttalam Muslims or Muslims from the north. However, in the realm of what Bourdieu (1992) calls, "practical kinship," all kinds of alliances and marriages occurred with tacit silence. The desire and anxiety for regrowth and recuperation meant that refugees had to materially and symbolically invest in new forms of life in Puttalam. Shafiqa told me,

When we arrived we put up a kottil in a school grounds. There were about a hundred other families in kottils in the grounds. We waited to return home. Ten years passed just like that. Then we gave up and built a house, and now they say we can go back. How were we to know? It's not that we don't want to go back, but we've built a house, people have married and settled here. You can't just get up just like that and go home. But believe me it's not because we don't want to. But it's not that easy.

From 1995, families began taking up the opportunity to buy small lots in new refugee settlements. Forced by the pressure of the necessity to make new marriages, to continue the reproductive cycles of families and land, the community as composed of its families could not stand still. The Muslim community began to invest in Puttalam, even while denying that Puttalam could become an *ur*. Nazleen told me in the midst of the 2002 ceasefire (which ended violently a few years later),

> To go back now [north], it is difficult. This is our own (*sonta/sontam*) place. We gave money and built this. We can't just leave it now. We can't tell how the situation will change, maybe who knows. It's only now there is peace. In Jaffna, the people who went saw that everything is destroyed. The Muslim area is completely gone. If you see it, the desire to go back dies in your mind. . . . Maybe things will change in the future, but right now . . . how can anyone go?

For those in the settlements, with the creation of neighborhood-like structures with fences and land, memories of *ur* were able to be reinvested in the present practices of life. One could actively remake *ur* as a safe, neighborly place with secure transmission. But ownership and resumption of dowry were double-edged: as refugees reinvested in homes in the present, the home in the past began to recede along with the possibility of return. However, as the final part of this chapter discusses, longing for home was never quite extinguished. It had become structurally part of who Northern Muslims were. Nazleen who earlier told me she would not return also said later on

> I'll never sell [dowry land in Jaffna]. If I sell it and then the situation changes then what can we do. We'll keep it and see what happens. . . . I tell my husband . . . my son has a marriage being arranged, I say that we will see him married and settle him here, and then me and my husband will go back. . . . We are old people now. So I tell him "let's go and live in Jaffna." [laughs] When I talk about it, my heart burns. If there is a good situation, then I won't say that we won't go. . . . To

think about it is depressing. To think of leaving the home you were born in and lived in, is so filled with sorrow.

Landscapes of Return

Many northern Muslims explained to me that at the time of the 1995 peace talks they had been much more ready to return to the north. It was after all only five years after Eviction and they had not fully settled in Puttalam. However, soon the peace talks collapsed and war broke out again. This was clear in Shafiqa's story above, where she and her family waited for ten years before finally in 2000 moving to a more permanent structure. When I went to the camps in 2003, it was in the midst of another ceasefire that had begun in 2002 and at the time was still uncertainly holding. By 2005 it had broken down.

In 2003, very few northern Muslims took the opportunity to return to former *ur*, though of course some families did. Most of my research with refugees in 2003 (and conversations in a subsequent brief informal visit to friends in 2006) was centered on the difficulty of returning home. It was not clear then that even if there was a ceasefire the war would end. The LTTE remained dominant, and it seemed that Muslims would always have to negotiate with their former evictors if return was to be possible. One Centre for Policy Alternatives (CPA) report relates the story of the 100 families who returned to Tharapuram in Mannar, where "the uncertainty with which the Muslim community live is epitomized by the numerous large cracks across the wall of the mosque trustee board president's house. He says that each year he tells himself he will do up the house the following year when the situation improves" (CPA 2003a, 59). This hesitance about future prospects meant that visions of return would always be vulnerable. When I went to visit my friend Nazima in 2006, she made it clear: "who wants to go home and die?" she asked me.

In 2009, the Sri Lankan army eliminated the LTTE leadership completely, and it is now clear that the LTTE will never be a military force in the north again. In September 2009, I met a friend Rinaz, originally from Mannar. He immediately told me that he, his family, and a thousand others were preparing to leave Puttalam and return to their former villages in the northern Mannar district. They had been in talks with some Tamil community groups and Tamils living in their area, and were now preparing to go back and reclaim their properties. Their only problem now, he told me, was the Sri Lankan navy, which had occupied the coastline and maintained an aggressive attitude toward locals. Hopefully they and the Tamils in the area would soon be able to go back to fishing, he told me. Return has become possible in a way it was not two years ago. Not all Northern Muslims will return; it is clear that a sizeable proportion of the younger generation will stay in their current places of residence. But thousands will return. They will return not to their past homes but to future homes, a new collective group with a new collective identity born through displacement. Here, I wish to contemplate this future through going back to the various figurations of the future as the possibility of return that I encountered in my research with Northern Muslims, and how these became generationally divergent. These past conversations are far from extinguished in 2009, they haunt and structure these new possibilities.

Liisa Malkki argues that, rather than seeing "the past and the future . . . placed in stable and commonsensical opposition to each other, like truth and fabrication, reality and fantasy" (2001: 327), "once we start looking, it becomes clear that much of our political energy and cultural imagination is expended in personal and collective efforts to direct and shape (and sometimes see) the future" (328). Here, I take her suggestion that we must understand the kinds of "figures of the future" that people employ and which are important in their emplotment of their pasts and presents, though these do not fit into our conventional understandings of "history." Prognostications, speculations, political energies, and social imaginations about the future of Northern Muslims as a whole were discussed in individual families around the possibility of "return" to the north. Return was the figuration by which the future was understood, utopist and dystrophic, practical and symbolic. The possibility of return located the past and future in relation to each other.

Return was also a question that IDPs could not avoid. Life in refugee camps and settlements was practically constituted around relationships to the state and UNHCR where the primary questions and tasks were about the possibilities of relocation and settlement (see Brun 2003). In countless surveys to gauge funding needs and applications, IDPs were asked if they wished to return or not, with different percentages given by different agencies. Northern Muslims were addressed and were addressing themselves as displaced people. It was not surprising, then, that it was around the possibility of desired or undesired return, which most conversations tended to discuss, planning for one's futures, that divergences and disjunctures between different generations emerged. Any individual has visions of the future, from immediate to long term. Here I talk about a collectively produced "horizon

of expectation" (Koselleck 2004). These dilemmas surrounding return in-
dexed refugees' conversations about family, social differentiation, the relationship of the past to the future, the passage of years, and the process of
becoming Northern Muslim itself.

However, stressing this figuration of "Return-as-Future" is not only about
the density of conversations about return by displaced people. It is also to
understand Reinhart Koselleck's insistence that concepts are not just deriva-
tions, but "have a semantic function and performance" in social and political
life (2004: 86). A concept is "not simply indicative of the relations which it
covers; it is also a factor within them. Each concept establishes a particular horizon for potential experience and conceivable theory and in this way
sets a limit." For him words such as "democracy" and "revolution" are such
concepts, as "the entirety of meaning and experience within a socio-political
context within which and for which a word is used can be condensed into a
one word" (85, 75–92). Here I suggest that in Northern Muslim communities
"return" has come to be such a concept, which not only describes but structures, is claimed, imagined, and also occludes. Return, thus, as "a figure of
the future" forces particular conversations (Malkki 2001) and sets particular
limits for other imaginations of community. It means that other figures of the
future have had to measure themselves against "return."

Important to this discussion is Koselleck's notion of the two general historical categories of the "space of experience" and "the horizon of expectation." Experience, both direct and alien (conveyed across generations and
institutions), is the "present past." Expectation is the "not yet," the nonexpe-
rienced, the "future made present." These are not, for Koselleck, symmetri-
cal: one is collected (experienced), while the other can never be experienced
and can always be revised (expectation); "the presence of the past is distinct
from the presence of the future" (2004: 260). However, Koselleck suggests
that while events may have happened, experience of them alters over time;
this is the temporal structure of experience I first explored in Chapter 2. This
structure is made possible by the temporal structure of "retroactive expectation"; new expectations, new futures continually become possible which were
not always anticipated. New imaginations of possible futures continually alter
our experiences of the past.

Expectations are also temporally structured and can be "temporally exceeded"; new experiences transform and exceed the limit of our possible futures, for instance, the end of the war, which I never thought possible a year

ago. However, Koselleck argues that "past futures" that have been exceeded do not by any means disappear neutralized; sometimes they can continue to "emit impulses" reformulated here more strongly as ghostly warnings. Past futures may have not happened, but they can continue to have a life that exceeds their actualization, the hidden surplus of new imagined futures.

Northern Muslim ideas about future return (Return-as-Future) are structured by a continual working through of past experiences (Eviction-as-Past). This relationship has had to be reimagined as histories around them have changed possible futures. Not least, experiences of regrowth through practical kinship and reproduction, and regrowth as historical loss, increasingly came to be in tension with each other given they involved different relationships to the question of return. It is to this we now move.

Eviction-as-Past?

Those times . . . we can't tell about that kind of life. Now when I think about it I have to laugh. When I think of it I feel frightened. That's why we have to guard our lives carefully. It should never happen again. It won't happen again and it should never happen again. They say it won't happen again.

Nazleen trails off. She resumes,

These thoughts will always come again and again. Some things you can forget, some things you can never forget. We think about Tamil people still and their difficulties back home. We were used to them; we all lived together. Only after the eviction did we think about that.

Nazleen was only one of many who spoke of the Eviction as that which should never happen again. She articulated this together with the uncertainty that indeed perhaps it could happen again, and that the Eviction could never be forgotten and had altered the basic frames of certainty and life itself. The LTTE's refusal in 2003 to give a guarantee that Muslims would not be collectively evicted again if they returned home always served to underline the vulnerability of Muslims and the possibility that the Eviction could happen again.

Moreover, the Eviction was not in the distant past. The Eviction as a foundational event of a collective past was everywhere in Puttalam. It is hard to express the density of stories of the Eviction. While there was undoubted reticence on the part of parents to express their feelings fully to their children and me, I found that there was not a house where the larger story of the Eviction as personal and social loss was not narrated. Children too young to have been part of the Eviction would tell me that their family arrived in Puttalam as a result of being evicted by the LTTE. I found a larger commitment to retelling the Eviction in families, and that those who were too young to have been part of identified themselves as primarily Northern Muslims. Not only did the Eviction as a collective event bring about a new demographic, Northern Muslims (as explored in Chapter 3), but constantly rememorializing it through retelling Eviction narratives and living in residences and settlements structured around loss actively maintained this collectivity. The Eviction as loss gave historicity. However, this commitment to retelling Eviction stories also concealed deep disjunctures, of status, class and gender as explored above, and here between generations, first, in relation to the question of "return" to the north, and second, to different experiences and identifications to home in the north and Puttalam.

Formerly, for northern Tamils and Muslims there had been no injunction to marry within *ur*. The *ur* of the child and one of its parents, most often the father, was rarely the same. Families where different generations had different *ur* were not uncommon in kinship systems in the north.[17] Marrying across area would have also been common for Muslims in the north. Jaffna town may have been an exception given that almost 90 percent of Jaffna Muslimsthere, and they were from the same *ur*. Nonetheless, *ur* in itself could always be different between generations and families. There have always been families with different *ur*, and the central question was of transmission of food, stories, and caste, family, and neighborhood relations to bind a child to one. *Ur* was about one way of relating and one vocabulary of love, but it was not exhaustive. Displacement, however, has for Muslims heightened anxieties about the plasticity of *ur* and belonging through residence.

When, after Eviction, *ur* also became the repository of emotional work toward the home that needs to be maintained outside residence, such discontinuities within families became more problematic. That is, they became understood *as* discontinuities. Displacement brought the desire to fix what became revealed in crisis to be fluid and yet deeply potent. Rapid social change brought a desire to *fix* ways of belonging, here those reckoned through *ur*, which are in themselves plastic and mobile. The idea of belonging through *ur* itself means that one is nourished, grows within that environ, and is related to the people who share this experience. Considerable emotional labor was required to maintain former homes in the north as *ur* against the practical and present claims of Puttalam and its land. The possibility of "becoming of this place," Puttalam, was obvious for Northern Muslims, but they remained ambivalent about that possibility.

As time passed, the possibility of forgetting home, if not the Eviction, and the impossibility of returning home became more apparent as children begin to marry and settle down in Puttalam. People talked of the consequences of making new kin, marriages, and households in Puttalam and thus potentially making kin with Puttalam, the place. The problem of forgetting was not a collective problem of forgetting Eviction but of the forgetting involved in regrowth of families and procreative and practical transmission of personhood. If sociality and difference were created by holding onto the stories about former homes, and if residence, sharing, and nourishment made *ur*, was Puttalam a potential *ur*? Relationships to former *ur* were direct for the older generation, who indeed had been nourished in their former homes but, people asked, what of their children? Were these children, children of this *ur*? And if so, did that make them different persons from their parents even though they were kin? Could these children ever be at home in their parents' *ur*? Sometimes people even wondered whether their children had an *ur*. Could a refugee camp be considered a proper *ur* even if it made people similar?

One elderly woman, Jezima, told me "these children are losing their Tamil," gesticulating at her grandchildren who were running around speaking fluent Tamil. The children in question had been born in Puttalam, so their loss was not in their life cycle but in their cultural identity. Jezima complained how little children were using "sully" to mean money, like the Sinhalese and the Puttalam Muslims, rather than "kasu," which for her was how proper Jaffna Muslims and Tamils spoke. For Jezima, while her grandchildren were indubitably her kin, the kinds of differences she detailed to me also made it clear that they could be different kinds of persons from her. Anxieties about return were referred to discussions of children born or brought up in the camps and family obligations of love and duty, and also mapped evident emergent discontinuities of experience between generations and their relationships to *ur* and memory.

This is where very different ideas about the possibility of returning home

to the north emerged. At the time I first went in 2003, thirteen years of displacement was already long enough to create three distinct generations with
different imaginings of the promise of return.[18] These generations can be
loosely mapped onto age: the elderly, the young, and those "in-between,"
as people defined themselves. Significantly, the generations mapped onto
people's relation to former homes as "memory of place" or the "memory of
the Eviction story." These follow age-span designations (Abrams 1970), but
those who are young do represent the possibility of being a generation in the
larger sense, one that will maintain a common set of orientations and attitudes beyond its youth as a more general sense of sharing a common destiny
as Northern Muslims (Mannheim 1952) (see Chapter 1).

Memory of Home—"The Elderly"

For the older generation, in 2003 thirteen, now twenty-one years was a rela-
tively small segment of time in their biographies, albeit a segment that had
assumed cataclysmic proportions. The Eviction marked a turning point and
rupture, but memories of home always overwhelmed them: life as it became
recreated in Puttalam was always contingent, always a pale shadow of what
they had once lived and which they assumed was character forming. Neighbors, schooling, marriage, employment, those crucial material and affective
relations one builds up in life, had been primarily conducted in their former
ur. Living in Puttalam was an aftermath; it was a struggle to survive that intimately recalled loss in every possible way. Strategies of person-making were
not for themselves: the former home had made persons of them. Rather, they
were for children and grandchildren.

Thus, elderly people strongly desired a possible return home. Of those
who did not desire to return, the pain of being evicted again was given as a
reason not to return. Asked about his ur, Nazleen's father turned his face toward the wall, rheumy eyes brimming, and refused to talk to me. On another
occasion, Farook pointed out his uncle on a street staring into space. He had
come and worked and brought up his children but, Farook said, he would
never recover from the Eviction. Jezima told me, "these are stories made of
tears." "If I live to be a thousand," she said, "I can never forget my motherland,
my ur." Sitting in the back of her house in Puttalam as she deftly changed her
granddaughter's clothing, she told me, "Jaffna was land that God gave life
to, even the vegetables here have no taste, drumsticks, bananas, they have

no taste . . . there is no Tamil like the one that Jaffna people speak." As older people they had memories of former homes in peacetime, not only in war.

Memory of Story—"The Young"

The formative experience of being from the north for the younger generation was of growing up in Puttalam. Many could not recall *ur* clearly, but they could recollect or tell me stories of the Eviction. The Eviction itself had become the genitive point of their identity and their relationship to home. In Puttalam, stories of former *ur* and displacement were about orienting their relationships *within* Puttalam, about differentiation from locals, and how life was lived there. It was *they* who were *Northern Muslims*; their identity is fueled by expulsion and by Puttalam as an *ur* and their position as refugees there.

For many Northern Muslims, children are their kin through sharing houses and marriage and birth. However, children are different persons, for their imagination of social relations springs entirely from Puttalam. Often for the young, home is an absence that is related solely through the memory of the Eviction and the memory of their home that their parents must pass on to them. Thus, for many young people, the promise of return is an immanent story written into the Eviction story, but the possibility of actual return is not a constitutive part of their identities. I return to the difference between the promise of return and the possibility of return below. For those who remembered their former *ur*, generally in their early twenties, *ur* was impossible to return to, either because their marriages were made in Puttalam, or because the memory of their former homes as battlefields made the memories too painful. They had incorporated the journey to Puttalam as part of their life stories, as opposed to the older generation, for whom the Eviction was the rupture that negated their life stories.

Examples from each end of the spectrum can be found in Amina and Mumida, from Kilinochchi and Mannar respectively, Amina told me:

> We have a place at home, but we are going to sell it. Our Umma [mother] and Dada [father] went to see it, no one else went. . . . In my house my Umma used to say that when they married me, then she and Dada would go back and live there, now Dada has gone [deceased] she can't do anything about it . . . Umma seeing our situation here is going to stay here. . . .
>
> Now I tell you, they will all say if you ask, where their home is,

they will say Kilinochchi and that we came as refugees. Now I won't, if anyone asks me I will say Puttalam. I came when I was small; if they ask me where I was born then I will say Jaffna, or Kilinochchi.

Yet when I interviewed her family, when Amina's mother and her aunt faltered in their stories, Amina prompted them with questions and explanations, showing her own detailed knowledge of their Eviction stories.

Mumida, on the other hand, remembers home very well. She told me with great sorrow that children now in Puttalam "do not care any more" about their homes. But she also felt that she could not go back. For Mumida, home is gone, it is no longer what it was. Unlike her parents who, embedded within that home, can imagine regrowing within it, working and building again, for Mumida home is her past and cannot be her future.

> Now I don't have even the desire to go home. Before I had it. When I went home again for the first time [in 1997], I thought, this is the soil I was born in. This is the smell of my land, the red fields, the earth as red as blood. This is what my own land (*conta munn*) looks like. That was when we went. I wept. I screamed. All the memories I had as a child of every place.
>
> When we came home from school we would find the bodies of the slain. Once the helicopter came, the army and bombed us. I remember all of this. When I went all these memories came. . . . In this life, we should all live together, we should have our rights and nobody should have to suffer. But to go and live at home . . . I have no interest. What was there before is no longer there. Now it is all jungle filled with places where people have died.
>
> Now we are like tourists. If we go there, when we think of our homes, we cry with our memories, we left this and came. We left our brick house and came to live in cadjan houses with the rain and snakes. How we used to live there! Our house is bombed, the walls are not even there. The LTTE had taken everything there was. Even the doors were carried away by looters.

For Mumida not only does home no longer exist, but its physicality reminds her of everything she has lost. She cannot return. Mumida, who left at ten, and Amina, who left at five, represent a transition toward the new young generation who will have no memories of home like Mumida, but will, like Amina, know stories of the Eviction. Without the memories of former homes, they are pulled

toward the future and toward performing *ur* and belonging in radically different ways from their parents. They saw *ur* as an unknown past and a potentially
deferred future, whereas for their parents *ur* was a real place that is now lost.

In-Between

Between these two generations were those who either married in the camps
or came with young children. They were often represented as torn between
their parents and their children, with different ways of relating to home. For
this middle generation, memories of home and the eviction were double-
edged. They remembered *ur*, not Eviction, as the genitive point in their life
stories. Memories of home were constantly emplotted as ideal ways of living.
However, they also felt that their obligations lay with their children, who increasingly were marrying and settling in Puttalam. Home was remembered
strongly, but was also written through the Eviction, through fear and uncertainty about the future.

Life stories stressed survival and growth in the aftermath of a devastating
event. They stressed regrowth, marrying, having children, sending their children to school, and working for dowry for their daughters as ways in which
they have survived and carry on. These stories of growth and survival also
recall loss because they are often used to represent the provisionality of return now that their children have settled in Puttalam. Both materially and
emotionally, many use their children as the figures that made it impossible for
them to return home. The languages of home, movement, and kinship mir-
rored and were interwoven as the children came to stand between a place that
was receding and the place that was assuming reality. I choose Yusuf's story
out of many similar conversations to illustrate the complex way in which children are made to figure in relation to the structures in which Northern Muslims are enmeshed. He told me,

> Think about this, three of them marry here, each have two children.
> The UNHCR and the government will give us Rs. 25,000 to go back
> but only as one family. But what about the children? Think about this
> situation. Are these people to leave their children here? Are these chil-
> dren a citizen of this home? If 5,000 people left there is only money
> for 5,000 people to go back. So what do my children do? . . . They're
> saying go to Jaffna we will give you rations there. How are we to go?

There is no space for us to even put up a hut. We have to clear it before
we can do anything. So where are we going to go? Where can we live?

The money offered by aid agencies and the government to IDPs as resettlement money, as Yusuf pointed out, does not account for children, and is not
enough for the children to return home too.

We have to think about the children that we have here and what situation we will give them. They live here. Now my daughter's son, his
birth certificate is in Sinhala. Will the LTTE tolerate this? Now you
take this man in our camp: his daughter was born there, her birth
certificate is in Tamil, even her name is written in Tamil. The birth
certificates there are in Tamil, here they are in Sinhalese. And in the
"Place of Birth" section, they write "Salterns camp B, Puttalam." Our
children are born in refugee camps.
   Now this man here, he said his son was going to get married in
two years. Now that child who comes out of that marriage will be
from here. And that child's child will be a citizen of this home. The
birth certificate you get in this home, will it be enough for there?

For many IDPs like Yusuf, whose children were born in Puttalam, birth
certificates encapsulated practical and symbolic issues. The children's birth
certificates in Sinhala displayed two things, their non-northern place of birth,
and their displacement in Puttalam. Most IDPs could not read Sinhala even
if they had acquired spoken Sinhala. Some wanted the place of birth to be
entered, not as Puttalam, but as Jaffna, or Mannar, the place that they *ought*
to belong to, something that might give their children in the future a claim to
lost property, history, and home. Many IDPs found that their children's birth
certificate was not even inscribed just "Puttalam," but "Salterns camp B." The
children in Puttalam are born into the Sri Lankan state as displaced people: as
one man told me, "my child will be a refugee forever." It is not just that children
might, by acquiring new *ur*, forget that they came from elsewhere; the fright-
ening possibility arose that perhaps children didn't even have *ur*. They might
have lost what they never had. Thus the desire to maintain a former home is
also tinged with the understanding that the children will have only an identity
as "displaced." In their parents' *ur*, they may be displaced too on return, for
they have none of the markers to show that they have been raised there.
   In 2003, Yusuf's final question to me, "the birth certificate you get in this

home, will it be enough for there?" referred to the shadow that underlay all conversation about the Eviction and "return." It was not only children settling in Puttalam who could prevent return. The authority that could prevent Northern Muslims from being at home in the north was in fact the LTTE. Yusuf rhetorically asked me whether the LTTE would tolerate a child's birth certificate being written in Sinhala. Children came to figure as the manner in which home can recede, but accompanying and shaping these anxieties about settlement in Puttalam was also LTTE refusal to guarantee Muslim Eviction would not happen in the future. Children here thus came to doubly figure in thinking of return-as-future. Would the LTTE accept Muslim regrowth in the north? The barrel of a gun lay then in 2003 as an ever present shadow over Muslim return.

Moreover, the north had become inhabited over two decades as Tamil only. Return was not to the past. Many Muslims talked of how, like people, places too age and transform. Some villages in the north, especially in Mannar, no longer exist. In others, houses and shops are occupied by other displaced people. Homes, when abandoned, die. Thus to "return" is to return to something new. Yusuf points out how going home, but living in refugee camps rather than their own houses, means not emplacement, but that Northern Muslims would be once again displaced and dependent on relief. The point Muslims made, in the aftermath of the Eviction and its destabilization of the past, was that becoming Northern Muslim was to embark on a journey that only unfolded into the future. It was not certain that the past could ever meet the future entirely through return. Return-as-Future was laden with difficulties.

To Dream of Return

However, while there was real generational divergence within Northern Muslim communities about returning home, this did not necessarily exhaust narratives of return as central to the merging collective identity of Northern Muslims. In Puttalam, return plaited together two different kinds of conversations, the first (explored above) about the actual possibility of relocation and the renewal of actual neighborhoods, and the second about the acknowledgment of the legitimacy of return, two coexisting visions. The former was generationally structured in the ways I outline above, but the latter as I develop below was, and continues to be, central to the constitution of the community.

These different visions evoked different spatiotemporal futures, at times they came together, and at other times they could not answer each other. They were also addressed to different kinds of listeners, different audiences.

It was clear to me in my fieldwork (also with Tamils) that while people were talking to me their conversations also addressed others not present, dead or alive, or that seeming "world" outside me who could be addressed. I was the least of their interlocutors. I came to understand how temporally these conversations gestured beyond the immediate to a larger "super-addressee," a "third" (Bakhtin 1992) who was not within the conversation. This "super-addressee" was differently constituted across the two different discourses of return.

The first discourse of return was about possibility/actuality. These conversations were structured along the timelines of the war and people talked of return as impossible to undertake without rehabilitation funds to rebuild lost homes. These are of course the fundamental material necessities of reconstruction for displaced people, and should not be considered by any means only prosaic. To demand material help to return home is also to assert a claim for recognition as a people wronged. The other side of the possibility of return was, as I show above, not just about relationships to institutions, but also about the lifecycles of community and family regrowth. For the younger generation "return" could always be just another relocation. These conversations and representations around the actual possibility of return were addressed to specific listeners: the LTTE, the Sri Lankan government, UNHCR, and so on. These are the frames in which Northern Muslims are enmeshed and in which they negotiate and are transformed as *ahathi*, local, IDP, Northern Muslims, and citizens (or not). These are the "appellate agencies" that have immediate worldly power over people's lives and with which, despite appeals to justice and provision, negotiations were often attended by feelings of compromise and disappointment.[19]

While most examinations of return in the popular media and NGO reports in Sri Lanka understand return only in terms of a narrative of the possibility/actuality of relocation home, this does not obviate the other second discourse of "return," one that is shared across generations and is constitutive of Northern Muslim identity. Other scholars working with people who have been displaced for a protracted period have also remarked on how younger generations increasingly do not desire to return to their former homes, that new emotional landscapes have emerged within which return and former homes are situated in mythic rather than practical relations (e.g., Allan 2005 on Palestinian refugees in Lebanon). Return in Puttalam, as indeed for many populations (e.g., Palestinians) displaced by political violence, is more than compensation or even physical relocation. It is a profound social and emotional question about one's place in the world, about recognition of injustice; it opens a horizon of expectations and dreams whose longings can never be fully satisfied.

This other mythic vision of the "promise of return to-come" organizes the rightful location of past, present, and future. The "promise of return" stresses that the wounds of the Eviction and Tamil/Muslim relations can only be healed when future return repairs the past. The symbolism of return is a story about belonging that is written into the making of Northern Muslim communities. Whether Muslims can physically return or not, the emotional landscape of "return" remained central. Even for the young, who did not intend to return, identities were rooted in displacement and the story of a terrible injustice. Retelling their stories opened up the emotional landscape of the past to be healed, and injustice righted, through the political legitimacy of return. Thus the legitimacy of return, as a promise that the Eviction was a terrible wrong that should be righted, is never extinguished from Northern Muslim stories regardless of how and where people settled.

As Bakhtin stresses, while we are always seen and enacted in the space/ time of the other, there is always the ability to imagine, in Holquist's words, what "any space and . . . time [would] be like, in which I might define myself against an otherness that is other from that which has been 'given' to me" (Holquist 1990: 38). In other words, people hope that "outside the tyranny of the present there is a possible addressee who will understand them." For Bakhtin, all dialogue is undertaken in our faith that someday, somehow, we will be understood by somebody. Otherwise, he argues, we would not speak at all. If we believe that somewhere, someone will listen to us, then Northern Muslims address themselves to a time/space where they will belong. These promise-of-return conversations were often addressed to idealized and eternalized listeners beyond the present (not the appellate agencies) that are seen to perceive injustice outside the frames that are presently available: Allah, referred to as the only one who knows people's troubles; future generations of Northern Muslims; the Tamil community in the present and past; and always an idea of *ur* that did not forget the people who remember it.

I heard these differing visions, and the interplay of these two kinds of discourses of return and these two different sets of super-addressees, in many houses and in many stories, in relation to children, land, Tamil neighbors, and me. The pain involved in this bifurcation in 2003 was that the impossibility of physical return indicated the inability of this future and the past to be reconciled, the inability to return to a time before the Eviction.

To Return to Whom?

In this chapter, I have examined the ways Northern Muslims have striven to survive in their new homes in Puttalam and to remember their old homes, pointing to how their former homes/*ur* form the basis for remaking life in Puttalam. The spaces where memory inheres and the practice of making these spaces is here considered fundamental to the production of memory and these stories. For Northern Muslims, loss itself provides historicity. Discourses of "kinship" and "place" and the relationship between them represent both loss and regrowth at their heart, regrowth through loss and regrowth that makes loss. As Northern Muslims make and remake kin and *ur* within Puttalam, memory itself becomes displaced in their children. Continuity was created between generations through the retelling of the Eviction story, but this could not escape the discontinuities of space itself as time aged homes and people. As the children came to remember the Eviction as the genitive point of their identity, home/*ur* itself receded into a past that is not entirely made into the future. Love and obligation to children then sometimes came to defer love of *ur* itself. Thus homes became possible to be erased in the remembering process itself. At times the success of becoming and surviving as Northern Muslims is undercut with the knowledge that this may foreclose the possibility of return. These dilemmas and anxieties are now only magnified given that what was thought impossible and mythic, has become possible: the end of the LTTE and the opportunity to go home to the north.

Those who contemplate actual return know that the future is difficult. While some Muslim houses retreated back into the jungle that grew over them, many were reoccupied and Muslim lands were redistributed by the LTTE to Tamils. As long as the LTTE was the aggressive intermediary between Tamils and Muslims, opposition between northern Tamils and Muslims was constantly posited and reaffirmed by the LTTE. One optimistic possibility is that now that the LTTE is not longer there, Tamils and Muslims may come to forge new alliances. Certainly Rinaz and his family and the returnees to his village in Mannar had negotiated with church and Tamil civil organizations and did not anticipate any problems in returning. On the other hand, the disappearance of the LTTE yanks the veil from between Tamil and Muslim neighbors. If it was the LTTE who forced Muslims to go, it is no longer the LTTE who could potentially make it difficult for Muslims to return. Tamils and Muslims stand before each other, confronting for the first time Tamil complicity and accommodation with Muslim eviction, LTTE aggression aside.

While Tamils did not partake directly in the Eviction, they condoned it by their guilty silence afterward. The only Tamils I found willing to openly speak about Muslim Eviction were the younger generation who identified with Muslim Eviction as another instance of victimization of northern people by the LTTE, forced displacements they too had experienced (see Chapter 1). Tamil complicity was assured by their accommodation with the aftereffects of the Eviction. Some months after Eviction, the LTTE held an auction of Muslim goods in Jaffna, which many Tamils attended, and many Tamils accepted LTTE redistribution of Muslim lands and houses. The LTTE thus made Tamils *beneficiaries* of the Eviction if not perpetrators, and this odd status of beneficiary without perpetration is part of the complications of possible reconciliation processes in Sri Lanka.

Moreover, in most cases the Tamils living in Muslim houses and properties are unknown to Muslims. The new inhabitants are themselves refugees, often from oppressed castes and with few resources to leave the north. Furthermore, in 2006, the Sri Lankan government noted that because of the ten-year law of prescription (those who leave houses and land for more than ten years lose rights to them), some Tamils had also acquired land deeds for formerly Muslim houses. When Muslims talk about reconciliation with Tamils, and when Tamils confront the necessity of repairing Muslim and Tamil relations in the advent of possible Muslim return, houses and their journeys present the most difficult objects of negotiation. Who owns them? Is it the Muslims who owned them originally? Is it the Tamils who have squatted in them for the last 21 years? Who has the right to pass them on, to keep them imagined as potential dowry houses? Those abandoned houses have made another journey, from owned to occupied/squatted. Tamil refugees have fashioned dwellings from Muslim ruins. Returning home is not to old and familiar neighbors; it is to entirely new neighbors, new relationships, and new realities.

Shahul Hasbullah alludes to this, albeit less dystopically, in his 2007 article in the web blog *Countercurrents* on the "needs and aspirations of ethnically cleansed Muslims." He points out that

the social fabric of the north has also changed in the last seventeen years. Younger generations of the Northern Tamils have no memories or experiences of the formerly multi-ethnic northern communities where Tamils and Muslims co-existed peacefully for hundreds of years. There should be attempts to revive such memories and undertake initiatives to promote the renewal of relationships between Tamils and Muslims.

Hasbullah argues that the inability of Northern Muslims to return to their former homes is a national not local problem and must be solved as such." To make a "durable solution," he points out, is not to rely on some underlying hope that all will be well, but to actively engage in processes that reinstate imaginations of the north as multiethnic in the past and multiethnic in the future. Those generations of Northern Muslims and northern Tamils who have grown up with each other only as either spoken or unspoken absence will now have to initiate new relationships and create new realities.

It is here that Northern Muslim return can also become our figure of the future. In the years to come there will be increasing tension around Northern Muslim decisions to stay in Puttalam and their decisions to return to the north. There will be tensions with other communities and institutions, as well as within Northern Muslim families and communities. The working through of these tensions, the assertion of the right to return for Northern Muslims, active engagement at all levels for making new relationships between Tamils and Muslims twenty-one years after Eviction, the attempt to make ordinary life that does not iron over conflicts but accepts these conflicts as fundamental to new forms of recognitions . . . these are possible futures which are not just about local futures but also about national ones for Sri Lanka. As we shall see in coming chapters, this is just one of the many questions that confront the new future that the ending of the civil war presents us with.

CHAPTER FIVE

———

The Generation of Militancy:
Gender Militancy, and Self-Transformation

We were, those of us born in the 1960s, we were born into a time of
ethnic awareness and conflict. . . . We were those who grew up with the
influence of those, the disturbances of that time

　　It is an experience isn't it. People who were outside, their
opinions, their experience was different. Many of them cannot
understand. . . . There is a limit to our understanding once you enter a
movement. . . . People outside could see things clearer.

Kugamoorthy, now in his forties and living in London, was reflecting on his
youth in Sri Lanka. He was one of many young Tamils now in their forties and
fifties who joined militant movements by the thousands in the mid- to late
1980s. Kugamoorthy had joined TELO as an eighteen-year-old in the early
1980s, been imprisoned by the Sri Lankan state for most of the late 1980s,
and on his release renounced militancy and migrated abroad. This chapter
is about these young people and the biography, personal and collective, of
militancy. Not least, it is about the enormous social transformation that this
generation of militants produced, as well as the failure of the radical and egalitarian social transformation that such militancy promised to bring about.

　　The LTTE has represented Tamil militancy as merely the prelude to themselves in their own teleology, a genealogy that academics have uncritically
reproduced. Thus the first aim of this chapter is to reexamine "popular" Tamil
militancy in this period from the perspectives of the thousands who joined
many different groups in the 1970s and 1980s, forming a distinct generational

experience that cannot be deduced only from individual groups. I focus on Sakthi, a former female militant in the EPRLF, and weave her story together with others from her generation—Kugamoorthy, Vijitharan, Parmini, and others not named. The chapter thus attempts to look at the scale and penetration of popular militancy into Tamil lives in Jaffna without automatically putting the LTTE at the center of this history.

Following sentiments expressed again and again in my interviews and sociologist Francesco Alberoni's (1984) theorizations of the temporal and affective aspects of group formation, I treat militancy as a generational, affective, and personal transformation rising from perceptions of personal and familial oppression as much as political discrimination. Ideas about the household, caste, and marriage, rather than being the preexistent and stable foundation of nonpolitical "cultural life," were in fact the very subject of potential political transformation, part of the struggle for this generation to produce a new sense of Tamilness. After Benedict Anderson's (1991) formalization, it has become a truism to say that nationalism speaks in the name of the family and draws on the family for its metaphors of belonging. However, analysis often merely restates the symbolic representation of kin relations at the level of nationalist propaganda.[1] Here, I attempt to explore the concrete families and kin relations that militants drew upon in imagining militant kinships. I show how reimagining kinship within the militant movements equally transformed and repurified the kinship and households outside the movements, locking the two together symbiotically. I also look at how militancy, maintained as an exceptional space, ultimately failed to fundamentally transform the "unexceptional" normative order of Jaffna Tamil kinship and society to a more egalitarian order, even though the violent break up of the militant movements and the ensuing war and violent political culture have reimported political violence, war, and deprivation into the heart of the family. Instead, the normative hierarchical order of the Tamil family became reformulated around the "national liberation struggle" by the LTTE, producing conservative national movements and national families side by side. Tamil kinship and militant kinship have become constructed together by being explicitly and performatively excluded from each other.

This story begins with middle-aged men and women remembering their youth. I attempt to understand the ambivalence and contingency of ex-militants' lives now as they look back on their past, one that has been removed from the history of freedom fighting and placed in a history of treachery instead. This chapter attempts to understand how it is that belonging to such movements remade and transformed young people from different backgrounds into sharing the same collective love object and group (which became, in the case of the LTTE, the leader as group), and the eros and alchemy of belonging to movements and groups, which were to mark the people I interviewed indelibly. For the young who came after them these biographies, these choices, have shaped all Sri Lankan Tamil lives either for better or for worse.

Reframing Militancy

Who Were the Militants?

One of the major aims of this book is to reframe conventional academic and journalistic accounts of the Sri Lankan civil war, and in particular, accounts of Tamil militancy. The LTTE is most commonly represented as the major protagonist of Tamil militancy from the very *beginning* of militancy in the 1970s, and used often as shorthand for Tamil aspirations and responses to state discrimination. This chapter argues in contrast that the LTTE were one of multiple groups, and cannot encompass a much larger phenomenon of Tamil militancy.

Most standard academic accounts (e.g., Tambiah 1986; Spencer 1990a; Manogaran and Pfaffenberger 1994) written in the 1980s and 1990s describe that in the 1970s small militant groups began forming in the northern Jaffna peninsula (later extending their reach to eastern Sri Lanka) in response to continued discrimination by the Sri Lankan state and the seeming failure of the Tamil parliamentary parties to end this discrimination. Militancy was also inspired in part by the 1971 (failed and brutally repressed) insurrection against the Sri Lankan state by the southern Maoist JVP, as well as the 1971 Bangladesh liberation war and 1972 creation of Bangladesh with India's help (Krishna 1999: 96–98). The five groups that dominated the militant scene were the TELO, LTTE, PLOTE, EPRLF, and EROS.[2] All five were formed before the 1983 riots, though, as all accounts rightly point out, it was the riots that saw their membership rise (e.g., Tambiah 1996), transforming conflict into the possibility of war. After 1983, the Indian central government began to provide arms and training for groups in South India (Krishna 1999: 115–27). Soon there were multiple militant groups, though many of these were tiny and endlessly fracturing. The big five continued to dominate until the LTTE became supreme over others from 1986 onward.

This standard account is not factually inaccurate, but the paucity of writing on this era and the subjective transformations wrought has led to the inability to theorize militancy's interpenetration in Sri Lankan Tamil life, the rise of the LTTE, and not least the legacy of this period. The sparse literature on the period treats popular militancy through discussions of the LTTE, which has led to accounts treating the period only as part of the LTTE's rise to power and equating the LTTE with popular militancy and Tamils at large.

The last ethnographic accounts of the Jaffna peninsula were those of David (1973, 1977), Banks (1960), and Pffaffenberger (1982), all based on fieldwork (1940s–1970s) conducted before open violence. The only exception was the popular journalistic account by Narayan Swamy (1994) entitled *The Tigers of Lanka*, which, based on interviews with Tamil militants, remains a history of sorts for the internal happenings of Tamil militancy in that era. As the emphasis in academic work shifted from ethnic conflict to war and violence, so did work on militancy shift from factual description to a fascination with the Tigers. All the extant work on Tamil militancy, most of it coming after 1990, has been on the internal rituals and rhetoric of the LTTE (e.g., Schalk 1994, 1997; Hellman-Rajanayagam 1994; Roberts 1996, 2005), cemeteries and symbolism of the dead (e.g., Natali 2005; Hellman-Rajanayagam 2005), the LTTE state (e.g., Stokke 2006), and LTTE cadres more generally (e.g., Trawick 2007), though most often the LTTE female cadre (e.g., Balasingham 2003; Alison and Trawick 1999, 2007). These works identify popular Tamil militancy, post facto, with the internal dynamics and effects of the Tigers. Both sets of literature occlude any in-depth look at the Tamil militancy of the 1980s.

The only two in-depth panoramic accounts of Tamil militancy are Sumantra Bose's (1994) *States, Nations, Sovereignty* and Sankaran Krishna's (1999) *Postcolonial Insecurities*. Krishna's excellent account focuses on Tamil militancy in relation to India and the Dravidian movement, not the internal dynamics of the Tamil militant movements, so here I concentrate on Bose, who does attempt to tackle both the internal and external dynamics of the rise of Tamil nationalism. However, because his informants about Tamil militancy were Tiger "activists" and cadres, Bose gives the five critical factors about Tamil militancy as (1) the break between "*the LTTE phase* of Tamil nationalist politics" (my emphasis) and that of the Tamil parliamentary parties in their commitment to armed struggle; (2) the "genuine commitment" to the creation of a separate state; (3) the social origins of "the pioneer activists of the *Tiger movement*" as different from the traditionally Colombo-based elite Tamil politicians, with the militant leadership predominantly school dropouts from lower-middle-class Jaffna families; (4) "a comprehensive generational turnover . . . young men in their twenties had replaced established politicians in their fifties and sixties as the popular representatives of the Tamil struggle"; and (5) that "the movement led by the LTTE is significantly *more broad based, in terms of mass participation*" than earlier forms of Tamil nationalism and, furthermore, that "it was with *the rise of the Tigers* that a concern for progressive social change *within* the Tamil national formation first explicitly entered into the discourse and practice of Tamil nationalism" (1994: 82–83, my emphasis). While this chapter traces these five factors within the lives of those I interviewed, part of the work done here is to challenge how these social phenomena are mapped onto and naturalize the rise of the Tigers.

First, I name militancy in the 1980s as "popular militancy" to distinguish it from the years of recruitment to the LTTE in the 1990s. In the 1980s, young people voluntarily left their homes to join militant groups who were considered at that time marginal, risky, and foolish. After the LTTE became supreme, militancy and recruitment were of a different order. Recruitment was within a militarized quasistate structure set up by the LTTE with some voluntary joining, but overwhelmingly rising forced conscription resembling and using the language of national conscription to a national army (UTHR 1998; HRW 2004). The LTTE became increasingly a conventional army, with clearly laid out lines of reward and mobility and delimitation of distinct wings, brigades, and chains of command. Tiger cadres who die become martyrs and their families martyr families, giving them preferential treatment in LTTE taxation, relief, and dispensations (Hoole 2001).[3] Thus, the large-scale militancy of the 1980s, haphazard and less organized, has to be viewed as distinct in its own right.

There are few statistics for militant recruitment in this period; the only comprehensive set of figures for recruitment was put together by the journalist Dharmaratnam Sivaram, a former member of the militant group PLOTE and later the pro-LTTE editor of the Tamil news website Tamilnet before his murder, probably by pro-state forces. Even if taken as approximate, these figures are instructive. Sivaram (1997) states that the peak years of recruitment were 1984 and 1985[4] and that the number of militarily deployable youth (that is, those who were actively engaged in militancy) in the north and east in these years were around 44,800. All the major groups had two active sets of military cadres, the first the cadres being trained in Indian military camps, and the second those in "local training camps" in Sri Lanka who could be moved into regular units headed by Indian trainees. PLOTE, TELO, EPRLF, and EROS also had political wings (the Tigers only introduced a division between political and military wings much later in its history). PLOTE, the largest, had 6,000 members in India and 12,000 local trainees; TELO had 4,000 in India and 2,000 in Sri Lanka; EPRLF had more than 7,000 in its military wing; and EROS had 1,800. The LTTE had, in the mid-1980s, fewer than 3,000 full-time trained cadres.[5] Even Bose relates that only in 1987 did the LTTE number even 4,000. Added to these (which Sivaram does not count) are the thousands mobilized in PLOTE and EPRLF's youth wings and village committees, those not military cadres but affiliated with the groups through their "consciousness raising" efforts. So in popular militancy, hailed as the popular response to state discrimination and anti-Tamil riots, around 80 to 90 percent of those (Sivaram's approximate figure of 44,800 people) who joined militant groups did *not* join the LTTE.

Thus, in the 1970s and 1980s, the LTTE was one of many different militant groups rather than the only significant one. Its power derived not from being a popular group, which it never sought to be until the 1990s, but by, unlike others, having a small, secretive, and highly disciplined militarily structured group with little attempt at popular outreach beyond recruitment—never doing consciousness raising until after it was supremely in control and in a very different capacity as quasi-state. Thus, the widespread mobilization of Tamil youth into militancy cannot be explained through the LTTE's own account of its rise to power as an organic fact and evolution of Tamil nationalism and Sinhala chauvinism.

Moreover, Sivaram's figure of 44,800 people is around 2.8 percent of the overall 1984–1985 Sri Lankan Tamil population in the northeast. This 2.8 percent were almost all from the same generation—approximately ages sixteen to twenty-nine.[6] This concentration of militancy in a particular sizable age range gave it intensity and high visibility in Tamil life in the north as a whole. In this, Tamil youth fitted into a larger pattern within Sri Lanka. In his analysis of the JVP and the Tamil militant movements and their youthful character, Pieris (2008) draws on the global phenomenon of the "youth bulge"—the emergence of a new category of unmarried youth as a result of increasing education, aspiration, and marriage delay in the 1960s and 1970s—that has been linked to the growth of insurrection and violence in those periods around the world.[7] As he points out, what is significant is the transitional nature of this age range—post-school, pre-marriage, and pre-work. While Pieris develops this argument very plausibly in relation to the JVP, his data and analysis falter in relation to Tamil militancy, not only because figures are hard to obtain, but also because while he identifies the JVP with a mass base, he can only note that the LTTE only numbered around 3,000 in the 1980s. If we do not take participation in non-LTTE groups into consideration we cannot understand the penetration of militancy into Tamil public and private life.

This slow parsing through statistics illuminates how central and yet completely unexamined the phenomenon of popular Tamil militancy was, one that haunts the life of Tamils in their forties and fifties. The LTTE rise to supremacy saw 80–90 percent of those who had "risen up" against state discrimination imagining themselves freedom fighters become labeled potential Tamil traitors instead. While current accounts have treated other Tamil militant groups as marginal to the story of Tamil nationalism, and the LTTE, I attempt to shed light on the marginal who were in fact the majority.

The Nascent State

In 1990, Tambiah observed that profound and unaccounted changes in gender, generation, and caste relations were occurring within Tamil society; linking these to militancy, he argued that they were more fateful than the more "dramatic" war between Tamils and Sinhalese (Tambiah 1990: 28). My understanding of popular militancy is based on an ethnographic exploration of militancy as a subjective and transformative experience, itself the major lacuna in the literature on this period. In Sri Lanka, there are clear demographic, political, and sociological explanations for why a generation of young people could become alienated from their elders and the political system and turn to militancy. That will be part of the story in what follows. One can explain why certain movements arise, but not as easily why and how people come to see themselves in relation to each other as a group and the kinds of affective solidarity generated. Sociological categorization of the class and caste backgrounds of movements does not in itself help us understand the movement as an affective phenomenon that imparted radically new ways of seeing and feeling to its participants, which "homogenized" the heterogeneous individuals it gathered in, however briefly. From Marxist Maoist to conservative nationalist, Christian to Hindu, from those who had experienced violence to those who had heard about violence, they all joined, taking new names and turning into acronymed identities. Years after they had left the movements, I was told "you should go and talk to "TELO Sundar" and "EPRLF Kumari." When people entered militant groups, they spoke of their lives being transformed forever; they talked about their disillusionment and departure in equally emotional terms.

Here I draw on Alberoni's seminal (1984) *Movement and Institution* and his attempt to understand the affective and far reaching processes of group formation through showing the ways that participation itself engenders new forms of collective identity. While his work and investigation ranges from small Christian sects and couples in love to political iconoclasm, the uniting theme is the specific temporal shifts and states in which we experience forms of collectivity, significant in thinking through here how militancy can have a personal, political, and generational biography. From the first, Alberoni is at pains to establish the difference between aggregate group behavior where large groups behave in the same way (e.g., a fashion trend) and "collective group behavior" in which the participant

> calls into question the social and cultural background in which he found himself prior to the collective process itself and establishes a new kind of solidarity with fellow participants. Correspondingly, the participants in the collective process are conscious of belonging to a collectivity which has something outside of itself with which it is either in rapport or is in conflict—an external system. (1984: 17)

Alberoni defines thus three different "states": the institutional, the everyday, and the nascent. The nascent state is a "phase of discontinuity from both the institutional and every-day life point of view" (1984: 2), a transitional, liminal, experimental phase, emerging when, Alberoni argues, there is some failure or crisis in forms of social "solidarity"—a period of enormous social rupture or circumstances perceived as rupture. It is in this perceived rupture that the nascent state, of finite duration, flowers and then dies. Alberoni suggests that the nascent state is both a social phenomenon and an incipient possibility of social life:

> Broadly speaking, the nascent state is a proposal for reconstruction made by one part of the social system. By creating an *alternative solidarity*, the nascent state unites active participants who were previously independent and sets itself up in opposition to the existing order. (20)

If, as Alberoni suggests, "the nascent state can be studied either as a social phenomenon or as the restructuring of the subject's field of experience"

(1984: 126), here I analyze the early years of militancy as such a nascent state, ethnographic interviews providing the basis by which this process can be seen as *both* a social phenomenon and the restructuring of individual fields of experience. Joining such a group is first and foremost, Alberoni suggests, about denaturalizing reality and asserting one's own desires and aspirations as necessary human needs. While in our daily life we may not be happy with our actions, reactions, and events, we do not attempt to make our desires the frame through which life is possible. We accept that which exists as "real" and the existent seems more "real" than the "desirable": "it would not enter anyone's head to consider one's personal desires, however authentic they may seem to the individual, as something to be set up as an ethical principle valid for everyone" (1984: 58). Nascent states transform the existent into what is contingent, the product of particular choices and histories rather than natural. Moreover,

> in the nascent state it is also the personal history of the individual that is re-examined. He discovers his past and looks back over it reviewing every phase, and in this fashion explains his present and the reason for it being the way it is and not otherwise. But at the same time he realizes that it might have been different because nothing was ever natural or a matter of course; rather, on the contrary, everything was the result of decision, acceptance, compromise. (1984: 60)

Those who participate in such groups engage in a radical historicization of the past and thus the present. This historicization and the mutual search for new meanings for the past itself provides solidarity; searching and reappraising the past together in the group makes possible "a future reality, at once "mine, the others, and ours."

Thus these groups provide new epistemologies, a radical turning around of perspective. To those inside, those outside seem misguided, trapped, unenlightened, and unable to see what they are enmeshed in. This is why, Alberoni suggests, for many within groups, there seems a radical incommunicability between those internal and external. Belonging to the group itself has provided a radical new way of seeing; thus for those inside the only way for those outside to understand is to "join" them. *Intelligibility is through participation.* It is recognition of affinity through new common categories of reevaluating the world at large, which is more significant in bestowing membership and a sense of rebirth than a common sociological or homogeneous background.

This recognition of mutual affinity is linked to Alberoni's central proposition that group formation in the nascent state is about libidinal investment, love, and thus, guilt. Joining a group is thus posited around a fundamental ethical dilemma. In fracturing from larger society, the realignment fundamentally demands that each participant choose the solidarity of the movement and group over another. The other order, even if heavily repressive, is also affective. This is a choice between two collective love objects, such as the family and the movement, the latter choice a classic generator of anxiety, guilt, and feelings of betrayal in accounts of groups all across the world. Groups present those who enter with transgression; their promise of rebirth comes with a renunciation of another love. This is particularly apposite in the case of Tamil militants. Their narratives of militancy are not about the coexistence of militancy and ordinary family life; both are imagined as collective love objects that generate inimical responsibilities and duties. To enter into one seems to betray the other.

Alberoni argues that this betrayal itself is constitutive. Those who join groups are held together by a sense of mutual doubled betrayal—the betrayal and guilt of choosing the group over the love object left behind and the constant sense of betraying others in the group in longing for the life left behind (1984: 142).[8] The love, guilt, and renunciation between what is chosen and what seems forsaken means that, "precisely for this reason, however, the two sides are bound together and constitute a single social field in which each is forced to change, whether such change leads in time to a new arrangement of relationships or to mortal conflict" (131, 135). This emphasis on love, guilt, and renunciation is critical to my focus here on the idealized kinship of Jaffna Tamil homes as an external system that was invoked and formulated as a problem in the militant movements, tying together the Tamil family and the militant kinship.

Transforming Society, Transforming Oneself

Every week for some months in Colombo in 2003 I went to see Sakthi, then in her late forties. After going through an elaborate network of trust and recommendations, Sakthi, a member of the (formerly militant) group EPRLF, agreed to meet me. She was careful because the LTTE, taking the opportunity of the 2002 ceasefire to "put its own house in order," had escalated assassinations of Tamils from other organizations such as EPRLF. Sakthi was a virtual prisoner in her home.

That house is still imprinted in my mind. I can recall ascending the stairs curling around the inside of the complex of apartments, passing upward past children playing in the courtyard, and innumerable doors with shoes neatly laid outside them. Sakthi's door opened straight onto the living room and I would enter to find her patiently waiting, sitting on the sofa that faced the door. The only thing on the walls was a familiar sight in Tamil homes, a framed and garlanded photograph of those dead: Sakthi's brother, formerly a member of the group EROS, with his birth and death date written underneath. Uthayan, Sakthi's husband and also in EPRLF, was in and out. Occasionally Sakthi would get visitors, a trusted small network of people that now constituted an informal family for Sakthi and others like her. As assassinations by the LTTE continued and the situation deteriorated, Sakthi's ten-year-old daughter Vasuki began to retreat into silence. She would sometimes sit mutely listening to our long conversations about politics, her expression unfathomable. Sometimes she would lock herself into the bedroom and Sakthi would have to coax her out.

Born in the 1960s, Sakthi was one of five children—three boys and two girls—from a Tamil-speaking Vellala background. She grew up in a tightly knit network of maternal kin. Like many others, Sakthi recalled that as discrimination against Tamils grew, political discussions became increasingly common within the home. Sakthi and her sister as young girls began to be involved with the Tamil parliamentary coalition, the TULF. Soon Sakthi followed many other young, politicized Tamils and moved from TULF politics into the more dynamic sphere of militant politics, joining EPRLF in 1981. EPRLF was one of the first militant groups to include women in militant groups, and by 1982 it had a functioning women's committee. The emphasis was initially on political education and consciousness-raising. Between 1982 and 1986, the women's wing went to villages to hold political meetings and form women's committees to deal with issues of caste, education, and labor. By 1986, around 1,500 women cadres were receiving political education, with some receiving military training, which Sakthi and other women had fought to make EPRLF leadership accede to. Sakthi's brothers were not immune to militant politics either, with two out of three joining EROS. However, Sakthi's family supported EPRLF (rather than EROS) after she began working for them.

Sakthi was part of a generation of young people who came into adolescence and adulthood shaped by the increasing violence and discrimination of the Sri Lankan state and a feeling of uncertainty about their futures in Sri Lanka. They were the first *swabasha* generation, the immediate product of the

1956 language legislation, which though a "Sinhala only" act also instituted regional language education for all in Sri Lanka, replacing English as the medium (Obeysekere 1974; Pieris 2008). These young people were educated in Tamil, unlike their elders who had been educated in English, in a country with a disproportionately large Anglophone elite—on independence nearly 9.5 percent of the population spoke English (Kearney 1978: 526)—where politicians from left to right came from an elite Tamil, Sinhala, and Muslim background, went to the same schools, married one another, and spoke English at home and in public (Obeysekere 1974).

The global economic slowdown in the 1970s had an enormous impact in Sri Lanka. The expansion of universal education after independence produced thousands of young people with aspirations toward white-collar work (higher than any other generation), who were then subject to high rates of unemployment and an increasingly stagnant economy (Moore 1990; Kearney and Miller 1985). Obeysekere (1974) has analyzed in detail the emergence of youth insurrectionary groups in southern Sri Lanka from this incendiary mix of the expansion of education and aspiration. In Tamil areas youth frustration was further reinforced by policies that discriminated against Tamil-speakers as the economy was progressively Sinhalicized (Moore 1990: 349). University standardization in 1972 and the restriction of Tamil entry into university hit Jaffna in particular with its highly educated and aspirational population.[9] Pfaffenberger (1994) reports finding groups of young men in Jaffna in the late 1970s with absolutely nothing to do, sitting around listlessly.

Many young people had ambivalent attitudes to the Tamil parliamentary party, the TULF. The TULF was formed from a coalition of preexisting Tamil parties representing the formerly conservative upper-middle-class stratum of Tamil society and the old elites of Jaffna Tamil society. The same older high caste Vellala English-speaking professional men dominated families and Jaffna society. For young Tamils, frustrations about employment, education, and state discrimination were compounded by the gerontocratic and caste-based politics of home and village. Whittaker (1990) describes the *maccan* in Batticaloa in Eastern Sri Lanka, groups of young unmarried Tamil men who were more inclined to radical political agendas than their elders. For

> a young man with many sisters, much money to earn, and both his own and his *attan's* [mother's brother] work to attend to, it can be endless drudgery. . . . Hence it is often among *maccan* that one finds the hope often expressed with varying degrees of articulateness, that

things as a whole might change; that is, dowry might be done away with, or caste or even temples. It was also, at least in 1984, the *maccan* who showed the most admiration for "the boys," the radical separatist guerrilla fighters. (Whittaker 1990: 152)

Militancy emerged opposing itself to both the Sri Lankan state and their elders at home. School was the site of many discussions. Vijitharan recalled seeing, as a fourteen-year-old, public boards where notices with political slogans were pinned up among the notices for tuition masters and private classes. In school, young people discussed among themselves the increasing violence of the Sri Lankan state, the anti-Tamil riots, the Sri Lankan police force. Militant groups appeared within the secret languages of the young, the conversations that fell silent when those in authority, parents and teachers, appeared. The line was drawn within Tamil society as much as without.

The Militancy of the Young; Caste, Marriage, and Kin

Muthu had initially been active in the TULF youth wing before becoming a member of GUES (later EPRLF). He related the youth wing's growing frustration with the elder statesmen of the TULF, who they felt engaged in political rhetoric and speeches while issuing orders to young activists to do the work. All the while, he said, these older politicians would stand back in public from actions that brought police attention to the young men. Muthu felt that they were just the hired hands of the older politicians. Young Tamils increasingly became dissatisfied with the ability of these men to bring about change; they wanted to claim this public space of action and potential heroism as their own.

These claims were ideological and elective rather based on preexisting class, caste, and family structures. The new militants were young men and women who proclaimed their freedom from caste boundaries, with some like EPRLF actively organizing those considered "lower castes" and others like the LTTE having a core of *karaiyar* (fishing caste) members. This was significant because the 1960s had been the stage for high profile conflicts over caste, such as the 1968 Temple entry crisis at Maviddapuram Temple (Pfaffenberger 1990). The "high caste" parliamentary parties such as the Federal Party consistently sidestepped the potentially divisive issue of caste. When the militant movements began they all professed to be anti-caste and organized differently from the caste patronage that they saw informed the old Jaffna political parties. However, many of the militant groups were viewed obliquely through caste, recruiting as they did through village, friendship groups, and sibling connections: PLOTE was considered a "high caste" movement, EPRLF a "low caste" movement, and the LTTE core from a matrix of village and caste loyalty based around Valvettithurai in northern Jaffna famous for its smuggling and "hard men" (Fuglerud 1999: 35). This early emphasis on freedom from caste oppression was subsumed in the late 1980s by an attempt to create a pan-caste, transcendent Tamil identity, with the national question trumping the caste question, as we will explore later.[10] Nonetheless, it is important to remember that in the 1970s and early 1980s, many young militants were openly frustrated with caste orders.

Moreover, young people's desire for radical change was most pressingly related to household and family expectations and obligations for marriage and dowry.[11] Young unmarried men and women saw joining the militant movements as freeing themselves from these obligations, particularly that of dowry. Dowry weighed heavily on young men who had to work to make dowry for their sisters—sons do not inherit land easily in Jaffna, they are expected to "marry land." It was even more difficult for women, who were both the objects and process by which new households were reconstituted.

Sakthi's family supported her in her political ambitions, allowing her to hold meetings in their home and not constraining her movements. But many young women who joined the militant movements faced condemnation from their families. Even Sakthi faced much gossip and censure by others in her caste-conscious village, when she began to work for EPRLF, commonly represented as a "low caste movement." Sakthi was criticized for holding meetings in dalit/oppressed caste villages and eating and drinking in dalit homes. Such activities, it was felt, would compromise young unmarried women's chances of marriage, which would then reflect on the family itself. Young militant women found that the everyday acts of eating with unknown others, walking at night, moving across villages, and associating with young men outside the house were considered shameful, not just involvement in politics per se. Sakthi says,

> The women were looked at and talked about if they even stayed the night in another house. So they would always have to return home at night . . . some families were fine about their sons joining the movements, but not their daughters. One, they were worried about their daughters' safety. The other thing is they were worried about

what other people would say about their daughters working like this . . . what would happen to their marriage prospects.

For women involved in the militant movements, it was precisely their experiences of their position as unmarried young women that led them toward the movements. And it was the threat of unmarriageability that senior family members used to exert pressure against their involvement. In Jaffna, marriage is the central lifecycle and property relation, as Thesawalamai, the customary code enshrined in Jaffna, makes clear (Kantawala 1930). It is through marriage, not birth as in North India, that new houses are founded and new alliances formed; the family reconstitutes itself around each marriage (Kantawala 1930: 17). The primary mode of capital and social accumulation in Jaffna society is through the transfer of property through dowry, thus through women (Tambiah 1973).[12]

Women were thus centrally associated with the reproduction of the household, whether they worked outside the home or not (many did). Pfaffenberger (1982) argues that the house is symbolically constructed in order to harness the *sakthi*/power of the high-caste Vellala woman in the same way that the temple is built to secure the *sakthi*/power of the god.[13] The temple contains dangerous and fertile divine power in much the same way the household contains and protects the fertile power of the wife from others. Given that the household is the central institution in Jaffna society, there is in fact considerable power for women within the scripted household roles—David (1980) describes Jaffna women as "outwardly enslaved and inwardly powerful" (104). However, while women did and continue to wield a great deal of power in Jaffna Tamil society, it is by being a chaste senior wife, and it is the discourse of chastity through which women's lives are managed. They were only allowed to be the carriers of property and the managers of kin at a senior stage in their life cycle. The entrance of women into militancy and crossing caste lines irrevocably challenged the allotted script. Being involved in the militant movements involved moving outside the household mode of gendered power that intimately involved them in clashes with the gerontocratic and gendered structure of kinship.

Thus, for the young people who joined the militant movements and the groups as they emerged, Tamil society itself, as well as Sinhala majoritarianism and state discrimination, posed problems that had to be fixed, particularly the perceptions of unequal caste, generation, and to some extent (for the women who joined) gender relations. For both young men and women in this era, unmarried and often economically junior, the militant movements offered a horizontal form of kinship—one based on mutuality, a feeling of togetherness, ideological commitment—the kind of relationships that were perceived to be totally absent from the caste and hierarchically structured family and household with its vertical forms of inheritance, based on land and marriage.

The movements stressed new loyalties and allegiances through parallel forms of kinship. When young people joined militant groups, they were meant to be "transformed," taking or being given different "movement names," loyalties, and duties. Even after leaving militant organizations, the majority of my informants still know each other by their "movement names," not their birth names. Even if sibling relations in the family were those of mutual dependency and obligation, the militant groups, like many such groups globally, instituted sibling relations as the valorized mode of egalitarian relations. Thus all called each other elder brother (*anna*), younger brother (*thambi*), elder sister (*akka*), and younger sister (*thangachi*). There were no elder generation terms used in the militant movements, with only a few more recently named as "uncles" (*amman*). The militant movements celebrated the power of youth, traditionally considered to be junior and powerless in the household, to initiate and make change for the whole of society.

The representation of household and militancy as inimical spaces of loyalty, if not love, was highlighted by the way in which most of the young men joined militant movements. Given the highly secret and dangerous nature of militancy, most who joined did not tell their families until the last minute. Initially, though this was to change when women were increasingly sent for training in camps too, Sakthi and many other female militants stayed in Jaffna. However, the young men who joined the armed wings of the militant groups were sent for combat training in India. When Kugamoorthy joined TELO in 1982 as an eighteen-year-old, he was immediately sent to India. He presented it to his family as a fait accompli.

> The day before I left, I told my mother that I was leaving for India. Amma was scared and I told her not to tell anyone. The next evening I went and took the boat to India for training. I had only seen the man [from TELO] for four times before I went.

A number of my male interviewees told me similar stories: one day they would leave home and their families would find out long after the fact that they had joined one group or another. When the 1983 riots occurred, fifteen-year-old Vijitharan and the other school boys in his class began discussing taking action.

> We felt that we should definitely also go and fight . . . in our school
> there was already someone who had gone to the LTTE. . . . me and
> another boy, my cousin, he is dead now . . . we thought that we would
> go. . . . We had no idea [laughs]. We didn't know what liberation was!
> None of us knew. We weren't politically aware; all we knew is that we
> wanted to beat the Sinhala army. Why the army? Because they were
> attacking us.

Furthermore, for Vijitharan, who was uncertain how he was going to perform in his exams, this was perhaps a way to gain respect by other means.

> I was studying for my O levels exams. That was also a big pressure that
> if you fail the people at home won't respect you if you don't get a pass.
> [laughs] That was not the reason, but that also played its part.

Vijitharan and his cousin went to a neighboring village and waited near a known temple with a group of other boys where the LTTE recruiter would come.

> Even more than me, it was my cousin. He had lots of trouble with his
> *mama* (mother's brother), who used to beat him a lot. He didn't want
> to go home either. After two days, at about 9 p.m., we were taken to
> the sea shore and put on a boat.

> *S:* You never went home?
> *V:* No, I never went. With that I was gone.

It would be some years before Vijitharan saw his family again. Many militants' families did not have news of them for months or see them for a year or more. Militancy and the household were not spaces that could be combined. Tamil militancy from the very beginning separated household and training spaces.

This was especially heightened in the LTTE, where loyalty to the movement and the leader was considered the new supreme value. Ranjan, from Vavuniya in north central Sri Lanka, ran away and joined the LTTE as a fourteen-year-old in 1988. Ranjan and his family had moved to Vavuniya from Anuradhapura after they had lost everything in the 1977 anti-Tamil riots. Ranjan joined in the period after the LTTE had become supreme and cannot be considered part of the upsurge of the mid-1980s in the same way as the others I write about, but his memories of what the transformation wrought on his relationship to his family after joining are symptomatic of many others. Ranjan underwent the compulsory camp training and separation from his family that the LTTE insisted upon.

> At the time that the LTTE took me, I heard that my mother was going around crying and looking for me. But I went to the movement basically because of the problems in our country . . . in my mind I became convinced that this was the only solution. But this was not the same for my family. They had thought they would send me to Colombo, or somewhere else and educate me. My mother had tried several times after I had gone to get me out. The movement would not let me go of course. If you go then you can't leave. As a young person the LTTE will never let you out. Until you are older they will not even show you outside. I was much older when I went outside and came to see them [his family].

As a young, strong man growing up, Ranjan had been continually harassed by the Sri Lankan police and the Indian forces under suspicion of being an LTTE member. He saw himself as giving in to a label he was already wearing.

> Those days when you left the camp you had to wear the capsule. When I went I was wearing a cyanide capsule. I had become part of the movement. We could not live just ordinarily in our *ur* without being taken for being part of the movement [LTTE]. After we had become part of the movement we couldn't live at home either. There was nothing I could do. I had landed in the movement now I had to carry on, that was how I then carried on with my life. . . . I had gone to fight, I learned to fight, so I fought.

Ranjan's face was indescribably sad as he told me of going home wearing the cyanide capsule, the trademark of the LTTE which cadres on capture by enemies were supposed to swallow rather than be taken alive. The capsule had made him a stranger at home. After his time in the LTTE camp, he refers in Tamil, not to "returning" home but to going "outside" from the camp. Inside and outside had been transformed.

For all the ex-militants of all groups I interviewed, foremost was the sense of new selves and transformation through participation in the movements. This is why I choose to highlight group formation around mutual recognition of affinity through common participation rather than sociological homogeneity. Following Alberoni, it was very clear for militants that joining the groups was in effect drawing a new line between inside and outside. The movement and the family present themselves as opposed love objects, a fundamental ethical dilemma between the gerontocratic perpetuation of the family and a new collective self. Understanding the sense of personal transformation effected by militancy is also critical in comprehending the extent to which disillusionment and departure from militancy, which came in the late 1980s and 1990s, was both a personal and political crisis for young people.

Householders, Fighters, and Traitors

In 1985, the militant groups wielded considerable power in the Jaffna peninsula; the Sri Lankan army was largely confined to areas around their barracks and the peninsula was carved up among different militant groups who all had their zones of operation and strongholds. Militants were increasingly unaccountable to civilians, taking their own initiative to police and "eliminate" those they saw as antisocial and traitorous elements. In April 1985, the LTTE, TELO, EPRLF, and EROS came together in the ENLF (Eelam National Liberation Front) to work together against the Sri Lankan Army. However, by 1986 cracks had already appeared, within movements and in the formal unity between them.

All the militants had headquarters in India, where they were being trained by Indira Gandhi's RAW (Swamy 1994; Krishna 1999). Increasingly there were conflicts between the high command of militant groups in India and local leaders in Jaffna. In 1985, the novel *Puthiyathor Ullakam?* (*A New World?*) was published by the Sparks (Theepori) group in PLOTE.[14] The novel centered on a group of young men who, drawn into a militant movement, found their ideals sacrificed and themselves subject to a internal regime of brutal conformity and internal killings. The group related around 90 internal killings they said had already happened in PLOTE. The book was the first acknowledgment of the internal killings and factional fights convulsing all the militant movements, particularly PLOTE, LTTE, and TELO.[15] The new recruits found that the "freedom fighting" organizations were military outfits demanding complete obedience. Many attempted to leave, but this was no easy task. Dissenting recruits were already being purged. Vijitharan who joined the LTTE as a sixteen-year-old and was trained in India recalls this vividly:

> They thought that these people would disturb the others. . . . If you didn't know anything then you were clean and then someone would come along and tell you something and then you become disturbed. . . . When we were inside, these many small problems became big issues for us . . . the answer [given to them] was do what Prabhakaran tells you and remain quiet. That was the order and our career. He will tell someone, they will tell another person and then they will tell us. We were soldiers and we had to do what we were told. . . . That was the system.

Moreover, all the militant movements were in competition with each other in Jaffna and Chennai, India. Vijitharan remembers that in 1984, at his first meeting with Prabhakaran, the LTTE leader in India,

> He asked me, "Do you have anything to do with PLOTE?. . . . " I told him no, but that my elder brother supports them. "Why didn't you go to PLOTE," he asked me. I told him that it had not occurred to me to go to them; it was to the LTTE that I wanted to come. Anyway, I said to him, "you are all the same aren't you, you are all one, we are all doing the same thing, we are all joined." He told me "we have to eliminate Uma Maheswaran [the leader of PLOTE][16] He is a traitor. You don't know, little brother, he is a traitor. We are the ones who will bring liberation and we have to wipe him out first."

On 29 April 1986, the LTTE launched a surprise attack on TELO camps. Within one week the camps were overrun and TELO cadres arrested and killed; estimates of the number of dead vary between 200 and 400.[17] In Jaffna, a high number of the TELO cadres were of eastern origin (particularly Trincomalee), didn't know Jaffna, and thus were especially vulnerable.[18] PLOTE cadres disobeyed the LTTE and helped some TELO cadres escape. It was clear that it would be the next organization to be attacked. On 29 October PLOTE voluntarily announced that it was withdrawing from Jaffna, upon which the LTTE promptly banned it and demanded that PLOTE cadres hand over their weapons.

The next group the LTTE turned its attention to was the EPRLF. Sakthi's memories of this year are bitter:

> We never thought that the situation would be like this. We started in 1982 but by 1986 we were banned. First we thought we would fight for political rights against the government, then we began to realize that we also needed to fight for women's rights, and then the movements began to split among themselves. Then we began to say whether just for women or for ordinary people we must not splinter like this. Now it is one against another.

EPRLF were the only organization to protest the banning of the other militant groups. EROS remained quiet, allying with the LTTE campaign in return for its continued existence. On 12 December the EPRLF women launched a large women's protest march appealing for unity and an end to all political killings. Sakthi was foremost in the organization of this.

> This came from the women's movement . . . we wanted to be united, to discuss our nation and women together, and we wanted to say that you shouldn't use violence against each other. The march wasn't just women who were in our movement; it was also women from outside the movement who supported us. Many women came for that march from all ages: young, old, and middle-aged.

The march would be the last action the EPRLF women's wing would ever organize. On 13 December the LTTE announced that EPRLF and TEA were now banned. Though EPRLF was probably the best armed of the militant movements, internally the group was reluctant to fight other Tamils and capitulated easily. EPRLF cadres were arrested and their offices raided. Sakthi's cousin was one of the many EPRLF cadres who disappeared.

Few defied the LTTE publicly, though UTHR reported that some of the lone protests came from women from oppressed caste villages near Keeri-malai and Mallakam, who sat on the road around their villages armed with kitchen knives and chili powder to defend EPRLF members (Hoole et al.

1990).[19] In the absence of any political structures or public voices to protect these young people, village and family structures were closing around their children to keep them safe. If militant and household spaces had been hitherto kept separate, now they were being rapidly folded together.

Sakthi herself was placed under house arrest, and her mother, aunt, and sister came together to protect her. The household became a fortress protecting Sakthi and at the same time a prison keeping her in.

> My elder sister locked me in one of the rooms and told me not to come out . . . . My cousin had also been taken. They [her mother, sister, and aunt] stood there and fought with these boys, they told them "if you are going to shoot, shoot us." "Who are you? We have been supporting the struggle, you are not the only people in the struggle. We have helped your movement and we will help other movements too, they have also come to fight just like you, we see all of you as one. . . . My aunt even grabbed their shirt. . . . and told them "If you shoot, then shoot me." . . . In the beginning people didn't consider so much the differences between, EPRLF, EROS, LTTE . . . when they thought of the "movements" they thought of them as the boys who have gone to fight for our liberation and so they helped them. Because they had all set out to help, we had even helped the LTTE. . . . So that is why they were so angry when the LTTE came to take away their children. . . . They [the LTTE] told them that I was not allowed to leave the house and not to talk to anyone. If you had been living from the beginning and working as I had been you cannot live like this. It was so difficult.

It was a deeply disillusioning moment for her as for others; as the militant movements splintered, the model of inter-movement kinship could no longer be maintained. Having moved from a role in the household to militancy, here she was confined to the household again.

EROS, the movement in which all Sakthi's brothers were members, was in alliance with the LTTE and refused to condemn its actions in banning the EPRLF. Sakthi and her youngest brother still active in EROS suddenly found themselves positioned on opposing lines. After the "banning," Sakthi's brother took leave from active combat duty in Mullaithivu and returned home to see her. She recalls with great sadness that he had looked very troubled in the few days he had stayed. He had tried to initiate conversation, telling her "I have some things to tell you," but in the end they had not had a full conversation about things. All she knew was that he was troubled by EROS's unquestioning support for the LTTE and the internecine warfare. Perhaps, she speculates now, he would have left EROS. When his leave was over he returned to Mullaithivu. They never saw him again. A few months later EROS sent word to them that he had been killed fighting the Sri Lankan Army in March 1987. He was twenty-four at the time of his death. Sakthi remembers,

> My brother's death was constantly on my mind. . . . I was really distressed at the time, I had lost most of my contacts, I could not move around freely. Always having to stay at home, I was thinking about it all the time and becoming sad and sadder. My mother was crying all the time about my brother's death. We had no body. If we could have at least seen it.

Sakthi's brother and her cousin and their disappearance in this time exemplify the invisible and secret deaths that many families close their ranks around. This was becoming numbingly normal: almost every family from the north and east has one member who is dead or disappeared due to the war, and is thus forced to shape some parts of itself around the presence of violent and untimely death.

The Indian Peace Keeping Forces

The entrance of the Indian Peace Keeping Forces in 1987 to maintain the Indo-Lankan accord further destroyed popular militancy. After the Sri Lankan government bombarded the peninsula in Operation Liberation, India intervened directly in the island to broker a peace accord to grant increased autonomy to the north and other amendments. If implemented, it would have made considerable difference in the lives of Tamils and Muslims. In 1987, Indian Peace Keeping Forces (IPKF) entered Jaffna to maintain the Indo-Lankan accord. The Indian command of TELO, ENDLF, and EPRLF brokered the alliance and entered with the Indian army.[20] The situation soon broke down into an all-out war between the IPKF and the LTTE, a war with a shadowy guerrilla force that melted into and used civilian spaces and civilian bodies as decoys and disguises. Indian forces could not tell if all Tamils were Tigers or not, and became embroiled in a full-blown counter-insurgency campaign in the towns and villages. As Jaffna's landscape was raked into sandbags and checkpoints, the Indians conducted nightly patrols and arrested thousands of young men and women. Rape by soldiers became rife. The allied militant groups became inextricably associated with the IPKF's actions both through their defence and their participation in IPKF operations.

The militant allies of the IPKF, smarting from their Sri Lankan banning by the LTTE, began to make clear their anger with the LTTE and their resentment of ordinary people's seeming quiescence at their banning (Bose 1994; Hoole et al. 1990). Many of the cadres backed by the IPKF began to abuse their newfound powers against civilians. Conservative Jaffna society derided and mistreated EPRLF cadres as lacking legitimacy as a "low caste" movement, which further stoked resentment. EPRLF was engaged with internal and often fruitless struggles to prevent cadres from abusing their positions. While EPRLF members themselves find it hard to discuss this era, it was clear that their actions and collaboration with the IPKF has led to their declining popularity among Tamils.

In contrast, the LTTE emerged as the only militant group that opposed the Indian campaign against Tamils. It had seized a moral advantage it itself had fought to create; it became the "sole defender" of Tamils against all attackers, Indians and Sinhalese. As the IPKF campaign proceeded, the LTTE continued to gather behind it the bitterness of those who felt betrayed by the Indians they thought had come to save them.

Sakthi's family and village were caught in one of the first battles of the 1987 war as the IPKF advanced into Jaffna up Urimpirai road (Hoole et al. 1990). Hundreds were killed in her area, one of the worst affected in the campaign. One night while most of the family escaped to the fields to hide from the shelling, her youngest uncle and his family had remained in their house. After the army withdrew, two of her uncles went to see what had happened. One uncle returned with her youngest uncle's son, daughter, and their nine-month-old baby. Their parents, her uncle and aunt, and the three other children had died. Her uncle had found the three surviving children and the little boy running into his arms had told him what had happened.

Indian soldiers from Tamil Nadu had come into the house and spoken to them in Tamil. At the time my uncle and the children were ill with fever. . . . and the soldiers had let them go, telling them, "we are going, other soldiers from the north [of India] are coming behind us; we don't know what they are going to do." The other soldiers had come and without asking a single question they had fired at my uncle. My uncle was holding the baby. He had immediately fallen to the ground, and his blood had covered the baby but the baby had not taken any direct fire. . . .

My uncle, aunt, and three children had died on the spot. Three children survived, the eldest son, the three-year-old daughter, and the nine-month baby. The children had lain down as if they were dead amid the bodies during the firing. The boy had told his little sister to lie down when she tried to rise and they lay with the blood flowing over them. After an hour, they rose and looked and saw the army was no longer there.

The three surviving children are now being raised by their other uncles.

Unlike the other stories we discussed often, we only talked about the deaths of Sakthi's family once. It had struck at the roots of her close-knit family. Sakthi and her family managed to burn the bodies of her uncle and family in their garden. Many others could not even recover the bodies of their dead. Because of curfews and roundups, some of her family could not be informed of the deaths, neither her sister who only lived 1 km away nor her brother who lived abroad. The inability to tell others within the family and the breaking of everyday kinship networks of information and shared grief is another aspect of the painful process of mourning these deaths (Lawrence 2002).

Sakthi's bitterness was heightened by the fact that she had witnessed Indian atrocities even while EPRLF high command issued denials:

We were at home; the command was all in India . . . we were so angry. We had suffered already under the IPKF; we could not believe it. Not just our family, but we had seen what had happened in front of our eyes. All the deaths. . . . We were so affected by this and on the radio they [EPRLF in India] were saying that the IPKF had not hurt anybody, that women had not been raped and so on, just lies, we were so angry.

She was isolated from her own movement and unable to convince EPRLF leadership in India that the IPKF were committing daily atrocities.

We were telling them [EPRLF leadership] that people won't accept us if we ally with the IPKF. At the beginning we thought that good things would come from the Accord, but then after the fighting started . . . after you see these problems with your eyes, of course you have a problem with the Indian Army.

Sakthi left EPRLF in 1987 in protest, though eventually she and some other senior figures returned to the movement. The abuse of power by individual EPRLF cadres and the defence of the Indian alliance has become a difficult legacy for EPRLF who recognize that their dwindled support today relates to this alliance.[21] It is this that led senior members of EPRLF after the departure of the Indians to abandon militant politics, give up arms, and move into parliamentary politics. Sakthi to this day continues to be a member of EPRLF, campaigning for them in municipal council elections. Nonetheless, the deaths of Sakthi's uncle and family and the surviving three children are a constant reminder of the difficult memories for many of the potential betrayal of the household by their own movements.

The final withdrawal of the IPKF in 1990 and the renewal of the LTTE came courtesy of the Sri Lankan government. Eager to get the Indians out by 1989/1990, President Premadasa entered into secret talks with the LTTE. India withdrew when the Sri Lankan government rearmed and renewed the LTTE. The 1990 peace talks between the LTTE and the Sri Lankan government soon broke down in October into Eelam War II. Members of the other militant groups began fleeing for their lives again, confronted with some hard lessons.

"I was kept safe by the Sinhala captor"

Kugamoorthy had been arrested in 1983 and had been severely tortured in a series of army and police camps before being transferred to prison in Colombo.

Being inside in a way was good for me. There were many different people from different movements inside, and we could see and learn about each other's views and ways. When we were outside, we were just inside our own movements.

In 1986, Kugamoorthy's mother came to visit him after the LTTE/TELO clash and told him of the fighting in the streets and the LTTE order that no help was to be given to any other movement.

She said to me, "good thing that you were caught. If you had been outside, the LTTE would have shot you." That had an immense effect on me. Because I was in the keeping of the enemy . . . I was kept safe by the Sinhala captor. It was so dishonorable that it was the enemy who kept my life safe. I wrote a poem called "Amma vanthal," "Mother came." . . . When they put the handcuffs back on, I was sad to go back into the place knowing that was the reason I had my life.

Kugamoorthy went and found his notebooks that he had kept while in prison, and then recited to me his poem "Amma vanthal"/"Mother Came." When he was released from prison in 1987 he left all militant activity and went abroad. How was he to understand that the enemy he had sworn to fight, the Sri Lankan state, through no intention of its own was the reason he was alive? The most immediate "enemy" and threat to his life and liberty had in fact turned out to be contained in Tamil militancy itself. Years later, he reflected on his TELO past with discomfort:

The problem was that all the movements turned quickly to violence for everything. Whenever anyone talked something different, then they said that he was someone against the movement then immediately the response was to repress him within the movement or chase him out, or kill them. . . . We became movements that . . . didn't know how to stand together with different opinions. . . . We have responsibility. We cannot deny that we are involved in creating what has happened. We could have changed it and we didn't.

While others did not articulate as clearly as Kugamoorthy the problems within the militant movements, nonetheless most talked about the escalation of violence and the intolerance of different opinions that came to mark the Tamil political sphere. It is undeniably this that has led to the current political climate of suspicion and fear. Culpability, guilt, and a sense of nostalgia for the movement linger on.

Moreover, for all these young people, their constitution of themselves as political subjects was through their perception of the Sri Lankan government as a Sinhalese majoritarian government, an enemy of Tamil people, unrelentingly violent and discriminatory and unwilling to concede any political reform. There were multiple reasons why young people had felt alienated from their families and society, from unemployment to intra-family pressures and conflicts. But the move toward militancy was formed around a collective story and reality of anti-Tamil discrimination, which gave a framework in which one could situate one's own biography. In 1986, however, the certainties of who was "the enemy" dissolved. The majority of the young people who had joined militancy were suddenly sundered not only from the history of Tamil nationalism but also from the selves they had constructed. Whom were they to support now? Did they face greater danger from other Tamils or Sinhalese? How could they play a part in Sri Lankan politics? If they were not freedom fighters, then who were they?

After 1990 militancy was over for most of these young people, and if any remained active against the LTTE, their lives were at risk. Those who remained active in politics in Sri Lanka pursued dangerous options. With their own groups unable to offer them protection, many joined the Sri Lankan army as specialized units.[22] These proceeded to enact the same violence against Tamil civilians that they once swore to fight against. Some moved in-between into the EPDP, which became a functioning political party allied to the national political party the People's Alliance, although EPDP continued to maintain a private arsenal and was, in tandem with the Sri Lankan government, responsible for recent abductions and deaths of Tamils. Others joined the LTTE, even from the group Sakthi belonged to, meaning that EPRLF too split between those who remained part of EPRLF proper and a small faction who joined the LTTE.[23]

Most of this generation left the groups totally disillusioned, resuming their jobs and family lives and striving to survive (Fuglerud 1999). Those who could went abroad to India, Europe, and Canada. I encountered countless ex-militants in London and Toronto. Some continued to support their respective groups at a distance; some rejected militant politics altogether. When Kugamoorthy came to England, he initially imagined that he would get involved in some political activity and "do something," but then "twenty years went." This was also a common theme from those I interviewed abroad: at first they would imagine that they would still be politically active but after a while mortgages, jobs, and new realities would slowly take over.

Many felt guilty about leaving the country to live a normal life *and not* putting their lives in danger,[24] indicative of the newly set stakes of the Tamil political sphere. While death should not be the stake of meaningful and sustainable politics, people like Kugamoorthy and others felt that somehow they had betrayed others, perhaps Sri Lanka itself, in living a life free from the possibility of being killed. Meaningful politics seemed to then be about what put your life at stake. Guilt and responsibility mingled equally with fear and disappointment.

Sakthi and her husband Uthayan were among those who had refused to leave Sri Lanka even though members of EPRLF were being killed throughout the ceasefire, both former and current members.[25] Even minor members, supporters, or family members of EPRLF came under threat. As assassinations increased, there was increasing controversy about how they were reported. The LTTE labeled all these as the killings by "paramilitaries," recusing themselves from such a label. Groups such as Amnesty International would only report the deaths of those who were not members or attributed members of formerly arms-bearing groups ("paramilitaries"). Given that a large proportion of the Sri Lankan population, Tamil and Sinhala, had been at one time involved in one form or another of militant politics, the label "paramilitary" reached deep into the roots of Sri Lankan community, family, and individual lives. Furthermore, the SLMM (the Sri Lankan Monitoring Mission) comprised of the five Nordic nations overseeing the ceasefire did not count these assassinations as violations of the ceasefire. These deaths were considered flotsam and jetsam from another era (Thiranagama 2010). (In more recent years, government aided Tamil groups such as EPDP have also been given impunity to carry out all manner of extra-judicial actions against Tamils they accuse of being LTTE, adding to the general fear of other Tamils by Tamils (see UTHR 2009b and recent UTHR reports)).

When I came to interview people, it had been 10 or 15 years for many since they had left militancy. They were now parents themselves, struggling with raising children and negotiating their own Tamilness afresh. Many of the female militants from non-LTTE groups had retreated into the home. Here, I move from personal to societal transformation. Why did those I interview who spoke of personal transformation continue in exile to give dowry and reinforce the socially conservative practices they rebelled against, while scholars in Sri Lanka increasingly identified transformations of traditional gender and caste roles within the LTTE? This is where the biography of militancy, and, thus, our analysis, merges with the LTTE.

Exceptional Spaces and Normative Orders

From 1990 onward the LTTE produced itself as a quasi-state within the Sri Lankan state, mimicking it by setting up its own law, taxation systems, army, and even, it later turned out, its own air force. The violence of the Sri Lankan state against ordinary Tamils (military campaigns and arrests and brutal torture) pushed Tamils out of Sri Lanka and many of those in Sri Lanka toward the LTTE. This has been well documented by the human rights group UTHR; here I concentrate instead on the internal story: why the promised social transformation of the 1970s and 1980s, the rebellion against dowry, caste, and normative family orders did not materialize in the larger Tamil society and the lives of ex-militants in middle age. Why was it that militancy, which transformed Sri Lanka indelibly in so many ways, failed to transform Tamil society in the way it wanted to?

One answer, given by all the militants I interviewed, is the way nationalism subsumed issues about caste and gender under the seemingly more burning question of "national self-determination." The national question and the seeming necessity of "militarization" were assumed to trump other forms of transformation; other forms of change would be secondary and come along organically as a result of fighting for (gendered and caste) ideologies of land and nation. The kinds of new social life engendered by militarization fall very short of what most aspired to previously—arranged marriages, caste societies, and dowries persist among Tamils in Sri Lanka and abroad.

Equally significant is, I suggest, something more intrinsic to the militant groups themselves and their attempt to set themselves up as zones of exceptional life. The divisions between life within the movement and life without—the equation of transformation with recruitment, the constant purification and maintenance of a line between the normative order and the militant order—while maintaining militancy, did not allow transgression and transformation to cross boundaries.

Scholarship on Tamils in the last decade have been dominated by either studies of the Tamil diaspora or developments within the LTTE, its state, rituals, cemeteries, martyr ideology, cadres, and especially its 30–40 percent female fighting force, which is analysed as the basis by which gender transformation as whole can be evaluated (e.g., Trawick 2007; Alison 2003). The major problem with this new scholarship is the implicit equation of the LTTE as an extraction of, and explainable by Tamil "culture," and the concomitant folding of Tamil civilians into a study of the LTTE. For example, Margaret Trawick writes that "the radical aspects of Tiger culture [are] explicable within the larger frame of Tamil and other Dravidian culture" (2007: 81). Trawick explains devotion to Prabhakaran within *bhakhti* traditions of offering love to those who harbor something divine and where, in relation to the three forms of love in Tamil culture—*pacam* (attachment), *pattu* (devotion), and *anbu* (selfless love): "among the Tigers, *anbu* for the people, *pattu* for Prabhakaran, and the breaking of ties of *pacam* for kin and friends are all fully in accord with wider Tamil cultural values." There are manifold problems with this logic.

First, Tamil militancy and relations within the movement are not examples of Tamil society as a whole. This is the difference between what Giorgio Agamben (1998) calls an example and an exception. The example is an "exclusive inclusion": an example is distinguished from what it belongs to in order to reveal its belonging, the classic anthropological anecdote or object. The exception, Agamben, argues is symmetrically opposite, an "inclusive exclusion"—"the exception is included in the normal case precisely because it does not belong to it" (1998: 22). The relationship of the exclusion to the rule is not that what is excluded no longer pertains; instead, what is excluded is governed by a withdrawal, and the rule/law applies in willed withdrawal. Tamil militancy explicitly pitched itself as at odds with normative kinship orders, carried to the extreme in the LTTE, where Tamil militants are presented as extraordinary figures who sacrifice themselves and their bodies for Tamils. For the LTTE, only LTTE cadres are considered martyrs, it is not a role open to ordinary civilians.[26] Visions of new roles and personal transformations were restricted to *within* the movement, not outside. The LTTE created its own purifying boundaries by which bodies and loyalties could be transformed and separated. Domesticating this exception was begun in the 1990s, when the LTTE set up a special office, the "Office of Great Heroes of the LTTE," devoted toward researching, evolving, and producing hero symbolism and new sacrificial and religious terminology (Schalk 1997) that would explain LTTE customs within Tamil tradition, while maintaining the boundaries between exception and norm, LTTE and Tamil society.[27] This LTTE continuance and condensation of militancy as a zone of exceptional life has produced a peculiarly deradicalized Tamil society out of a formerly highly politicized youth.

I use the phrase "zones of exceptional life" deliberately in keeping with Agamben's (1998, 2005) theorization of the exception, though with some constitutive clarifications. Agamben's widely discussed notion of the exception is drawn out in his two volumes, *Homo Sacer* (1998), which concerns itself with life, and *The State of Exception* (2005), which concerns itself more with law. Agamben argues, with Foucault, that our modern age is constituted around the management of us as biological life, *bare life* (Arendt's *homo laborans*)—a force in potentia, our humanity, excluded from political life by the Greeks. This, he argues (against Foucault), is not about the supplementation of older forms of sovereignty with new forms of governmentality, but about the constant intrusion of sovereignty, which is centrally about the production of life as *bare life*, into every corner of modern political governance and law. This appears in *State of Exception* as the institutionalization of regular exception/ emergency rule within western democracies, a indistinct space between the sovereign authorizing *auctoritas* and the juridico-political normative order *potestas*, threatening all the time in our modern age to be collapsed into each other.

Sovereignty, Agamben argues, is that which can decide on life and death, the sovereign is he who can institute a state of exception. The exception is "that which is included through being excluded"—that which is expelled, or held in suspension—and is thus not marginal but central, continually constitutive through its very exclusion. In the state of exception we are only *bare life*, nothing else, made by the withdrawal of the law, *bare* in the sense of nakedness, exposure, killable without retribution. This is where Agamben places the figure of the *Homo Sacer*, a life that is unsacrificeable and killable without retribution, from an occasional figure produced within Roman law as migrating to the heart of political life.

This emphasis on sovereignty as concerned with life and death is of immediate significance in thinking about the LTTE's claims to sovereignty. However, we have to think of sovereignty, following Hansen and Stepputtat (2006) as potentialities that can be *performed* rather than self-evident pre-existing power or coherent occasions—the major problem with Agamben's theorization.[28] The identification and elimination of traitors, as I have argued elsewhere, included through exclusion, was central to the LTTE's attempt to institute its own governance, a search for unity, which had to be constantly performed and maintained (Thiranagama 2010).[29] The sovereign is not pre-given, but attempts to become so *by* instituting states of exception where some lives become killable without retribution, haunted by the real possibility of failure. Thus the state and the law are not without elaboration the natural source of sovereignty per se; sovereignty has to be performed (Hansen and Stepputat 2006), and insurrectionary groups like the LTTE are continually attempting to institute themselves as sovereign through particular organization of life and death.

The LTTE more than any other group made the administration of death its center (Hellman-Rajanayagam 2005; Schalk 1997; Sornarajah 2004). Entry into the LTTE is ritualized through the very promise of death, the cyanide capsule. Militant life is presented as an exceptional zone, governed by different kinds of rules about death and dying, and animated by the will of their leader, Prabhakaran. *Tiyakam*, the Tamil word the LTTE uses to describe death in battle/combat, is not martyrdom in the Christian sense; it means in Tamil "abandonment," the voluntary abandonment of life (Schalk 1997). The *tiyaki* is s/he who dies while killing, abandoning life (Fuglerud 1999: 170). From 1991 onward, LTTE cadres were not allowed religious family funerals or cremations, but were given LTTE ones pledging their loyalty toward the state coming—Tamil Eelam (Schalk 1997). Their graves are engraved with cadres' LTTE name and rank, not the names they were born with, and they are "buried" in total contradiction to Hindu rituals. As Peter Schalk observes:

> The camati [the stone or wooden head plate for the grave] is also a public place and so are the rituals around it. The social identity of the dead is that of a fighter and not that of a brother or cousin . . . there is then a change from about 1990–91 toward an elimination of the private and kinship-based ritual system of the dead toward a public "state based" ritual. (Schalk 1997)

Most significantly, being an LTTE cadre and ready to die or commit suicide in the service of the leader as a prerequisite to combat—a requirement no other Tamil militant group ever instituted—is also about another form of sacralized life and death placed in abeyance to be activated by the sovereign. Here we can qualify Agamben's quick move beyond sacrifice[30] itself to assert the specialness of the category of *homo sacer*, by talking of what is also central to sovereignty, lives that are ritualized and sacralized but nonetheless can also be killed without retribution—the soldier whose life is only of value inasmuch as it is at the disposal of the sovereign.[31] The tragedy of the last battles of the LTTE was the cynical forced recruitment of thousands of civilians who were pushed into the battlefront to defend the LTTE leadership (UTHR 2009), expendable lives par excellence because the LTTE had never evolved an ideology of life that was not simultaneously about the potential for death. Two kinds of life and death are thus central to the constitution of the LTTE, that of the traitor and that of the LTTE cadre/martyr; both become killable when held in the zone of exception, but in different ways.

The LTTE thus arrogated itself the right to govern all Tamil life and death, but with its own fighting force maintained as a zone of exceptional life. This structure of hierarchical separation is most apparent in its treatment of gender relations within and outside the movement, a question that returns us to our inquiry about the failure of militant visions of a new society.

The vision of horizontal kinship offered by the militant movements never offered a sustainable alternative to the gerontocratic sexualized household, as the valorization of sibling relations in reality did not radically challenge gendered roles in Jaffna society. As Nanthini Sornarajah (2004) points out, the celebration of sibling relationship and the sexual distance implied, "masked and restrained interaction between the sexes, while at the same time attempting to maintain a familial cohesion and unity within the movement."[32] None of the movements effectively challenged strictures of chastity and the role of the wife in Jaffna society. Personal transformation was unmatched by societal transformation. It was belonging to the movement alone that licensed new forms of life. In maintaining a distinction between the exceptional and the ordinary, the militant and Tamil society at large, roles of gender, generation, and caste challenged within the movement were contained and separated from wider society.

The LTTE accentuated this position into an article of faith, valorizing women only on the basis of their LTTE membership and their willingness to sacrifice themselves for the nation. Always emphasizing the celibacy of its male cadres in the 1970s, when it began to recruit women, the LTTE highlighted its rigid control of the sexuality of its women cadres, representing them as "virgin warriors" (Schalk 1994). LTTE propaganda describes women cadres as preserving their *katpu* (chastity) and expending their sexual energy on the battlefield (Sornarajah 2004; Fuglerud 199: 167–68). This appealed to conservative Jaffna society far more than did some of the other militant groups (Hoole et al. 1990). Notions of appropriate womanhood continued to be reproduced in the household, regardless of the arming of female cadres.

Arming of women thus failed to successfully challenge the key discourse of chastity linked to the movement of property/dowry through women. The distance between militant and civilian women was instead emphasized. In 1986, leaflets issued by the LTTE women's wing asked Tamil women to remember dictates of modesty and to dress in sari and pottu "as the changes which have been taking part in our culture will only demean our society" (quoted in Maunaguru 1995: 169). Similar leaflets were issued in 2002 by the LTTE's cultural wing in eastern Sri Lanka, prescribing appropriate forms of dress (sari) for noncombatant Tamil women. The kinds of kinship the militant movements produced thus ultimately remained parasitic on the sexualized kinship of the household, which continued to be reproduced as the appropriate mode for sexual relations. As long as social forms of marriage were not challenged, neither was caste, which is continually reproduced precisely through control of household land and marriage.

The LTTE then purged itself of any radical social agenda toward Tamil society and instead represented itself clearly as the supreme upholder (through non embodiment) of the Tamil family, the Tamil nation, and Tamil culture more generally. In this manner, the confused muddle of proposed agendas for radical social transformation, Tamil nationalism, and of arms and military training that characterized the 1980s was clearly resolved. The LTTE disavowed any hint of the agenda for social transformation that had characterized youth mobilization, and concentrated on building the vertical ties of Tamil nationalism. LTTE ideology settled on the pursuit of land, tradition, and inheritance, all that the 1980s youth were frustrated with. The lives and deaths of traitors and martyrs, lives that were sacrificeable without retribution, became the central premise around which politics and Tamil life could be produced.

Doubly Traitor—
"Today I have not told my daughter, but one day I will"

Into this separation between militancy and the family emerge the figures of the non-LTTE female cadres like Sakthi. They were doubly traitor, transgressing societal strictures to become militants and then condemned as traitors by the LTTE. At the time of the banning many of the women were arrested; the majority were questioned and released, to disappear from political public life. Many of them married and, unlike the men I interviewed, suppressed their pasts, with even their affiliations extinguished from memory. Sakthi constantly told me stories of other women who had been peripherally involved with them, most often the mothers of the young women and men who had often suffered as a consequence of their support for EPRLF.[33]

> All the women, if we were one, we would have some strength. Somehow we can get through troubles together, but we became separated

from each other and dispersed everywhere. We can't get contacts with
each other; we can't meet each other anymore. We knew each other
but when the movement went, we were also broken.

Separated from each other, many EPRLF women also disappear from the
public gaze. Yet, as I found from my time with Sakthi, affiliations between the
women are not renounced; often kept secret from their children and husbands,
sometimes women come together to share old memories. Sakthi still took
phone calls from many women who, now abroad, had wiped out their pasts.

I met Parmini when she came to visit Sakthi, dragging along her two
youngest children squirming under her tight grasp and quick eyes, speaking sharp idiomatic Tamil with barely contained restlessness. Parmini was
formerly an EPRLF cadre. She told me immediately, "I'm not like before." She
had become noted by the LTTE because of her sharp tongue.

When the troubles came I had problems, because I had argued with
them so much. The LTTE came and talked to me directly. I told them,
"if you are going to shoot me, shoot me" and I stood there with my
eyes closed. What kind of talk! Why should I tell them anything? This
is my work and this is what I do. They shouted at me. They kept me
under house arrest.

Parmini had finally signed a letter renouncing all connection to the EPRLF
and given up politics permanently. She, like Sakthi, had profound difficulty
with the IPKF and EPRLF alliance.

My sister was taken by the IPKF. They took everything off her, her clothing. God! My mother was there and was screaming. The soldier had
told my sister not to say anything and turned the light off, attacked her.
The major came and asked her what happened but she could not tell
him. My mother has now come to Colombo; she was displaced in 1995.

Shortly after this she married a man whom she describes as hard working and
caring, but who disapproves of her militant past, to which he also attributes
her temperament.

He is a very good man; it is just this he doesn't like. I have stayed with
him. For what reason, for the children of course! What else can I do?

One son, two daughters. . . . It is because of my children that I have a husband. I tell him this directly "if not for the children you think I am going to live with you!" . . . My normal way is to argue not just because I joined the movement. He thinks it's just because I joined the movement. Now I don't say anything whether he's right or wrong, I accept it.

Politics, he is frightened that women will move out of their place. I argue, but do you think that any woman who is involved in politics, that their husband or their children are happy? It is a life of tension too.

Partly prompted by her own bitterness at the end of her political life and partly because of her husband's disapproval, the only part of her past life that Parmini holds onto is her friendship with Sakthi.

I told him, you can stop me doing anything political, but you can't stop my friendship. I just come here. I was alone and isolated for a long time. I did not even look at the paper so I couldn't get any news about politics . . . I have left it so much, this is how much I have controlled it. Sometimes little things come out where I don't realise when I talk to someone.

She looks at me,

We used to see you and your sister in Jaffna, and people used to say "there are the daughters" when you walked to school after your mother was killed. Look at your life! . . . I tell you one thing, it's difficult to work in the women's movement and have a family. If you want to work then you shouldn't get married.

Sharika: My mother had children.

Exactly, now your mother is not your mother any more. You have moved to foreign so you can't see the problem. In Sri Lanka you will see the problem immediately. If I go to my *ur* they see me and they say "there goes that EPRLF woman," the children will also get that name "EPRLF woman's children." You can't lose the name.

Parmini's life, anonymous in Colombo, is openly available as a poisonous inheritance in Jaffna, as is my own, as she points out to me. Her children will

inherit her name just as I have inherited my mother's. She smiles as Sakthi
remonstrates with her.

> Sakthi: Why are you talking like this, this is awful! What we set out
>   to do is for our children too.
> Parmini: Now look, I was not involved in a big way, I was not big,
>   but now I have a big name to carry. I don't like it any more. I
>   don't mind being in a union, but nothing political. Two years of
>   happiness is all I ask for.
>   I have nothing for national liberation any more. Pack of
>   dogs. They [LTTE] wander around with their guns. You can
>   see them everywhere. To go, you will feel angry seeing this,
>   who won't? Of course it is my home, my soil, but my land has
>   been despoiled by them. How can one go there after we had to
>   surrender to them after the banning, and to see those people
>   who did this to me? There is no freedom to go and live in a
>   place where everything is done at gunpoint. Let them learn our
>   Tamil people! Let them live with them and realise how they
>   are. . . .
> Sakthi: But this only helps them if you are like this. By keeping quiet,
>   then you think that you are safe. But you don't realise what they
>   are doing is wrong.
> Parmini: I know they are wrong. But it is difficult for us here
>   [Colombo] too. The people here are also frightened of them.

Parmini looks at me soberly. I realize that this is a conversation that she
has had with Sakthi and internally many times. Parmini's life has been secured at the cost of her own past, which hidden from others has become a
second secret and disavowed self. She has not told her eldest daughter, whom
she never brings to Sakthi's house, the truth about her past.

> The eldest. . . . She is full support for the LTTE. The thing is that we
> don't talk politics at home. When you live here (Colombo) there is
> constant checking, police come home all the time to check and we
> are always frightened. She is only ten years old, but she supports
> the LTTE. Now only I started to say slowly to her, there were other
> people who were fighting, other people also were working. I never
> talked to her about this before. Because of my previous situation I

didn't talk about anything political. Now the LTTE are appearing on
TV . . . she was against the Sri Lankan military, because they check
only Tamils. She would ask me, "why do they only check Tamils?"
It is only now I told her "there are so many problems for Tamils you
don't know . . . you don't know what the LTTE has done to us Tamils."
But this thing I didn't tell her. To my husband I told everything, but I
didn't want to tell her I was involved. When she comes to an age . . .

I raise them in such a traditional way. A woman is like this, a man
is like this. Sometimes when I think about it I feel a shock. I don't
know why. Without thinking.

Parmini says this, her face twisted. Life will be easier for them, she tells
us, easier than it was for her if they conform to Jaffna strictures. They may
never really know their mother in this light; Parmini only talks in this tone
with Sakthi, both of them tell me. With us, Parmini speaks in two voices, in
the past and the present simultaneously. With Sakthi, who knows both her
lives, and the past she is forced to erase in every other part of her life, Parmini
can relate this story with a note of irony in her voice. She plays two women
who are the same. Her reconciliation with life has come through her faith and
the evangelical Christian church she has joined in Colombo. This gives her a
public life of sorts. This church, she tells me, does not allow women to sit at
the front of the church as they are "responsible" for "original sin." She laughs
uproariously to see my expression. More seriously, she says,

We have to have faith in some power (*sakthi*). Now I have found my
faith in God, and in preaching and prayers. I have been beaten by
life. For so long I was arguing with him [husband], now I have even
stopped arguing with him. Life has stopped. We have to have satisfac-
tion in something. Mine has gone to God. We have to have something,
don't we? Today I have not told my daughter, but one day I will.

I bring in my encounter with Parmini for a number of reasons. Parmini,
more than anyone else, brings to light the hidden histories that perhaps one
day will be told from mother to daughter (it is her daughter, after all, that
Parmini both fears and is compelled to tell) and a particular kind of past that
creates its own manner of hesitant transmission in its active suppression. Parmini, like many ex-militant women, hesitates to tell her children about her
past, which is instead made to feature unspoken and oblique in their present

lives. There is also an affiliation and construction of affinity through togetherness that is kept alive by these "traitor" women, another kind of relationship of kinship and politics that is constructed through what is seen as togetherness in household and militant experience, but at the same time slips beyond them.

I Survive, But We Are Broken

> We don't know each other anymore. We are broken. A movement is like a family for sure, as soon as we become alone, all our ideas and our experiences, and the things we need to talk about, become lost. (Sakthi)

The fundamental feeling of loss in Sakthi's life is the loss of others. Often, especially when dealing with narrative and biography, it has increasingly become a truism that possessing and retelling one's story is a means of gaining agency and voice (e.g., Bruner 2004; Crapanzano 1980; Caverero 2000; and see essays in Anztze and Lambek 1996 for critique). However, my work with Sakthi and others showed me that the question of where agency and voice was to come from was far more complicated for this generation of women and men. Sakthi's loneliness was an existential condition born out of very concrete social and political causes. It was about her separation from the public world, from a world of kin, and finally from a collective group identity on which her political subjectivity had been built.

> I can go home, but only secretly, I can't go freely. To go home in happiness like I lived there and see the people I knew, go to houses, and talk with our minds as we used to do, can we do that? . . . You have to live in silence. Live as if you don't exist. Talk to your kindred without speaking your mind. These are our problems.

Sakthi was denied a public world in which her life had value. She and her husband Uthayan could not mix freely with other people; they had to be constantly careful about who they met and who came to their house. As with Sakthi's house arrest and her dependence on her family in 1986, the house is both a fortress and a prison. It is protection but also the sign of a public world denuded of meaningful interaction. Their lives were an extreme expression of a more general modality of public sociality among Sri Lankan Tamils, as this book has aimed to draw out.

There is not only no freedom for people like us, but also just for ordinary people. . . . Everyone is frightened . . . but we can't talk with everyone. Even with our school friends we can't talk, not even small talk. Even if we go home, we are frightened, we can't even ask or answer the basic questions, how are you, where are you living, what work are you doing? That is what is being lonely is like.

Sakthi has become excluded from everyday rounds of sociality and a world of kin that she, as part of a large family from a rural village, had been at the heart of.

We have learned to be only with our friends, people between whom there is trust. Now if you think of kindred, we do not go to their weddings or anything. We do not go to the temple, we do not go home. . . . We only talk to those who have trust with us and who know all our histories. . . . people who are kin to us, with our mother or father . . . are not in this kind of world.

The necessity for trust, as she says "with our history we have to be careful," means that those who do not share risk cannot become "intimate," house visits cannot be exchanged, food and conversation about personal matters cannot be shared. For Sakthi, "*Uravu* [kindred] is for us only those who we have worked with in the struggle."

This individual life Sakthi has found constantly reminds her that it is in collective life that she believes that she can truly flourish. In one exchange between Sakthi and I she told me,

As soon as we become alone, all our ideas and our experiences, and the things we need to talk about, become lost . . . when we are alone, then it is only one person's experiences and one person's story. I am telling you as one person now, if I could have talked to you as part of a movement, if a group could have talked then it would be greater . . . now it will be just one person's documents, one person's conversation.

My own elevation of the individual story and agency was for Sakthi secondary. While she welcomed our conversations as means by which loneliness and isolation could be combated, she understood the circumstances of our meeting and her own story not as a sign of strength but as a symptom of loss. For Sakthi, our conversations were made possible because the women's EPRLF movement had "failed"; we were merely two women talking of this on our own, and the manner of these interviews was built on that invisibility. She reminded me that what she offered me was "only one person's experiences and one person's story." The possibilities of these stories and her own individual story were limited, compared to a collective voice which she longed for renewed dialogue with and on which she had built her sense of political strength and subjectivity. What it meant to be an individual and only offer an individual story for Sakthi was a sign of political marginalization and profound loneliness.

Politics and political activism are not individual affairs for Sakthi; they are collective activities. This is perhaps what Hannah Arendt means when she reminds us that there is nothing "political *in* man that belongs to his essence . . . *man* is apolitical." Instead, Arendt argues "politics arises in what lies *between* men and is established as relationships" (2005: 95). This is certainly what Sakthi points to. Second, and most important, this exchange illuminates the immense significance of belonging to movements, and ideas about "group" and collective identities for this generation. For all the militants that I interviewed, the very idea of "movements" was foundational, an identity that produces both the togetherness and the depth of disillusionment, abandonment, and betrayal that many feel. It was strongly defined groups that served to nurture their identities and political consciousness.

I began this chapter with Kugamoorthy's reflection, a decade on, that the experience of being in these movements marked you in some ineffable way,

It is an experience isn't it? People who were outside, their opinions their experience was different. Many of them cannot understand. But there is a limit to your understanding once you enter a movement. People outside could see things clearer.

These ideas about the movement as the ultimate bestower of agency and identity are still clear and carried to the extreme in the LTTE. They come out of the histories of these militant groups and more general legacy of political activism—especially left political activism—in post-independence Sri Lanka; many Sinhalese and Tamils in their forties are still more likely to identify their youth through groups they affiliated with or belonged to. We cannot really understand political affiliation and agency for these now older ex-militants and activists without discussing how group affiliation provided means of social and political recognition that were the source of agency for them. Even after this "exceptional life" is gone, it still prevails for many as a memory that cannot be shared with those outside the movements, a memory that haunts one's life.

For political subjectivities where groups are the means by which one nurtures one's identity and gains recognition, to be only an individual, as Sakthi explained, is sometimes to show that you have lost one kind of battle. Perhaps one of the consequences was that the strength of ideas about group affiliation, obligation, and loyalty precluded the growth of strong dissent cultures *within* the movements, only possible when one left. For us as anthropologists, especially those like myself who work with individual biographies and life stories, it means that the very notions of inside and outside, household and public world, individual and collective are, as I hope I have shown, never to be taken for granted but in fact are distinctions that are morally and politically constructed and invested in.

Moreover, as I have argued above, if, following Alberoni, we can see the process of group formation as an investment in a mutual quest for meaning, investment in a collective love object—the group—where meaning and emotion were generated while participating, then being alone is more than just being on one's own. Alberoni argues that when the nascent state ends through extinction, then on return to the love objects and life once abjured and rejected, one is conscious of a sense of falsity. Once what was real had been made contingent, return to that "real" lends hollowness to continuing on a life path that has been revealed to be chosen rather than inevitable. Pamini is not the only one who leads a life marked by doubleness. Sakthi put it as starkly:

This life, this is one without any feeling, we have lived here and there, in India, in Colombo, in different houses.

The few years when Sakthi was actively political, from her school years to EPRLF, appear to her as the life lived most vividly, the decades after is of a life "without any feeling." Moreover, that former "reality" itself no longer exists, as Sakthi's husband Uthayan told me once:

We fought for *ur*/home, but this is what has happened. One day *ur* will go away. For you and your generation none of you know what Jaffna was like in peacetime. Now for us, we have gone around it freely, watched dramas, bathed in Keerimalai, remembered when the army was not there, when there were no arms on the street . . . *ur* is a feeling, an understanding. It is a lived in, looking like, smelling feeling. It is a life.

This chapter attempts to give a picture of a generation fighting multiple political wars, against the state, against their gerontocratic societies, as well as finally, against each other. Rather than taking boundaries between the household and the political sphere for granted, I have attempted to show the shifting relationships between them that maintained a moralized binary between the two while being in constant dialogue, one defined through the other. In the early years of militancy, the household was seen as a restrictive space, and political associations and militant organizations were perceived as the sites of discussion and debate. However, after the LTTE began to eliminate and incorporate Tamil political life into itself, small "private" networks and households absorbed memories of violence and dissent into themselves. Militancy along with fear and secrecy was folded back into the same "familial" structures and small networks of trust within houses. Looking back as they did twenty years later, for many of them, militancy had transformed them personally, but had not transformed Tamil society in the way they had intended. What had transformed Tamil society was the unbelievable privations of war, upheaval, displacement, death, and disappearance, but not liberation from oppressive caste, gender, or generational structures. This purification of the boundaries between households and movements, making them into forms of ordinary and exceptional life, reinvested households with the task of upholding the nation through appropriate reproduction, even as they were dismembered by the plucking out of those who were chosen to die for the nation.

If now, many commentators discuss how LTTE cadres will be reintegrated into Tamil society after the fall of the LTTE, our history tells us that Tamil families are more than capable of tacitly absorbing thousands of young militants as they did in 1990. The question for another person in the future is what kinds of transformations of the household lie ahead? These houses that kept secrets were also at times prisons. They recalled to those trapped inside that they had been sundered from a public world that had nourished their identities, and this present and future had possibly been built on their past. Ex-militants returned to ordinary life but with one part of them "out of joint," haunted memories. This other side, this past militancy and shared biography, in ambiguous ways ties even those who actively oppose the LTTE to the LTTE. Now they, like all of us, contemplate a new future. If fear of the LTTE imprisoned so many ex-militants in Sri Lanka and colonized the pasts of those abroad, then what will the sudden collapse of the feared but heavily invested in presence of the LTTE do? Will this mean that Tamils will have to reflect more on their culpability for a culture of violence? If many saw their withdrawal from public life as the result of LTTE violence, now what will happen? One of the things I hope I have done here is at least to make it possible to understand and formulate more critically some of the pressing concerns for Sri Lanka today, not least the way in which Tamil political culture has been shaped and why it continues to produce particular politics of guilt, nostalgia, "failure," and grief.

CHAPTER SIX

Conclusions from Tamil Colombo

In here it's deliberately dark so that one may sigh
in peace. Please come in. How long has it been?
Upstairs—climb slowly—the touch is more certain.
You've been, they say, everywhere. What city's left?
I've brought the world indoors . . .

. . . Listen, my friend. But for quick hands, my walls
would be mirrors. A house? A work in progress,
always . . .

—Agha Shahid Ali, "Rooms Are Never Finished" (2002: 55–57)

Colombo, a recurring site of anti-Tamil riots in Sri Lanka, is at the same time a city of many Tamil-speaking and other minorities, Malaiyaha Tamil, Muslim, "Colombo Tamil," and Sri Lankan Tamil, along with Malays, Borahs, Burghers, and Europeans. Prime target of attacks by the LTTE in wartime, Colombo is also one of the places where Tamil remittances flow, where the call for prayer, the *azaan*, is broadcast daily on national Tamil radio, where famous Indian Tamil eateries and businesses abound.

There are many sights that recall Colombo for me. They are, in keeping with my own linguistic bias, visions of a Tamil-speaking city. The long bustling markets in Pettah and Wellawatte, two of Colombo's major Tamil areas (the former more Hill Country and the latter more Sri Lankan Tamil). The early evening chatter of children and adults out walking on Galle Face Green by the beach side favored by Tamils, Muslims, and Sinhalese alike of all classes, who come in their hundreds invading one of the more exclusive ends of the city. The lodges that house rooms and rooms of Tamil transients, with all their belongings crammed in and their door open to greet those who walk up the stairs. The army and police checkpoints all across the city. The food huts by the wayside where I go to order the street food that all Sri Lankans love, which seems to easily transgress ethnic boundaries. The Muslim "hotels," open late at night, where we stop sometimes when I go out with friends to drink faluda and have a late night snack. So many sights I can list. These are crisscrossed with sweaty crammed bus rides with conductors shouting out the stops, their fingers interlaced with banknotes, and three-wheeler drivers with whom I constantly have to negotiate, talking sometimes about who I am and why I am in the city.

I traveled Colombo on buses memorizing money and destinations, and like many Tamils through Tamil. I became skilled at picking out another Tamil-speaking person to ask directions, eating lunch at Tamil canteens and eateries, memorizing certain kinds of ritualized buying encounters in markets, and going to Tamil area markets for everything complicated. The months I would come back from Puttalam to Colombo late on Friday night for the weekend, I always went straight from the bus to the many Muslim shops dotted around the central bus station, where one could wait in safety to ask them to help finding a reliable three-wheeler driver. The money markets I changed my pounds in were in Pettah, the heavily Tamil central marketplace of Colombo. I took my grandparents to the Wellawatte Church of South India (CSI) church. There we met all those from the north whom we had known all our lives, now permanent residents in Colombo, supported by the remittances of overseas children. I very quickly slipped into a particular segment of life in the city, which was ever present but concealed. This is just one such segment in a city that is essentially comprised of constant presence and absence: 50 percent of Colombo live in multiple small slums and shanties positioned at the doorways and thresholds of respectable neighborhoods.

Thus the city with all its securitization had a place for me and other Tamils. And, as I discovered it has historically always been a place *of* minority life. The question remains to what extent it can become a place *for* minority life. In this chapter, I explore, by way of conclusion, Tamil life in Colombo past, present, and future. The chapter traces a phenomenology of Colombo as a Tamil-speaking city that I was only one of thousands in traversing. The city appears both through the jostling ethnographic journeys traveled along ethnic lines, and also through a historical lens which shows that Colombo has to perform its Sinhala nationalist credentials constantly because it is "a city which is not one" (Tagg 1996).[1] Colombo is a city of many discrete intimate ethnic lives rather than distant proximity.

Violence is critical to Tamil phenomenologies of the city, and here I attempt to excavate the means by which the city is traversed through flows of "anticipatory violence" (Jeganathan 2002) these sites, past, present, and future folded into each other, constantly re-encoded. Riots, bombs, and the checkpoints that crisscross Colombo make violence a constant feared spectacle of the urban, images of the possible bound by past violence that "flash up" as Walter Benjamin (1974) might argue, to be grasped at a "moment of danger."[2] Yet Tamil spaces of relative safety also present themselves, due to fear of the LTTE and exploitation by other Tamils, as spaces of un-safety. Colombo is a crucible for the complexities of this conflict, from the intense surveillance and violence enacted against Sri Lankan Tamils to the reality of multiple Tamil-speaking minorities which cannot be represented by the resolution of the conflict around Sri Lankan Tamil concerns alone. Sri Lanka now stands at a crossroads. Colombo epitomizes that crossroads, whether or not there is now the possibility of making a home for minorities in the larger Sri Lankan nation-state.

Colombo Past

Hansen and Verkaaik suggest that cities are both the ground of lived experience and also a mythologized supra-being or space. Moreover, dwellers by "invoking the name of the city as their own, also incorporate, and bring into existence, the myth of the city as something that lives within themselves" (Hansen and Verkaaik 2009: 5). It is no accident that the cities that the authors themselves work on are Bombay/Mumbai and Karachi respectively, cities that are both sites of enormous imaginative and political postcolonial labor (see Hansen 2001; Verkaaik 2009). These cities have been actively worked on and transformed from their colonial or migratory histories into sites of modern Indian and Pakistani life (ibid). Conversely, when one asks oneself, what is the soul of Colombo, the answer still points to a disavowed uncertainty about the uneasy place of Colombo in the national imagination. Colombo, while the economic and political nerve center of Sri Lanka, has failed to be rendered fully for later nationalist imaginations. Instead, it is the ancient cities of Anuradhapura and Polonannaruva (Jeganathan 1996; Nissan 1988, 1989), the city of Kandy and its long lost aristocracy (Duncan 2005), and not least the rural

Sinhala village with its idealized temple, dagoba, and tank (Spencer 1990b, c),
that have taken prime representational space in the nation. These spoke to
an imagined pre-colonial uncontaminated space which lay waiting, to paraphrase Serena Tennekoon for the postcolonial nation to reclaim the past as
their future (1988: 297–98). Colombo does not offer a redemptive pre-colonial "pure" Sinhalized past with its diversity, mixed architecture, and colonial
buildings marking the city as their own. Colombo's own elite have sought their
"national" origins not in Colombo, but in the more all embracing vocabulary
of Sinhala nationalism, purified Buddhism, and the upholding of a seemingly
declining and idealized rural past (Spencer 1990a, b). Given Sri Lanka's sizable
postcolonial Anglophone elite (Kearney 1978; Obeysekere 1974) and lack of
large-scale anticolonial revolt, it is not suprising that not only is there rela-
tively little writing on Colombo, but that the literature that there is traces these
uncertainties and faultlines: Jayawardena (1972) traces the urban proletariat
and labor action at the turn of the century, some of the strongest challenges to
colonial rule; Perera (1998, 2002) writes of the indigenization of Colombo by
elites and non-elites—as a means of reconfiguring the city as ours; and Francesca Bremner (2004) writes of how parts of the city are worked on and claimed
by watta/slum dwellers as "Ape Gama"—our village. Colombo's soul has thus
always been up for grabs by those who lived in it, fearing that it is in fact
marked by the other, the minorities from Tamils and Muslims to Burghers, the
English-speaking elite, the colonial rulers, the slum dwellers.

Some figures immediately give a picture of Colombo's ethnic density. Colombo Municipal Council census data in 1981 and 2001 revealed that nearly
50 percent of those living within the boundaries of Colombo city were minorities.[3] In 2001, the ethnic composition of Colombo Municipal Council was
Sinhalese 41.36 percent (nationally, 74.5 percent), Sri Lankan Tamils 28.91
percent, Indian Tamils 2.17 percent, Muslims 23.87 percent, and other communities (Malays, Burghers, Chetties, Bharatha, etc.) 3.69 percent (Sevanatha
2003: 5). Thus, in 2001 58.64 percent of people living in Colombo city were
not from the majority community, and 54.95 percent of these could claim
Tamil as their mother tongue. The Municipal Council itself represents around
one million, with 642,000 residents (in 2001) and a daily floating population
of 400,000 coming into work in the city (Sevanatha 2003: 3). These figures
mark particular densities within the city proper.[4] Central Colombo, even in
2001 before the newest influx of Sri Lankan Tamils from the north and east,[5]
was marked by being overwhelmingly Tamil-speaking, even as the calligra-
phy of the city and its institutions remained Sinhalese.

This heterogeneity, as this section will trace, is of long standing. The
Tamil Colombo I describe is not purely produced by the war. Instead, Tamil
life in Colombo builds upon—however aphasic the memory of the nation
has been—a longer history of trilingual and racially divided life in the city.
This deeper knowledge buried within the city and manifest in its extraordinary ethnic diversity, means that Tamil speakers are a historical presence
in Colombo. Tamil-speaking minorities of all kinds cannot be declared in
Colombo to be recent migrants or newcomers to the city; the city itself testi-
fies to a different history which in the process of being domesticated into the
nation cannot yet fully expel its minority dwellers who continue to find ways
to dwell, however marginally, within the life it offers.

Colonial Colombo

Colombo emerged through colonial conquest by the three powers: the Portuguese (1505–1658), the Dutch (1658–1796), and finally the British (1796–
1948). Under the Dutch, Colombo was the center of one of the three Maritime
Provinces: the Colombo *disava* and the Commandments of Jaffna and Galle.
This did not include the large interior Kandyan kingdom that remained free of
colonial rule. When the British took over in 1796, they brought the provinces
together. They made Ceylon a crown colony in 1802, governed as a separate
political territory from India. It was ruled directly by the Colonial Office in
London through its agent in Ceylon, the governor, based in Colombo, the new
imperial city (Perera 1998: 38). The fortification and centralization of power at
Colombo was central to the British conquest and the disinterring of the Kandyan kingdom and aristocracy in 1815. After the defeat of the Kandyans, the
island was imagined and governed as one for the first time in its long history.

On unification, the British sought to create a wholly new, highly centralized,
administrative system with Colombo at the center, where "as the node of the
imperial urban structure as well as the political center of Ceylon . . . [Colombo]
was the pivotal link between the British imperial and the Ceylonese colonial
urban systems" (Perera 1998: 38) and "monopolized all urban functions for the
island as a whole" (Rhoads Murphey 1989: 192). Though it was a seaport under
the Portuguese (Kolamba for Arab and South Indian traders) after 1825 and
the building of roads and beginning of plantation agriculture, British Colombo
became one of the most important ports within the Empire (Rhoads Murphey
1989: 204). It stood on three major routes: Europe to Madras via Cape Town;

Coromandel coast and Calcutta; and Bombay and the far East (Perera 1998; Rhoads Murphey 1989) and in the 1900s was known as the "Clapham junction of the East" (Turner 1927 quoted in Perera 1998: 76). Within Ceylon, new communication and transportation systems all converged toward Colombo from where flows of information and files, military action, and, civil servants emanated (Munasinghe 2002; Perera 1998: 41). In postcolonial Sri Lanka most roads and railways do still converge in Colombo, and, most important for Tamil migrants, the only international airport out of Sri Lanka is in Colombo.

The residential city itself also continued to mutate with an ever-growing population. Yet its mutation was deeply marked by its racialized colonial economy. As Hansen and Verkaaik point out, "colonial cities were founded on a distinction between the proper colonial citizens, living in regulated and planned spaces, and the masses of urban poor and recent migrants who were concentrated in the slums, favelas, souks, and bidonvilles" (2009: 10). Colombo was also marked by the entrances and exits of three different colonial powers displacing each other into new zones in the city. Until the mid-nineteenth century, Colombo was divided into three major zones, the "Fort," the "Pettah," and the "outer Pettah," based on different racial groups and thus different functions (Perera 1998: 48). The British occupied the fort area and kept it clear not only of "natives," but also of Dutch and Portuguese descendants. The Fort was the center of British rule and residence combining both military and residential spaces (unlike the separation of the canton and civil spaces in other colonial cities) (Perera 1998: 48–52). The Fort itself had been originally occupied by the Portuguese and the Dutch in turn, who had "Europeanized" its space (49). The Portuguese and Dutch were instead confined to outside the fort in the Pettah region, which they called Oude Stad. Unlike the Fort, the Pettah was a largely residential district laid out in neat and regular grids, only encroached upon in the late nineteenth century pushed from both ends from the Ceylonese suburbs and the Fort on the other. The Ceylonese were pushed into the "outer Pettah" suburbs in the Hultsdorf area. The outer Pettah had no administrative or military functions but was the bustling heart of the native city, filled with bazaars, houses, merchants, and traffic (Perera 1998: 51–52). It was here where the bullock carts poured in with people and goods from other areas in Sri Lanka.[6]

Colombo's size and population were transformed in the mid-nineteenth century with the expansion of the colonial economy, industrialization, creation of new docklands, and intensification of traffic through Colombo's port (Jayawardena 1972; Perera 1998). A massive influx of migrants from the rest of Sri Lanka and from India pushed the municipal boundaries of Colombo beyond the three zones, and expanded the "native" part of the city, which increasingly encroached on the rest. The transportation network built by the British to bring crops and goods into Colombo and out into the colonial empire was now bringing people into the city. The adaptations of new migrants and longer-term residents increasingly led to the "proletarianisation and ruralisation" of Colombo's population (Perera 2002: 1718). In 1880 the municipal area of Colombo was 13 times larger than the fort area (1716); the population between 1824 and 1891 increased by 300 percent, and expanded again, from 154,000 in 1901 to 200,000 in 1911, an increase of 30 percent (Jayawardena 1972: 5).

Tamil-speaking minorities were far from absent in this major population boom. Colombo has been historically a trilingual (English, Sinhala, Tamil) city throughout the twentieth century. This is still evident all across Colombo, not only in the billboards in Sinhala, Tamil, and English, but also in the calligraphies of the historically Tamil neighborhood of Wellawatte or the famous Sea Street with its concentration of Indian jewelers. In colonial Colombo non-European trade was primarily Indian (e.g., Memons, Borahs, Parsis, and Sindhis) and local Ceylonese trade was dominated by Chettiars, Colombo Chetties, and Muslims (Jayawardena 2002),[7] making Tamil, the lingua franca of South India and Sri Lankan Tamils and Muslims, one of the major language of non-European trade. In the dockland areas of the port, Tamil was spoken as much as Sinhala both as a lingua franca of trade and because of the high numbers of Tamil-speaking workers (Jayawardena 1972, 2002). The well-educated northern Jaffna Tamils, trained in English in an extensive network of (especially American) missionary schools in the north, entered the colonial economy as brokers and intermediaries, "shroffs" between "native trade" (Chetties and Muslims) and European banks and firms (Jayawardena 2002: 207). They also increasingly provided a large proportion of the clerical staff of the colonial government. Blue-collar trade and labor within the city was also heavily Tamilized—the Sinhalese monopolized skilled labor while most of the unskilled labor was by immigrant Indian workers. In 1931 there were 33,000 Indian workers in Colombo, mainly engaged in unskilled labor in the municipality, harbor, railways, public works, and factories (Jayawardena 1972: 318). The majority were Tamils from the Madras presidency and Malayalis from Travancore-Cochin. A large population of separately categorized "Indian Muslims" (close to 33,000 in 1911) scattered across the island were quickly absorbed after independence into the larger Ceylonese Muslim communities (unlike Indian Tamils, who were never absorbed into the Sri Lankan Tamil population).

This brief picture of Tamil Colombo folds in rather profound and con-sequential differences between northern and eastern, here Jaffna Tamils, the Malaiyaha/Hill Country and Colombo Tamils of Indian descent, and the mul-tiple Muslim communities. The very distinct Muslim communities are well established in Colombo, with well-designated Muslim areas and mosques and an internally class-divided community further divided into Borah, Sri Lankan Muslim, Malay, and so on. Many of the Muslim elite politicians of the early twentieth century came from Colombo, and Muslim schools, institutes, newspapers, and community associations are of long stand-ing. Muslims (like Malaiyaha/Hill Country Tamils, and Colombo Tamils of Indian descent), though Tamil is mostly their mother tongue, are fluent in Sinhala, having lived continuously in Sinhala majority areas. Thus they move flexibly between the many grammars of the city. At the same time, Muslim communities are found across class differences and predominate in some of the historically working-class "slums."

Ethnically Tamil communities too are profoundly divided by class, mi-gration economies, and regional origin and these divisions have profoundly shaped the kind of Tamilness in Tamil Colombo. As I have suggested above, until the 1920s, Tamils of Indian descent were found in large numbers in Co-lombo. Some of this is postcolonial, there have been large migrations of Ma-layaha/Hill Country Tamils to Colombo in the 1970s and 1980s, often into "slum areas" (see below). However, the major ethnic demographic changes that marks the transition from colonial to postcolonial Colombo is in fact the uprooting of its Indian Tamil population. Formerly bustling with migrants from South India, Colombo's population of Indian Tamils has declined con-siderably in the post-independence period.[8] Growing resentment against Indian workers saw Sinhala nationalist leaders such as Buddhist reformer Anagarika Dharmapala[9] campaign extensively against Tamil, Malayali, and Muslim immigrants from India (Jayawardena 1972: 318). Communal ten-sion was rife in the late 1920s and early 1930s as the world economy and that of Sri Lanka began to decline. While initially Indian laborers were part of the Ceylonese trade unions, the latter began to turn against Indian workers when some strikes were broken by the direct importation of new labor from South India, though earlier Unionists had relied on the support of Tamil and Malayali workers (318–21). Campaigns against Indian workers took on new fervor and virulence in the 1930s (see also Wickramasinghe 2007: 131–38). The campaigns against South Indian workers also marked the real beginnings of sharply communalist language within Sinhala nationalist movements, from newly active monks and unions, that only later directed itself at Sri Lankan Tamils.

Conversely, until the war began to transform migration patterns, Jaffna Tamils in Colombo were predominantly middle-class migrants. The famous upper-class Tamil elite of more distant Jaffna origins, the "Tamils of Cinnamon Gardens,"—Cinnamon Gardens being the suburb in which Sinhala, Tamil, and Burgher colonial elites constructed colonial-style mansions— were one kind of Colombo Jaffna Tamil. More numerous were well-educated lower-middle-class clerks, shroffs (see above), and professionals of all kinds who moved to Colombo for employment and shuttled back and forth between Colombo and Jaffna, either on a weekly basis or for holidays. This shuttling was greatly facilitated by the opening of the railways between Jaffna and Colombo in 1911. Denham reports in his comments on the 1911 census that already "the passenger traffic is heavy, especially at the holiday seasons, when there is an exodus of clerks from Colombo to their homes in Jaffna" (1912: 70). As Don Arachchige showed, there has been for a long time a major migration route between Jaffna and Colombo, as well-educated young Jaffna Tamil men and women moved out of the risky and stagnant northern economy into the south (1994: 30).

Despite the Sinhalization of the Sri Lankan public sector in the 1970s (Moore 1990), Jaffna Tamils continued to find work as professionals and in other businesses. Thus by the 1980s, as Tambiah pointed out, Colombo and its suburbs could reliably be called an area that was sensitive to Sinhala and Tamil tensions, given that " large numbers of Sri Lankan Tamils are concentrated as clerical and administrative personnel in government departments and business firms, and as members of professions such as medicine, law, and accounting" (1986: 9–10). These Tamils were not necessarily all from middle-class backgrounds, but their educational aspirations marked them as such. They often lived together or in ways that reflected their aspirations: they were not found in large numbers in Colombo's slums, unlike Hill Country and Colombo Tamils of Indian origin or Sri Lankan Muslims.

Adjacent Marginalities: Class, Ethnicity, and Riots

The absence of Sri Lankan Tamils in Colombo's "slums" is significant for a number of reasons. One dominant (and undoubtedly important) way of understanding marginality within postcolonial cities has been through focusing on slums and urban poverty. In Colombo, from the late 1870s onward and throughout the twentieth century, small settlements, slums, and shanty towns sprang up to accommodate a new urban (initially primarily male) population.[10] Now around 50 percent of Colombo's population live in a variety of "slums" called wattas (Silva and Athukorala 1991: 1).[11] Colombo's wattas are rather different from others in South Asia. They have not become consolidated into larger areas (like Bombay's Dharavi), and they vary greatly in size, though most are very small communities.[12] In 2001 74 percent of these settlements had less than 50 housing units while larger settlements with more than 500 units count for only 0.7 percent of the total watta population of Colombo (Sevanatha 2003: 6–7). There are different kinds of wattas, from the colonial, tenement gardens (working-class neighborhoods that have deteriorated) and "slum housing" (formerly affluent housing that has been endlessly partitioned), to postcolonial structures: shanty communities of "temporary" structures erected in marginal land such as river banks, railway lines, often at the outskirts of the city, and now unserviced semi-urban neighborhoods in Colombo's suburbs or in satellite towns becoming suburbs (Sevanatha 2003).

Watta communities, especially the small inner-city ones, are thus of longstanding. Silva and Athukorala's (1991) study conducted in the early to mid-1980s shows that there was little rural migration into the inner-city slums with most migrating into specific wattas coming from other urban areas. Rural migration is more often to shanties and deteriorating suburbs. The only exceptions are Hill Country Tamils migrating from plantation areas into Colombo Tamil slum areas, particularly to the "colonies" as they are sometimes called, as happened in large numbers in the 1980s.

In Colombo, inner-city wattas are located next to, sometimes internal to, hidden parts of respectable and affluent neighborhoods. Sometimes they are just a few streets between larger parallel roads, as was the watta next to one of the flats where my grandfather lived for a little while. In those small streets between the big, men and women sat in chairs outside their subdivided houses, playing cards and watching life on both ends. It was there that many of the young three-wheeler drivers who serviced the area rented rooms.

The wattas, as Silva and Athukorala (1991) show, are mainly working-class Sinhalese of many castes, Muslims, working-class Colombo Tamils of Indian descent, and Hill Country Tamils who have migrated to Colombo over the last twenty years. One of the case studies for Silva and Athukorala was a watta they call Swarna Mawatha, which was overwhelmingly Malaiyaha/Hill Country Tamil. In their study, they made the more general case that it was rare for a Sri Lankan Tamil to live in the wattas in the 1980s (1991: 118–23). Thus, there are enormous class divides between forms of marginality. This is not an issue of language. In fact as Silva and Athurokala are joined by others in noting, Tamil is also a language of the wattas. Tamil-speaking minorities were fluent in Sinhalese, but Sinhalese watta dwellers were also often fluent in colloquial Tamil (121–22). If we take Tamil as purely a language, then the wattas are central to Tamil Colombo. However, for watta dwellers of all ethnicities in Colombo we might surmise that Sri Lankan Tamils were perceived primarily as part of the other half of Colombo, the educated middle class, often English-speaking (see Bremner 2004). Silva and Athukorala conclude that poverty among Sri Lankan Tamils was primarily confined to the northern and eastern areas and was not a characteristic of how Sri Lankan Tamils were perceived in Colombo or Kandy.

This absence of Sri Lankan Tamils from the slum areas and the concomitant perception of them as English speaking and middle class is significant because the transformation of Colombo's Sri Lankan Tamil population in the 1990s and from 2000 onward has been one of class and caste. The war has propelled all kinds of Tamils out of the north and east, moving into forms of transient housing. However, it seems that this transient housing prevails mainly in predominantly Tamil areas or suburban satellites. There has been no large-scale move into the wattas, which are longstanding tightly knit communities, opaque and difficult areas for new migrants to move into. Forms of adjacent marginality structured by class and ethnicity coexist uneasily. Thus Colombo's subterranean and transient worlds are many, and they do not map onto each other with ease. Nonetheless, at times these worlds have been more than adjacent; they have come into violent confrontation in the case of anti-Tamil riots, in which invariably, as Silva and Athukorala point out, watta dwellers are invoked as a "mob"-in-waiting, those who burned down Tamil homes and businesses and murdered hundreds. If the Sri Lankan war has created new forms of sociality, then these are uneasily grafted onto longer histories of violence in the city, Sri Lanka's numerous postcolonial riots in 1956, 1958, 1977, and 1983.

Riots

Eliathamby recalled going to the Colombo Fort train station in August 1977. It was a momentous year: a new government had been elected in such a landslide that the small Tamil parliamentary party TULF had ended up the official opposition. The TULF itself had just declared its support for a separate state for Tamils, so tensions in the country ran high. Eliathamby was waiting for his wife and two children to come from Jaffna. He had booked them reserved special seats. The train was delayed, so he continued to wait. Some hours later he was still waiting for the train. Finally it rolled in. He told me of running to the carriages to find many of them empty, some with blood staining the walls. Some passengers came off the train reeling, disheveled and bearing marks of violent struggles. There was no sign of his wife and children. Finally Eliathamby went to the railway staff who had traveled on the train to ask for the list of reserved seating. He told me of his great relief when he realized that his wife and children had not gotten on the train; their names were not marked as having boarded. As he walked out of the station, he walked into the midst of the 1977 riots.

The 1977 anti-Tamil riots had started, though their origins remain ever clouded. The beginnings are attributed to an incident involving violent police action in Jaffna that led to rumblings of discontent, and some incidents involving attacks on police which in turn provoked a clampdown (Hoole 2001: 22–38). Rumors, all false, traveled rapidly of purported Tamil violence against Sinhalese.[13] The results of the rumors were tragic. Passengers were attacked on the train from Jaffna to Colombo. Violence moved through the country from Anuradhapura to Colombo and then up to Hill Country areas, leading to around 300 dead and 25,000 displaced. Sri Lanka president J. R Jayawardene issued a speech warning that though the deaths were regrettable, the action had come out of a natural reaction to Tamil separatist claims. The outcome of the first riots since 1958 was a persistent insecurity that lay over Tamil life in Sri Lanka and the movement of many Hill Country Tamils toward India to settle in northern border areas.

While 1977 left its mark on Colombo, its homegrown riot came in 1983. After the deaths of 13 soldiers in the north at the hands of the LTTE, riots against Tamils began again with Colombo and Hill Country areas the most vulnerable. The numbers of affected and displaced increased exponentially, with some putting the death toll at around 2,000, and the estimated displaced hovering at 80,000–100,000 (Tambiah 1986: 22). While earlier riots had begun elsewhere and been exported to Colombo, the 1983 riots began in Colombo and moved upward through the country in waves of violence. The 1983 riots showed evidence of well-organized violence and (as in 1977) indifference of police, army, and established politicians toward Tamil victims. Colombo's

Tamil landscapes were burned out. Not only individuals but Indian Tamil businesses, factories belonging to industrialists, and even the Indian embassy were
attacked—an obliteration of the complex and long history of Tamil-speakers
in Colombo (Tambiah 1986; Kanathipathipillai 1990). Tamils for the first time
as Tambiah (1986) points out, through their mutual targeting, felt Tamil across
class, caste, and religion. The riots bridged class differentiations between Sri
Lankan and Malaiyaha/Hill Country Tamils; they marked all Tamils as one by
the violence enacted against them (see Kanathipathipillai 1990).[14]

These stories remained sedimented in Colombo's landscape for Tamils, a
secret history of violence that marked the whole city, passed on to those who
had never experienced them directly. After I moved to Colombo to conduct
research, my grandparents from Jaffna, when they stayed with me, insisted
that all mail to them be addressed to me with my (father's) Sinhalese sur-
name, as in 1983 rioters had identified Tamils through postal registers. On
one walk to buy food, my grandfather pointed to the railway tracks and told
me that this was where mobs had swarmed down to kill Tamils in that area.
He had not lived in Colombo in 1983, but even now this seemingly innocu-
ous crossing was marked by a history of violence forgotten by most Sinhalese
in that area. This ordinary reference to the riot histories of landscapes was not
uncommon. Passing by the popular and very cheap Saraswathi lodge eatery
in the central artery of the city, Galle Road, run by Tamils of Indian origin
but frequented by both Tamils and Sinhalese, another Tamil casually told me
that the Saraswathi lodge had been one of the hundreds of Tamil businesses
burned down in 1983. The riots implicitly drew Colombo dwellers into different spaces of possibility and a differently inhabited city. One cartography of
Colombo for Tamils constantly reinstates the intimate history of past violence
buried in various sites in the city, seemingly ready to be ignited again at any
point.[15] Riots, far from being merely Colombo's past, were forms of knowing
that constantly lay in wait, always potentially available. They are the violent
remainders of seemingly ordinary streets and mobs waiting to kill Tamils.

Yet those who imagined themselves as one at a moment of violence nonetheless remain differentiated after the riots. Sri Lankan Tamils and Malaiyaha/
Hill Country Tamils have seen no profound realignment of interests in Colombo. Tamilness under attack proved ephemeral in the face of longer histories of class and caste separation. Middle-class Sri Lankan Tamils still mostly
have employee to domestic worker relationships to Malaiyaha/Hill Country
Tamils. Thus Malaiyaha/Hill Country and Colombo Tamils of Indian descent
continue to bridge the adjacency of wattas and ethnic discrimination, part of

both histories. They have been neglected and rendered silent in discussions of minority Tamil rights, which I briefly return to later.

Many have argued (e.g., Tambiah 1986; Kapferer 1988) that Colombo's urban poor were instrumental in the 1983 anti-Tamil riots, albeit organized by other agencies. Undoubtedly, watta dwellers were at the forefront of 1983. Yet, as Silva and Athukorala (1991) argue, the involvement of watta dwellers involved a complex calculation of class and their own marginal position toward the police. They show that riot violence was often directed in areas outside the wattas and less common within, and that watta dwellers engaged in widespread looting of Tamil businesses and homes in the belief that "the law enforcement agencies would turn a blind eye toward offenses committed against Tamils" (125). Indeed, this would be the beginning of the forging of particular relationships between watta dwellers and police around Sri Lankan Tamils and their marginality. The influx of northeast Tamils into areas surrounding wattas saw the recruitment of watta dwellers by the police to inform on Tamil movements (Bremner 2004: 149) New forms of violence and securitization against Tamils simultaneously mobilized watta dwellers into Sri Lankan patriots, defenders of a nation in which they ordinarily they teetered on the edge.

However, as Bremner (2004) points out, the fragility of these links between the nation and wattas could always become evident, and Colombo's two adjacent marginalities come into odd and violent symbiosis. After the widespread looting and murder encouraged by authorities in 1983, police raided and increased police surveillance of the wattas, alarmed by the spontaneous spreading of watta dwellers across the city (Silva and Athukorala 1991: 126; Bremner 2004). The people could be released in service of the nation, but at the same time they had to be restrained. As Bremner points out, residents "were part of the Sinhala Buddhists for whom the nation had been built and looked to the state to provide them with viable strategies for living, but the links that the agents of the state built with them fractured their unity and were sometimes brutal and unpredictable" (2004: 142). Police incursions into wattas have only increased in the war era. A spate of mysterious killings of underworld figures in 2006–2009 was rumored to be partly the work of state security forces nominally mobilized against the LTTE, and increased police boldness, given the extension of powers in wartime.

However, while the riots drew in watta dwellers, politicians, police, and Tamils of all kinds, the alliances created to defend the nation against Tamils have now mutated. In 1995, rumors spread through Colombo that the

LTTE had poisoned the water supply with cyanide. Angry people thronged the street. Tamils hid in their houses, afraid that new riots would erupt. Sri Lankan officials went on TV to assure the public that nothing of this kind had happened, and the moment passed. For all, it summoned up the riot as part of Colombo's past that seemed to be potentially a future possibility. Yet it was unlikely that another riot would happen in Colombo after 1990. Anti-Tamil riots posed the attacks against Tamils as one of popular feeling, of Sinhalese anger against Tamils. Indeed, statements made after 1977 and 1983 by President Jayawardene only reinforced the idea that riots were the result of spontaneous popular anger (Hoole 2001) despite the well-organized nature of the 1983 riot. After 1990, however, the state moved into a new phase of securitization. Tamils became no longer the target of popular "sovereignty," a place in Sri Lanka, however nominal; they became the targets of state sovereignty of overwhelming police and army powers within Colombo. Increasingly, securitization and militarization of Sri Lankan society have argued the language of necessity, and those at the heart of this process are Sri Lankan Tamils. The mob, in its anti-Tamil anger, has turned into the police officer, and it is in exploring this that I move to Colombo present. Despite its seemingly "contaminated" colonial and ethnic pasts and presents, Colombo's actual centrality to the nation was graphically and symbolically reaffirmed by the sequence of LTTE attacks unleashed on it, and the sense that an attack on Colombo was an attack on the southern polity at large. It is Colombo as a city that provides invisible histories of violence and Colombo as a city under siege, to which we now proceed.

Colombo Present

The City as Violent Expectation

To allude to the weaving of Colombo's pasts into an ongoing *lived* experience of Colombo's present is to turn to a phenomenological account of urban space, what a phenomenology of Tamil Colombo trades in. In doing this, I am clearly inspired by Michel de Certeau's (1988) influential account of urban space as a traversed space, contrasting the Daedalus-like bird's eye view of the planner with the crisscrossing paths of pedestrians whose frozen footprints constantly recreate new spatial and social contours. De Certeau from the very beginning distinguishes between what he calls "place" and "space." Place implies an ordered distribution of properties; place is, he suggests, "an instantaneous configuration of positions. [I]t implies an indication of stability" (117). Space is differently composed: it is 'intersections of mobile elements,' an actuated "ensemble" of movements. Space comes out of the multiple elements that emerge as a present operation, like a "word when it is spoken," which has to negotiate and be understood within multiple conventions and possible misapprehensions. Space has nothing of the proper; for De Certeau, space is a "practiced place." This interplay between place and space is continually mediated by stories that cut across maps to constantly destabilize the order of place. To some extent, what follows is an attempt to discuss stories of itineraries that traverse and reorient the order of the city. At the same time, there is something celebratory in De Certeau's account, which contrasts, however implicitly, two different orders in which one becomes subversive and the other stabilizing, less portable. In a multi-ethnic society, however, spatial operations themselves, while mobile, are hierarchically and socially coded.

The spatial operations I describe to some extent combine an understanding of the multiple irreducible space(s) of urban life, but with the understanding that our itineraries and mobile intersections are themselves structured and lived, in this case by mobilizations of ethnicity and class (which De Certeau would not argue against but does not flesh out in favor of walking as a way of doing). One example can easily be found in statistically derived studies such as Gould and White's (1974) cognitive mapping, their analysis of composite maps and surveys of topographic stress found that "people tend to define their neighborhoods as an area whose size seems to be quite independent of the density of the people living in it," and that "neighborhoods in outer middle-class suburbs and high-density slums are perceived as about the same size" (34). Gould and White (1974) discuss this through the data gathered by geographer Peter Orleans's study of Los Angeles, where very different composite maps of urban space were drawn by different social and ethnic groups.[16] For Gould and White, one of the most significant results is the composite map created by a small Spanish-speaking minority in Boyle Heights: "their collective map includes only the immediate area, the City Hall, and pathetically, the bus depot—the major entrance and exit to their tiny urban world" (1974, 37).

If we take mapping as one entry point, then Tamil Colombo as reconstructed from spatial stories would be a composite of particular ethnic neighborhoods and important sites, a map that, while marking durable landscapes, simultaneously points to an institutionalized transience. It includes the Tamil areas and markets, the temples and churches, certain schools, post offices,

hospitals (especially those with a Tamil-speaking doctor), the lodges, and individual houses connected by bus routes across the city, as well as the police
stations one must avoid and the foreign embassies one must queue at in the
hope of getting a visa out of Sri Lanka. Most of all for Sri Lankan Tamils, the
international airport is clearly marked; this is why most come to Colombo,
after all. This characterization might change for Muslims and Malaiyaha/
Hill Country Tamils. For both migrating abroad to western countries is rare.
The Indian and Middle Eastern embassies and employment agencies collect
queues of working-class Sinhalese, Muslims, and Tamils. For many Malai-
yaha/Hill Country Tamils who engage in domestic service, the city opens
wide as a series of back doors and kitchens. Temples may be shared with Sri
Lankan Tamils, though Sri Lankan Tamils and their expatriate relations who
send donations sometimes edge out other Tamil participants.

Preeminent, however, and here prioritized as an understanding of the
phenomenologies of urban Colombo, is what united all inhabitants of wartime Colombo: differently inhabited and ethnicized practices of anxiety
around the possibility of state and LTTE violence. In his insightful essay on
walking through violence, that is, walking in Colombo, Pradeep Jeganathan
(2002) points to the ways Colombo is (dis)ordered and known through flows
of anticipatory violence. Jeganathan's essay begins with the renewed attempts
of residents of an upper-middle-class neighborhood to get a nearby military
installation removed after the massive LTTE bombing of the Central Bank in
1995, fearing that such proximity to military targets would make them the
next targets of an LTTE bomb. Made up of hard targets (military and administrative buildings) and soft targets (human beings, buses, trains), Colombo
is a series of actual and potential sites of attack by bombs and suicide blasts.
For its residents Colombo is constantly rerouted through the anticipation
of such violence, both as everyday fears for civilians and as ever-accreting
state surveillance apparatus. Jeganathan writes, "into the social cartographies
of targets, then, there can arise cartographies that become in turn cartographies of anticipated violence—mappings of a terrifying future" (2002: 358).
He refuses to create such a cartography, for "the tactics that accompany such
anticipation do not map out a cartography in a stable way"; instead, "what
might be subjected to 'violence' shifts, and the targets themselves flitter like
shadows across the landscape of the city." The city offers itself constantly as a
space of life and death simultaneously, its sounds and sights to be read with
an anxious gaze and speculative ear.

A few months into the ceasefire, I was at one of the iconic Hindu temples in Colombo, Bambalapitiya Pillaiyar Kovil, for the 6 p.m. *puja*. The evening puja was one of the busiest, with Tamils and a regular small stream of Sinhalese coming in to worship, a steady crowd of Tamil women walking around the Amman (Mother Goddess) shrine praying for children and/or marriage. It was a time of cautious celebration. As we stood at the entrance of the main doorway, a firework went off loudly and unannounced near the preening peacocks in the courtyard. Everyone jumped visibly, and people started looking around anxiously. The Brahmin purohit distributing ash called out loudly "it is only a firework, what did you all think it was!" The second part of the sentence was uttered with a knowing laugh. He knew as we all did that we all thought it was a bomb, a normal rather than exceptional happening, but one attended with enormous consequence, not just for the city but for how Colombo's Tamils would continue to be seen.

As Vyjayanthi Rao (2007) writes, the bomb blasts that have ripped through urban terrain (Mumbai in her case), reveal through grotesque undoing, the skeleton of the city and its urban infrastructure. Bombs that attack the city have created a geography of undifferentiated sites that, by signifying attack on a city at large, have, she argues, created a city that corresponds to its municipal boundaries, a public city. This map of violence overlies and supersedes an older geography of "sensitive points" that signified the riot with its intimate pinpointing of neighborhoods and fraught intimacies (583). She points out how such "coordinated, simultaneous attack turns connectivity into collapse" by "using the very connectivity afforded by the infrastructural network itself—the underlying systemic bases that form the conditions of possibility of modern urban planning and indeed contemporary urban life " (572).

If forms of urban terrorism turn "connectivity into collapse," then in Colombo the institutionalization of urban terrorism as a permanent feature of wartime life has turned collapse back into connectivity. Colombo's landscape is crisscrossed with checkpoints, police stations, and evident signs of the state as surveillance. This pattern has become so normalized that checkpoints in Colombo frequently bear commercial advertisements. As Jeganathan points out,

> the checkpoint configures practices of anticipation in a double way. On the one hand, to pass through one is to remember why they exist—it is to recall the possibility of a bomb . . . on the other hand is another kind of anticipation, that of the soldiers who are checking the flow of traffic and people asking questions. They, the not-so-diffuse

tentacles of the state are . . . anticipating violence in an organized way.
(2002: 361)

To extend his argument farther, we could contend that such anticipated violence builds up a regular exchange of differentiated relationships between the
state and its various citizens.

Checkpoints were just one part of the organized surveillance and anticipation of violence. All kinds of social relations also bound together citizens
and surveillance, from the deals struck between the police and the Tamil and
Sinhala landlords of the lodges that have sprung up to house transient Tamils, to the watta/slum dwellers recruited to watch neighborhoods for suspicious Tamils (Bremner 2004). A mental and physical surveillance apparatus
coproduced by civilians and the state has become a regular habituated way of
thinking of the city as a whole. Neighborhoods became drawn next to each
other across class by their possibility of attack, even as in everyday life they
are separated by gulfs of experience and class. These intangible bonds, as well
as those consecrated by regular checking and illegal economies, produced
Colombo's Tamils as potential shadowy threats.

For Colombo's ordinary Tamils, the checkpoint is one of many nodes in
an anticipated violence that is qualitatively different from how non-Tamil residents in Colombo fear violence. If non-Tamil residents have flickering and
constantly adjustable mappings of targets, Tamils fear that their own bodies
are mapped onto such cartographies. By blurring the lines between Tamil civilian and suicide bomber in Colombo, the LTTE folded the two in together.
As one man told me bitterly "the Sinhala chauvinists and the LTTE are the
same, they both think that all Tamils are Tigers." This intense surveillance and
attempt to keep seemingly mobile Tamils "in place" made for an institutionalized permanent transience in the city as an effect of a constantly reinforced
transience within the nation.

Tamil Colombo as Permanent Transience

"In life one gets little possessions and builds up a home and shelter. Can one
take these when you are asked to leave with only two bags? Can one take
tables, or chairs?" Murugan asked me. He gestured to the room they were
living in. Thangamma sat on the ramshackle bed. On the floor was a small
cooking stove, and neatly arranged around it were the various foodstuffs and

spices she was cooking for our lunch. Under the bed, Murugan showed me suitcases and boxes packed with paper—what he had brought as vital items—documents of all kinds, from those they needed to show in Colombo, to the school certificates and letters of recommendation that Murugan was trying to use in his continuing attempts to migrate abroad.

I have known Murugan and Thangamma, who are friends of my family, on and off for most of my life. When I was born, it was a younger Murugan who was around and, as he reminds me with affection, ran with my birth time to the astrologer for a horoscope I have never read. They were both from the Jaffna peninsula part of the war zone. As Murugan ruminates, none of us knew then that what was in store for us and Tamils more generally was constant displacement. Murugan had brought them to Colombo after many failed attempts to continue his life in the northern Jaffna peninsula. A mechanic, he was unable to make a living in the north, trapped between the LTTE and the Sri Lankan army and their requirements. Any work done for either would put him in danger, but refusal was often not an option. Finally he and Thangamma left Jaffna in 1995, when the Sri Lankan army advanced upon Jaffna town and the LTTE had forced the 450,000 people living there to leave the city, the event now called the "Exodus." (see Chapter 1; UTHR 1996). Murugan recalled how they had walked alongside the thousands streaming out of their Jaffna home, another phase in the continued displacement that Tamils undergo. They both at times slept under trees and drank rain water collected in an umbrella. There was nothing shocking about Murugan's story; I had heard similar stories from many Jaffna Tamils who had left in the Exodus. They talked of Jaffna with love and pragmatism. It was their home, but they felt there was no future there for them. So, Murugan and Thangamma, like thousands of other Tamils, had come to Colombo, the most ethnically plural city in Sri Lanka, with its international airport the only route out of Sri Lanka.

The Colombo I knew was filled with Sri Lankan Tamils from the north and east, and most had come to Colombo in the hope of finding a way out of the country. It is, for many of these migrants, a temporary stopping place. Yet the waiting place had transformed for many into permanent limbo. Some had been "waiting" for more than ten years. Most remained stuck there, unable to leave. They are the unacknowledged part of the much-studied Sri Lankan Tamil diaspora,[17] the *shadow diaspora*, those who cannot leave Sri Lanka, but who possess dreams of migration and betterment as potently as those who do leave.

Anthony, the young Jaffna Tamil man we encountered in Chapter 1, was also part of this amorphous clustering of Tamil hopes around foreign futures. He and another young Tamil shared a room and dreamed of leaving. His roommate still had a piece of shrapnel embedded in his head and lived under the constant fear that the shrapnel would work its way farther in and end his life. Anthony feared the possibility that he would remain stuck in limbo and not become a full person, able to marry and provide for his family. After his education suffered as a result of the war, and he abjured joining the LTTE, Anthony was left with only migration as the final plank of Tamil aspirations. As discussed in earlier chapters, "migration" is buried deep in Jaffna cultural aspirations (McDowell 1996). But Anthony constantly found himself unable to access the financial and other resources to obtain a visa or imagine a sustainable life abroad. He was alone in Colombo; his immediate family and extended kin were in India and other countries. Jaffna for him, though the object of love as his *sonta ur* (real home) as he readily identified it, was empty of kin. His kin had become "splintered and separated"; his home "withered" away. Migration had come to pose the only answer. After all, Anthony pointed out to me, many of those who had gone abroad without an education were earning well and sending money back to their relatives and those who had stayed like him were earning nothing. As he told me on one occasion,

> now look, you are doing your degree; you have done well. It is because you were able to go abroad. Otherwise you would not have been able to do all these things. People who were able to go abroad are all doing well. Those who could not, most are like me.

For Anthony, the distinction I draw between the shadow diaspora and the diaspora had become an obvious structural inequality in Sri Lankan Tamil society, one observed in other South Asian communities who adopted migration as a form of social mobility (e.g., Gardner 1993 on Bangladesh; Osella and Osella 2006 on Kerala, India). As Anthony told me,

> Everyone is trying to go abroad. In Colombo most people who are there have relatives abroad who support them. . . . In Jaffna people there don't have these resources, the young men and women who join can't go abroad. . . . Everyone wants to leave as soon as possible.

For Anthony the choice between migration and staying in Sri Lanka is a choice also between his family and his country:

For me, the opportunity to go abroad is about helping my family, one must look after one's family too, not just one's country. If one does not look after one's family one cannot look after one's country. It is foolish to go and fight for your country if you cannot help your own family when they are suffering. You must do whatever you can first for them before going to take up the country's trouble.

Coming to Colombo was for Anthony part of his journey toward full personhood. He himself could only get married after he had helped obtain his sister's dowry and seen her married, so he remained constantly poised between two life projects, youthful achievement, and adult reproduction. Yet leaving Jaffna for Colombo was not to leave a life of insecurity for one of security. Instead as a young man, he found himself the target of constant suspicion. Many Tamil parents taking their young children out of Jaffna to escape recruitment by the LTTE found instead that the children were being picked up by the Sri Lankan army and police for being LTTE.

In the intense years of war between 1995 and 2002, Tamils fleeing to Colombo and its satellite suburbs moved into countless lodges, large, often hazardous and over-crammed buildings that promised temporary accommodation on a monthly basis, providing for those who could not mobilize financial resources to buy or rent houses in Colombo or the social resources to stay with family and friends. Murugan and Thangamma lived in a lodge in the (historically Sri Lankan Tamil) Wellawatta neighborhood in Colombo. They were renting a room, and were one of the many Tamil families and individuals packed together in small rooms and shared bathrooms. There were an odd assortment of people in the lodge that Murugan and Thangamma lived in, from the young women who had come to Colombo to wait for an overseas marriage with a diaspora Tamil to be arranged, to elderly people who were waiting for visas. Mainly Sri Lankan Tamil, in the Pettah area in central Colombo some lodges also housed Malaiyaha/Hill Country Tamils coming down from plantation areas to find work and marriage in Colombo too. These lodges often existed just on the right side of the law, and stories abounded about unscrupulous landlords who had links to the police or underworld and were rumored to exploit female tenants. For Tamils who had no family or established links in Colombo, lodges were the only places they could move into. But they were dangerous and insecure, the first port of call for the Sri Lankan army and police after any hint of trouble.

In one high profile case, on 7 June 2007, after a week of LTTE bomb

attacks, 376 Tamils were summarily evicted from lodges in the (predominantly Sri Lankan and Hill Country Tamil) Wellawatte, Kotahena, Pettah,
and Wattala areas of Colombo by the Sri Lankan police for "security reasons." The arrests were directed precisely at temporary accommodation and
lodges. The 376 Tamils were rushed suddenly out of their homes and put
on seven buses out of the city toward "their homes" in the war zone areas.
They managed to alert others when one Tamil man called the private Sinhala radio station Sirasa FM while on the bus and spoke on air of what was
happening.[18] As a consequence an immediate petition to halt the eviction
filed by the group Centre for Policy Alternatives, Sri Lanka's Supreme Court
ordered a halt to the evictions on 8 June, and 185 of those deported to north
central Vavuniya were transported back. The Tamils concerned had come
to the lodges for a variety of reasons, some waiting to go abroad, some for
work, some to be treated at Colombo hospitals. While in this case the cleansing of Tamils in retribution for LTTE attacks out of Colombo was halted, this
harassment and the possibility of arrest were a constant probability for all
Tamils in Colombo.

Restrictions on northeast Tamils in Colombo were numerous. The major
restriction was the mandatory police registration of northeast Tamils. On arriving in the city, Tamils had to register their address with a local police station, and had to carry their certificate with them at all times. If found at an
address that was not that on their certificate, they would be arrested. It was
rare to stay over at other people's houses purely because of the fear of arrest.
I recalled traveling around Colombo in the 1990s with my young male Tamil
cousin, carrying his police certificate like a talisman, tense and frightened
whenever we were stopped by police or army. Even in the 2002 ceasefire when
these restrictions were suspended, in their retelling of the stories of the 1990s,
people could not shake themselves of the fear that restrictions would return.
They were right. By the tail end of the ceasefire the restrictions were reinstated and ever more checkpoints reappeared.

In 2002, as we walked through mainly Tamil Wellawatte market, Murugan told me of the years prior to my visit, when young people were constantly
taken away from the lodge by the army or police. "We would never stand
and talk," he told me, indicating the busy scenes in the market. People were
simply too frightened to hang around. The lifting of restrictions under the
ceasefire prompted constant reflection on the years preceding it, guided at
all times by the (accurate) fear that these would return. People kept on trying

to make me visualize or understand what it could be like to be "too scared to speak your own language" or display Tamil script. I heard women talk of wiping the vermilion pottu that marked them as Tamil from their faces, and being afraid to speak Tamil on the streets. One Muslim woman remarked pointedly to me, "we were the ones to keep Tamil alive on the street, your people were too frightened," describing how Muslims were the ones to openly speak Tamil and maintain the sounds of Tamil as a language of Colombo when Sri Lankan Tamils effaced themselves for fear of being picked up by the army.

These conversations were about the inability to have a public identity as a Tamil, since this public identity would put one at risk. One half-Tamil half-Sinhalese man living in a working-class Sinhalese neighborhood told me of how his neighbors had complained to him about Tamils visiting his house and threatened to inform the police. As a matter of patriotism, Sinhalese were enjoined to inform on suspicious Tamils to the police throughout the 1990s, leading to a climate of fear and division and Tamils clustering in predominantly well-established Tamil pockets in Colombo. Questions of "passing" and possibilities of an underground Tamil life were thus often related also to Tamil areas in which Tamil public life could at least display itself. Tamil areas thus were imagined as ethnic interiors within a largely Sinhala city. Tamil areas were imbued with a peculiar economy of psychic stress, particularly the predominantly (and thus favored) Sri Lankan Tamil areas of Wellawatte, Dehiwela, Bambalapitiya, and Wattala. On one hand, they represented community and comfort. One could speak Tamil, eat Tamil food, and order Tamil goods. All one's relatives lived nearby; odd assortments of people one had lost contact with years ago turned up suddenly in those areas. I myself frequently went to buy things in Wellawatte market. On the other hand, as many Tamils complained, the problem with Tamil areas was the astronomical prices. Food, housing, commodities were all more expensive in Tamil areas than in other sections of Colombo. Knowledge of a literally captive market and the remittances that flowed in from overseas relatives for many Tamil migrants kept prices artificially high. Rents especially were incredible. Living together was expensive. Furthermore, congregating together invited further surveillance and regular police incursions. There was an uneasy balance between being together and forming a collective target.

Other Tamils also made being together a site of anxious ambivalent enjoyment. Given the LTTE penetration of Tamil families through forced recruitment, and their control over Tamils more generally, that I have consistently documented in this book, Tamils constantly feared other Tamils being LTTE informers. Even in Colombo, the LTTE were feared to be everywhere. I was hushed many times in the street, in the temple, and in the church by those I talked to. "One never knows," I was told all the time. In my interviews with Tamil dissidents, I would have to take long and circuitous bus routes, varying my journey many times to make sure I was not followed. Unusually tall for a Sri Lankan, my informants were convinced that I stood out like a sore thumb. Perhaps indeed I did. Some of the dissidents I interviewed, like Sakthi (see Chapter 5), lived on the periphery of a Tamil area, caught between her fear of other Tamils and her longing for them.

This ambivalence toward togetherness marked Tamil life in Sri Lanka more generally. Ethnic interiors were comforting and yet laced through with fear of each other as a result of the penetration of the LTTE into ordinary civilian life. The internal gaze of the community on itself is often missed in accounts that narrate the way marginal/transient communities live within spaces. Often we focus only on the policing of the state and the ways communities become intelligible to the state. In the case of Tamils, this gaze is doubled. While the state and police looked at all Tamils as potential tigers to be unmasked with their stripes revealed, other Tamils, who afford intelligibility, conversation, and exchange of comfort at most times, were also still those one had to guard against. If this ambivalence of being together is a feature of wartime life, it is in less heightened contexts a more general feature of life in enclaves. Even in Puttalam, within refugee camps and settlements, people complained constantly of gossip and being watched and judged within the community. At the point of desired intelligibility intrudes the doubled life of kinship and intimacy, both amity and anxiety simultaneously (Geschiere 1997; Thiranagama 2010). Not least, to return to earlier discussions of the class and caste distinctions that constantly ordered interaction between Sri Lankan Tamils and Malaiyaha/Hill Country Tamils or working-class Colombo Tamils of Indian origin, all Tamils were not Tamil in the same way. Tamil life fractured around class and caste. Tamilness was given life as a collectivity by state discrimination and the LTTE, and at the same time was undone continually by this violence.

This comfort and discomfort generated by other Tamils nestles within the larger and new connectivities and economies of the city, generated by the anticipation of violence that we began with. The state as an ensemble of actors, as well as a representation of an entity larger than these actors (Abrams 1988;

Hansen and Stepputat 2001), has come to represent itself ever more through an institutionalized surveillance apparatus as an entity under siege. This apparatus orders and places at its heart the control and fixing of Tamil movement. Tamil Colombo thus traverses operations of particular ethnic journeys, which are at the same time the everyday instantiation of Sri Lanka at war, as a state under siege, as proliferating wartime economies.

The Future of Tamil Colombo

Michael Gilsenan ends one of his books with a rumination on walking: "this book has been a kind of excavation and a wandering" ([1982]2000: 269). He retells his own attempts to walk self-confidently with others through spaces which he only "dimly intuited" and the routes that, while seemingly aimless, didn't take him to just any house but to a particular house. Recalling this he writes, "It is that way of walking that now comes unexpectedly to teach me about that culture and its unspoken premises . . . to absorb that walk into one's own body was far closer to speaking 'the language' . . . behind its apparent formlessness and disinterest, there was readiness, a sense of options, even a practical and quite specific awareness of risk" (270–71).

I take inspiration from both this kind of walking and this kind of ending. In many ways it seemed apt to me to close this book with an account of being a Tamil dweller in Colombo. All that I learned about Tamil sociality in wartime years came from the cues that picked up as I learned to navigate the city the way others did. I have not been able to write about Colombo except to call upon this phenomenology, and in doing so I have more directly than at any other time in the book had to recall what it is that I learned from others in this journey, and perhaps why it is that I took this path. I have also thus abjured a direct conclusion; each chapter has ended with questions, and here I can only add more questions as we move into a critical postwar future in Sri Lanka, a cessation of war—ironically in a chapter about the anticipation of violence—that was unanticipated.

Home and the impossibility of homeliness have been the underlying theme of this chapter. The stories I have told about *ur* and Jaffna in this book have been just one set of stories about belonging and home. Jaffna, while culturally nourishing, has over the war years become aspirationally disappointing. Colombo, the heart of the southern polity, has indeed become for many a possible future. Yet, as I have argued in this chapter, Colombo has institutionalized its Tamils as permanent transients. This transience has not come out of literal transience in the city, because Tamil speakers of all kinds have long been part of Colombo's disavowed soul. It is instead how the nation state is lived and trodden into the everyday spaces of urban life. Colombo was a city where Tamil life was constantly shot through with the anticipation of violence. Colombo's present was one where Tamils effaced themselves. Tamils in the city, male and female, posed the threat of constant illegibility to the state. Ordinary Tamils were both extremely vulnerable and feared.

Yet this chapter and the book also argues that the dream of racial purity, of being together, of the complete legibility of a Tamil-only space, whether Tamil Eelam or the gossipy expensive enclaves of Tamil neighborhoods in Colombo, is deeply ambivalent as a lived reality for Tamils despite their imaginative promise as a safe space. Not least, the mono-ethnic identities encoded in visions of Tamil Eelam were not self-evident, but were built on the continual purging of Muslims from Tamil spaces in the north and east (Chapter Three). Tamil life in Colombo is always intimately concerned with Sinhalese and other ethnic minorities. In turn, the many Tamil-speaking minorities of Colombo themselves through their constant presence and absence threaten the idea of a Sinhala-only city. The complexity and interlaced density of ethnic life in Sri Lanka will always threaten dreams of racial purity.

That said, the particular ways in which ethnicity, class, and caste has structured life in Sri Lanka, and in particular the policing of Tamil movement in the war years, will not, alongside the other kinds of investments I describe in the book, vanish with the end of the war. This book has detailed the ways wartime life has been, for those living through it, a terrain where Tamil movement has been the major focus of the performance of stateness by the LTTE and the Sri Lankan state. Earlier chapters detailed the LTTE control of movement through pass laws, and its forcing of large-scale movements such as the Exodus and the Eviction. In turn, this chapter has alluded to the building of the Sri Lankan state's surveillance apparatus in Colombo city around the movement of Tamils, an apparatus that is nonetheless tested constantly by its inability to make Tamils fully legible.

For the last two decades, Tamils have become the feared center of new constructions and routes of the city. What of those forms of connectivity and licit and illicit exchanges that have constituted a particular wartime economy and cartography of Colombo? How can Sri Lankan Tamils themselves imagine a future in Sri Lanka when still in 2011 there has been little attempt by the

Sri Lankan state to institute real processes of reconciliation after the defeat of the LTTE? How is it that the end of the war has not brought about large-scale commitment to rethinking and finding political and constitutional resolution to the uncertain status and transience of all minority life in Sri Lanka? These are the questions that lie ahead for ordinary civilians in their ongoing prognostications of their future possibilities.

One of the major themes of this book has been the intense investment in place and the contours of that investment handed down as forms of loss, as a means of negotiating relationships, as well as the more obvious institution of it as an empty metaphor for political struggle by Tamil militant groups such as the LTTE. The racially differentiated landscape of neglect of the north and east, the need for development, devolution of power, and democratic governance in those regions, means that any Sri Lankan state has to be prepared to take regional power and representation seriously. However, any form of political solution that treats only limited devolution for northern and eastern Tamils within the areas they live, and not minority rights and entitlements for all Sri Lanka's minorities wherever they live, would have ignored what Colombo can tell us, and why I present Colombo and not Jaffna as a model for reimagining Sri Lanka.

First, increasing control by the LTTE and the Sri Lankan state over Tamil movement has been played out against a longer and different marking of histories of movement, most specifically within the Jaffna Tamil community, with migration and internal movement as forms of aspiration and social mobility. Those I interviewed in the shadow diaspora in Colombo and elsewhere did not contrast displacement to sedentary lives, but contrasted forced and chosen movement, displacement, and migration. This is why any long-term solution to minority issues in Sri Lanka must come up with solutions that acknowledge that minorities in Sri Lanka are also highly mobile. Second, if one has rights only by coming from a designated Tamil majority area, what will happen to Colombo Tamils from nowhere else but Colombo, or Malaiyaha/Hill Country Tamils in Sinhala majority areas, or the Colombo Muslims who live all across the city? What do we do when people have homes but no homeland? When the places they live in are not places they are recognized to belong in? Retrenchment of entitlement solely in the relationship between people and certain places without a meaningful entitlement for minorities in a larger national space will be inadequate for all these people on the move: Sri Lankan Tamils, and "landless" but emplaced minorities such as Sri Lankan

Muslims, and the formerly Indian Tamil, Malaiyaha Tamil, and Colombo Tamil population who have no defined territory of their own. Colombo has for generations provided a site for minority and majority futures, even when these futures were centered on Sri Lanka as a dystopia. To be able to understand the city that has never "been one" is perhaps to begin to imagine a future for Sri Lanka, the nation that has never been one.

ABBREVIATIONS

ENDLF - Eelam National Democratic Liberation Front
ENLF - Eelam National Liberation Front
EPDP - Eelam People's Democratic Party
EPRLF - Eelam People's Revolutionary Liberation Front
EROS - Eelam Revolutionary Organization of Students
ESLMF - East Sri Lanka Muslim Front
GUES - General Union of Eelam Students, later became EPRLF
IPKF - Indian Peace Keeping Force
ICRC- International Committee of the Red Cross
JVP - Janatha Vimukthi Perumuna (National Liberation Front)
LTTE - Liberation Tigers of Tamil Eelam
MULF - Muslim United Liberation Front
PLOTE - People's Liberation Organization of Tamil Eelam
RAAF - Research and Action Forum for Social Development
RAW - Research and Analysis Wing (Indian external intelligence agency)
SLFP - Sri Lanka Freedom Party
SLMC - Sri Lanka Muslim Congress
SLMM - Sri Lankan Monitoring Mission
TEA - Tamil Eelam Army
TELO - Tamil Eelam Liberation Organization
TNA - Tamil National Army
TULF - Tamil United Liberation Front
UNP - United National Party
UTHR(J) - University Teachers for Human Rights (Jaffna)

NOTES

Foreword

1. Linda Colley, *Britons: Forging the Nation 1707–1837* (New Haven, Conn.: Yale University Press, 1992); Eugen Weber, *Peasants into Frenchmen: The Modernization of Rural France, 1870–1914* (Stanford, Calif.: Stanford University Press, 1976).

2. Gananath Obeyesekere, "Religious Symbolism and Political Change in Ceylon," *Modern Ceylon Studies: Journal of the Social Sciences* 1, 1 (1970): 43–63; reprinted in *The Two Wheels of the Dhamma*, ed. Bardwell L. Smith (Chambersburg, Pa.: Wilson Books, 1972), 58–78.

Introduction: In My Mother's House

1. Ponnambalam Memorial Hospital was bombed on 6 February 2009 and Puthuk-kudiyiruppu hospital was hit thrice by artillery fire on 1 February, killing nine (UTHR 2009a).

2. See items such as http://news.bbc.co.uk/2/hi/south_asia/8017945.stm; http://english.aljazeera.net/news/asia/2009/05/2009569856222191.html; http://english.aljazeera.net/news/americas/2009/05/2009513222013221256.html.

3. Nordstrom explicitly abjures studying war in one community and/or in one place, arguing that war is a process and necessarily fluidly studied as such a process (1997: 10).

4. Our libidinal dependency on our own subjectification does not circumvent any possibility of agentive power. Butler points out that while power subordinates and forms the subject, it does not mean that this power remains untransformed (for her elaboration on the relationship between power and agency see 1997: 10–19).

5. The 2001 Census could only survey 18 (southern and central) districts and showed the population to be "Sinhalese 82.0 percent, Sri Lanka Tamil 4.3 percent, Indian Tamil 5.1 percent and Sri Lanka Moor 7.9 percent." However, Census compilers point out that if one includes the unsurveyed northern and eastern districts, " according to the 2001 estimated population of Sri Lanka as a whole, Sinhalese, Sri Lanka Tamil, Indian Tamil, and Sri Lanka Moor population comprise of 74.5 percent, 11.9 percent, 4.6 percent and 8.3 percent respectively" (2001 Census, Population and Housing, 9)

6. The "North" includes the Jaffna Peninsula and those regions immediately lower, the "East" includes Trincomalee and Batticaloa Districts and the "Vanni" districts of the North Central province is centred on Vavuniya.

7. As Pfaffenberger (1982) points out, different dominant castes (Jaffna's symboli-cally dominant caste is Vellala and the east coast Batticaloa region's is Mukkuva) and patterns of kinship and marriage (Jaffna bilateral, East Coast matrilineal) give the areas markedly different social structures.

8. Dennis McGilvray (2008) gives the only comprehensive account of the distinc-tive matrilineal structures of Tamils and Muslims on the east coast—where both caste and mosque membership are passed through *thay vali* (mother way) and one's mother's "clan" (*kuti*).

9. There has been more work with Northern Muslims subsequent to displacement (see Brun 2003; Hasbullah 2001; Shanmugaratnam 2000; etc.), but only Hasbullah has attempted to bring together analyses of Tamils and Muslims (Hasbullah n.d).

10. There is been little ethnographic work on the north. Some work conducted in the eras prior to the 1970s such as David (1977, 1973, 1980), Pfaffenberger (1982), and Banks (1960), concentrated on kin and caste patterns while post-1970s Jaffna is dis-cussed in all kinds of writings on ethnic conflict, violence, and war but has not been the basis of actual ethnographic research.

11. See UTHR(J) (University Teachers for Human Rights-Jaffna), CPA (Centre for Policy Alternatives), RAAF (Research and Action Forum), HRW (Human Rights Watch).

12. The census of 1871 reported that almost 10.3 percent of the total population of the island lived in the Jaffna peninsula. Between 1816 and 1827 the population of Jaffna increased by 19 percent and doubled in the next 44 years from 1827 to 1871. In 1921 the Jaffna Peninsula was the most densely populated area of cultivated territory in Sri Lanka (Arasaratnam1994)

13. Denham (1912) relates that in 1911 there were close to 7,000 Tamils in Kuala Lumpur, which soon became referred to as Little Jaffna. By 1930 there were 10,000 Tam-ils in the Federated Malay States (Bastin 1997: 418).

14. In 1981 the Tamil population of Sri Lanka numbered 1,900,000 people; by 1995 almost three-quarters of them were either internally displaced or seeking asylum over-seas (McDowell 1996).

15. Indeed, most have experienced multiple displacements; the Danish Refugee Council (2000) estimates that since 1983 around 1,700,000 have been displaced one or more times.

16. Around 280,000 Tamils were interned in government camps such as Menik Farm after May 2009. By late November 2009 only 150,000 had been released; the gov-ernment announced that there were "only" 127,000 remaining (see IDMC 2009).

17. Canada houses 200,000–250,000 by official estimates, though other sources fol-lowing UNHCR estimate Canada's Tamil population at 400,000 (Sriskandarajah 2002: 293). Europe houses 200,000 and India 67,000. These figures were last tallied in 2002, and the numbers, especially in India, have increased following the resumption of con-flict in 2004.

18. While Daniel glosses *ur* as the English "home," and I use this and also use the English word "village" because in Sri Lanka ordinary people translate Tamil *ur* and

Sinhala *gama* as village. However, the sense of "village" found in *kiramam*, as Daniel argues and I found too, is used for abstract administrative and political boundaries, to which the person by using *kiramam* ascribes distance or objectification.

19. The 1977 university standardizations sought to redress the dominance of urban youth over rural youth by standardizing quotas via district but which, accompanied by language standardization, directed against perceived Tamil "dominance," meant that Tamils had to get higher marks than their Sinhala counterparts for the same university places.

20. A common Tamil way of describing militancy in the media and ordinary conversations.

21. Thus the effects of the faltering Sri Lankan economy of the 1960s onward were doubly exacerbated for Tamils.

22. Moreover, criticism of the LTTE often came from Sinhala chauvinist elements not out of concern for Tamils. Thus it was even more "our secret."

23. The debate is structured around Dumont's (1953) discussion of the southern subcontinent, characterised by those speaking "Dravidian languages" (Tamil, Malayalam, Kannada, etc.) as providing examples of bilateral systems based on alliance, marked by a distinction between cross cousin (marriageable) and parallel cousin (unmarriageable). He suggests these structural relations are passed down from generation to generation, becoming divided into "terminological affines" and "terminological kin." I follow Anthony Good, who comprehensively demonstrates through his detailed data that Dravidian kinship as it has been defined does not exist (1996: 2). As Good points out, the observance of systematic features is important but does not necessarily commit us to a notion of a kinship system (1996: 11)

24. See Daniel (1989) for his discussion and coining of the term, *Tanimai tosam* (loneliness disorder), and also Fuglerud (1999: 78–80).

25. Peletz's argument is implicitly Freudian as is mine

26. Kapadia argues that non-brahmanical castes often invest in the whole kindred group, *sondam,* rather than solely patrilineal kin and the intense *pasam* (affection/love) that a mother's brother is said to have for his sister's children is seen as axiomatic. Among her informants "it is widely accepted that the link between brothers and sisters is exceptionally close and it endures throughout life, even after a sister's marriage" (1995: 20; Trawick 1990, 179). {1992?}

27. Jaffna Tamils and Batticaloa Tamils stand in contrast to Tamil Nadu Tamils in their stress on maternal kin, though the eastern Muslim and Tamil *kuti* matri-clan system is unmatched in Jaffna (McGilvray 1982)

28. The *uravuvalamai* (lineage tradition) that Sivathamby (1989) argues is practiced in Tamil Nadu is less stressed in Jaffna, where the concept of *pakuti* (division/section) is more lateral than vertical (Sivathamby 1989). Yalman has also argued for the importance of lateral kin over lineage in Sri Lanka for Kandyan Sinhalese too (1962: 552).

29. Jaffna follows the customary code Thesawalamai and Batticaloa the Mukkuva code (the latter became legally defunct in the early twentieth century), in defining three

kinds of property: (1) *mutucom* passing from father to son in Thesawalamai and brought into the marriage by the husband; (2) *thediathetam*, property or profits acquired by the couple together; sons generally inherit from this, though dowry provision for daughters is prioritized; (3) *chidenam*, the dowry payment that accompanies most marriages, comprising land, jewels, and cash (Kantawala 1930; McGilvray 1982b; Tambiah 1973; Sivathamby 1989).

30. Furthermore, in Jaffna the preferred pattern for the first phase of postmarital residence is uxorilocal (living with the bride's family) or ambilocal (though uxorilocality is high when couples are able to live on the given dowry land) (Tambiah 1973; Sivathamby 1989; McGilvray; 1982). This understanding of houses as "mother's house" is a taken-for-granted assumption by my informants.

Chapter 1. Growing Up at War: Self-Formation, Individuality, and the LTTE

1. The LTTE continued a covert presence in Jaffna after the government takeover in 1995 and was in full control of the north central areas surrounding the peninsula, rendering government control of the north highly precarious.

2. With a typically South Asian interpretation of rule when I was in government-controlled Jaffna in 2003, I noticed that ice cream vans had "ice kully or "kuli cream" written on them.

3. Anthony says *viduthalai* (liberation) sarcastically, a reference to the LTTE's name (Liberation Tigers of Tamil Eelam) known in Tamil in shortened form as *viduthalai puligal* (Liberation Tigers).

4. See Chapter 5 for an explanation of the "youth bulge" theory.

5. See also UTHR Briefing No. 2 (June 1995)

6. Under the British five different missionary bodies arrived in Sri Lanka: the London Missionary Society (1804–5), the Baptist Mission (1812), the Wesleyan Missionary Society (1814), the American Mission Society (1817) and the Church Missionary Society (Bastin 1997: 406). The American mission concentrated its activities exclusively in the North, though all the missionary bodies set up schools in Jaffna (Wickremeratne 1973).

7. By 1822 there were 42 schools in the peninsula (Arasaratnam 1994)

8. Within Sri Lanka, in 1921, a total of 10,185 Tamils were employed in public administration and the liberal arts (ibid.).

9. Stories of scarcity in Jaffna always stress the scarcity of kerosene and thus of light.

Chapter 2. The House of Secrets: Mothers, Daughters, and Inheritance

1. Don Arachchige notes that one of the most consistent migration routes to Colombo in the twentieth century was from Jaffna, chiefly for employment (1994: 30).

2. In fact, as Tambiah (1986) points out, the effects of the 1956, 1958, 1977, 1981, and 1983 anti-Tamil riots in southern Sinhalese majority areas were possible because Tamil minorities (SLT from all areas and hill-country Tamils) were to be found in large numbers throughout the island, not just in the "Tamil areas" of the north and east. It is

the movement of people in riots and the civil war that has polarized Sri Lanka into more clearly defined Tamil and Sinhala-speaking areas.

3. This collective identity still excluded hill-country and "Indian" Tamils who, though directly affected by the riots (with many of the arson attacks in Colombo directed against businesses run by Tamils of recent Indian descent and with every riot moving up the country into plantation areas), were not woven into the story of Sri Lankan Tamil nationalism (see Daniel 1996). The retelling and resignification of 1983 as a climactic event in the story of the civil war is also a story of Sri Lankan Tamil nationalism.

4. Sri Sabaratnam is the TELO leader murdered brutally by the LTTE. Later on, EPRLF leader Padmanabha would be similarly brutally murdered in Chennai by the LTTE in an event that sent shock waves through India and Sri Lanka.

5. I am influenced by and extending in a different direction Peletz's (2001) excellent "Ambivalence in Kinship."

6. The way I think of kin is as primarily processual rather than ascribed. The processual nature of kinship animates contemporary anthropological work on kinship, but this also takes as its subject distinctions between kin and non-kin (cf. Carsten 2010). As Weston (1997) points out in her study of "gay kinship," new models of making kinship refer constantly to making distinctions between kin and non-kin even though those included in kin are (in this case close friends and ex-lovers) conventionally in Euro-American kinship considered to be non-kin. Her discussion still preserves kinship as providing a structure of "recognition," which is essentially what I am arguing here.

7. Bourdieu in particular points out the distinctness of the family which, even though injunctions are worked out in relation to achievement in the workplace or education, et cetera, nonetheless "imposes injunctions that are contradictory either in themselves or relative to the conditions available for these injunctions to be realized or fulfilled" (1999: 511).

8. Leach argues that in Pul Eliya kinship does not order landholding patterns; the reverse is true (1961: 301). Thus, Leach argues that "kinship systems have no "reality" at all except in relation to land and property . . . kinship structure is just a way of talking about property relations which can also be talked about in other ways" (305). Instead, Spencer argues that "property relations in this context are themselves the means of "talking about" many things beside the drudgery of everyday subsistence: things like standing or status, gender, caste, ultimately what manner of person you profess to be" (1990b: 101). Given the potency of land as an idiom and that in Sri Lanka the areas of common concern in making personhood are centred around land and property, all kinds of disputes are "generated and worked through" these areas..

9. The inevitable disjuncture between "the disposition of the inheritor and the destiny contained within the inheritance itself" (Bourdieu 1999: 508) are contradictions which, to paraphrase Bourdieu heavily, are both "generic" and "specific," tied as they are to each family's necessity of perpetuating itself and the specific contents or characteristics of that inheritance. Bourdieu here focuses particularly on the various dilemmas

relating to fathers and sons and both downward and upward mobility in French families. The most difficult situation is when the father sets goals which are impossible for
the child to realize, which Bourdieu identifies as a "major source of contradictions and
suffering" in French society, where "many people are long-term sufferers from the gap
between the accomplishments and the parental expectations they can neither satisfy nor
repudiate" (508)

10. See note 8 for Spencer's argument

Chapter 3. From Muslims to Northern Muslims:
Ethnicity, Eviction, and Displacement

1. The LTTE lost control of Jaffna in 1995.

2. By this he meant that I too had experienced LTTE "terror."

3. Even the excellent (2007) *Sri Lanka in the Modern Age: A History of Contested Identities*, by Nira Wickramasinghe, largely ignores Muslim identity production. Muslims are
discussed in a small section on Tamil-speaking Muslims in a chapter on Tamils.

4. The title of this section is of course a reference to Partha Chatterjee's (1993) chapter title " The Nation and its Women."

5. Such insistence can be understood in Sri Lanka, where claims to ethnicity are
claims to legal and political recognition, even as these also bring discrimination. An
Indian analogy would be caste status.

6. See McGilvray's (1998) comprehensive comparison of Sri Lankan Muslims,
Marakkayar Muslims of Tamil Nadu and Mappila Muslims in Kerala. As McGilvray
points out, all three see themselves as communities founded by Indian Ocean commerce, are Sunni Muslims of the Shafii legal school with strong Sufi practices also. All
three retain some elements of a matrilineal, matrilocal structure, share Tamil kinship
terms, and have historically attested links of commerce, migration, and pilgrimage etc.
However, McGilvray also points to strong differences. Sri Lankan Muslims, while class
differentiated along occupational and rural/urban structures, do not have hereditary
endogamous caste-like structures like most South Indian Muslim groups. South Indian
Muslim groups also played strong roles in precolonial, colonial, and postcolonial contexts, which Sri Lankan Muslims until now have not done. They also have a large rural
peasantry, which Marrakayars of Tamil Nadu do not have, and are regionally dispersed
in a manner Mappilas of Kerala are not.

7. North India saw far more Turkic and Persian influence (McGilvray 1998).

8. Philip Baldeus's 1672 "description of the great and most famous isle of Ceylon"
describes his disapproval of the Jaffna village of "Nalour" (modern-day Nallur), where
paganism had been allowed to flourish because of Calico printer immigrants from the
Coramandel Coast and where Moors "have had their publick schools allow'd them of
late Years" (Baldaeus [1672] 1998: 803).

9. In November 1884 Siddi Lebbe oversaw the opening of the first Muslim English
educational school, Al Madurasathul Khairiyyatul Islamiah, in Colombo. He went on to
found the Muslim Educational Society in 1891.

10. The Kandyan kingdom was parceled out among the different provinces with the new Kandyan province a shadow of its former self.

11. The other practical exception were low-country Sinhalese who had been well-integrated into various colonial economies and who formed the foundations of new lay institutions and ideas of Sinhaleseness. Kandyans were integrated into the island as first a conquered people and then, in subsequent British eyes, a romantic noble people in decline.

12. Manu Goswami (2004) has argued that this simultaneous homogenization and differentiation is a critical feature of colonial state space more generally.

13. The Council kept the secretary of state and London in touch with local opinions and provided an alternative source of information from the governor.

14. In 1923 when territorial representation was more widely introduced, of 37 unofficial members, 23 represented territorial electorates and 11 special communal electorates (Nissan and Stirrat 1990: 29).

15. See Jayawardena (1985: 24) on the virulent anti-Muslim sentiments expressed by the leading figure of Sinhala Buddhist revivalism, Anagarika Dharmapala, in 1915

16. Ismail remarks on the persistence of various colonial and postcolonial representations of Muslims as a trading community even though Denham in the 1911 census recorded that "Ceylon Moors for the most part are small farmers cultivating their own lands" (quoted in Ismail 1995: 78). Despite their own 1973 statistics that only 28 percent of the Muslim workforce was involved in trade, Dawood and Samarasinghe claim that the Muslims were a "business community" (Ismail 1995: 79).

17. The Donoughmore constitution was bitterly opposed by many of Sri Lanka's minority politicians, who saw territorial representation as favoring the numerically strong Sinhalese (Russell 1982).

18. These fissures were also more general. Both Kandyan Sinhalese and the Jaffna Depressed ("lower") caste league also petitioned the Dounoughmore commissioners, asking for separate representation from low-country Sinhalese and Sri Lankan Tamils respectively.

19. The pseudonym of the late journalist Dharmaratnam Sivaram.

20. Some Muslim cadres reached very high positions such as Jaan Master of PLOTE, Cader of EROS, and Farook of the LTTE. In addition cadres, both Tamil and Muslim took movement nicknames that crossed ethnicity.

21. In this agreement specific clauses asserted that the North and East were the homeland for Tamil-speaking peoples and Muslims were acknowledged as a distinct ethnic community. Muslim communities were awarded 30 percent representation in a provincial cabinet and council, and that in any future land distribution the Muslim people would be entitled to not less than 35 percent in the Eastern Province, not less than 30 percent in the Mannar (in the North) district and not less than 5 percent in other areas.

22. See http://www.reliefweb.int/rw/rwb.nsf/db900SID/YAOI6TK5WA?OpenDocu ment&RSS20=18–P.

23. Though this splintering is also reflective of perhaps a greater democratic franchise and more contestation within Sri Lankan Muslim parliamentary politics.

24. S. H. Hasbullah, President, Northern Muslims' Rights Organization, Speech (30-10-1995) in Colombo to commemorate the fifth anniversary of the expulsion. (Hasbullah 2001: 1)

25. The border between LTTE and government control is unrecognized as a border by international law. Therefore, the legal category for UNDP is IDPs, "Internally Displaced Persons." UNDP officials repeatedly (sometimes very callously) told them not to call themselves "refugees," a different legal category. In Tamil, however, Muslims always referred to themselves as *idam peyrntha* (displaced) and as *ahathi* (refugee). They saw *ahathi* as a term that expressed the enormous wrench of the Eviction and their feelings of having been moved into entirely unfamiliar terrain. While as Malkki's ([1992] 1999) seminal essay points out how historically "refugees" as a category have been seen as impure and as half- or nonpersons in territorialized national imaginations, for IDPs even lower down the scale, the term refugee in Tamil imbues one with a sense of legitimacy and dignity.

26. In the Kathankuddy massacre of August 1990, the LTTE surrounded two mosques in Kathankuddy, cut the electricity, and opened fire inside on the backs of the men kneeling in prayer. The final death count is reckoned as 149 though many were left injured, many with limbs severed from the knee down. The Kathankuddy massacres began the long cycle of killings and counterkillings in the eastern province, which has led to the present tense situation between Tamils and Muslims there.

27. Moreover, the Eviction is crucially linked in the memories of Jaffna people to the later Exodus of Tamils in 1995, as I illustrated in Chapter 1.

28. I borrow the tenor of this argument from Bakhtin's analysis of the *Bildungsroman* novels of becoming, where the hero and the world emerge simultaneously (Bakhtin 1986: 21–23).

Chapter 4. Becoming of This Place? Northern Muslim Futures After Eviction

1. One woman retold me the commonly held story among Jaffna Muslims, that Nallur itself, formerly the seat of the kings of Jaffna, had been the original habitation of Muslims and the site of their dispersal into the peninsula (cf. Hasbullah 2001).

2. http://www.resettlementmin.gov.lk/instancefiles/67933145/Operation%20ManualPHP.pdf

3. http://www.ancsdaap.org/cencon2002/papers/Sri%20Lanka/SriLanka.pdf.

4. http://www.muslimaffairs.gov.lk/siteview.php?rightmenue=1&pid=152&title=Muslim%20Population%20in%20Puttalam.

5. For the refugees, 90 percent still on dry rations provided by the World Food Programme and the Sri Lankan state in 2000 (Hasbullah 1996) and the majority living in appalling conditions, this resentment was highly unwelcome and restrictions on employment sent them further into impoverishment.

6. Shanmugaratnam's 2000 paper "Forced Migration and Changing Local Political Economies: A Study from North-Western Sri Lanka" is an excellent guide.

7. When I went to Puttalam and Kalpitiya in 2003, it had only been six months since refugees were allowed to drive three-wheelers in Puttalam town though they could in rural areas.

8. Brun (2003) extensively discusses the problems faced by "people out of place" within Puttalam in the humanitarian and governmental structures where refugee Muslims found themselves. My work takes a different angle from Brun and Shanmugaratnam (2000) through examining relationships to former homes and the Eviction as stories of belonging, while they focus on the political economy of internal displacement within Puttalam and governmental and humanitarian structures.

9. http://www.resettlementmin.gov.lk/instancefiles/67933145/Operation%20Manual PHP.pdf.

10. The average daily wage for displaced women was Rs. 50 in 1990 and Rs. 75–100 in 1998–1999 (Shanmugaratnam 2000: 36).

11. Community building activities are thus of very different character in Puttalam from eastern Sri Lanka, where mosque committees are highly influential in distributing aid and community assistance and there have been considerable religious clashes between Sufi and Sunni Maulavis and their followers.

12. While Sinhala medium education was sufficiently staffed, the Tamil medium was of very poor quality and understaffed. An assessment of Puttalam district in November 2003 found a 46 percent deficit of teachers in the Tamil medium (a shortfall of 843) (ADB/UN/ World Bank 2003). Education in the Tamil medium in the Puttalam district, they concluded, was not only poor but insufficient to deal with IDP children. The report identified many well-qualified Tamil medium teachers among the IDP population who, because they are not registered in the Puttalam district but in northern divisions, are offered jobs in districts that they cannot even live in (15). More generally, aside from Colombo and Jaffna, Tamil medium education is chronically under-resourced.

13. The moving out process had been quite gradual. In 2003 most houses in settlements were temporary housing, as refugees could not do without rations and rations were not given to those who had built permanent housing.

14. http://www.resettlementmin.gov.lk/instancefiles/67933145/Operation%20Manual PHP.pdf.

15. Nazima nominally had her deceased father's shop in Jaffna as dowry. This was now occupied by a Tamil family. When she went to argue her case for claiming it to the LTTE political commander in Jaffna, he told her that " it is nothing to do with us, you can take the case through our [LTTE] courts, but remember they are our people." She had told them "it is only because of you I am in this situation." For many the property or goods left in Jaffna are dowries in name only. In addition, the law of prescription in Jaffna means that after ten years of absenteeism "without good reason," land can be appropriated. Dislocation from Jaffna as the years stretch on made the possibility of regrowing through land and property in Jaffna increasingly insecure.

16. Bachelard argues it is not enough to describe houses without trying to

understand attachment to houses and homes as structured by specific ways of inhabiting them ([1960] 1994: 4)

17. In the east the man always joins the *kuti* of his wife and never carries the *kuti* of his birth, but in the bilateral systems of the North one potentially keeps *ur* for only one generation.

18. I am grateful to Zulfika for first pointing my attention to this phenomenon

19. I am grateful to Stephen Feuchtwang for suggesting this elaboration of this distinction and his notion of these agencies as "appellate agencies" who can right wrongs but from whom disappointment also is learned.

Chapter 5. The Generation of Militancy: Kinship, Militancy, and Self-Transformation

1. Begoña Aretxaga (1997) is a notable exception.

2. TELO was the first to begin operations under different names, though formally instituted as TELO after the 1977 anti-Tamil riots. The TNT formed in 1972, becoming LTTE (Liberation Tigers of Tamil Eelam) in 1976. In 1979 Prabhakaran briefly joined and worked with TELO before returning to LTTE. In 1980 Uma Maheswaran split from LTTE and formed PLOTE. In 1975 a group of Tamil students in London formed EROS, which also soon acquired an active youth wing GUES. In 1980 a split in EROS led to the formation of EPRLF by Padmanabha, who took with him GUES. PLOTE and EPRLF were more openly Marxist and involved in village level consciousness raising; LTTE and TELO were always more straightforwardly militant nationalist groups and their espousal of left-wing rhetoric was purely nominal.

3. See also Schalk (1997).

4. We do not have accurate figures for the more recent period. Some estimate LTTE numbers between 1990 and 2008 as 10,000–15,000 active members. This is still a fraction of total militant numbers in 1984 and 1985.

5. Sivaram adds to these figures another 3,000 to both the members of the political wings of PLOTE, TELO, EPRLF, and EROS and the militarily trained cadres of some of the smaller organizations like NLFT, TPP, and TEA.

6. After the 1980s, statistics for the percentage of the population of the north and east in the age group 15–24 are no longer reliable; in 1975 the percentage of the Sri Lankan population as a whole in the 15–24 category was 34 percent (Peiris 2008)

7. See Pieris (2008).

8. Alberoni sees the love of the leader as straddling and condensing this ethical dilemma.

9. Standardization by district actually opened up education for eastern Tamils and Muslims who had previously seen Tamil medium education dominated by Jaffna Tamils and Muslims.

10. One example was the obscuring of the expressed prewar preference of many lower caste villages to have Sinhala rather than Tamil upper caste Vellala police (Santhasilan Kadirgamar pers comm).

11. Pathiraja's 1977 film *Ponmani* focuses on a young Jaffna Vellala woman Ponmani

and her elder unmarried brother and sister Ganesh and Saroja. Ganesh works as a clerk in Colombo, returning only on weekends, to pay off the dowry debts incurred on the marriage of his elder sister Pavalam and to obtain dowry for his as yet unmarried second sister Saroja. The central tensions within the film are the unhappiness of Ganesh and Saroja and the dependency their obligations force on them, one that Ponmani attempts to escape through her elopement to her Karaiyar caste boyfriend Ananthan, though her escape ends in tragedy.

12. The most preferred and high status dowry goods given by the wife's family to the groom were land and jewelry (Tambiah 1973). Land and jewelry given in dowry are also considered to be (with restrictions in the case of land) the property of the woman; her rights to these even after marriage can only be alienated by legal process. Traditionally, to belong to Jaffna land one had to marry a Jaffna woman. The cash donation, a gift straight to the groom (exclusively for him and his family), has only gained favor since the 1980s after the civil war rendered land insecure.

13. See Fuller (2004) on hot and cold goddesses.

14. Norbert, the leader, and some others from the Theepori group were later arrested by the LTTE in the early 1990s. Most were killed in LTTE camps after some years of detention.

15. The most prominent case was the murder in April 1986 of Das, one of the founding members of TELO, and some of his followers outside Jaffna hospital by the Bobby faction of the TELO. TELO fired on the university student demonstration protesting these killings, and students had to negotiate with EPRLF and PLOTE to protect demonstrators.

16. Uma Maheswaran was expelled by Prabhakaran from the LTTE after his affair with a female member. He subsequently set up PLOTE.

17. Initially the internecine war was only in Jaffna. LTTE commander Kaduvul of eastern Batticaloa tried to prevent fighting in the east, but high command dispatched Kumarappa to take over and eliminate TELO in the east. http://www.atimes.com/ind-pak/DC30Df04.html

18. George, now in Canada, a schoolboy at the time, remembered seeing young TELO cadres huddled together at one of the main Jaffna bus stops, appealing for help from anyone who could give it. George, who did help some of the TELO cadres and, whose brother was a prominent member of EPRLF was then arrested and tortured by the LTTE.

19. The LTTE were unable to remove one PLOTE member who had retreated to his home village and whom villagers surrounded and protected. Villagers then arranged for the boy to leave Jaffna and go abroad.

20. PLOTE maintained its independence and some presence in the Vanni, though dislodged by the early 1990s by the LTTE. Uma Maheswaran was assassinated by the LTTE in Colombo in July 1989.

21. The final blow to the Tri-Star credibility came in the last desperate days of Indian withdrawal. The Indian agency RAW, determined and desperate not to lose influence to

the LTTE ordered its partner organizations and administration in the north and east, EPRLF, TELO and ENDLF, to forcibly recruit young boys (particularly harshly enacted in the east) to form the TNA (Tamil National Army) to fight against the LTTE. There are many stories of individual EPRLF and TELO members who attempted to aid some of the conscripted to flee, but this was another low point for EPRLF (Hoole et al. 1990). After the Indians left, the LTTE helped by the Sri Lankan government (with whom it was now maintaining some operational links as well as talks) pounced on the TNA camps slaughtering most of these young boys.

22. The Razeek group, a breakaway faction of EPRLF, became a highly feared and brutal fighting unit in eastern Sri Lanka.

23. In 1999 EPRLF General Secretary Suresh Premachandran and his faction walked out with much of the EPRLF funds and joined the LTTE. EPRLF split into two factions: the LTTE-allied small Suresh Premachandran faction and the anti-LTTE parliamentary party EPRLF (P) headed by Varatharaja Perumal (Sakthi's group). This splintering affected the militant groups too; a TELO faction led by Adaikalingam and EROS under Balakumar also joined the LTTE.

24. Santhan, an ex-LTTE member, was silent for large parts of our interview. His voice was halting as he talked about the deaths of fellow cadres and the loyalty between rank and file, the only positive memory of the LTTE that he had.

25. On 14 June 2003 Subathiran, known as Robert, the deputy leader of the EPRLF, was murdered by an LTTE sniper in Jaffna. His assassination was one of the weekly, sometimes daily assassinations of militants, as well as ex-militants who no longer had any affiliation to any group, that peppered my fieldwork. Eleven days after Robert, the LTTE killed Pakyarasa Kumaranadan, who had not been a member of EPRLF since 1998 and was working as a mason (UTHR(J) press release 06-15-2003).

26. This is in contrast to Palestine, where any Palestinian who dies as a result of occupation could be thought of as a martyr.

27. These new rituals and national ideologies range from a calendrical year based on LTTE martyr rituals to pamphlets and poetry drawing from imagery from ancient Tamil epics and likening LTTE cadres to ancient Tamil heroes. LTTE leader Prabhakaran, formerly referred to as "Thambi" (little brother) or "Anna" (elder brother), was most recently deified as a "sun god."

28. This performative aspect is only highlighted if one combines the connection between the rise of biopower and the management of human welfare within governmentality with the twentieth-century globalization of speaking "in the name of the people" as the principle of political organization and representation (Laclau 2005; Thiranagama and Kelly 2010)

29. To speak in the name of Tamils meant constantly purging to make Tamils fit subjects of Tamil homeland, purging which has normalized LTTE rule and governance in areas under its control and at the same time represents for them a constant anxiety and fear about traitors that need to be rooted out continually (Thiranagama 2010).

30. Thanks to Parvis Ghassem Fachandi, this formulation arose through later

reflections on a conversation with him on Agamben and anthropological notions of sacrifice, though I take this in a very different direction from him.

31. This blind spot emerges from Agamben's oscillation in these two books between the state of exception as a "zone/location" (within which there is a implicit comparison between those whose lives are that of the *homo sacer* and those that are not . . . as yet) and "a temporality," a state of emergency in which supplements are continually created and maintained. Moreover, the gray zone of life, in *The State of Exception*, as a zone of indistinction between two orders remains taken for granted though such zones require intense purification of boundaries to appear.

32. Nanthini Sornarajah is the pseudonym of Nirmala Rajasingam

33. Stories ranged from the elderly seamstress whose daughter was a member of EPRLF and who took food to EPRLF detainees in LTTE camps, who was detained and killed, to the young widow of a dead EPRLF cadre, whose head was shaved and publicly displayed in LTTE camps as a sign of her disgrace.

Chapter 6. Conclusions from Tamil Colombo

1. Tagg of course refers to Luce Irigiray

2. "To articulate the past historically does not mean to recognize it 'the way it was' (Ranke). It means to seize hold of a memory as it flashes up at a moment of danger." Walter Benjamin, Thesis VI, Theses on the Philosophy of History (Benjamin 1974)

3. Census data for 1981 report that around 49 percent of the city was non-Sinhala. Sinhalese made up 50.1 percent (nationally 74.5 percent), Sri Lankan Tamils 22.2 percent (12.7 percent), Indian Tamils 1.9 percent (5.5 percent), Muslims 23.4 percent (7.1 percent) and others 2.4 percent (0.8 percent)

4. Colombo district (2.2 million) in 2001 was less mixed and represented the distribution of population nationally, with Sinhalese at 76 percent and Sri Lankan Tamils and Muslims at 11 and 9 percent respectively.

5. Moreover, since 2001, Sri Lankan Tamils fleeing from the north east have also flocked to satellite towns such as Wattala, which have now become included within the imagination of Colombo proper.

6. This bullock cart trade was later destroyed by the building of the railway into the center of Pettah.

7. See Jayawardena 2002 for an explanation of the dominance of Indians in trade and the difficulty of accessing banks and capital for Ceylonese, which led to an increased concentration on plantations and liquor and other "rents."

8. The first act of newly independent Ceylon was the citizenship act of 1948 in which the Indian Tamil population of Sri Lanka was disenfranchised. Citizenship for Indian/ Hill Country Tamils was not resolved until the 1970s, when the Srimavo Shastri pact saw a third offered citizenship and two thirds immediately deported or scheduled for deportation. Many of Colombo's Indian Tamils and Malayalis went back to India, leaving Colombo with a far smaller proportion of its population from India than previously and with Indian Tamils in Sri Lanka predominantly the Hill Country Tamils, the

descendants of plantation labor. Now Hill Country Tamils are nationally only around 5.5 percent of the population, though they were above 12 percent before independence.

9. See Seneviratne 1999 for more on Anagarika Dharmapala.

10. This population was initially heavily gendered. Perera notes that until 1921, 61 percent of Colombo's population was male, it was only after independence that Colombo became more feminized with migrant families settling in (2002, 1717).

11. Watta, often translated "garden," is more appropriately translated "estate" (Silva and Athukorala 1991: 1).

12. In 1984 an average community size was about 35 households and with an estimated total population of 210 (Sevanatha 2003, 21). In 2001 a survey by the Colombo Municipal council and the NGO Sevanantha documented 1,614 low-income settlements/wattas, though varying in size, access to resources, and built materials (2002, 21–25).

13. As the 1977 Sansoni Report found, a false message was sent from police in Jaffna to others on radio, telling of crowds of Tamils waiting to kill Sinhalese passengers arriving in Jaffna (Hoole 2001: 22–38).

14. Kanathipathipillai 1990 provides an excellent ethnographic account of the 1983 riots and its aftermath in the lives of Tamils.

15. See Burton 2001 on Paris.

16. Upper-class white respondents from Westwood had a rich and diverse knowledge of the city spanning most of the city, while Black residents from Avalon had a far less detailed knowledge with far fewer interstitial links (Gould and Whitney 1974).

17. Fuglerud 1999; McDowell 1996; Daniel and Thangarajah 1995; etc. The Sri Lankan diaspora has emerged as the test case for studies of diasporic life and asylum seekers.

18. http://news.bbc.co.uk/2/hi/south_asia/6729555.stm

REFERENCES

Abraham, Nicolas, and Maria Torok. 1994. *The Shell and the Kernel: Renewals of Psycho-analysis*. Vol. 1. Chicago: University of Chicago Press.

Abrams, Philip. 1970. "Rites de Passage: The Conflict of Generations in Industrial Society," *Journal of Contemporary History* 5: 175–90.

———. 1988. "*Notes* on the Difficulty of Studying the *State.*" *(1977). Journal of Historical Sociology* 1 (1): 58–89.

———. Agamben, Giorgio. 1998. *Homo Sacer: Sovereign Power and Bare Life*. Stanford, Calif.: Stanford University Press.

———. 2005. *State of Exception*. Trans. Kevin Attell. Chicago: University of Chicago Press.

Alberoni, Francesco. 1984. *Movement and Institution*. Trans. Patricia C. Arden Delmoro. New York: Columbia University Press.

Ali, Agha Shahid. 1997. *The Country Without a Post Office*. New York: Norton.

———. 2002. *Rooms Are Never Finished*. New Delhi: Permanent Black.

Alison, Miranda, 2003. "Cogs in the Wheel? Women in the Liberation Tigers of Tamil Eelam." *Civil Wars* 6 (4): 37–54.

Allan, Diana. 2005. "Mythologizing al-Nakba: Narratives, Collective Identity and Cultural Practice Among Palestinian Refugees in Lebanon." *Oral History* 33: 47–56.

Amin, Shahid. 1995. *Event, Metaphor, Memory: Chauri Chaura 1922–1992*. Berkeley: University of California Press,

Ameer Ali, A. C. L. 1981. "The Genesis of the Muslim Community in Ceylon (Sri Lanka): A Historical Summary." *Asian Studies* 19: 65–82.

Amnesty International. 1996. *Sri Lanka: Wavering Commitment to Human Rights*. Index Number ASA 37/008/1996. http://www.amnesty.org/en/library/info/ASA37/008/1996/en. Accessed February 2011.

Anderson, Benedict. 1991. *Imagined Communities: Reflections on the Origin and Spread of Nationalism*. London: Verso.

Antze, Paul and Michael Lambek. 1996. *Tense Pasts: Cultural Essays in Trauma and Memory*. London: Routledge.

Apel, Dora. 2002. *Memory Effects: The Holocaust and the Art of Secondary Witnessing*. New Brunswick, N.J.: Rutgers University Press.

Appiah, K. Anthony. 1992. "Epilogue: In my Father's House." In *In My Father's House: Africa in the Philosophy of Culture*. Oxford: Oxford University Press.

Arasaratnam, Sinnappah. 1982/1986. "Historical Foundation of the Economy of the Tamils of North Sri Lanka". In *Chelvanayagam Memorial Lectures*, ed. Fr. Xavier S. Thaninayagam. Jaffna: Saiva Press.

——. 1994. "Sri Lanka's Tamils Under Colonial Rule." In *The Sri Lankan Tamils: Ethnicity and Identity*, ed. Chelvadurai Manogaran and Bryan Pffafenberger. Boulder, Colo.: Westview Press.

Arendt, Hannah. 2005. *The Promise of Politics*. Ed. Jerome Kohn. New York: Schocken.

Aretxaga, Begona. 1997. *Shattering Silence: Women Nationalism and Political Subjectivity in Northern Ireland*. Princeton, N.J.: Princeton University Press, 1997.

Arnold, David and Stuart Blackburn. 2004. "Introduction." In *Telling Lives in India: Biography, Autobiography, and Life History*, ed. David Arnold and Stuart H. Blackburn. Bloomington: Indiana University Press.

Asad, K. M. N. M. 1993. *Muslims of Sri Lanka Under the British Rule*. New Delhi: Navrang.

Asian Development Bank, United Nations, World Bank. 2003. "Sri Lanka, Assessment of Conflict-Related Needs in the Districts of Puttalam, Anaradhapura, Polonnaruwa and Moneragala." http://www.peaceinsrilanka.org/Downloads/Assessment%20of%20 Needs2.pdf. Accessed June 2006.

Bachelard, Gaston. 1994 [1969]. *The Poetics of Space*. London: Beacon Press.

Bakhtin, Mikhail M. 1996. "Forms of Time and of the Chronotope in the Novel." In *The Dialogic Imagination: Four Essays*, ed. Michael Holquist, trans. Caroline Emerson and Michael Holquist. Austin: University of Texas Press.

Bahloul, Joelle. 1996. *The Architecture of Memory: A Jewish-Muslim Household in Colonial Algeria, 1937–1962*. Cambridge: Cambridge University Press.

Balasingham, Adele. 2003. *The Will to Freedom: An Inside View of Tamil Resistance*. Mitcham: Fairmax.

Baldaeus, Philip. 1998 [1732]. *Description of the Great and Most Famous Isle of Ceylon*. New Delhi: Asian Educational Services.

Bandarage, Asoka. 2008. *The Separatist Conflict in Sri Lanka: Terrorism, Ethnicity, Political Economy*. London: Routledge.

Banks, Michael. 1960. "Caste in Jaffna." In *Aspects of Caste in South India, Ceylon, and North-West Pakistan*, ed. Edmund R. Leach. Cambridge: Cambridge University Press.

Bass, Daniel. 2001. *Landscapes of Malaiyaha Tamil Identity*. Marga Monograph Series on Ethnic Reconciliation 8. Colombo: Marga Institute.

Bastin, Rohan. 1997. "The Authentic Inner Life: Complicity and Resistance in the Tamil Hindu Revival." In *Sri Lanka: Collective Identities Revisited*, vol. 1, ed. Michael Roberts. Colombo: Marga Institute, 1997.

Bate, Bernard. 2009. *Tamil Oratory and the Dravidian Aesthetic: Democratic Practice in South India*. New York: Columbia University Press.

Benjamin, Walter. 1974. *On the Concept of History*. Trans. Dennis Redmond.

Gesammelten Schriften I, 2. Frankfurt am Main: Suhrkamp. http://www.efn.org/~dredmond/Theses_on_History.pdf.

Bose, Sumantra. 1994. *States, Nations, Sovereignty: Sri Lanka, India and the Tamil Eelam Movement.* New Delhi: Sage.

Bourdieu, Pierre. 1992. *The Logic of Practice.* Stanford, Calif.: Stanford University Press.

———. 1999. *The Weight of the World: Social Suffering and Impoverishment in Contemporary Society.* Cambridge: Polity Press.

Boyden, Jo. 2007. *Of Tigers, Ghosts and Snakes: Children's Social Cognition in the Context of Conflict in Eastern Sri Lanka.* Oxford: Queen Elizabeth House Working Papers. http://ideas.repec.org/p/qeh/qehwps/qehwps151.html.

Bremner, Francesca. 2004. "Fragments of Memory; Processes of State: Ethnic Violence Through the Life History of Participants." In *Economy, Culture, and Civil War in Sri Lanka,* ed. Deborah Winslow and Michael D. Woost. Bloomington: Indiana University Press, 2004.

Brun, Catherine. 2003. "Local Citizens or Internally Displaced Persons? Dilemmas of Long Term Displacement in Sri Lanka." *Journal of Refugee Studies* 16 (4): 376–97.

Bruner, Jerome. 2004. "Life as Narrative." *Social Research* 17 (3): 691–710.

Burton, Richard D. E. 2001. *Blood in the City: Violence and Revelation in Paris, 1789–1945.* Ithaca, N.Y.: Cornell University Press.

Busby, Cecilia. 1997. "Of Marriage and Marriageability: Gender and Dravidian Kinship." *Journal of the Royal Anthropological Institute* 3: 21–42

Butler, Judith. 1997. *The Psychic Life of Power.* Stanford, Calif.: Stanford University Press.

———. 2004. *Precarious Life: The Powers of Mourning and Violence.* New York: Verso.

Carsten, Janet, ed. 2007. *Ghosts of Memory: Essays on Remembrance and Relatedness.* Oxford: Blackwell.

Caverero, Adriana. 2000. *Relating Narratives: Storytelling and Selfhood.* Warwick Studies in European Philosophy. London: Routledge.

Centre for Policy Alternatives. 2003a. *Informal Dispute Resolution in the North East and Puttalam.* http://www.reliefweb.int/library/documents/2003/cpa-lka-12aug.pdf

———. 2003b. *Land and Property Rights of Internally Displaced Persons.* www.cpalanka.org

Cheran, R. 2001. *The Sixth Genre: Memory, History and the Tamil Diaspora Imagination.* Marga Monograph Series on Ethnic Reconciliation 7. Colombo: Marga Institute.

———. 2007. "Transnationalism, Development and Social Capital: Tamil Community Networks in Canada." In *Organizing the Transnational: Labour, Politics, and Social Change,* ed. Luin Goldring and Sailaja Krishnamurti, 129–44. Vancouver: University of British Columbia Press.

Cohn, Bernard. 1987. "The Census, Social Structure, and Objectification in South Asia." In *An Anthropologist Among the Historians and Other Essays,* 224–54. Delhi: Oxford University Press.

Consortium of Humanitarian Agencies. 2003. "National Peace Audit, Puttalam

District." November. http://www.humanitarian-srilanka.org/Pages/npa_reports_pdf/puttalam.pdf.

Crapanzano, Vincent. 1980. *Tuhami, Portrait of a Moroccan*. Chicago: University of Chicago Press.

Daniel, E. Valentine. 1984. *Fluid Signs: Being a Person the Tamil Way*. Berkeley: University of California Press, 1984.

———. 1989. "The Semeiosis of Suicide." In *Semiotics, Self and Society*, ed. Greg Urban and Benjamin Lee. New York: de Gruyter.

———. 1996. *Charred Lullabies: Chapters in an Anthropography of Violence*. Princeton, N.J.: Princeton University Press, 1996.

Daniel, E. Valentine and Yuvi Thangarajah. 1995. "Forms, Formations, and Transformations of the Tamil Refugee." In *Mistrusting Refugees*, ed. E. Valentine Daniel and John Knudsen. Berkeley: University of California Press.

Danish Refugee Council. 2002. "Program Document, DRC Sri Lanka 2000–2003." Colombo. http://www.db.idpproject.org/Sites/idpSurvey.nsf/AllDocWeb/B10B95B330 791EC1C12569990052D57D/$file/DRC_May+2000.pdf. Accessed June 2006.

Das, Veena. 1995. *Critical Events: An Anthropological Perspective on Contemporary India*. Delhi: Oxford University Press.

———. 2000. "The Act of Witnessing: Violence, Poisonous Knowledge, and Subjectivity." In *Violence and Subjectivity*, ed. Veena Das, Arthur Kleinman, Mamphele Ramphele, and Pamela Reynolds. Berkeley: University of California Press.

———. 2001. "Communities as Political Actors: The Question of Cultural Rights." In *Gender and Politics in India*, ed. Nivedita Menon. New Delhi: Oxford University Press

———. 2006. *Life and Words: Violence and the Descent into the Ordinary*. Philip E. Lilienthal Book in Asian Studies. Berkeley: University of California Press.

David, Kenneth. 1973. "Until Marriage Do Us Part: A Cultural Account of Jaffna Tamil Categories for Kinsmen." *Man* 8: 521–35.

———. 1977. "Hierarchy and Equivalence in Jaffna, North Sri Lanka: Normative Codes as Mediator." In *The New Wind: Changing Identities in South Asia*, ed. Kenneth David. The Hague: Mouton.

———. 1980. "Hidden Powers; Cultural and Socio-Economic Accounts of Jaffna Women." In *The Powers of Tamil Women*, ed. Susan Wadley. Syracuse, N.Y.: Maxwell School of Citizenship and Public Affairs.

Denham, Edward Brandis. 1912. *Ceylon at the Census of 1911, Being the Review of the Results of the Census of 1911*. Colombo: H.C. Cottle.

De Certeau, Michel. 1988. *The Practice of Everyday Life*. Berkeley: University of California Press.

De Silva, K. M. 1973a. "The Reform and Nationalist Movements in the Early Twentieth Century." In *History of Ceylon*, vol. 3, ed. K. M. De Silva. Peradeniya: University of Ceylon.

———. 1973b. "The History and Politics of the Transfer of Power." In *History of Ceylon*, vol. 3, ed. K. M. De Silva. Peradeniya: University of Ceylon.

———. 1973c. " The Legislative Council in the Nineteenth Century" In *History of Ceylon*, vol. 3, ed. K. M. De Silva. Peradeniya: University of Ceylon.

Dewaraja, Lorna. 1994. *The Muslims of Sri Lanka: One Thousand Years of Ethnic Harmony, 900–1915 AD*. Colombo: Lanka Foundation.

Don Arachchige, Neville. 1994. *Patterns of Community Structure in Colombo, Sri Lanka: An Investigation of Contemporary Urban Life in South Asia*. Lanham, Md.: University Press of America.

Donzelot, Jacques. 1979. *The Policing of Families*. New York: Pantheon.

Dumont, Louis. 1953. "The Dravidian Kinship Terminology as an Expression of Marriage." *Man* 53: 34–39.

———. 1994. *German Ideology: From France to Germany and Back*. Chicago: University of Chicago Press.

Duncan, James S. 2005. *The City as Text: The Politics of Landscape Interpretation in the Kandyan. Kingdom*. Cambridge: Cambridge University Press.

Durham, Deborah. 2000. "Youth and the Social Imagination in Africa: Introduction to Parts 1 and 2." *Anthropological Quarterly* 73 (3): 112–20.

———. 2004. "Disappearing Youth: Youth as a Social Shifter in Botswana." *American Ethnologist* 31 (4): 589–605.

Englund, Harri. 2005. "Conflicts in Context: Political Violence and Anthropological Puzzles." In *Violence and Belonging: The Quest for Identity in Post-Colonial Africa*, ed. Virgis Broch Due. London: Routledge.

Feldman, Ilana. 2006. "Home as a Refrain: Remembering and Living Displacement in Gaza." *History & Memory* 18 (2): 10–47.

Fortes, Mayer. 1970. *Kinship and the Social Order: The Legacy of Henry Lewis Morgan*. London: Routledge.

Fuglerud, Oivind. 1999. *Life on the Outside: The Tamil Diaspora and Long Distance Nationalism*. London: Pluto.

———. 2009. "Fractured Sovereignty: The LTTE's State-Building in an Interconnected World." In *Spatializing Politics: Culture and Geography in Postcolonial Sri Lanka*, ed. Catherine Brun and Tariq Jazeel. London: Sage.

Fuller, Christopher. 2004. *The Camphor Flame: Popular Hinduism and Society in India*. Princeton, N.J.: Princeton University Press.

Gardner, Katy. 1993. "Desh-Bidesh: Sylheti Images of Home and Away." *Man* 28 (9): 1–15.

Geschiere, Peter. 1997. *The Modernity of Witchcraft: Politics and the Occult in Postcolonial Africa*. Trans. Janet Roitman. Charlottesville: University of Virginia Press.

Giddens, Anthony. 1992. *The Transformation of Intimacy*. Stanford, Calif.: Stanford University Press.

Gilsenan, Michael. 2000 [1982]. *Recognizing Islam: Religion and Society in the Modern Middle East*. London: Tauris.

Good, Anthony. 1991. *The Female Bridegroom: A Comparative Study of Life-Crisis Rituals in South India and Sri Lanka*. Oxford: Oxford University Press.

———. 1996. *On the Non-Existence of Dravidian Kinship*. Edinburgh Papers in South Asian Studies 6. Edinburgh: Centre for South Asian Studies, University of Edinburgh.

Goswami, Manu. 2004. *Producing India: From Colonial Economy to National Space*. Chicago: University of Chicago Press.

Government of Sri Lanka, Department of Census and Statistics. 2001. "Brief Analysis of Population and Housing Characteristics". http://www.statistics.gov.lk/PopHouSat/PDF/p7%20population%20and%20Housing%20Text-11–12–06.pdf. Accessed February 2011

Gould, Peter and Rodney White. 1974. *Mental maps*. Harmondsworth, UK: Penguin Books

Gunawardena, R. A. L. H. 1990. "The People of the Lion: The Sinhala Identity and Ideology in History and Historiography." In *Sri Lanka: History and the Roots of Conflict* ed. Jonathan Spencer, 45–86. New York: Routledge.

Hage, Ghassan. 1997. "At Home in the Entrails of the West: Multiculturalism, "Ethnic Food" and Migrant Home-Building." In *Home/World: Space, Community, and Marginality in Sydney's West*, ed. Helen Grace et al. Annandale: Pluto, 1997.

Hansen, Thomas Blom. 2001. *Wages of Violence: Naming and Identity in Postcolonial Bombay*. Princeton, NJ: Princeton University Press

Hansen, Thomas Blom and Finn Stepputat, eds. 2001. *States of Imagination: Ethnographic Explorations of the Postcolonial State*. Durham, N.C.: Duke University Press.

———. 2006. "Sovereignty Revisited." *Annual Review of Anthropology* 35: 295–315.

Hansen, Thomas Blom and Oskar Verkaaik. 2009. "Introduction: Urban Charisma—Everyday Mythologies in the City." *Critique of Anthropology* 29 (1): 5–26.

Hasbullah, Shahul H. 2007. "Needs and Aspirations of Ethnically Cleansed Northern Muslims." *Crosscurrents.org*, 2007. http://www.countercurrents.org/hasullah241007.htm

———. 2001 *Muslim Refugees: The Forgotten People in Sri Lanka's Ethnic Conflict – (Volume -1)* Nuraicholai: Research and Action Forum for Social Development

Havel, Václav. 1986. *Living in Truth: 22 Essays on the Occasion of the Award of the Erasmus Prize to Václav Havel*, ed. Jan Valdislav. Amsterdam: Meulenhoff.

Hellmann-Rajanayagam, Dagmar. 1990. "The Politics of the Tamil Past." In *Sri Lanka: History and the Roots of Conflict*, ed. Jonathan Spencer. New York: Routledge, 1990.

———. 1994. *The Tamil Tigers: Armed Struggle for Identity*. Stuttgart: Franz Steiner, 1994.

———. 2005. "And Heroes Die: Poetry of the Tamil Liberation Movement in Northern Sri Lanka." *South Asia* 28 (2005): 112–53.

Hewamanne, Sandya. 2009. "Duty Bound? Militarization, Romances, and New Forms of Violence Among Sri Lanka's Free Trade Zone Factory Workers." *Cultural Dynamics* 21 (July): 153–84.

Hirschon, Renee. 1989. *Heirs of the Greek Catastrophe: The Social Life of Asia Minor Refugees in Piraeus*. New York: Oxford University Press.

Holland, Debora and Jean Lave. 2001. "Introduction." In *History in Person: Enduring Struggles, Contentious Practice, Intimate Identities*, ed. Dorothy C. Holland and Jean Lave. Santa Fe: School of American Research Press.

Holquist, Michael. 1990. *Dialogism: Bakhtin and His World*. London: Routledge, 1990.

Hoole, Rajan, Kopalasingam Sritharan, Daya Somasunderam, and Rajani Thiranagama. 1990. *The Broken Palmyra: The Tamil Crisis in Sri Lanka, an Inside Account*. Claremont, Calif.: Sri Lanka Studies Institute.

Hoole, Rajan. 2001. *Sri Lanka: The Arrogance of Power: Myths, Decadence & Murder*. Jaffna: University Teachers for Human Rights.

Human Rights Watch. 2004. *Living in Fear: Child Soldiers and the Tamil Tigers in Sri Lanka*. New York: Human Rights Watch. http://hrw.org/reports/2004/srilanka1104/

Internal Displacement Monitoring Centre. 2009. *Sri Lanka: Continuing Humanitarian Concerns and Obstacles to Durable Solutions for Recent and Longer-Term IDPs*. http://www.internal-displacement.org/countries/srilanka.

Ismail, Qadri. 1995. "Unmooring Identity: The Antinomies of Elite Muslim Self-Representation in Modern Sri Lanka." In *Unmaking the Nation: The Politics of Identity and History in Modern Sri Lanka*, ed. Pradeep Jeganathan and Qadri Ismail. Colombo: Social Scientists Association.

Jansen, Stef. 2002. "The Violence of Memories: Local Narratives of the Past After Ethnic Cleansing in Croatia." *Rethinking History* 6 (1): 77–93.

Jansen, Stef and Steffan Löfving. 2009. *Struggle for Home: Violence, Hope and the Movement of People*. Oxford: Berghahn.

Jayawardena, Kumari. 1972. *The Rise of the Labor Movement in Ceylon*. Durham, N.C.: Duke University Press.

———. 1984. "Class Formation and Communalism." *Race and Class: Sri Lanka: Racism and the Authoritarian State* 26 (1): 51–63.

———. 1985. *Ethnicity and Class conflicts in Sri Lanka*. Colombo: Sanjiva Books.

———. 2002. *Nobodies to Somebodies: The Rise of the Colonial Bourgeoisie in Sri Lanka*. London: Zed.

Jeganathan, Pradeep. 2002. "Walking Through Violence: 'Everyday Life' and Anthropology." In *Everyday Life in South Asia*, ed. Diane P. Mines and Sarah Lamb. Bloomington: Indiana University Press, 2002.

Jeganathan, Pradeep, and Qadri Ismail, eds. 1995. *Unmaking the Nation: The Politics of Identity and History in Modern Sri Lanka*. Colombo: Social Scientists Association, 1995.

Jeyaraj, D. B. S. 2000. "Obituary; A pioneering leader, M. H. M Ashraff 1948–2000." *Frontline* 17 (20) (30 September–13 October). http://www.flonnet.com/fl1720/17201260.htm. Accessed February 2011.

———. 2002. "Need for SLMC-LTTE MoU." www.tamilcanadian.comhttp://www.tamil-canadian.com/page.php?cat=39&id=111&page=0. Accessed February 2011.

Kanathipathipillai, Valli. 1990. "The Survivor's Experience." In *Mirrors of Violence: Communities, Riots and Survivors in South Asia*, ed. Veena Das. New Delhi: Oxford University Press.

———. 2009. *Citizenship and Statelessness in Sri Lanka: The Case of the Tamil Estate Workers*. London: Anthem Press, 2009.

Kantawala, Mohan H. 1930. *A Thesis on the Thesawalamai*. Jaffna: Saiva Prakasa Press.

Kapadia, Karin. 1995. *Siva and Her Sisters: Gender, Caste, and Class in Rural South India*. Boulder, Colo.: Westview Press.

Kapferer, Bruce. 1988. *Legends of the People, Myths of the State: Violence, Intolerance and Political Culture in Sri Lanka and Australia*. Washington, D.C.: Smithsonian Institution Press.

Kearney, Robert N. 1978. "Language and the Rise of Tamil Separatism in Sri Lanka." *Asian Survey* 18 (5): 521–34.

———. 1987 "Territorial Elements of Tamil Separatism in Sri Lanka." *Pacific Affairs* 60 (4): 561–77.

Kearney, Robert N., and Barbara D. Miller. 1985. "The Spiral of Suicide and Social Change in Sri Lanka." *Journal of Asian Studies* 45 (1): 81–101.

Kelly, Tobias. 2008. "The Attractions of Accountancy: Living an Ordinary Life During the Second Palestinian Intifada." *Ethnography* 9 (3): 351–76.

Kelly, Tobias, and Sharika Thiranagama. 2010. "Introduction: Specters of Treason." In *Traitors: Suspicion, Intimacy, and the Ethics of State-Building*, ed. Kelly Tobias and Sharika Thiranagama Philadelphia: University of Pennsylvania Press, 2010.

Koselleck, Rheinhart. 2004. *Futures Past: On the Semantics of Historical Time*. Trans. Keith Tribe. New York: Columbia University Press.

Krishna, Sankaran. 1999. *Postcolonial Insecurities: India, Sri Lanka, and the Question of Nationhood*. Minneapolis: University of Minnesota Press.

Laclau, Ernesto. 2005. *On Populist Reason*. London: Verso.

Lawrence, Patricia. 2002. "Violence, Suffering, Amman: The Work of Oracles in Eastern Sri Lanka." In *Violence and Subjectivity*, ed. Veena Das, Arthur Kleinman, Mamphela Ramphele, and Pamela Reynolds. Berkeley: University of California Press.

Leach, Edmund Ronald. 1961. *Pul Eliya, a Village in Ceylon: A Study of Land Tenure and Kinship*. Cambridge: Cambridge University Press.

Levi, Primo. 1996. *Survival in Auschwitz: The Nazi Assault on Humanity*. Trans. Stuart Woolf. New York: Simon & Schuster.

Lubkemann, Stephen C. 2008. *Culture in Chaos: An Anthropology of the Social Condition in War*. Chicago: University of Chicago Press, 2008.

Malkki, Liisa. 1995. "Refugees and Exile: From 'Refugee Studies' to the National Order of Things." *Annual Review of Anthropology* 24: 495–523.

———. 1999 [1992]. "National Geographic: The Rooting of Peoples and the Territorialization of National Identity Among Scholars and Refugees." In *Culture, Power, Place: Explorations in Critical Anthropology*, ed. Akhil Gupta and James Ferguson. Durham, N.C.: Duke University Press.

———. 2001. "Figures of the Future: Dystopia and Subjectivity in the Social Imagination of the Future." In *History in Person: Enduring Struggles, Contentious Practice, Intimate Identities*, ed. Debora Holland and Jean Lave, 325–48. Santa Fe: School of American Research Press. 325–48.

Mannheim, Karl. 1952. *Essays on the Sociology of Knowledge*. Ed. Paul Kecskemeti. London: Routledge.

Manogaran, Chelvadurai and Bryan Pffafenberger, eds. 1994. *The Sri Lankan Tamils: Ethnicity and Identity*. Boulder, Colo.: Westview Press, 1994.

Maunaguru, Sitralega. 1995. "Gendering Tamil Nationalism: The Construction of 'Woman' in Projects of Protest and Control." In *Unmaking the Nation: The Politics of Identity and History in Modern Sri Lanka*, ed. Pradeep Jeganathan and Qadri Ismail. Colombo: Social Scientists Association, 1995.

McDowell, Christopher. 1996. *A Tamil Asylum Diaspora: Sri Lankan Migration, Settlement and Politics in Switzerland*. Oxford: Berghahn.

McGilvray, Dennis B. 1982. "Sexual Power and Fertility in Sri Lanka: Batticaloa Tamils and Moors." In *Ethnography of Fertility and Birth*, ed. Carol P. MacCormack, 25–73. London: Academic Press.

———. 1998. "Arabs, Moors and Muslims: Sri Lankan Muslim Ethnicity in Regional Perspective." *Contributions to Indian Sociology* 32 (2): 433–83.

———. 2008. *Crucible of Conflict: Tamil and Muslim Society on the East Coast of Sri Lanka*. Durham, N.C.: Duke University Press.

McGilvray, Dennis B., and Mirak Raheem. 2007. *Muslim Perspectives on the Sri Lankan Conflict*. Washington, D.C.: East-West Center.

Mines, Mattison. 1994. *Public Faces, Private Voices: Community and Individuality in South India*. Berkeley: University of California Press.

Mohideen, M.I.M. 2004. Resettlement of IDPs : North East Muslims ignored. *Sunday Observer*, June 27. http://www.sundayobserver.lk/2004/06/27/fea34..html. Accessed February 2011

Moore, Mick. 1990. "Economic Liberalisation Versus Political Pluralism in Sri Lanka?" *Modern Asian Studies* 24 (2): 341–83.

———. 1993. "Thoroughly Modern Revolutionaries: The JVP in Sri Lanka." *Modern Asian Studies* 27 (3): 593–642.

Munasinghe, Indrani. 2002. *The Colonial Economy on track: Roads, Railways in Sri Lanka (1800–1905)*. Colombo: Social Scientists Association

Murphey, Rhoads.1997. "Colombo and the Re-Making of Ceylon." *Gateways of Asia: Port Cities of Asia in the 13th–20th Centuries*, ed Frank Broeze , London and New York: Kegan Paul

Natali, Cristina. 2005. "Building Cemeteries, Constructing Identities. Funerary Practices and Nationalist Discourse Among the Tamil Tigers of Sri Lanka." Paper presented at BASAS Annual Conference, University of Leeds, 30 March–1 April. http://www.basas.ac.uk/conference05/natali,%20cristiana.pdf.

Nissan, Elizabeth, 1988. "Polity and Pilgrimage Centres in Sri Lanka." *Man* n.s. 23 (2): 253–74.

———. 1989. "History in the Making: Anuradhapura and the Sinhala Buddhist Nation." *Social Analysis* 25(1): 64–77.

Nissan, Elizabeth, and Roderick L. Stirrat. 1990. "The Generation of Communal Identities." In *Sri Lanka: History and the Roots of Conflict*, ed. Jonathan Spencer. New York: Routledge.

Nordstrom, Carolyn. 1997. *A Different Kind of War Story*. Philadelphia: University of Pennsylvania Press.

Nuhuman, M. A. 2003 [1999]. "Ethnic Identity, Religious Fundamentalism and Muslim Women in Sri Lanka." *Lines Magazine*. http://issues.lines-magazine.org/articles/nuhuman.htm and http://www.wluml.org/node/322. Accessed September 2010.

Obeysekere, Gananath. 1974. "Some Comments on the Social Backgrounds of the April 1971 Insurgency in Sri Lanka (Ceylon)." *Journal of Asian Studies* 33 (3): 367–84.

Osella, Filippo, and Caroline Osella. 2006. "Once upon a Time in the West: Stories of Migration and Modernity from Kerala, South India." *Journal of the Royal Anthropological Institute* 12 (3): 569–88.

Peiris, G. H. 2008. "Sri Lanka: Youth Unrest and Inter-Group Conflict." *Faultlines* 19. http://www.satp.org/satporgtp/publication/faultlines/volume19/Article5.htm.

Peletz, Michael. 2001. "Ambivalence in Kinship Since the 1940s." In *Relative Values: Reconfiguring Kinship Studies*, ed. Sarah Franklin and Susan McKinnon. Durham, N.C.: Duke University Press.

Perera, Nihal. 2002. "Indigenising the Colonial City: Late 19th Century Colombo and Its Landscape." *Urban Studies* 39 (9): 1703–21.

———. 1998. *Society and Space: Colonialism, Nationalism, and Postcolonial Identity in Sri Lanka*. Boulder, Colo.: Westview Press, 1998.

Peribanayagam, Robert. S. 1982. *The Karmic Theater: Self, Society, and Astrology in Jaffna*. Amherst: University of Massachusetts Press, 1982.

Pfaffenberger, Bryan. 1982. *Caste in Tamil Culture: The Religious Foundations of Sudra Domination in Tamil Sri Lanka*. Syracuse, N.Y.: Maxwell School of Citizenship and Public Affairs.

———. 1994. "Introduction: The Sri Lankan Tamils." In *The Sri Lankan Tamils: Ethnicity and Identity*, ed. Chelvadurai Manogaran and Bryan Pffafenberger. Boulder, Colo.: Westview Press.

———. 1990. "The Political Construction of Defensive Nationalism: The 1968 Temple-Entry Crisis in Northern Sri Lanka." *Journal of Asian Studies* 49 (1): 78–96.

Rajasingam, Nirmala. 2009. "The Tamil Diaspora: Solidarities and Realities." 17 May. http://www/opendemocracy.net/article/the-tamil-diaspora-solidarities-and-realities. Accessed 26 November.

Ramanujan, A. K. 1985. *Poems of Love and War*. New York: Columbia University Press.

———. 2001. *Uncollected Poems and Prose*. Ed. Molly A. Daniels-Ramanujan and Keith Harrison. New Delhi: Oxford University Press.

Ramaswamy, Sumanthi. 1997. *Passions of the Tongue: Language Devotion in Tamil India, 1891–1970*. Berkeley: University of California Press.

Rao, Vyjayanthi. 2007. "How to Read a Bomb: Scenes from Bombay's Black Friday." *Public Culture* 19 (3): 567–92.

Richards, Paul. 1996. *Fighting for the Rain Forest: War, Youth, & Resources in Sierra Leone*. Oxford: James Currey

———. 2005a. "War as Smoke and Mirrors: Sierra Leone 1991–2, 1994–5, 1995–6." *Anthropological Quarterly* 78 (2): 377–402.

———, ed. 2005b. *No Peace, No War: An Anthropology of Contemporary Armed Conflicts*. Athens: Ohio University Press.

Roberts, Michael. 1994. *Exploring Confrontation: Sri Lanka: Politics, Culture, and History*. Reading: Harwood.

———. 1996. "Filial Devotion in Tamil Culture and the Tiger Cult of Martyrdom." *Contributions to Indian Sociology* 30 (2): 245–72.

———. 2005. "Tamil Tiger 'Martyrs': Regenerating Divine Potency?" *Studies in Conflict & Terrorism* 28 (6): 493–514.

Rogers, John D. 1990. "Historical Images in the British Period." In *Sri Lanka: History and the Roots of Conflict*, ed. Jonathan Spencer. New York: Routledge.

Rose, Jacqueline. 2004 [1996]. *States of Fantasy*. Oxford: Clarendon Press.

Rouner, Leroy. 1996. *The Longing for Home*. Notre Dame, Ind.: University of Notre Dame Press.

Russell, Jane. 1982. *Communal Politics Under the Donoughmore Constitution, 1931–1947*. Colombo: Tisara Prakasakayo.

Samaddar, Ranabir. 1999. *The Marginal Nation: Transborder Migration from Bangladesh to West Bengal*. New Delhi: Sage.

Samaraweera, Vijaya. 1973. "The Development of the Administrative System from 1802 to 1832." In *History of Ceylon*, Vol. 3. Peradeniya: University of Ceylon.

———. 1979. "The Muslim Revivalist Movement, 1880–1915." In *Collective Identities, Nationalism, and Protest in Modern Sri Lanka*, ed. Michael Roberts. Colombo: Marga Institute.

Scarry, Elaine. 1987. *The Body in Pain*. Oxford: Oxford University Press, 1987.

Schalk, Peter. 1992. "Birds of Independence: On the Participation of Tamil Women in Armed Struggle." *Lanka* 7: 44–142.

———. 1994. "Women Fighters of the Liberation Tigers in Tamilijam. The Martial Feminism of Atel Palacinkam." *South Asia Research* 14: 163–83.

———. 1997. "The Revival of Martyr Cults Among Illavar." *Temenos* 33. http://www.tamilnation.org/ideology/schalk01.htm#Sacrilisation. Accessed January 2010.

Seneviratne, H. L. 1999. *The Work of Kings: The New Buddhism in Sri Lanka*. Chicago: University of Chicago Press.

Sevanatha. 2002. *Poverty Profile: City of Colombo Urban Poverty Reduction through Community Empowerment*. Colombo, Sri Lanka

———. 2003. "The Case of Colombo." In *Understanding Slums: Case Studies for Global Reports on Human Settlements*. http://www.ucl.ac.uk/dpu-projects/Global_Report/cities/colombo.htm.

Shanmugaratnam, N. 2000. "Forced Migration and Changing Local Political Economies: A Study from North-Western Sri Lanka." Noragric Working Papers, Noragric/

Agricultural University of Norway. http://www.nlh.no/noragric/publications/work-ingpapers/noragric-wp-22.pdf.

Silva, Kalinga Tudor, and Karunatissa Athukorala. 1991. *The Watta-Dwellers: A Sociological Study of Selected Urban Low-Income Communities in Sri Lanka*. Lanham, Md.: University Press of America

Simmel, Georg. 1972. *On Individuality and Social Forms*. Ed. Donald N. Levine. Chicago: University of Chicago Press.

Simons, Anna. 1999. "War: Back to the Future." *Annual Review of Anthropology* 28: 73–108.

Sivanandan, A. 1984. "Sri Lanka: Racism and the Politics of Underdevelopment." In *Sri Lanka: Racism and the Authoritarian State. Race and Class* 26 (1): 1–39.

Sivaram, Dharmaratnam. 1997. "The Cat, a Bell, and a Few Strategists." May. www.tamilcanadian.com/page.php?cat=121&id=677. Accessed October 2008.

Sivaramani, S. 1992. "A Night in War Time." In *Women in War Time*. Colombo: Women and Media Collective.

———. 1994. *Sivaramani Kavithaigal*. Toronto: Vizhippu.

Sivathamby, Karthigesu. 1984. "Some Aspects of the Social Composition of the Tamils of Sri Lanka." In *Ethnicity and Social Change in Sri Lanka: Papers Presented at a Seminar Organised by the Social Scientists Association*. Colombo: SSA.

———. 1989. "Tamils of Sri Lanka: An Ethnological Introduction." In *Sri Lankan Tamil Society and Politics*. http://www.tamilnation.org/heritage/sivathamby.pdf.

Skjonsberg, E. 1982. *A Special Caste? Tamil Women of Sri Lanka*. London: Zed.

Sornarajah, Nanthini. 2004. "The Experiences of Tamil Women: Nationalism, Construction of Gender, and Women's Political Agency." Parts 1–3. February, May, August. http://www.lines-magazine.org

Spencer, Jonathan. 1990a. "Introduction: The Power of the Past." In *Sri Lanka: History and the Roots of Conflict*, ed. Jonathan Spencer. New York: Routledge.

———. 1990b. *A Sinhala Village in a Time of Trouble: Politics and Change in Rural Sri Lanka*. Delhi: Oxford University Press.

———. 1990c. "Writing Within: Anthropology, Nationalism, and Culture in Sri Lanka." *Current Anthropology* 31 (3): 283–300.

———. 1990d. "Collective Violence and Everyday Practice in Sri Lanka." *Modern Asian Studies* 24 (3): 603–23.

———. n.d. "People in a Landscape: Writing Anti-Essentialist Histories in Sri Lanka." University of Edinburgh, unpublished paper.

Sriskandarajah, Dhananjayan. 2002. "The Migration-Development Nexus: Sri Lanka Case Study." *International Migration* 40 (5): 283–307.

———. 2004. "Forced Migration Online: Sri Lanka." http://www.forcedmigration.org/guides/fmo032/. Accessed August 2010

Stepputat, Finn. 2008. "Forced Migration, Land and Sovereignty." *Government and Opposition* 43 (2): 337–57.

Stokke, Kristian. 2006a. *State Formation and Political Change in LTTE-Controlled Areas in Sri Lanka.* http://www.tamilnation.org/conflictresolution/tamileelam/seminar_06_Zurich/ 05kristian_stokke.html.

———. 2006b. "Building the Tamil Eelam State: Emerging State Institutions and Forms of Governance in LTTE-Controlled Areas in Sri Lanka." *Third World Quarterly* 27 (6): 1021–40.

Strathern, Marilyn. 1990. *The Gender of the Gift: Problems with Women and Problems with Society in Melanesia.* Berkeley: University of California Press.

———. 1992. *After Nature: English Kinship in the Late Twentieth Century.* Lewis Henry Morgan Lectures) Cambridge: Cambridge University Press

Swamy, M. R. Narayan. 199. *Tigers of Lanka: From Boys to Guerrillas.* Delhi: Konark.

Tagg, John.1996. "This City Which Is Not One." *In Re-Presenting the City: Ethnicity, Capital and Culture in the Twenty-First Century Metropolis,* ed. Anthony D. King. New York: New York University Press.

Tambiah, Stanley J. 1973. "Dowry and Bridewealth and the Property Rights of Women in South Asia." In *Bridewealth and Dowry,* ed. J. Goody and Stanley J. Tambiah. London: Cambridge University Press, 1973.

———.1986. *Sri Lanka: Ethnic Fratricide and the Dismantling of Democracy.* Chicago: University of Chicago Press, 1986.

———. 1990. "Introduction." *Journal of Asian Studies* 49 (1): 26–29.

———. 1996. *Leveling Crowds: Ethnonationalist Conflicts and Collective Violence in South Asia.* Berkeley: University of California Press

Taraki. 1991 [1990]. *The Eluding Peace:An Insider's Political Analysis of the Ethnic Conflict in Sri Lanka.* Paris: ASSEAY.

Taylor, Charles. 1989. *Sources of the Self: The Making of Modern Identity.* Cambridge: Cambridge University Press.

Tennekoon, Serena. 1988. "Rituals of Development: The Accelerated Mahavali Development Program of Sri Lanka." *American Ethnologist* 15 (2): 294–310.

Thiranagama, Sharika. 2010. "In Praise of Traitors: Intimacy, Betrayal, and the Sri Lankan Tamil Community." In *Traitors: Suspicion, Intimacy and the Ethics of State Building,* ed. Sharika Thiranagama and Tobias Kelly. Philadelphia: University of Pennsylvania Press, 2010.

———. n.d. "Generating the LTTE from Abroad: Memory, Moral Projects, and the Sri Lankan Tamil Diaspora in Toronto."

Thiruchandran, Selvy. 1997. *Ideology, Caste, Class and Gender.* New Delhi: Vikas.

Thomas, Nicholas. 1991. *Entangled Objects: Exchange, Material Culture and Colonialism in the Pacific.* Cambridge, Mass.: Harvard University Press.

Trautmann, Thomas R. 1981.*.Dravidian Kinship.* London: Cambridge University Press,

Trawick, Margaret. 1992. *Notes on Love in a Tamil Family.* Berkeley: University of California Press.

———. 1999. "Reasons for Violence: A Preliminary Ethnographic Account of the LTTE."

In *Conflict and Community in Contemporary Sri Lanka : "Pearl of the Indian Ocean"
or "The Island of Tears"*, ed. Siri Gamage and Ian B. Watson. New Delhi: Sage.

———. 2007. *Enemy Lines: Warfare, Childhood, and Play in Batticaloa.* Philip E. Lilienthal Book in Asian Studies. Berkeley: University of California Press.

University Teachers for Human Rights (Jaffna). Reports accessible at www.uthr.org.

———. 1991. *The Politics of Destruction and Human Tragedy.* Report 6. September–January.

———. 1994. *Someone Else's War.* MIRJE, Colombo

———. 1995. *The Exodus from Jaffna.* Special Report 6, December 6.

———. 1995. *Children in the North-East War: 1985–1995.* Briefing 2 June 20.

———. 1998. *Living Through Jaffna's Sultry Sunset.* Special Report 10. April 9.

———. 1998. *A Tamil Heroine Unmourned & The Sociology of Obfuscation.* Special Report 11. April 9.

———. 2003. *Child Conscription and Peace: A Tragedy of Contradictions.* Special Report
16, March 18.

———. 2004. *The Batticaloa Fiasco and the Tragedy of Missed Opportunities.* Information
Bulletin 36.

———. 2009a. *A Marred Victory and a Defeat Pregnant with Foreboding.* Special Report
32, June 10.

———. 2009b. *Let Them Speak: Truth About Sri Lanka's Victims of War.* Special Report
34, December 13.

Verkaik, Oskar. 2005. *Migrants and Militants: Fun and Urban Violence in Pakistan.*
Princeton, NJ: Princeton University Press

Watson, Rubie S. 1994. "Making Secret Histories: Memory and Mourning in Post-Mao
China." In *Memory, History, and Opposition Under State Socialism*, ed. Rubie Watson. Santa Fe: School of American Research.

Wedeen, Lisa. 1999. *Ambiguities of Domination: Politics, Rhetoric and Symbols in Contemporary Syria.* Chicago: University of Chicago Press.

———. 2004. "Acting 'As If': Symbolic Politics and Social Control in Syria." *Comparative
Studies in Society and History* 40: 503–23.

Weston, Kath. 1997. *Families We Choose: Lesbians, Gays, Kinship.* New York: Columbia
University Press, 1997.

Whittaker, Mark P. 1990. A Compound of Many Histories: The Many Pasts of an East
Coast Community." In *Sri Lanka: History and the Roots of Conflict*, ed. Jonathan
Spencer. New York: Routledge.

———. 2006. *Learning Politics from Sivaram.* Ann Arbor: University of Michigan Press,
2006.

Wickramasinghe, Nira. 2007. *Sri Lanka in the Modern Age: A History of Contested Identities.* London: Hurst.

Wickrematne, Lal. 1973. "Education and Social Change, 1832 to c. 1900." In *History of
Ceylon*, vol. 3, ed. K. M. De Silva. Peradeniya: University of Ceylon.

Yalman, Nur. 1962. "The Structure of Sinhalese Kindred: A Re-examination of the Dravidian Terminology." *American Anthropologist* 64: 548–75.

Yurchak, Alexei. 2006. *Everything Was Forever, Until It Was No More: The Last Soviet Generation*. Princeton, N.J.: Princeton University Press.

Zackariya, Faizun, and N. Shanmugaratnam. 1997. "Communalisation of Muslims in Sri Lanka: An Historical Perspective." In *Alternative Perspectives: A Collection of Essays on Contemporary Muslim Society*. Colombo: Muslim Women's Research and Action Forum.

INDEX

homeland. *See* Tamil Eelam
homeliness, 19, 89

IDPs (Internally Displaced Persons), 3,
16–17, 128, 146–47, 149–50, 167, 176,
266n25. *See also* refugees
individuality: and collectivity, 39, 42, 222–23;
and South Asia, 34–35; and war, 36–37, 76;
western idea of, 35
IPKF (Indian Peace Keeping Forces), 24, 46,
87, 205–8. *See also* RAW

Jaffna, 41–42; as home, 84, 89, 253; as
homeland, 15; and migration, 15, 63; and
war, 45
JVP (Janatha Vimukthi Peramuna-National
Liberation Front), 22–23, 103, 185, 188–89

Karuna, 28, 30
kinship, 31, 92, 263n6; and ambivalence,
92–93; "Dravidian kinship," 31, 261n23;
and political conflict, 93. *See also* family;
sontam
Koselleck, Rheinhart, 43, 168–69; "horizon
of expectation," 168; "space of experience,"
168; "temporal structure of experience,"
88, 168
Krishna, Sankaran, 186

Leach, Edmund, 93, 263n8
loss, 146–47, 180, 222–23
LTTE (Tamil Tigers), 2–3, 24–27, 46, 183–88,
201; against other militant movements,
85–86, 202; cadres, 25–26, 136–37, 213,
215; and caste, 195–96; control, 42–43, 51,
107, 254; defeat of, 30, 226–27, 254–55;
and Eelam War II, 25, 208; and everyday
life, 27; as exception, 213–15; female cadres, 29, 216; and ideology of death, 61, 215;
intelligence, 25; IPKF against, 46, 205–6;
and Muslims, 125–31, 137; as part of Tamil
culture, 28, 212; and popular culture, 48;
as a quasi state, 27, 39–40, 47, 63, 76, 187,
211; and recruitment, 26, 43, 47, 56–57,
59–61, 200; and sovereignty, 214; and Sri
Lankan state, 25; support of, 39; and Tamil
civilians, 4, 26,71,153; and Tamil family,
29, 62, 200; and Tamilization, 47, 217;
terror, 38
Lubkemann, Stephen, 5, 7–11

Mannheim, Karl, 44–45
migration, 15–18; as form of social mobility,
248–49, 255; overseas, 16–17, 74, 210, 248.
See also diaspora; displacement; IDPs
militancy, 5–6, 23–24, 59, 82–83, 184–85,
210; ethnography of, 186; and gender,
196–97, 203; internecine warfare, 86, 203;
and kinship, 184, 192, 198–99, 204–5, 226;
as nascent state, 191; and personhood,
201; and politics, 193–95, 211; "popular
militancy," 187–89, 205, 210; and social
transformation, 183, 184, 212, 226. *See also*
militant movements
militant movements, 6, 24, 83, 183, 202,
209, 224; and caste, 196; and IPKF, 206;
and Muslims, 124–25. *See also* EPRLF;
EROS; group formation; LTTE, PLOTE,
TELO
minorities, 4, 12–13, 127; Sri Lankan,
Malaiyaha/Hill Country Tamils, 240–41;
Tamil-speaking, 13, 79, 237. *See also*
Muslims
Muslims, 13–14, 109, 149; Eastern, 119,
122–23, 126; and homeland, 116; Northern, 16, 29, 64, 106–9, 119, 122, 126–27,
131–32, 137–44, 150–55, 157, 163–66, 168,
170, 173, 178–82; and political representation, 117–18, 121–23; and racial identity,
117–18, 157; regionalization of 110–12,
115, 118–22; and religious identity,
111–13; Southwest, 119; Tamil relation
with, 13, 109–11, 119, 121–23, 126, 142,
179–82. *See also* Eviction

narration: of the Eviction, 131–36, 138–39;
of the Exodus, 66–73; of militancy, 204,
209, 218–21, 169; of return, 173–76; of
violence, 48–50
nationalism, Tamil, 23, 122–24, 217
Nordstrom, Carolyn, 7, 259n3

Operation Liberation, 46, 205

PLOTE (People's Liberation Organization for
Tamil Eelam), 86, 185, 187–88, 196, 203,
268n2, 269n20
Prabhakaran, Vellupillai, 3, 25
Puttalam, 106–7, 143, 146, 149–10, 155–56,
165, 175–76; and female labor, 156. *See*
also refugees

ACKNOWLEDGMENTS

This book from fieldwork to its various reincarnations in writing has taken me close to a decade and left me indebted to more people than I can possibly name. The greatest debt is of course to those I interviewed in Sri Lanka, in Britain, and in Canada whom I keep anonymous but who have left an indelible mark on me. There are many stories that are not explicitly in this book but are the scaffolding which holds it together.

My original fieldwork was fully funded by an ESRC Postgraduate studentship. Subsequent work was funded by a one year Nancy L. Buc Postdoctoral Fellowship at the Pembroke center, Brown University, and a one year ESRC Postdoctoral Fellowship at Edinburgh University. I would like to thank all my fellow participants in the Pembroke Seminar and the Pembroke Center for a wonderful and intellectually stimulating year. The Department of Anthropology and the South Asia Center at University of Edinburgh were my homes for more than seven years, and I have to thank all my colleagues, cohort, and friends for their help, intellectual support, and many cups of tea over these years. Needless to say some of the greatest input has come from Jonathan Spencer and Janet Carsten, who have always sustained me over the years with their intellectual inspiration and directions, mentoring, and ongoing friendship and love. The Department of Anthropology at Johns Hopkins also provided me with a home away from home, and I wish to thank the department and my graduate cohort for taking me in for a very influential semester. Thanks to Veena Das, who has continued to have faith in me over these years, I have written the book that she would have liked my dissertation to be . . . finally! I am ever grateful to Gerd Baumann, Anthony Good, Stephen Feuchtwang, and Chris Fuller all of whom for different reasons believed in me and have continued to support me and my work. Thanks to Joke Schrivers and David Kloos for their wonderful and indispensable gift of Peter Kloos's library of Sri Lanka books, and Stephen Champion who allowed me to use his amazing photograph for the front cover.

My colleagues and students at the New School for Social Research and Eugene Lang College, The New School University have been a source of enormous intellectual stimulation, fun, and community. Thanks especially to Lawrence Hirschfeld, Nicolas Langlitz, Hugh Raffles, Vyjayanthi Rao, Janet Roitman, Ann Stoler, and Miriam Ticktin. Thanks to Tyler Boersen who painstakingly went through the first draft of this manuscript! Dilshanie Perera has been my indispensable Girl Friday, editing and getting my manuscript ready for production, sending me efficient emails and enduring my rambling emails. Thanks to Ana Ulloa Garzon who did a fantastic index (again!).

In Sri Lanka, I have to thank Mr. and Mrs. Balasubramaniam, staff at the MDDR, the staff in the Colombo National Archives, and ICES. I am ever grateful to Dr. Hasbullah (Peradeniya) who introduced me to people in Puttalam and has helped me throughout the years. I received more than my fair share of help from those working with Northern Muslims. I extend thanks to Zulfika from MWRAF, Jeweria and Farwhin at RDF (Puttalam), and Aneis, Rizni, and Farim at RAAF in Puttalam, and Sharmila. I am continually indebted to Indrakanthi Perera and Audrey Rebeira. There are so many in Sri Lanka I wish to thank, who spoke to me but whom I cannot name. One I can is the late Maheshwary Velautham. Thanks to Aathavan and Vasuki, Dr. Rajaratnam, Vasantha, and Kirupa. In Canada I would like to thank Rajmohan, Jacob, Regi, and Viji for all their help and friendship; I especially owe a lot to Manoranjan who enabled my work on treason and pushed me to find something that was important to say. Thanks to Helene Klodawsky, who helped my family find some peace with our past. Thanks to Rasanayagam and all the various dissident families in London. Of these, Keeran, Anushan, and Kandeepan, ex-militants and dear family friends, have been ever present in my life and my research. The greatest inspiration for my work has been the determination and work of K. Sritharan and Rajan Hoole of the UTHR (J) (University Teachers for Human Rights, Jaffna), who continue to stand up for human rights, integrity, and truth, and the women from Poorani women's refuge (Jaffna), now dispersed and disappeared.

Thanks especially to dear friends and colleagues across many different places, who have invaluably commented on various versions of these chapters at different stages or endured long conversations about all the things I wanted it to be: Emma Wasserman, Kelly Davis, Jun Hwan Park, Kim Masson, Naveeda Khan, Lori Allen, Steffen Jensen, Hester Betlem, Ahilan Kadirgamar, Miriam Ticktin, Hylton White, Devika Bordia, Peter Geschiere, Malini Sur, and of course Mirak Raheem. Working on "treason" with Tobias Kelly was invaluable, not to mention his reading of countless drafts of these chapters at the last minute, and his characteristically calm advice. The above have also kept me sane with their friendship; to those names I add more: Debora King, Rebecca Walker, Abirami Rasaratnam, Anil Patel, Ben Bavinck, and Ramani Muttettuwegama, (and Ram Mannikalingam!). Elisha Davar has made this book and so much more possible.

My editor at Penn Press, Peter Agree has been amazing. He has shown unflagging enthusiasm for this project despite crises of confidence and breaks to accommodate a baby and a new job. Thanks to all the staff at the Press, who were extremely helpful and professional in seeing this project through. Gananath Obeyesekere and Valentine Daniel have consistently pushed me to make this book much more than I knew it could be. I wish to thank them for their invaluable critical engagement and encouragement.

I end here as my journey began, with my family in life and love. My grandparents Mahila (Amma) and Rajasingam (Appa) gave me a precious year with them in my fieldwork in Sri Lanka. Thanks to Amma's monitoring of my "click-clacking" and Appa's bus and A-Z training, I have some field notes and interviews. Amma, my second mother, is now dead, but Appa is my Jaffna, he is my home. My aunts and uncles, Nirmala and Ragavan, Vasuki and Mick, Sumathy and Pathi, have listened to me over the years, patiently read things at last minute, cut me down to size, and generally made me. Vasuki in particular has read almost everything I have written. My sister Narmada and I share our history; this is also for her. Athamma and all my father's family have always showered me with affection that luckily transcends language. I want to say especial thanks to my cousins Valluvan, Maithreyi, and Kausikan who valiantly proofread and helped me get my original dissertation in (!), and who with Sarujan and Ramya continue to be the most fun siblings anyone could want. It has been my good fortune to be born into a family that mixes irreverence with intellect, even if at times I find it difficult to be in a family of ex-militants, experts, and eccentrics. Thanks to my newer family, Thomas Blom Hansen, Laerke Blom Madsen, Malte Blom Madsen, and Mirak Blom Hansen. They have brought me immeasurable happiness. This book owes everything to the careful and critical eyes of Thomas, my dearest intellectual companion, my "pep squad," and the love of my life.

This book is dedicated to my grandparents, my parents, and my "uncle" Kugamoorthy. My mother Rajani Thiranagama (Daji) and father Dayapala Thiranagama (Thatha) raised me with integrity, responsibility, intellect, and love. From north to south, because of them, I know that individuals and their struggles and actions can, and do, transform history, and that one has to be responsible for and learn from one's mistakes. They taught me that ordinary people should not be made spectators in their own history. Without these lessons I would have never written this kind of book. Kumaraguru Kugamoorthy, my favorite uncle, a journalist who helped so many and who I remember for his kindness, his big smiles, explosive laughter, and his many stories, disappeared in Colombo on September 13, 1990, falsely accused as an LTTE supporter and taken into an army camp. We have never heard from him again. He leaves behind Thenmoli, his widow who searched for him for years, and Manoujitha, his daughter born in Jaffna days before he disappeared in Colombo, who has never seen him. Their lives are the lives of so many in Sri Lanka—for whom this book is ultimately written.

CPSIA information can be obtained
at www.ICGtesting.com
Printed in the USA
LVHW091357240321
682323LV00007B/31